Margaret Atwood: The Open Eye

30   REAPPRAISALS:
CANADIAN
WRITERS

Margaret Atwood: The Open Eye

Edited by
John Moss and Tobi Kozakewich

University of
Ottawa Press

REAPPRAISALS: CANADIAN WRITERS
Gerald Lynch, General Editor

Library and Archives Canada Cataloguing in Publication

Margaret Atwood : the open eye / edited by John Moss & Tobi Kozakewich.

(Reappraisals, Canadian writers, ISSN 1189-6787 ; 30)
Includes bibliographical references and index.
ISBN-13: 978-0-7766-0613-2
ISBN-10: 0-7766-0613-1

1. Atwood, Margaret, 1939- --Criticism and interpretation. I. Moss, John, 1940-
II. Kozakewich, Tobi, 1975- III. Series.

PS8501.T86Z732 2006   C818'.5409   C2006-902920-2

University of Ottawa Press gratefully acknowledges the support extended to its publishing program by the Canada Council and the University of Ottawa. We also acknowledge the support of the Faculty of Arts of the University of Ottawa for the publication of this book.

We acknowledge the financial support of the Government of Canada through the Book Publishing Industry Development Program (BPIDP) for our publishing activities.

All rights reserved. No parts of this publication may be reproduced or transmitted in any form or by any means, electronic or mechanical, including photocopy, recording, or any information storage and retrieval system, without permission in writing from the publisher.

Copy-editing: Angela Lombardi
Typesetting: Sharon Katz and Brad Horning
Cover design and layout: Sharon Katz
Proofreading: Stephanie VanderMeulen

© University of Ottawa Press, 2006
  542 King Edward Street, Ottawa, Ont. Canada K1N 6N5
  press@uottawa.ca   http://www.uopress.ca

Typeset in Minion 11/13

Contents

Contributors   xi

Abbreviated Titles   xix

Haunting Ourselves in Her Words
JOHN MOSS   1

Open Eyes: An Introduction
TOBI KOZAKEWICH   9

Subject/Object

Margaret Atwood: Branding an Icon Abroad
LAURA MOSS   19

"A Slightly Uneasy Eminence": The Celebrity of Margaret Atwood
LORRAINE YORK   35

Eyes Wide Shut: Atwood, Bill C-32, and the Rights of the Author
RENÉE HULAN   49

"Les talents de la voisine": Margaret Atwood and Quebec
EVA-MARIE KRÖLLER   65

P.K. Page and Margaret Atwood: Continuity in Canadian Writing
SANDRA DJWA   81

Negotiations with the Living Archive
ROBERT MCGILL   95

Writing History, from *The Journals of Susanna Moodie* to *The Blind Assassin*
CORAL ANN HOWELLS   107

Atwood and the "Autobiographical Pact"—*for Reingard Nischik*
SHERRILL GRACE   121

Earlier Novels

"Saying Boo to Colonialism": *Surfacing*, Tom Thomson, and the National Ghost
CYNTHIA SUGARS   137

A Silhouette of Madness: Reading Atwood's *Surfacing*
TINA TRIGG   159

"It looked at me with its mashed eye": Animal and Human Suffering in *Surfacing*
JANICE FIAMENGO   171

Having It Both Ways? Romance, Realism, and
Irony in *Lady Oracle*'s Adulterous Affairs
        TOBI KOZAKEWICH   185

How Can a Feminist Read *The Handmaid's Tale*?
A Study of Offred's Narrative
        TAE YAMAMOTO   195

"Lurid Yet Muted": Narrative and the Sabotage of
Dissident Voice in Margaret Atwood's *Alias Grace*
        JULIE GODIN   207

A Contemporary Psychologist Looks at Atwood's
Construction of Personality in *Alias Grace*
        REGINA M. EDMONDS   217

Atwood and Class: *Lady Oracle, Cat's Eye*, and
Alias Grace
        FRANK DAVEY   231

Short Fiction and Poetry

Funny Bones Are Good Bones: Atwood and
Humour
        WANDA CAMPBELL   243

"Back from the Dead": Journeys to the
Underworld in *Wilderness Tips*
        PAMELA S. BROMBERG   257

"*It's still you*": Aging and Identity in Atwood's
Poetry
        SARA JAMIESON   269

"Com[ing] Through Darkness": Margaret
Atwood's "I"-Opening Lyricism
        DAVID R. JARRAWAY   279

Power Politics/Power Politics: Atwood and Foucault
    PILAR SOMACARRERA   291

The Two-Headed Opus
    CHRISTINE EVAIN   305

Incandescence: "the power of what is not there" in Margaret Atwood's *Morning in the Burned House*
    ROSE LUCAS   319

Eye-Openers: Photography in Margaret Atwood's Poetry
    REINGARD M. NISCHIK AND JULIA BREITBACH   331

The Blind Assassin and Oryx and Crake

Negotiating with the Looking Glass: Atwood, Her Protagonists, and the Journey to the Dead
    PHYLLIS STERNBERG PERRAKIS   349

The Body of/as Evidence: Margaret Atwood, *The Blind Assassin*, and the Feminist Literary Mystery
    WENDY ROY   361

The Dead Are in the Hands of the Living: Memory Haunting Storytelling in Margaret Atwood's *The Blind Assassin*
    HELENA HYTTINEN   373

Margaret Atwood and the Critical Limits of Embodiment
    SALLY CHIVERS   385

Frankenstein's Gaze and Atwood's Sexual Politics
in *Oryx and Crake*
    SHARON R. WILSON   397

The Representation of the Absent Mother in
Margaret Atwood's *Oryx and Crake*
    NATHALIE FOY   407

Resistance in Futility: The Cyborg Identities of
Oryx and Crake
    MICHÈLE LACOMBE   421

Oryx and Crake: Atwood's Ironic Inversion of
Frankenstein
    HILDE STAELS   433

Atwood's Global Ethic: The Open Eye, The
Blinded Eye
    DIANA BRYDON   447

Postscript

Propositions from a (Reap)praising Margaret
Atwood Conference
    FRANK DAVEY   461

Index   465

Contributors

JULIA BREITBACH, MA, studied English and American Literature, German Literature, and Art and Media Studies at the University of Constance and Yale University. During her studies she received grants from the Studienstiftung des deutschen Volkes (German Study Foundation) and the German Academic Exchange Service. She is now a PhD student in North American Literature at the University of Constance with a special interest in the intersections between literature and photography.

PAMELA S. BROMBERG is Professor of English at Simmons College in Boston. She has published numerous articles on women's writing, narrative, and Romanticism, including "Learning to Listen: Teaching about the Talk of Miss Bates," "Buchi Emecheta: Dislocation and Discovery," and "Margaret Drabble's *The Radiant Way:* Feminist Metafiction." Her research interests include feminist literary theory, film, and popular culture.

DIANA BRYDON is Professor of English at the University of Western Ontario. She has published extensively, including books on Timothy Findley and Christina Stead, and has edited *Postcolonialism: Critical concepts in literary and cultural studies* and *Shakespeare in Canada: "a world elsewhere"?* with Irena R. Makaryk. Her current research focuses on globalization and autonomy and the ends of post-colonialism.

WANDA CAMPBELL has a master's degree in Creative Writing from the University of Windsor, and a PhD in Canadian Literature from the University of Western Ontario. She teaches Creative Writing and Women's Literature at Acadia University in Wolfville, Nova Scotia. She has edited several books, including *Hidden Rooms: Early Canadian Women Poets* and most recently the Canadian edition of *Literature: A Pocket Anthology* for Penguin. Her academic articles have appeared in the Reappraisals Series and in journals such as *Mosaic, Canadian Poetry, Studies in Canadian Literature, Essays in Canadian Writing, Canadian Literature*, and *Wascana Review*. She has also published two collections of poetry—*Sky Fishing* and *Haw-[Thorn]*—and her poems and stories have appeared in creative journals across Canada.

SALLY CHIVERS is Assistant Professor of Canadian Studies and English at Trent University. She has published extensively on women's literature, disability, and autobiography—for example, in *From Old Woman to Older Women: Contemporary Culture and Women's Narratives*. Her research interests include women and aging, gender studies, and the body.

FRANK DAVEY is the Carl F. Klinck Professor of Canadian Literature at the University of Western Ontario. He is the first to hold this chair. Frank Davey's writing makes a humorous and ironic comment on the ambiguous play of signs in contemporary culture, on the popular stories that lie behind them, and on the struggles between different groups in society—racial, regional, gender-based, ethnic, economic—that drive this play. He is the author of *Margaret Atwood: A Feminist Poetics* (1984), *Popular Narratives* (1991), and *Cultural Mischief: A Practical Guide to Multiculturalism* (1996). He is the editor of Talon's New Canadian Criticism Series and numerous books of poetry.

SANDRA DJWA is Professor of English in the Department of English at Simon Fraser University. Her research interests include national, modern, and post-colonial literatures, literary and institutional history, biography, poetry, textual studies and editing, as well as the writers E.J. Pratt, F.R. Scott, Roy Daniells, Margaret Atwood, and P.K. Page. She is the author of *E.J. Pratt: The Evolutionary Vision* and a biography of F.R. Scott, *The Politics of the Imagination* (1987). She has edited Carl Klinck's memoirs, *Giving Canada a Literary History: A Memoir* (1991). Her biography of Roy Daniells, entitled *Professing English*, was published by the University of Toronto Press in 2002. She is presently working on a biography of P.K. Page.

REGINA M. EDMONDS, a clinical psychologist, is Associate Professor of Psychology at Assumption College. Her specialty areas include family systems theory, trauma based disorders, eating disorders and the qualities that characterize successful mother-daughter relationships. She is currently the Director of Assumption's Women's Studies Program, working to provide a transnational emphasis to that program.

CHRISTINE EVAIN is a French lecturer at the École Centrale de Nantes. She is currently completing her dissertation on Margaret Atwood. Her research interests focus on Canadian and contemporary literature, including that by John Grisham, Alice Munro, and Kazuo Ishiguro.

JANICE FIAMENGO is Associate Professor of English at the University of Ottawa. She has published numerous articles on Canadian literature and is currently completing a monograph on the strategies of rhetoric and self-presentation of early Canadian women journalists, essayists, and activists. She is also editing an anthology of essays on animals in Canadian literature and a collection of Sara Jeannette Duncan's newspaper writing.

NATHALIE FOY is an instructor in the Department of English at the University of Toronto, where she recently completed her PhD. Her thesis examines the undermining of vision in Canadian fiction. Her work today forms part of her next project, on the representation of mothering in Canadian fiction.

JULIE GODIN is in the last year of her PhD at the University of Ottawa. Her work focuses on American Literature, specifically African-American literature of the twentieth century. She is currently writing her thesis "Uptown, Downbeat: Contestations of Space, Mobility and Masculine Self-Fashioning in African American Urban Discourse." Her interests include slave narratives, representations of criminality and marginality, and dissident subjectivities in American and Canadian texts.

SHERRILL GRACE is Professor of English, and Distinguished University Scholar at the University of British Columbia. Her research interests include twentieth-century Canadian literature and culture, drama, biography, and autobiography, as well as interdisciplinary studies in twentieth-century culture. She has published sixteen books and over two hundred articles. Her monograph, *Canada and the Idea of the North*, appeared in 2001 and her study of painter Tom Thomson, *Inventing Tom Thomson*, was published in 2004. Works on individual authors include articles in *Canadian Literature* and *Essays in Theatre* as well as monographs on Margaret Atwood and Malcolm Lowry. Her most recent book is the co-edited volume, *Theatre and Auto Biography* (Talonbooks, 2006), and she is currently writing a biography of Sharon Pollock.

CORAL ANN HOWELLS is Professor Emerita of English and Canadian Literature at the School of English and American Literature at the University of Reading. She has published extensively on contemporary Canadian women's literature, including a number of articles on Margaret Atwood, Alice Munro, and Carol Shields, as well as a book entitled *Margaret Atwood*. She has also co-edited a collection of essays on Atwood, entitled *Margaret Atwood: The Shape Shifter*, and another called *Narrative Strategies in Canadian Literature*. She has recently edited *The Cambridge Companion to Margaret Atwood*.

RENÉE HULAN is Associate Professor of English at St. Mary's University, where she teaches Canadian Literature. Her research interests include "Imagining the North" in Canadian literature, as witnessed by her most recent book, *Northern Experience and the Myths of Canadian Culture*; Native literature, on which she has edited a collection of essays entitled *Native North America*; and the interdisciplinarity of Canadian literary studies. Her individual author studies include articles on Marilyn Dumont, Thomas King, and Margaret Atwood, in such periodicals as *Essays on Canadian Writing* and the *Journal of Canadian Studies*.

HELENA HYTTINEN is a PhD student of the English department at Karlstad University, Sweden. She holds a degree in teaching and an MA in English literature. She is currently working on her dissertation on narrative strategies in Margaret Atwood's *The Blind Assassin* (2000). She also teaches Creative Writing at the university.

SARA JAMIESON teaches at the University of Alberta, where she is a postdoctoral student. She has published numerous articles on the elegy including "Now That I Am Dead: P.K. Page and the Self-Elegy" and "Mourning in the Burned House: Margaret Atwood and the Modern Elegy." Her research interests include contemporary Canadian literature and poetry, women's literature, and the elegy.

DAVID R. JARRAWAY is Professor of English at the University of Ottawa. His areas of specialization are American literature and cultural studies and queer theory. Recent publications include *Going the Distance: Dissident Subjectivity in Modernist American Literature* and articles on Ernest Hemingway, Wallace Stevens, William Carlos Williams, Lyn Hejinian, Allen Ginsberg, A.R. Ammons, Marjorie Perloff, Langston Hughes, Michael Cunningham, Mark Doty, Elizabeth Bishop, Gertrude Stein, William Faulkner, Tim O'Brien, Jim Grimsley, Marilyn Bowering, Erin Mouré, Wallace Thurman, theory and pedagogy, feminist modernism, and gay AIDS memoirs. His current research interests are modern (i.e., "Harlem Renaissance") and postmodern (i.e., "New York School") American poetry, and contemporary American fiction.

TOBI KOZAKEWICH is a doctoral candidate in English at the University of Ottawa. Her publications include articles on textual editing and the culture of sensibility. She is presently writing her thesis, which is a literary historical analysis of representations of adultery in twentieth-century English-Canadian prose fiction. Her work on Margaret Atwood is part of this larger project.

EVA-MARIE KRÖLLER is Professor of English and Comparative Literature at the University of British Columbia. Recent publications include *The Cambridge Companion to Canadian Literature* (2004; rpt. 2005) and *The Cambridge History of Canadian Literature*, ed. with Coral Ann Howells (forthcoming). She was Editor of *Canadian Literature* from 1995 to 2003.

MICHÈLE LACOMBE is Associate Professor in the Canadian Studies department at Trent University. Her research interests include Canadian nationalism, women's literature, and cultural theory. She has published extensively in

Journal of Canadian Studies/Canadian Literature, and *Canadian Theatre Review*, and, most recently, a number of articles about gender and landscape, theosophy and the Canadian idealist tradition, the immigrant novels of Mary Anne Sadlier, amputated speech in Atwood's *The Handmaid's Tale*, and the Acadian Theatre of Antoine Mallet.

ROSE LUCAS is a senior lecturer in the School of Literary, Visual, and Performance Studies at Monash University in Australia. Her research interests include feminist poetics, the intersections of psychoanalytic and feminist theories, women's fiction, and cinema analysis. Recent publications include the volume *Bridging: Critical Readings in Australian Women's Poetry*, which she co-authored with Lyn McCredden for Oxford University Press. She is currently working on a book-length research project entitled *Labours of Mourning: Trauma and Text*.

ROBERT MCGILL is a PhD candidate at the University of Toronto. He has published articles in *Textual Practice*, *Mosaic*, *The Journal of Commonwealth Literature*, and *Essays on Canadian Writing*. In addition to publishing this critical work, Robert McGill has also published a number of creative pieces as well as a novel, *The Mysteries*, with Jonathan Cape (in the United Kingdom) and McClelland & Stewart in 2004.

JOHN MOSS is Professor of English at the University of Ottawa. His publications include *Being Fiction*, *Invisible Among the Ruins*, and *Paradox of Meaning*.

LAURA MOSS is Associate Professor at the University of British Columbia. She has published articles on post-colonialism and Canadian literature in such periodicals as *Canadian Literature*, *ARIEL*, and *Wasafiri*, and has also edited a critical edition of *The History of Emily Montague* for the Tecumseh Press's Canadian Critical Editions Series. Her most recent book, *Is Canada Postcolonial? Unsettling Canadian Literature*, was published by Wilfrid Laurier University Press in 2003.

REINGARD M. NISCHIK has taught as a professor at the universities of Mainz (1988–1992), Freiburg (1992–1994), and Constance (1994–) in Germany; since 1994 she has been Chair of American Literature at the University of Constance. She has published some twenty-five books on Canadian, American, and Comparative literature, was editor of the German interdisciplinary journal *Zeitschrift für Kanada-Studien* from 1992 to 2005, and has been editor of the book series *European Studies in American Literature and Culture* (Camden House, Rochester, NY) since 1996. She has published some ten articles and three books on Atwood, among them *Margaret Atwood: Works and Impact* (2000), for which she received the Best Book Award of the Margaret Atwood Society.

PHYLLIS STERNBERG PERRAKIS teaches English Literature at the University of Ottawa and is interested in post-colonial literature and the works of Doris Lessing and Margaret Atwood. She is the editor of *Spiritual Exploration in the Works of Doris Lessing* and has written articles on Doris Lessing, Margaret Atwood, D.H. Lawrence, and Mary Shelley. She is presently working on editing the collection *Adventures of the Spirit: The Older Woman in the Works of Doris Lessing, Margaret Atwood, and Other Contemporary Women Writers*. She is the past president of the Doris Lessing Society and is currently co-editor of the journal *Doris Lessing Studies*.

WENDY ROY is a post-doctoral student in the Department of English at the University of Saskatchewan. She has written numerous articles about Canadian women's writing and post-colonialism. Recently, she has completed a book entitled *Maps of Difference: Canada, Women, and Travel, 1838–1963*. Her current research focuses on representations of geography, text, and the body.

PILAR SOMACARRERA is Professor of English at the Universidad Autónoma de Madrid. She has translated Atwood's *Power Politics* into Spanish and is currently writing a chapter about this book for the *Oxford Companion to Margaret Atwood*, edited by Coral Ann Howells.

HILDE STAELS is Professor of English Literature at the University of Leuven in Belgium. Her research interests include contemporary Canadian writing and the novels of Margaret Atwood. She has published a book entitled *Margaret Atwood's Novels: A Study of Narrative Discourse* as well as various articles in international journals such as *Modern Fiction Studies, Journal of Commonwealth and Postcolonial Studies,* and *English Studies: A Journal of Literature and Language.*

CYNTHIA SUGARS is Associate Professor in the Department of English at the University of Ottawa. She has published numerous articles on Canadian literature and has recently edited two collections of essays on Canadian literature and post-colonial theory: *Unhomely States: Theorizing English-Canadian Postcolonialism* (Broadview, 2004) and *Home-Work: Postcolonialism, Pedagogy, and Canadian Literature* (University of Ottawa Press, 2004).

TINA TRIGG is Assistant Professor at King's University College in Edmonton, where she teaches contemporary theory, the North American short story, postmodern literature, and Canadian literature. She completed her dissertation—a study of the strategic use of madness in Atwood's novels—at the University of Ottawa in 2003. Tina's current research includes reader-involvement strategies in Yann Martel's *Life of Pi* and in Atwood's fiction (novels, short stories, prose poems).

SHARON R. WILSON is Professor of English at the University of Northern Colorado and founding president of The Atwood Society. She is the author of *Margaret Atwood's Fairy-Tale Sexual Politics*, editor of *Margaret Atwood's Textual Assassinations: Recent Poetry and Fiction*, and co-editor of *Teaching Atwood's "The Handmaid's Tale" and Other Works*.

TAE YAMAMOTO is Associate Professor at the Institute of Language and Culture at Doshisha University in Japan. She has published a book entitled *Portraits of the British Writers of the 20th Century* and several articles on women writers such as Virginia Woolf, Mary Shelley, and Margaret Atwood. Her research interests are modern and contemporary women's writing, editing, and translation.

LORRAINE YORK is Professor of English at McMaster University, where she also serves on the Academic Advisory Committee in Women's Studies. Her current research interest pertains to theories of celebrity and authorship, and she has published several articles in this area in periodicals such as *Canadian Poetry* and *Essays on Canadian Writing*. She has also published a monograph entitled *Rethinking Women's Collaborative Writing: Power Difference, Property*, and edited a collection of essays on Margaret Atwood, called *Various Atwoods*.

Abbreviated Titles

Dancing Girls and Other Stories (DG)
In Search of Alias Grace (Search)
Negotiating with the Dead (ND)
Moving Targets (MT)
The Circle Game (CG
Wilderness Tips (WT)
Surfacing (Surfacing)
Survival (Survival)
The Metal and the Flower (MF)
The Sun and the Moon (SM)
The Robber Bride (RB)
The Journals of Susanna Moodie (JSM)
Alias Grace (AG)
The Blind Assassin (BA)
Lady Oracle (LO)
The Handmaid's Tale (HT)
Second Words (SW)
Selected Poems (SP)
Selected Poems II (SP II)
Selected Poems 1966–1984 (SP 1966–1984)
Good Bones (GB)
Oryx and Crake (OC)
Two Solitudes (TSS)

Morning in the Burned House (MBH)
Bodily Harm (BH)
Power Politics (PP)
True Stories (TS)
Two-Headed Poems (THP)
"Notes Towards a Poem That Can Never Be Written ("NTP")
Murder in the Dark (MD)
Procedures for Underground (PU)
The Edible Woman (EW)
You Are Happy (YAH)
Life Before Man (LBM)
Interlunar (I)
The Animals in That Country (ATC)
Eating Fire: Selected Poetry (EF)
Unit of Five (UF) (P.K. Page)
As Ten as Twenty (ATT) (P.K. Page)

Haunting Ourselves in Her Words

JOHN MOSS

I

IT IS INCONCEIVABLE to imagine a collection of short stories in English without Margaret Atwood's representation. It is highly unlikely a poetry anthology would exclude her work, whether it's of Canadian poetry or a survey from Beowulf to the present. Any canon of the novels of our time, in genres as diverse as speculative fiction, parody, social realism, and historical metafiction, would include an Atwood title or two. There can be no consideration of Canadian literary criticism without allusion or deference to Atwood's commentaries. There could be no discussion of Canadian cultural politics during the past fifty years that did not centre on the contributions of Margaret Atwood and her partner, Graeme Gibson. In any discourse on Canadian identity, she provides key terms of reference, maps and mirrors, reassurance and reproach. She has iconic status in Canada and she is our greatest emissary abroad, not because she is characteristically Canadian but because as a Canadian she is wholly herself, her work and her vision impossible to ignore. And she is an emissary of the world among us, showing in a turn of phrase, delineation of character, twist of plot, and subversion of generic conventions, how we connect, all of us to each other, if sometimes only through the differences that define us.

For all that, how little we know her. Behind the authorial voice and the public persona, behind the cultural edifice is a woman of singular talent and drive and achievement. Perhaps it is the commodification of her celebrity that protects her. We know the name, Margaret Atwood, but the person, when she writes, writes alone—in a room, I imagine, teeming with voices and ghosts. We hear these voices as they filter through, the voices of literature, voices of the past, memories of bubble gum and great events; we see the ghosts of our literary forebears, the ghosts of our human trek through the ages, ghosts of our childhood, of our future, of our dreams. That's what Virginia Woolf meant: all writers need rooms of their own, to hear, unimpeded, the voices and ghosts. And Margaret Atwood above all is a very great listener. When she plays on her own, the room is tumultuous.

We could become lost trying to know Margaret Atwood. She lives like the rest of us in a labyrinth of libraries that interconnect, her mind a treasury of infinite possibilities. Unlike the rest of us, she walks through those libraries, along those corridors, plucking books from the shelves, shaping their contents for others to share. She has the gift to be everywoman and to be unique, to give us access to universal particularities through her words, shaped on paper in startling and memorable design. We know all about her, for she shares what she hears, what she reads, what she imagines and schemes; and we do not know her at all.

II

In the twenties, Robert McAlmon gave his memoir of Paris the perfect title *Being Geniuses Together*. Margaret Atwood gave her most recent novel the unwieldy title *Oryx and Crake*. Interestingly, *Oryx and Crake*, after a while, seemed inevitable. As the novel embedded itself in the reader's consciousness and in the public mind, it became wonderfully allusive. McAlmon's title was the best part of his book. Atwood's book has now made her title seem perfect.

Margaret Atwood does this; she says things that, once said, seem inevitable. Her fiction, as well as her poetry and essays, displays that peculiar kind of originality that seems to coalesce our fragmented experience into coherent patterns that resonate inside the skull. Critics as critics are sometimes unnerved by her familiarity. Readers, including critics, find in even her most ominous and sinister writing something reassuring. For example, take "A Women's Issue" (listed portentously in the table of contents of her *Selected Poems 1966–1984* as "A woman's issue"). The images are gut-wrenchingly horrific; they are of abuses to women "we" all know about and try not to. In their rendering as poetry we are forced to confront them directly, but there is something profoundly positive in how she invites us, forces us, to share in the poem's outrage, to recognize the absurdity of moral relativism, that sometimes culturally sanctioned things are inherently evil. Although our recognition of this means we're not evil, it still means that we're complicit. It is familiar territory: an unnerving blend of ambivalence and certainty.

III

> You fit into me
> like a hook into an eye
>
> a fish hook
> an open eye
> (Atwood, *Power Politics* 1)

Quite possibly, Margaret Atwood dreads the thrill of three decades past, finding her open eye poem transcribed from raw nerves onto paper—it must haunt her like Earle Birney's "David," which became so much a signature epic that readers forgave him for murder, while the smashed and implacable David lurched through the years in pursuit, until Birney died. Who says it's by our lack of ghosts that we're haunted? Birney said it, of course, in a poem, but he was wrong. We live in a world teeming with ghosts; however, we don't always see them. Margaret Atwood apparently does. Reading her, we find ourselves haunting ourselves in her words.

Much has been said and will be said about Margaret Atwood's writing, about her themes and motifs and their ramifications; much has been and will be implied about the woman herself, based on research and gossip and perhaps on intimate insights through astral projection, but I would like to talk briefly about words. Most work on Atwood is concerned with what Saussure called *langue*; I would like to speak on *parole*. A brief sentence will do—to suggest how language in Atwood's jurisdiction may incarcerate the reader and still set us free.

On the front cover of a book by Alice Munro is a terse statement credited to Margaret Atwood: "These stories are real as kitchens." Now, when

I read that a generation ago, I felt I was in the presence of genius, perhaps more than one. And the interesting thing about "These stories are real as kitchens" is that I have no idea what it means.

Well, I do and I don't. I've been in kitchens and I've read stories, and I can appreciate the copula that binds them together. I am also aware of the differences on a literal level: phenomenologically, stories and kitchens are mutually exclusive. The terms of the equation are arbitrary, their connection both self-evident and absurd—but that's their impossible alliance, that's the hook. And we know about the startling efficacy of Atwood and hooks—how when you think you've caught the glory, you've also fished up something unexpected, like a drowned walleye with a ring in its gut, or an old rubber boot with the remains of a foot inside.

The refusal of her brief description to settle into meaning excites the mind on a visceral plane. Of course you know what the words mean; these stories are as real as kitchens, it's as simple as that. You just do not know how to put what she means into words; you end up repeating her words. They are your words, their meaning inside you assimilated as a quality of the thing she is talking about—kitchens and stories by Alice Munro, the equation between them.

Atwood has invented the postmodern analogue: her statement is neither metaphor nor metonym; her stories are not like kitchens, nor are they kitchen-like. It is not a statement redolent with symbolic possibilities; it is not a trope of any sort. It does not invite interpretation. It is placidly hostile to what used to be called explication and is now euphemistically described as close reading. I have no more idea what her sentence means on a figurative level than on the literal. But the ineluctable rightness of her analogue—its dazzling subversive resistance to rational explanation—is wondrously generous.

IV

I have been acquainted with Margaret Atwood for almost five decades, the first one from a distance as I listened to her read, back when we were young geniuses together. I think I remember her reading at the Bohemian Embassy in the early sixties, in Toronto, back when I was falling in love twice a month, and enthralled with her words, I wrote bad poetry in weak imitation. She might deny having read at the Bohemian Embassy. It doesn't matter, my memory is not about to collapse from an excess of truth. Over the years our lives intersected now and then. I grew to admire this woman who has become strangely iconic, strange because she remains one of us, the slightly eccentric neighbour in the apartment next door who might be clairvoyant or simply is able to see through adjoining walls. And yet she is a formidable high flier, totally at ease in the grand circus of international literature. Something I came to realize was her remarkable generosity—generosity not only to readers but to causes, to friends, and to fellow writers.

As years turned into eras, I discovered in Margaret Atwood's contributions to the Writer's Union of Canada and to Pen International, as well as in various other public causes whose sympathies I share, the stunning bounty of her sometimes obstreperous spirit. But what has been most exciting as her peer, in age if in nothing else, is having been able to follow the wondrously subversive and irrepressible social conscience in her writing as each new work appeared, and to recognize as I gained the soul and wit to appreciate such things, the evolving aesthetic of her creative vision. She has grown marvellously and yet, as Eliot observed about literature in general, this has not been a matter of improvement, for who would presume to improve on *Surfacing* or *The Journals of Susanna Moodie*? It has been a matter of shifting, refining, and developing, of keeping pace with her own and outpacing her readers' maturing sensibilities.

Teaching her work at the university level, I have watched as her name has become a rubric for what she has written, in the same way that Shakespeare and Austen stand for their canons more than for the man or woman behind them. "Atwood" means the novels and poems and essays, as well as the deftly deployed persona in the midst of public controversy, but it is also a label for feisty attitudes, a clear moral vision, devastating wit, and a genius for making words mean something. She has not fallen into the Hemingway trap, reprised by Leonard Cohen, in which the persona displaces the person, nor into the Virginia Woolf trap, reprised by Michael Ondaatje, in which the person appears as her achievement's creation. The personality of Margaret Atwood is forthright and steadfast, while Atwood, the work, is a creation of remarkable and diverse complexity.

I have taught Atwood to university students since the late sixties, sometimes in a context of Canadian literature and sometimes in courses on genre, courses shaped by critical theory, courses on themes in world literature, courses on Arctic narrative, courses on authorial subversions. I have never taught a course solely on Atwood but she has a way of dominating the courses in which she appears. This is because she has a knack for making the ineffable effable, for wringing the most astonishing meaning from words, for conspiring with readers to share a moral perspective on even the most arcane or unimaginable issues (imagined, of course); she has the capacity to be succinct about the wondrously complex and to expose complexity in the apparently simple. She creates memorable lines and memorable images, she creates memorable characters, she creates memorable visions of our world as it might have been, might be, and might possibly become. And perhaps the most telling aspect of Margaret Atwood's writing, from a pedagogical point of view: people love to talk about it. There is no other writer who connects to the reader on such a personal basis, on so many planes. She makes us more aware of ourselves.

v

I once said to Margaret Atwood that there is a strong postmodern tendency in her writing. She told me I was wrong. Being an academic I assumed she therefore did not understand my point. I now suspect she did. I have often been disconcerted to discover that she has my ideas before I think of them. Her denial of postmodernity was very postmodern. The crux of the postmodern analogue is not meaning but sense. It is this that resonates through much of her poetry, this refusal to explain that allows us to know, and it is in much of her fiction. Words are arranged; images, characters, and events are articulated in ways that refuse interpretation, invite speculation, and affirm the brilliance of her narrative and poetic imagination. They open, in the tension between various terms, the doors of perception, and the avenues in a private garden which fork and converge like Borges' fiction, and shift like a staircase at Hogwarts, thus enlarging the reader's life.

To read Atwood is a creative experience, the reader finding herself, himself, caught up in creation. I have sometimes written about Margaret Atwood's fiction and have written fiction about her. Her name provokes in me a deep desire to make things up, to tell resonant lies, to insert myself into parallel dimensions, some gothic, romantic, confessional, speculative, realistic; others psychological, moral, political, sexual, all of them originating in my reading of her polyphonous and multivariate canon. I want to transform myself into a character in something by Margaret Atwood, preferably a short story, but a poem or a novel will do. At the very least, I want to participate in making a book like this, where I can immerse myself in the words of some of the brightest, most imaginative, best-informed, and most engaged readers one is likely to encounter anywhere. The beauty of books is that desire and practice come together, as they have here, as we negotiate with the dead, the undead, and the yet-to-be-born.

Open Eyes:
An Introduction

TOBI KOZAKEWICH

AS A POET, literary scholar, recipient of the Governor General's Award (poetry), novelist, literary critic, cartoonist, social commentator, humanitarian, Guggenheim Fellow, Fellow of the Royal Society of Canada, recipient of the Governor General's Award (fiction), Woman of the Year, environmental journalist, recipient of the Giller Prize, recipient of the Booker Prize, and inductee to Canada's Walk of Fame, Margaret Atwood occupies vast terrain on the Canadian and international literary and cultural fields—terrain that extends beyond the parameters of W.H. New's modest 2003 description of her as one of the foremost Canadian writers of the 1980s and 1990s.

As New's *History of Canadian Literature* makes clear, however, Atwood has long been a force with which her critics and readers have had to reckon, and reckon they have. Atwood's novels consistently appear on Canadian and international bestseller lists, and on syllabi for Canadian, contemporary, and women's literature courses both in Canada and abroad. Her oeuvre, moreover, has provided material for a wide range of literary and cultural commentators, both those who admire her work and those who find it provoking, at best. Her presence in—one could say dominance of—Canadian literary history is shown by the number of monographs that leading scholars have produced focusing solely on her life and work: from Sherrill Grace's *Violent Duality* (1980) to the newest edition of Coral

Ann Howell's *Margaret Atwood* (released last year); from Frank Davey's *Margaret Atwood: A Feminist Poetics* (1984) to Karen Stein's *Margaret Atwood Revisited* (1999); and from Barbara Hill Rigney's *Margaret Atwood* (1987) to Rosemary Sullivan and Nathalie Cooke's 1998 critical biographies, *The Red Shoes: Margaret Atwood Starting Out* and *Margaret Atwood: A Biography*, respectively. There are, additionally, countless essay collections devoted to her work and innumerable theses on Atwood from Canada, the United States, Germany, Sweden, France, and China, among other countries.

Yet despite the range of existing critical work, Atwood continues to surprise and challenge her readers. Her latest novel, *Oryx and Crake*, while in some ways expanding on the sci-fi story inset in *The Blind Assassin* and in others echoing the dystopic *The Handmaid's Tale*, also marks a clear departure from her earlier, more representational novels, indicating the need for a cumulative and collective reappraisal of her life and, most especially, her work. That need was the inspiration for a conference on Atwood, originally proposed by John Moss, and was reflected by the overwhelming response to our call for papers, with more than one hundred submissions coming from countries in North America, Europe, Asia, and Australia. The essays in this book are for the most part a selection adapted from the "Margaret Atwood: The Open Eye" symposium held at the University of Ottawa in the spring of 2004, and although some very fine papers were left out due to publication exigencies beyond the editors' control, we have tried to convey a sense of both the symposium's international appeal and the breadth of interests that presenters addressed.

What follows, then, is a broad range of approaches to Margaret Atwood and her work—a range that coalesces in fruitful ways. For example, a shared focus on Atwood as she presents herself and is presented, in Canada and abroad, appears in the essays that frame Part One of this volume: Laura Moss's "Margaret Atwood: Branding an Icon Abroad," Lorraine York's "'A Slightly Uneasy Eminence': The Celebrity of Margaret Atwood," and Sherrill Grace's "Atwood and the 'Autobiographical Pact.'" These papers, while proclaiming at once Atwood's centrality as a literary figure within Canadian letters and as a cultural figure within Canada's national and international identities, also justify the close scholarly attention to Margaret Atwood that characterizes the essays in this book. Moreover, such implicit justification helps to clarify the role of this volume, and the symposium that inspired it, within a broader cultural and social context. As Laura Moss observes, in her capacity as "celebrity author," Atwood "speak[s] across a range of subjects that illustrate the relevance of the arts in discussions of important topics such as good governance, citizenship, and civil society." Moving beyond the mistaken assumption that "academic papers are written for academics" (as Paul Gessell had claimed in his column about the symposium), *Margaret Atwood: The Open Eye* foregrounds the extent to which concerns that we as scholars address resonate throughout Canadian society as a whole.

Also emphasizing the relation between literature and culture, for example, is Renée Hulan's "Eyes Wide Shut: Atwood, Bill C-32, and the Rights of the Author," which, in considering the ways a public figure like Atwood works to shape legislative policy, touches on issues of concern to any person who has borrowed books from a public library. Eva-Marie Kröller examines Atwood's role in shaping society through her focus on French Canada's changing responses to this dominant Anglo-Canadian author in "'Les talents de la voisine': Margaret Atwood and Quebec"; Sandra Djwa delves further back into Canadian literary history to delineate P.K. Page's influence on Atwood's writing in "P.K. Page and Margaret Atwood: Continuity in Canadian Writing." Coral Ann Howells similarly identifies key influences on Atwood's writing, beginning her essay "Writing History, from *The Journals of Susanna Moodie* to *The Blind Assassin*" with the premise that "Atwood has always had a historicising consciousness" before proceeding to stress that Atwood does not always treat history in the same way: whereas early in her career Atwood draws upon history to record lost or under-represented experiences, by the 1990s, she evinces a scepticism about the way history "forg[es] links with a past that may be already forged." Finally, using Atwood as a case study into the nature of archival work, Robert McGill asks questions that bear not only on critical or even biographical scholarship but on historical research as well: how does the availability of archival material shape what we know and understand? And how does the archive itself delimit knowledge?

Despite the body of criticism that Atwood's novels have generated, the complex subtleties of her work lend themselves to a variety of approaches and interpretations. Part Two, "Earlier Novels" provides new perspectives on some of Atwood's earlier fictions, ranging from *Surfacing* and *Lady Oracle*, both of which have been in print for some thirty years, through to *Alias Grace*, which first appeared ten years ago. In "'Saying Boo to Colonialism':

Surfacing, Tom Thomson, and the National Ghost," for instance, Cynthia Sugars undertakes a post-colonial analysis of *Surfacing* to uncover the ways Atwood both borrows from and impacts the national imaginary vis-à-vis the national mythic figures of Tom Thomson. "A Silhouette of Madness: Reading Atwood's *Surfacing*" expands on a previous project by Tina Trigg and clarifies the ways in which "Atwood's works implicitly criticize" the process whereby the reader as critic "*becomes* the analyst," privileged and authoritative, capable of "dismiss[ing] the narrator as a mad figure." Adding an eco-critical component to her reading of Atwood's nameless narrator in "'It looked at me with its mashed eye': Animal and Human Suffering in *Surfacing*," Janice Fiamengo connects the two kinds of suffering in an incisive analysis of the narrator's abortion, that vital act that motivates much of the narrator's self-exploration in the wilderness and ultimately serves as the measure against which readers can assess her growth. My own essay on *Lady Oracle* incorporates the notion of cultural capital, focusing on the production of Joan Foster's celebrated book of poetry with a view to considering literary production within a larger—and gendered—social context. Tae Yamamoto expresses analogous concerns about gender in her essay about Atwood's first dystopia in "How Can a Feminist Read *The Handmaid's Tale*? A Study of Offred's Narrative."

The final three essays in this part of the book all engage with *Alias Grace*. In the first of these, "'Lurid Yet Muted': Narrative and the Sabotage of Dissident Voice in Margaret Atwood's *Alias Grace*," Julie Godin explores Grace's fraught participation in the construction of her own story, ultimately arguing that "Grace's first-person 'answer' to the confessional framings of her story serves to catalogue and critique, but also to fulfil the cultural expectations that attend her self-revelation as a nineteenth-century murderess." Drawing on contemporary psychology, Regina M. Edmonds construes the split in Grace's subjectivity differently, conceiving of it as the result of a traumatized psyche rather than the manifestation of a conflicted or compromised dissidence, and, opening up the discussion to include other Atwood novels as well, Frank Davey's "Atwood and Class: *Lady Oracle, Cat's Eye,* and *Alias Grace*" posits the split as class-based, characterizing it as, among other things, a division in several of Atwood's characters between what he calls a "Wordsworthian childhood" and a mature, socially determined symbolic identity. Ultimately, however, he complicates his own opposition, contesting the claim "about unconditioned identity that runs throughout Atwood's writing," seeing both identities as equally conditioned by class.

In an effort to redress the comparative critical void regarding Atwood's shorter prose pieces and her poetry, the book's third section brings these genres into the spotlight. In the opening essay, for example, Wanda Campbell directs attention to the role of humour in Atwood's oeuvre, focusing largely on Atwood's shorter works since they engage with humour more explicitly than any of Atwood's novels, except perhaps *Lady Oracle*. The following essay, by Pamela S. Bromberg, draws primarily on the essays from *Negotiating with the Dead* as it allusively teases out of Atwood's writing an indication of the possibilities of narrative therapy.

Subsequent essays focus more exclusively on the books of poetry, evidencing, in the process, the extent to which Atwood's poetry simultaneously engages with the intensely personal and the openly public. The range here is remarkable: From Sara Jamieson's insights into aging and identity throughout Atwood's poetic canon to Pilar Somacarrera's reading of Atwood's *Power Politics* against Michel Foucault's conception of the same; from Christine Evain's interrogation of the relation between Atwood's poetry and fiction to Rose Lucas's deciphering of the subtext of grief, loss, and mourning in *Morning in the Burned House*, these essays insist that the diversity of Atwood's fiction has its counterpart in that of her poetry. Reingard M. Nischik and Julia Breitbach open the generic field still further in their essay "Eye-Openers: Photography in Margaret Atwood's Poetry," and David R. Jarraway's "'[Com]ing through Darkness': Atwood's 'I'-Opening Lyricism" theorizes Atwood's construction of the self, the Other, and the self as Other as it moves toward a hopeful conclusion in which a larger, more sophisticated identity comes just into view on the other side of an apparently dark abyss.

Appropriately, the last section of this volume of essays focuses on Atwood's last two novels. Taking as her starting point a *New York Times* review of *The Blind Assassin*, Wendy Roy suggests that, perhaps ironically, it is the humanity of the *female* characters that is compromised in the novel, and not only by Atwood but also by a society that must "turn a 'blind' eye to women's bodily experience"—including abuse—if it is to "maintain its conventional order." Helena Hyttinen also posits abuse as a gendered phenomenon in *The Blind Assassin* and consequently reads its presence throughout the narrative as reflecting the novel's participation in the genre of feminine gothic.

Concentrating on *Oryx and Crake*, the final grouping of essays looks outward and ahead to consider where our present social trajectory might lead, and the prognosis is not good. Phyllis Sternberg Perrakis's "Negotiating with the Looking-Glass: Atwood, Her Protagonists, and the Journey to the Dead," opens this section with a feminist consideration of the way Atwood's representations of corporality have changed in her recent novels, and Sally Chivers's "Margaret Atwood and the Critical Limits of Embodiment" follows that lead, asserting that "the elimination of physical difference in *Oryx and Crake* ... depends entirely on widespread investment in a normative bodily frame" and is predicated on the extermination of the "wider swath of human existence" that includes physical disability and variation. In "Frankenstein's Gaze and Atwood's Sexual Politics in *Oryx and Crake*," Sharon R. Wilson offers a provocative interpretation of Atwood's speculative world by suggesting that eradicating aggression could ensure our extinction just as surely as practising it could do, and Nathalie Foy, focusing more explicitly on feminist issues, considers what the gaps in *Oryx and Crake* imply about female sexuality and motherhood in particular. Hilde Staels examines how those gaps and absences impact Snowman's humanity, and Michèle Lacombe calls into question the relevance of concepts like humanity and family in a post-human world. The final essay, Diana Brydon's "Atwood's Global Ethic: The Open Eye, the Blinded Eye," recontextualizes the debate about the novel by foregrounding its separation of art and science and by calling for a more global view—one that sees with two eyes, not one, and can therefore validate both branches of human knowledge.

By way of concluding this introduction, John and I would like to acknowledge the support of a number of people who helped make the "Margaret Atwood: The Open Eye" symposium the success it was, and whose encouragement helped shape this volume arising from it. For advice and encouragement along the way, we are grateful to our colleagues in the Department of English at the University of Ottawa, especially Janice Fiamengo, Gerald Lynch, Seymour Mayne, Klaus Peter Stich, Cynthia Sugars, Lia Marie Talia, and Chair David Rampton. For facilitating Margaret Atwood's presentation at "The Open Eye" symposium, we thank Jennifer Osti. And for financial support of this project, we acknowledge the grants we received from the Social Sciences and Humanities Research Council of Canada, and the Faculty of Arts Research and Publications Committee, University of Ottawa.

WORKS CITED

Cooke, Nathalie. *Margaret Atwood: A Biography*. Toronto: ECW, 1998.
Davey, Frank. *Margaret Atwood: A Feminist Poetic*. Vancouver: Talonbooks, 1984.
Gessell, Paul. "Atwood Academics Dissect Her Work: Their Idol Says She Doesn't Read the Stuff." Ottawa Citizen, April 23, 2004. D1.
Grace, Sherrill. *Violent Duality: A Study of Margaret Atwood*. Montreal: Véhicule, 1980.
Howells, Coral. *Margaret Atwood*. 2nd ed. New York: Palgrave Macmillan, 2005.
Rigney, Barbara H. *Margaret Atwood*. London: Macmillan Education, 1987.
Stein, Karen F. *Margaret Atwood Revisited*. New York: Twayne, 1999.
Sullivan, Rosemary. *The Red Shoes: Margaret Atwood Starting Out*. Toronto: HarperFlamingoCanada, 1998.

SUBJECT/OBJECT

Margaret Atwood:
Branding an Icon Abroad

LAURA MOSS

IN THE FIFTH annual LaFontaine-Baldwin Symposium Lecture, "A Country Imagined: Democracy and National Identity in Global Culture," author David Malouf spoke in detail about Australian history, the notion of "fairness" as a national governing principle, and the failure of the 2000 referendum on Australia becoming a republic. He was at once a national historian, a cultural analyst, and a political commentator as he spoke unflinchingly and without irony of "we" and "us": "We are down-to-earth people, rooted, as most people are, in the particularities of daily living" (Malouf). At Convocation Hall on the University of Toronto campus, Malouf interpreted the democratic life of Australia for a Canadian audience. It seemed incumbent upon him to make the kinds of comprehensive statements about his nation that he might hesitate to make at home. Malouf, in Canada, was speaking as a national icon of Australia.

Malouf's lecture reminded me of Margaret Atwood's Clarendon lectures at Oxford. While Atwood demystifes the Canadian North in the four Clarendon lectures collected in *Strange Things: The Malevolent North in Canadian Literature*, she also approximates Gayatri Spivak's notion of the "native informant," speaking almost ethnographically about herself, her culture, and her people. Although the genre of the prestigious university lecture invites the positioning of the author as cultural guru, some writers play to expectation more than others. Margery Fee comments that in *Strange Things* "the lectures make it clear how nearly irresistible it is for colonials visiting England to play the colonial" (Fee 335). As she is an astute judge of audience and market, there is undoubtedly a link between what Atwood presents to a foreign audience and what she thinks they want to hear. Fee suspects that Atwood

> panders to what survives in the British ... of the sense that Canadians are a rough-hewn folk struggling to survive in a snow-and-bear-covered landscape. Her defence is that an account of literary uses of Canadian urban life would be boring to her audience. (335)

Un-boring Canadian literature in the Clarendon lectures is populated by the Wendigo, Grey Owl imitators, gallant exploring men, and linoleum caves. Going beyond the boring has always been important for Atwood. She speculates that "the beginning of Canadian cultural nationalism was not 'Am I really that oppressed' but 'Am I really that boring'?" (qtd. in Nischik 169). Sometimes avoiding the boring means acquiescing to expectation; sometimes it means bypassing some of the tedious details of debates that occur within Canada. As Atwood plays the role of international–national cultural commentator, she abridges some of the ongoing discussions in Canada and abbreviates their complexities for a non-Canadian audience.[1] She is not at Oxford to mediate debates about Canada; she is there as a cultural ambassador of Canada—or Icon Abroad. She plays her role well. In this paper, I am interested in three interrelated ways in which Atwood and Canada are linked beyond the borders of the nation, as she situates herself as Canadian, as she is promoted as part of a Canadian global brand, and as she is read popularly and academically outside Canada.

Atwood and Malouf are not alone as creative writers who (are called upon to) represent the culture, history, politics, and values of their home nations in foreign contexts. This is part of literary celebrity culture, the endowed university lecture genre, and the promotion of authors as cultural ambassadors abroad. In an age in which universities around the world are shifting funding emphasis away from the arts in the process of "businessification," the endowed lecture has gained prominence as a means for public institutions to publicly display support and validation of the arts. The literary celebrity puts a human face on the university's commitment to what UBC President Martha Piper labelled the "human sciences" in her 2002 Killam lecture. The celebrity author is asked to speak across a range of subjects that illustrate the relevance of the arts in discussions of important topics such as good governance, citizenship, and civil society. The author of international stature further helps to underline the degree to which the modern university projects itself as part of a global cultural community.

The apparent desire of the university to highlight its commitment to the arts and to a global community is emblematic of a broader institutional desire to link artists and international relations. The Canadian government, for instance, is eager to capitalize on the popularity and economic success of Canadian literature and other arts abroad. A recent publication of Foreign Affairs Canada (FAC) entitled "Canada World View, As Others See Us," packages a group of artists together as integral parts of "Canada's global brand":

> Filmmaker Atom Egoyan, multimedia director Robert Lepage, visual artist Jeff Wall, and author Margaret Atwood have made waves in Europe with individual, even quirky visions that are resolutely made in Canada. Such cultural figures are important elements of Canada's global brand, one that garners recognition all over the world but particularly in Europe. On a continent so deeply steeped in the arts, Canada's credibility in the cultural arena strengthens all aspects of our country's international relations. (FAC paragraph 4)

The image of Canada branded for export to a continent so steeped in culture is one of quirky individuality that is still resolutely Canadian. If, as Naomi Klein suggests, branding is about promoting "not a product but a way of life, an attitude, a set of values, an idea" (23), it is also about selling a product and making a profit. What is FAC promoting through Atwood, Egoyan, Wall, and Lepage? What does Canada want to sell? The literal answer (films, art, books, and photographs) meets the symbolic answer (respect, economic growth, and political strength). Canada is branded as culturally progressive and yet firmly located in a national sphere in much the same way that the endowed university lecture helps brand the university as committed to sustaining the values of culture.

Another publication, by the Department of Foreign Affairs and International Trade, "Why Trade Matters," reinforces the strong economic motivation behind the promotion of Canada though the promotion of art:

> Canadian authors, with their increasing high profile and international critical acclaim, could be described as Canada's 'other ambassadors.' Through their writing, they bring a particular vision of Canada to the world, promoting an image of a dynamic, bilingual, and multicultural nation. (paragraph 2)

As one of the senior "other ambassadors," Atwood promotes Canada promoting her books promoting Canada. It is a business relationship that is beneficial for Atwood and for Canada. Although Atwood states with characteristic bluntness that "I don't work for the tourist board" when asked "Is it important to you in your writing to sort of promote the Canadian identity?" she does take advantage of the ways in which the tourist board works for her. The unnamed author of the FAC article focuses on the economic impact of Canadian literature globally, noting that "in 2002, the total value of cultural goods exports was 2.3 billion. Nearly half of this was publishing and printing products, with books representing nearly 500 million of this figure (paragraph 2)." The Canadian government's commitment to "an image of a dynamic, bilingual, and multicultural nation (paragraph 20)" aside, half a billion dollars is big business. Although the article lists several writers (Margaret Atwood, Marie-Claire Blais, Nicole Brossard, Timothy Findley, Anne Hébert, Ann-Marie MacDonald, Alistair MacLeod, Yann Martel, Rohinton Mistry, Alice Munro, Michael Ondaatje, Nino Ricci, Carol Shields, and Michel Tremblay, to be precise), it highlights the role of Atwood as the most accomplished and celebrated of the list: "With her books in over twenty languages, Margaret Atwood is probably Canada's most translated author. Her novel *The Blind Assassin* can even be read in Bengali and Farsi!" (paragraph 10). The global reach of Atwood, extending as far as Bangladesh and Iran as FAC points out, is in part due to the quality of her work, but it is also at least in part due to the way she is marketed (by herself, her publishers, and the Canadian government) as an ambassador of Canada and an integral element of Canada's global brand, the way she performs the role with gusto, and the way she in turn is read as both Canadian and transnational.

As an "other ambassador," Atwood witnesses her country's national narratives. In doing so, she comes to exemplify what I see as the paradox of transnational-nationalism. According to Jana Evans Braziel and Anita Mannur, transnationalism is defined as the "flow of people, ideas, goods, and capital, across national territory, [which] undermines nationality and nationalism as discrete categories of identification, economic organization, and political constitution"(8). However, paradoxically, transnationalism often relies precisely on the designation of individuals, often well-known cultural figures, to represent the nation categorically beyond its borders. This is clearly the case with the publications of the Department of Foreign Affairs explicitly naming Atwood as an important element of the international image of Canada it wishes to project. Atwood is both representative of a very localized, often rather neatly packaged, national identity and a global figure who is worthy of representing the local for the international community. As an "other ambassador," Atwood is exemplary of such transnational-nationalism.

The 1970s image of Atwood as a medusa with a razorblade in her mouth has been replaced by twenty-first century images of her as the "first lady of Canadian literature" (Ferguson paragraph 2 and Queen of the Booker). As the British council website puts it, Atwood "is Canada's most eminent novelist and poet, and also writes short stories, critical studies, screenplays, radio scripts, and books for children, her works having been translated into over thirty languages" (Holcombe paragraph 2). For the British council, she is not one of Canada's most eminent writers; she is *the* most eminent writer. Although Canadians tend to avoid such absolutes, Atwood is still everywhere: locally, on the poster students put up outside my office door for the UBC student literary journal *Rant*: "churning out atwoods [sic] since 1918"; nationally, on the list of suggestions in the CBC search for the "Greatest Canadian" (although not one of the finalists); and globally, on hundreds of Internet web pages dedicated to her work; in newspaper articles by and about her; in megabox bookstore displays of her latest work; on high school and university course offerings in Denmark, Germany, Japan, Australia, England, the United States, China, and in Canadian studies centres around the world. More often than not, in the international references to Atwood, the word Canada and the Canadian flag are not far away. Atwood is not just an internationally recognizable icon; she is an internationally recognizable icon of Canada.

Atwood is undeniably an important writer, one who experiments with a variety of literary genres and one who comments on a range of subjects from national identity to food to war. In Canada, however, she is often discussed with ambivalence. It is just not "cool" to enjoy the works of

Atwood. German critic Caroline Rosenthal asserts that "much in contrast to the United States, Canadians often treat national icons with irony and self-deprecating humour ... Canada ritualizes the non-reverence of national icons and the absence of a coherent national mythology"(50). As is often the case, as a cultural figure is elevated to the level of icon nationally and then internationally, other writers, thinkers, and speakers rebel at the simplification of having one artist's voice paradigmatically represent many. Academic ambivalence to the icon further comes out in such statements as "if only Atwood were a better writer," as one senior colleague said to me when I told him I was going to the Atwood conference in Ottawa. Popular ambivalence is well illustrated by Will Ferguson in an article for *En Route* magazine on Canadians whom Canadians love to hate. Ferguson suggests that it is part of the Canadian identity to want to unsettle an icon: "it is Atwood the icon that people resent, not Atwood the Feminist ... no, it's not anything as grand as her gender politics or as petty as the tone of her voice. It is simply the fact that Atwood has become an icon, and icons were meant to be—if not toppled—at least pelted by snowballs (paragraphs 6 and 9)." Beyond fulfilling the stereotype of a national distrust of iconicity, the ambivalence with which Atwood is almost always met in Canada comes from her position as Ur-Canadian beyond Canada. Outside of Canada, snowballs tend to melt and icons tend to last.

An icon often begins symbolic life as an iconoclast.[2] The challenging of accepted beliefs may be considered heretical, but if such challenging leads to a change in public opinion, or in communal conceptions of culture or art, a shift occurs where what was once considered iconoclastic becomes recognizably representative of an epoch or a nation. Subsequently, with the forgetting of the iconoclastic beginnings, the icon is emptied of a history and instead becomes something to be reacted to by another iconoclast. However, context is key. The trajectory from iconoclasm to icon sometimes stops at the symbolic stage of iconicity outside of the original context. This is the case of Atwood as an icon abroad. The iconoclasm of the "political manifesto" of *Survival* has been enshrined and subsequently rendered iconic in the international canonization of Atwood as the figurehead of CanLit. Atwood herself is clearly aware of the fluidity and illusory nature of iconicity. In answer to a question posed in Wollongong, Australia, about how it feels to have "spent a quarter of a century as an icon of Canadian literature," she replied, "Well, number one, icons inspire iconoclasm;

number two, I'm never around when I'm being an icon. It's like the Virgin Mary: she's in heaven, her picture is down here" (Canadian Studies Address 23). Self-comparisons with the Virgin Mary aside, Atwood has a point about the way that iconicity is not sought but thrust upon one.

Atwood as national icon has followed the familiar trajectory—from iconoclast to icon. Donna Bennett and Nathalie Cooke argue that "[i]ronically, today Atwood in particular, and the writers of her generation in general, are seen as embodying the authority that they saw as external and inauthentic to their experience"(41). Such irony is the basis of the trajectory. Atwood is not alone on this trajectory in Canada. Think of the struggle of Emily Carr in the early part of the twentieth century to be considered an artist of merit. She did not paint the kinds of realist portraits of nature expected of her as a woman or as a Canadian. Indeed, she worked against what she considered to be the confining artistic conventions of her training in Paris, San Francisco, and Victoria. Carr was iconoclastic in her views on art, Haida culture, women, and family. Over time, however, and with the patronage of such an icon as Lawren Harris, Carr's work has become closely associated with the West Coast and with Canada. The largest permanent collection at the Vancouver Art Gallery is the Emily Carr collection. Her images are available on magnets, T-shirts, and shopping bags. As with Atwood, Carr's work is marketed as quintessentially Canadian. Carr's art has also become the target of more avant-garde artists. In her 1996 installation entitled "A Group of Sixty-Seven," Vancouver artist Jin-me Yoon reconfigured a *terra nullus* Canada by asserting the presence of Asian Canadians in the mountainous landscape as she poses sixty-seven figures who stand looking at a detail of Carr's painting "Old Time Coast Village."[3] The installation is a powerful and important reconfiguration of the Canadian landscape to include Asian Canadians, but it also relies on using the work of Carr as a stand-in for a racist Canada. Carr's own struggle as an artist, and the controversy over her representation of a vanishing and decaying Haida culture, are set aside in order to make a point about other kinds of struggles in Canada. Carr's work is decontextualized over time, much as some contemporary literary icons works are rendered less complex with chronological and geographic distance. Carr's painting is used as a cultural totem that stands in for a Canada that is natural and sublime—much like the iconic Canada associated with Atwood.

In his chapter on Atwood in *The Postcolonial Exotic*, Graham Huggan discusses the literary star system by way of Pierre Bourdieu's notion of cultural and symbolic capital (212). Huggan adds, "In Atwood's case, we are talking not just about a consecrated writer but about a *cultural celebrity*" (214 emphasis added). His nine reasons why Atwood is so celebrated range from the fact that she is a powerful performer to the argument that she has bridged the gap between academic discourse and popular audiences. The most compelling of Huggan's reasons, however, is that "Atwood's image as a no-holds-barred cultural commentator has been augmented by her international image as a translator and interpreter of Canadian culture. These images when taken together have fuelled the common (mis)perception of Atwood as a 'representative,' or even 'quintessential,' Canadian or Canadian writer" (214). As if providing evidence for Huggan, in Germany, Walter Pache writes that "Atwood has shaped our literary perception to such an extent that it is difficult to imagine how we might read Canadian literature and Canadian culture without her guidance"(133). While Pache is undoubtedly justified in saying that Atwood's work is vital in the development of Canadian literature, his comment also raises some questions about the role of the author as, to use his words, an "institution" (133), a "public figure" (120), and a "public persona" (123), or to use the language of FAC, a "global brand" and an "other ambassador." How much can or should an author (be expected to) represent a nation? What does it mean to be the quintessential Canadian writer? There is a tendency to configure Canada as reflected in Atwood's novels as white, middle-class, and Ontario based. This reaffirms a notion of who is central and who is marginal in Canada, beyond what I think is actually the case. If Atwood is central, then Thomas King, Michael Ondaatje, and Joy Kogawa must be marginal. This is clearly not so. These writers are as central to the current Canadian canon as Atwood, but they are written about outside of Canada as marginal because they do not depict versions of Canada like the one associated with Atwood.

In "Canonizing Atwood: Her Impact on Teaching in the US, Canada, and Europe," Rosenthal outlines the results of a survey she conducted on the teaching of literary works by Atwood. She notes that in Germany, Atwood has been taught more than any other Canadian author (taught as a science fiction writer, feminist writer, and most often as a Canadian writer). In the United Kingdom, according to Rosenthal, Atwood is generally identified as a post-colonial or feminist Canadian, whereas in the United States, she is rarely taught as Canadian. Rather, Rosenthal irately notes that "she is often included in American Literature courses which simply interpret 'American' as 'North American' (whatever that means) and efface Canada"(48). What is interesting in this excellent article is Rosenthal's insistence on Atwood's Canadianness and even her anger at how Atwood is "made into an international American author by overwriting her Canadian identity"(48). While I understand that the outrage is based on a fear of American cultural imperialism subsuming the "best" of Canada and claiming it as its own, I also wonder about the implications of the German critic bristling at such a suggestion. Whereas Diana Brydon points to constructive ways of addressing such an effacement by drawing on the post-colonial notion of subaltern agency as she reads it in *Survival*, Rosenthal is reluctant to relinquish the Canadianness of Atwood's work. Playing devil's advocate, I wonder if there is also a danger in Rosenthal's demand that the Canadianness of Atwood be front and centre. Has the branding of Atwood as Canada worked so thoroughly that when she is misrecognized the misrecognition of a larger sense of Canadian identity is also threatened?

My own research into the reception and teaching of Atwood around the world leads to slightly different conclusions than Rosenthal's. I looked at English course web pages and individual Canadian Studies program websites available in a variety of locations outside of Canada (Australia, Argentina, Brazil, China, Denmark, England, Germany, India, Israel, Japan, South Korea, Scotland, Spain, and Wales) to see if Atwood is mentioned and, if so, to consider how she is read in association with Canada.[4] While she is certainly not present on all the Canadian Studies web pages, if any writer is named, it is Atwood. The novels and poems offered in literature courses fall along a continuum that ranges from Canadian to Great. Often, Atwood is made to stand in metonymically for Canada (with reference to the recognizably Canadian works *Survival, Surfacing, The Journals of Susanna Moodie, The Blind Assassin,* and *Alias Grace*). Or she is read as a "novelist of our time" (or rather a "feminist of our time") who happens to be Canadian.[5] On non-Canadian Studies course web pages, and there are hundreds of them on which Atwood appears, Atwood is presented with an emphasis more often on Great than Canadian, under expansive versions of American literature, British literature, women's literature, or simply contemporary literature (with reference most often to *The Handmaid's Tale* and *Oryx and Crake*).

Still, it is striking how much the influence of *Survival* is felt around the world even now. Many Canadian Studies courses begin with *Survival* to establish a theoretical framework. An article published in Germany nearly thirty years after *Survival* by Helmut Bonheim argues the predominance of "Margaret Atwood's thesis that Canadian writing is about survival in a hostile environment: the typical subject of Canadian literature is a potential victim"(57). This version of Atwood is not in line with the prevalent view in Canada that *Survival* was important but is now outdated. Bennett and Cooke claim that Atwood's early articulation of a valid and coherent Canadian literature in *Survival* is now "rejected" within Canada because "the nationalism of Atwood's generation seems to speak neither to multiethnic reality of Canada's cities nor to the current split between Canada's traditional English-French solitudes. It seems, in fact, an ideal lost in a receding past"(41). While such nationalism is commonly rejected in Canada, it sometimes still holds sway abroad.

However, another kind of updated nationalism associated with Atwood is also prevalent outside Canada. Such a Canada is not a nostalgic or melancholic desire for a unified national identity based on a shared sense of victimization but, rather, a transnational-nationalism. It is a kind of nationalism that exists concomitantly within a global framework. It is a nationalism that has consumed the brand of Atwood as an ambassador of Canada in the world. The flip side of transnational-nationalism is evident when Atwood is read as a writer who touches on "global" concerns that transcend national borders. The emphasis is on the transnational rather than the national. This is where the ends of the continuum of Canadian to Great become cyclical and Atwood is a Great Canadian global citizen.

In exploring online responses to Atwood, I realized how much the reception and projection of Atwood as a national and/or transnational Canadian icon is dependent upon the subject matter and thematic focuses of her most recent novel. I compared a dozen reviews of *The Blind Assassin* and *Oryx and Crake* primarily in British newspapers to see how much the subject matter affects how Atwood is configured and which icon is drawn upon. In the *Blind Assassin* reviews, with the named Canadian setting (fictional as it is), the focus is on the Canadianness of Atwood, her biography, and the novel. Catherine Pepinster, in the *Independent on Sunday* to my mind hyperbolically illustrates an obsession with a nature-based Canada when she writes, "Canada also informed Atwood's writing, from layers of its history enhancing her own sense of identity to its wide open spaces and its wilderness where she spent her childhood, steeping her novels in otherness"(23). With the reception of *The Blind Assassin*, Atwood is interpreted as an icon of Canada. She is the local author globally representing her nation.

In stark contrast, in reviews of *Oryx and Crake* Canada is rarely mentioned. Instead, Atwood is presented as the prophetic writer of feminist dystopias—notably *The Handmaid's Tale*—who follows in the footsteps of George Orwell and Aldous Huxley rather than of her etymologist father. With *Oryx and Crake*, she is a global icon. In these reviews, Atwood is dislocated from Canada and relocated as a global figure with what Rosemary Goring calls a "bleak, soul-destroyingly isolated picture" of the future. Joan Smith writes that if *The Handmaid's Tale* is a warning about an "anti-feminist backlash," then "*Oryx and Crake* is about another set of dangers facing the human race; with its genetically modified viruses, it is particularly resonant during the current SARS outbreak" (15). Smith's emphasis on the human race appears to illustrate that Atwood's fictional interrogation of environmental degradation goes beyond the concerns of a single nation-space. With the recent revival of discussions of nature under the auspices of eco-criticism and environmental studies, Atwood's concerns about the devastating effects of nature forced into an unnatural state resonates with her earlier focus on land, nature, and wildlife in Canada.

As the author of *Oryx and Crake*, Atwood remains a Canadian ambassador. It is no less part of Canada's global brand to be the globe's moral and ethical conscience than it is to represent wide open spaces of untamed wilderness and quirky individuals. Atwood is such a powerful icon of Canada outside of Canada because she can represent both the nation and the nation in a transnational globalized space. In the terms of cultural globalization, a literary icon like Atwood is a figure who personifies the paradox of transnational-nationalism. She is a figure who moves around the globe delivering lectures, selling books, reading poetry, and speaking on the affairs of her nation. As with the trajectory from iconoclast to icon, there is a shift from national to international icon that both reinforces and rejects the notion of the icon as an icon of the nation. Although I recognize the risks of using diaspora as a metaphor of global displacement and movement, there is an allure to reading Atwood's texts, and even more interestingly Atwood's iconicity, as diasporic subjects: moving away from the context of production, they are either read through a nationalistic lens of Canada or as emphatically transnational global subjects. There is a kind of diasporic connectedness with Atwood scholars, readers, consumers, and promoters. That is exactly what FAC is banking on.

—University of British Columbia

NOTES

It was with a clear sense of irony that I, a Canadian writing from within Canada, presented the original version of this paper about Atwood abroad at the Atwood conference in Ottawa to an audience of people from at least fourteen different countries. This subsequent paper has gained a great deal from the conversations I had at the conference with Atwood scholars from around the world. I am, however, still committed to thinking through the ways in which I see Atwood represented as a Canadian abroad.

1. In conversation, Sherrill Grace suggested to me that Atwood has long played the role of spokesperson for Canadian culture. Grace traces this role from the first-person voice in *Survival* through *Strange Things* to *Negotiating with the Dead*.
2. According to C.S. Peirce's triadic taxonomy of signs, a symbol is "related to its object only in consequence of a mental association, and depends upon a habit"; an icon is "a sign which stands for something (merely) because it resembles it," and an index is "a sign [which] signifies its object solely by virtue of being really connected with it" (qtd. in Adam 225–226). Ian Adam notes that "in general usage we often conflate indexes and icons—e.g. a moose doesn't resemble Canada but it is seen as an 'icon' of Canada." Similarly, although Atwood does not resemble Canada (or a moose for that matter), she has become a national icon. Indeed, the Lavin Agency, Atwood's PR company, makes no bones about listing her as "Margaret Atwood: Literary Icon."
3. Yoon combines the Group of Seven artists with the 1967 centenary celebrations in Canada, the date marked by some as the beginning of a new phase in Canadian nationalism.
4. My research assistant, UBC PhD student Kathryn Grafton, compiled the information on Canadian Studies websites available in English for me to draw on. I am indebted to Kathryn for all her hard work and valuable commentary on this paper.
5. In conversation, Gordon Bölling told me that he teaches *The Handmaid's Tale* beside *Famous Last Words* and *In the Skin of a Lion* precisely to show the depth of Canadian literature beyond texts that realistically represent Canada.

WORKS CITED

Adam, Ian. "Iconicity and the Place of Butala's 'The Prize.'" Paper presented at the *Iconicity and Narrative in Canadian Literature* Conference, St. John's College, University of Manitoba, MB. September 1995 [online]: <http://www.130.179.92.25/canlitx/Framed_Version/Conference/Adam.html> (accessed March 2004).

Atwood, Margaret. *Alias Grace*. New York: Bantam, 1997.

———. *The Blind Assassin*. Toronto: McClelland & Stewart, 2000.

———. "Entering the Labyrinth: Writing The Blind Assassin." In Nortel Networks Canadian Studies Address No. 2., 23. Wollongong, Australia: University of Wollongong Press, 2003.

———. *The Handmaid's Tale*. New York: Anchor, 1998.

———. *The Journals of Susanna Moodie*. Toronto: Oxford University Press, 1970.

———. *Negotiating with the Dead: A Writer on Writing*. Cambridge: Cambridge University Press, 2002.

———. *Oryx and Crake*. Toronto: McClelland & Stewart, 2003.

———. *Strange Things: The Malevolent North in Canadian Literature*. Oxford: Clarendon, 1995.

———. *Surfacing*. New York: Anchor, 1998.

———. *Survival: A Thematic Guide to Canadian Literature*. Toronto: Anansi, 1972.

———. *Wilderness Tips*. Toronto: McClelland & Stewart, 1999.

Bennett, Donna, and Nathalie Cooke. "A Feminist by Another Name: Atwood and the Canadian Canon." In *Approaches to Teaching Atwood's "The Handmaid's Tale" and Other Works*, edited by Sharon R. Wilson, Thomas B. Friedman, and Shannon Hengen, 33–42. New York: MLA of America, 1996.

Bethune, Brian. "Atwood Wins the Booker." *Maclean's*, November 20, 2000 [online] <http://www.macleans.ca/culture/books/article.jsp?content=42881> (accessed March 2004).

Bonheim, Helmut. "Models of Canadianness." In *New Worlds: Discovering and Constructing the Unknown in Anglophone Literature*, edited by Martin Kuester, Gabriele Christ, and Rudolf Beck, 51–71. Munich: Verlag Ernst Vögel, 2000.

Bourdieu, Pierre. *The Field of Cultural Production: Essays on Art and Literature*. Edited by Randal Johnson. Cambridge: Polity Press, 1993.

Braziel, Jana E., and Anita Mannur. "Introduction: Nation, Migration, Globalization: Points of Contention in Diaspora Studies." In *Theorizing Diaspora: A Reader*, edited by Jana Evans Braziel and Anita Mannur, 1–22. Malden, MA: Blackwell, 2003.

Brydon, Diana. "Beyond Violent Dualities: Atwood in Postcolonial Contexts." In *Approaches to Teaching Atwood's "The Handmaid's Tale" and Other Works*, edited by Sharon R. Wilson, Thomas B. Friedman, and Shannon Hengen, 49–54. New York: MLA of America, 1996.

Canada. Department of Foreign Affairs and International Trade. "Why Trade Matters." [online]: <http://www.dfait-maeci.gc.ca/latinamerica/wn-04-canadian-films-2-en.asp> (accessed April 2004)

Edemariam, Aida. "Us? Boring? Ha!" *Guardian* (Manchester), September 27, 2002. [online]: <http://books.guardian.co.uk/bookerprize2002/story/0,12350,800031,00.html> (accessed April 2004).

FAC (Foreign Affairs Canada). "Canada World View, As Others See Us." Summer 2004, issue 22 [online]: <http://www.dfait-maeci.gc.ca/canada-magazine/04-title-en.asp> A publication of Foreign Affairs Canada (accessed October 9, 2004).

Fee, Margery. "Review of *Strange Things: The Malevolent North in Canadian Literature*, by Margaret Atwood." *University of Toronto Quarterly* 67, no.1 (1997–1998): 335–36.

Ferguson, Will. "On Atwood." *En Route*, August 2001 [online]: <http://willferguson.ca/articles_interviews/article_onatwood.html> (accessed April 2004).

Goring, Rosemary. "Welcome to Your Worst Nightmare." *Herald* (Glasgow), April 26, 2003.

Holcombe, Garan. British council contemporary writers site [online]: <http://www.contemporarywriters.com/authors/?p=auth03C18N390512635243> (accessed June 2004).

Huggan, Graham. "Margaret Atwood Inc., or Some Thoughts on Literary Celebrity." *The Post-colonial Exotic: Marketing the Margins*, 209–227. London: Routledge, 2001.

Klein, Naomi. *No Logo: Taking Aim at the Brand Bullies*. Toronto: Vintage, 2000.

The Lavin Agency. "Margaret Atwood" [online]: <http://www.thelavinagency.com/canada/margaretatwood.html> (accessed April 2004).

Malouf, David. "A Country Imagined: Democracy and National Identity in a Global Culture." Paper presented at the LaFontaine-Baldwin Symposium 2004. Convocation Hall, University of Toronto, March 12, 2004 [online]: <http://www.operation-dialogue.com/lafontaine-baldwin/e/2004_speech_1.html> (accessed April 2004).

Nischik, Reingard M. ed. *Margaret Atwood: Works and Impact*. Rochester: Camden House, 2000.

Pache, Walter. "A Certain Frivolity: Margaret Atwood's Literary Criticism." In *Margaret Atwood: Works and Impact*, edited by Reingard M. Nischik, 120–136. Rochester: Camden House, 2000.

Pepinster, Catherine. "The IOS Profile: Margaret Atwood; Fear is Her Forté." *Independent on Sunday* (London), April 3, 2003. 23.

Piper, Martha. "Building a Civil Society: A New Role for the Human Sciences." Paper presented at the 2002 Annual Killam Lecture, University of British Columbia, October 24, 2002 [online]: <http://www.president.ubc.ca/president/speeches/24oct02_killam.pdf> (accessed April 2004).

Rosenthal, Caroline. "Canonizing Atwood: Her Impact on Teaching in the US, Canada, and Europe." In *Margaret Atwood: Works and Impact*, edited by Reingard M. Nischik, 41–56. Rochester: Camden House, 2000.

Smith, Joan. "And pigs might fly ... In Margaret Atwood's dystopian vision, Oryx and Crake, the perils of GM have come home to roost." *Observer*, May 11, 2003 [online]: <http://www.observer.guardian.co.uk/review/story/0,6903,953240,00.html> (accessed April 11, 2006).

Yoon, Jin-me. *Group of Sixty-Seven*. 1996–1997. Collection of the artist.

"A Slightly Uneasy Eminence": The Celebrity of Margaret Atwood

LORRAINE YORK

THE FIRST FOUR words of my title belong to Margaret Atwood. Asked by an Australian radio host how her Booker win for *The Blind Assassin* (2000) would be received in Canada, she responded:

> I think that they will, on the one hand, be very pleased. And on the other hand, you know, Canadians are very good at coming second. They may also like to share a thing. There's a wonderful line by our songwriter Nancy White, who says you can always tell a Canadian girl because if you ask her if she'd like some sex she says, "Only if you're having some yourself." And we do like to feel that ... all should have prizes. So when one person is singled out, it's a slightly uneasy eminence. (see ABC)

The "slightly uneasy eminence" that is the celebrity of Margaret Atwood is also arguably the condition of celebrity in Canada. This paper considers questions such as the following: Uneasy for whom? And why? In this nation, is celebrity, like the sex in Nancy White's song, something no nice girl would ever admit to wanting?

Students of Atwood's work have only recently begun to examine the phenomenon that is Atwood herself: Atwood as literary celebrity. In this respect, we have been somewhat slow out of the starting blocks, for

Atwood herself has been musing on stardom, and on variations of her own experience of literary stardom, for decades, whether in interviews, public addresses, or in her own fiction. Recently, though, Graham Huggan has devoted a chapter of his book *The Postcolonial Exotic* to an absorbing analysis of the stardom of Margaret Atwood (214). There, drawing on the work of French sociologist Pierre Bourdieu, he characterizes her literary fame as "a process of consecration in which Atwood herself continues to play an active role." He offers several explanations for Atwood's success: first and foremost, her hard work, her expertise on several cultural fronts as commentator and critic as well as creative writer, her quotability and "epigrammatic witticisms," and so forth. German critic Susanne Becker focuses on one of these contributing factors: Atwood's response to and management of media discourses about her. In her article "Celebrity, or a Disneyland of the Soul: Margaret Atwood and the Media," Becker offers a nuanced analysis of the way in which Atwood is able "to anticipate public demands and to counter rather than deny them" (33). Her unspoken assumption, however, is that celebrity is in and of itself a negative phenomenon: "the curse of celebrity" (30) that "precludes privacy" (38). Huggan, on the other hand, tends to see literary stardom as an intensification of ordinary processes of canon formation, and yet he draws on celebrity theorists who tend to see the formation of stars as culturally suspect, most notably the historian Daniel Boorstin who, in the 1960s, saw the phenomenon of stardom as one example of what he called the "pseudo-event," an instance of false cultural consciousness. And there is something of the same aura about Huggan's analysis of Atwood's fame, however much he grounds his explanations first and foremost on the fact that she has, simply, worked very hard to gain her success. He argues, for instance, that the subversiveness for which she is often praised by her admirers is actually "negotiated from the safety of the middle-class family, the middle-class educational system, the middle-class home" (217). Whether those spaces actually are safe is a question that Atwood's work persistently interrogates. My own analysis of Atwood's celebrity shares Becker's and Huggan's awareness of Atwood's canny interventions in her own media image, but it also tries to downplay the long tradition of seeing stardom as false consciousness. Instead, I want to consider the opportunities that stardom can open up, the possibilities it may present, particularly in the realm of public intervention. We can all, in this age of reality television, think of instances of stardom as false value, but what we spend less time thinking about is the possibility of stardom's social efficacy.

At first glance, it may seem absurdly out of proportion to understand a writer in terms of celebrity at all. After all, writers are notoriously private people, no matter how larger than life the persona of a Hemingway or a Mailer might be. The fact remains that the labour that gives rise to the renown of a writer is, except in the cases of literary collaboration or oral literatures, carried out in private. However, the parallels that exist among various manifestations of cultural celebrity are worth attending to; the similarities may outweigh those other, obvious differences. To begin with, our expectations about celebrity are, for better or worse, largely informed by the particular phenomenon that is Hollywood celebrity, to such an extent that we sometimes forget its cultural particularity. Not surprisingly, then, the growing field of celebrity theory has grown out of film studies, and it betrays some of the tendencies of its gestation: most notably, using film as a preferred site of analysis. And yet some theorists do appreciate that celebrity operates across institutions and media, forming no particular hierarchy. As Christine Gledhill notes, although "Hollywood has established the dominant paradigm of ... mainstream ... stardom," stars "cross disciplinary boundaries" (xiii). Borrowing from the influential work of film theorist Richard Dyer, Gledhill concludes that a star image (or what Dyer would call a "star text") is "an intertextual construct produced across a range of media and cultural practices" (xiv).

A photograph of Margaret Atwood that appeared in the *Globe and Mail* in 2001, when she received her star in our very own Walk of Fame in the Toronto theatre district, acts as a visual dramatization of this theoretical point about the institutional mobility of celebrity. [Fig. 1]. Atwood is crouching beside a beaming Joni Mitchell, both women pointing to their newly minted stars, a visual tableau of the institutional porousness of celebrity: writer and pop-folk singer-songwriter side-by-side. The caption punningly reads "Concrete evidence of fame," and, for my purposes, the observation is apt. Songwriting, after all, like the penning of novels and poems, requires its own measure of solitude and intense meditation, and yet its institutional packaging seems so much more public: concerts, photo shoots, album promotions. Suddenly, though, these two Canadian artists, linking hands and pointing at their stars on the Walk of Fame, seem to share more than their obvious differences would suggest.

38   "A Slightly Uneasy Eminence": The Celebrity of Margaret Atwood

The photograph is relaxed, charming even, and yet it discloses its own moment of cultural unease. Looked at more closely, the stars to which they point are, in fact, stylized maple leaves, a striking reminder of Atwood's own words about stardom and the body politic in Canada: "when one person is singled out, it's a slightly uneasy eminence." Atwood and Mitchell are present on this occasion as remarkably successful women in their respective areas of cultural endeavour, but they are first and foremost present as representative "Canadians." In fact, this morphed star-maple leaf seems almost admonitory in its collectivism: you, the individual, can have your stardom, it seems to say, but only if we, the national collectivity, are having some ourselves.

Figure 1
"Concrete Evidence of Fame." Photograph. Louie Palu. *Globe and Mail* (Toronto), October 20, 2001. A21.

Accordingly, many forms of uneasiness can be detected in media representations of the celebrity of Margaret Atwood. For example, in a *Chatelaine* article that certainly carries a boosterish title, "Margaret Atwood takes N.Y.C.," journalist Robert Collison observes, "for almost as long as she's been an adult, Margaret Atwood ... has been as famous as it is possible for a Canadian cultural figure to be" (100). As a formulation of praise, this encomium seems a lightly revised version of that old chestnut, "As Canadian as possible ... under the circumstances." Since celebrity tends to be confirmed both by America and by mass entertainment industries, Atwood's celebrity is here rendered doubly uneasy.

In media representations of Atwood that stretch over thirty-five years, a number of narratives about celebrity and uneasiness have taken shape. In the 1970s, Atwood and journalists interviewing her focused on the untoward consequences of her growing fame. Many of these stories have to do with Atwood becoming a type of visual spectacle whose collective ownership by the Canadian public was rapidly becoming invasive, disruptive of her privacy. One journalist, interviewing her in a restaurant near Alliston, slowly realizes that, while they're talking, "a heavy-set woman at another table picks up her meal and watches as if Atwood were a television set" (MacGregor 65). As she told Valerie Miner on another interview occasion, "Sometimes I would just like to be able to walk down the street and have no one notice me. But people talk to me when I'm on the airport bus, while I'm taking a quiet pee in Eaton's, when I'm walking down Bloor Street"(33). Ironically, of course, these comments reach the mass media as a result of that privacy having been broken. In the 1970s, at the very time that media coverage of Atwood emphasized the rupture of her privacy, it did so largely as a result of journalists being allowed the sort of entrée into Atwood's private spaces that she has not felt able to extend in recent years. Theoretically and historically, though, invasion of privacy has been seen as a crucial precondition of stardom. As film historian Richard deCordova argued, the phenomenon known as "stardom" arose in early twentieth-century North America as soon as "the question of the player's existence outside his or her work in film became the primary focus of discourse. The private lives of the players were constituted as a site of knowledge and truth"(98). Celebrity, in fact, collapsed the very dichotomy of public/private; whatever representations of privacy made their way to eager fans were always already public, filtered through media and often through public relations people. Celebrity both posed and rendered problematic the question: What is a public individual?

As this question gained momentum for Atwood in the 1980s, she, in turn, shifted gears in dealing with media, from a mainly defensive posture to an offensive stance. She realized that the advice she had been given about celebrity by a *very* public personality, writer Farley Mowat, was both wise and prescient. In the wake of Atwood's phenomenal success in the early seventies, he had warned her "Now you're a target ... and they will shoot at you" (qtd. in Atwood, "Survival" 54). Thinking about what Mowat had done in order to deal with this celebrity barrage, that is, to create a larger-than-life persona, she started to consider building herself one of her own. In 1976 she mused to Helen Slinger, "Maybe I should do what Farley Mowat does—construct a public persona that has nothing really to do with him. But he sends it out and he does his number, dancing on tables and whatnot, and everybody takes that as what he's really like. And he, himself, is not bothered" (6). In effect, then, the advice was to become a moving target. She briefly pondered the option of giving up interviews altogether (Timson 60), an option that surely her publishers would not have greeted with much enthusiasm. And around the same time, the early eighties, she lived briefly in London. As she explained to another disrupter of her privacy, William French, "It's just the price of fame. It was increasingly difficult to maintain privacy there, to get any writing done without being rude to people"(E1). The late 1970s was a period of re-evaluation for Atwood, of testing strategies for dealing with fame. In the end, her own version of Mowat's advice won the day, and she returned to Canada, continued to give interviews, but increasingly on her own terms and with a clear eye to protecting her boundaries and to policing both her persona and her privacy.

Other commentators on Atwood's fame have remarked on how well she handles the media to her own ends. Becker, for instance, argues convincingly that "she encounters—and uses—the publicity machine and the media business with superiority, dignity, and generosity"(29). Becker's detailed analysis is perceptive; she maintains that "Atwood's strategy to address, summarize, and thus control much of the media imagery about her" makes her able "to anticipate public demands and to counter rather than deny them" (32–33). I agree wholeheartedly with this assessment; preemptive critical strikes are an Atwoodian forté. She has assembled the most comprehensive list of media representations of her, and in the process of doing so she has, of course, skewered those representations: Man-eating Medusa, Ice Queen, Margaret the Monster, Margaret the Mother, and so on. This parodic performance of one's own celebrity is itself a means of simultaneously distancing and confirming it. Looking, briefly, to film, consider the occasional tendency of film stars to refer to their own "star texts" or self-images.

For example, Jim Carrey, in his numerous comic roles, often injects a moment of self-parody; when the character of his young son in *Liar, Liar*, for instance, capitalizing on his father's brief inability to lie, asks him whether making a funny face by stretching his mouth with his fingers will cause his face to stay that way (a common adult warning), Carrey's character solemnly replies that it won't; "in fact, some people make a good living that way." Some people like Jim Carrey, of course. We laugh: and Jim Carrey both parodies his fame and consolidates it with one stroke. In spite of my filmic example, film theorist Barry King's comments on stardom as parodic performance should apply to more than film. He suggests that "stardom is a strategy of performance that is an adaptive response to the limits and pressures exerted upon acting in the mainstream media"(167).

That Atwood has so adapted really isn't at issue; Becker and others have charted the ways in which she cannily manages her interactions with the media. What I want to focus on, instead, is the uneasiness that is persistently associated with her fame, whether that fame is pre-emptively constructed by herself or by others. A major form this uneasiness takes, as I would argue it takes in celebrity in general, is the question of what kinds of power celebrity is able or unable to harness. David Marshall has written cogently on this question in his book *Celebrity and Power*. As Marshall admits, celebrity is "a less definable form of power" operating "in contemporary culture," but he nevertheless gives definition a try. This isn't power, he says, in "any overt political sense," and I would add that in some senses the celebrity inhabits power and powerlessness simultaneously. The celebrity is assumed to be significant. He or she utters things and they are given cultural attention. At the same time, however, as Marshall puts it, "the celebrity is viewed in the most antipathetic manner." In our own, national literary culture, Atwood is the prime case; as I have written elsewhere, no figure in our literary world excites as much reverence or as much hostility as Margaret Atwood.

The hostility of which Marshall is thinking has to do with the celebrity possessing what many feel is unearned recognition, or, as he says, "success without ... work" (xi). As Richard Dyer pointed out years ago in his pioneering work *Stars*, classic Hollywood stars were often depicted in the media as revelling in consumption and leisure time. This representation, according to Dyer, effectively mystifies the labour that is involved in acting and in producing film (39). In the case of writing, there would seem to be less of a problem here; picture an author and a deeply absorbed, madly word-processing figure emerges in many of our imaginations. And yet the increasing publicizing of the authorial figure that dates from Lord Byron, and from the public reading tours of Charles Dickens and, later, Dylan Thomas, would seem to produce another, competing image, or "star text." This image is of the writer as public orator and performer rather than private scribbler. And with the recent, well-documented rise in the popularity of author readings, book tours, and book superstore and television talk-show appearances, writers must negotiate this strong injection of "visibility" into their star images. As literary visibility rises, the representation of labour becomes much more problematic. No wonder, then, that a writer as unquestionably industrious as Atwood still feels the need to end a section of her website devoted to favourite quotations with the following exchange: the Australian-born soprano Joan Sutherland was once asked by an interviewer, "To what do you attribute your success?" to which she replied, "Bloody hard work, Duckie!" (O.W. Toad, Margaret Atwood Reference Site).

This uneasy fame that both enables and undercuts finds its expression in Atwood's own conflicted responses to her celebrity. On one hand, she is given to modest rebuttals of fame, suggesting that she doesn't really live up to the label "celebrity." As she told *CBC National Magazine*, a performance artist made a video in which he complained that Canada was disappointing because you could get on the subway and run into Margaret Atwood. As she joked, "Surely celebrities ought to be driving around in limousines and wearing white fox fur and doing Hollywood things and what have we got, you know, Margaret Atwood with her shopping bag. How dowdy" (see CBC). On the occasion of having her novel *The Handmaid's Tale* placed on the French national qualifying exams for teachers, she once again downplayed her celebrity by offering a negative comparison with a normative celebrity system: "Anybody who has lived any length of time at all knows that you can be very popular one year, then not ... I don't think it's quite as bad in literature as it is in the world of pop singing, but there are fashions in these things and you more or less have to ignore them" (Spicer D11). Deflating similes are strategically useful here too; once asked how she felt to be favoured to win the Booker, she replied that it's like being "a big zucchini in the fall fair" (see ABC).

Beside all this strategic downplaying, however, there coexists a genuine awareness of her potential for some form of political intervention. There are the numerous causes that Atwood has supported and that have been well documented (Amnesty, protection of wilderness space, support for striking University of Toronto teaching assistants and striking *Calgary Herald* workers, the anti-freetrade movement, and so on). Obviously, Atwood believes to some extent in the efficacy of acting as a spokesperson for these causes, or else she would not devote so much valuable writing time to them; as she commented to Joel Yanofsky, "The most important thing about writers and why they are at the forefront of this or that controversy is that they can't be fired. I have power—the kind that allows me to continue to do what I do" (F1). And yet, in a revealing comment made to Val Ross, Atwood painted a much uneasier portrait of her cultural power: "I write so many letters to which I do not receive replies!" she indignantly told Ross. But on second thought she added, "The worst of it is, I do get some of my letters answered. And Joe Schmoe wouldn't" (19). Here is the paradox of celebrity power, set out in all its contradictoriness: if you don't get listened to, you lack power. If you do, then you possess unfair amounts of it.

In her writing, I have consistently noted that one sign of this ambivalence is the way in which fame operates both as power source and as spectre, as a sign of artistic vigour and as a ghostly emanation of death and decay. Painter Elaine Risley in *Cat's Eye* opens her Toronto daily paper and finds herself hailed as a famous Canadian artist. The article opens, "Eminent artist Elaine Risley returns to hometown Toronto this week for a long-overdue retrospective" (302), and right away Elaine perceives two verbal kisses of death in operation in one sentence: "eminent" and "retrospective." Elaine refers to the former as "*Eminent*, the mausoleum word" (302), and as for the latter, she mordantly reflects, "First the retrospective, then the morgue" (19). There's also the figure of Joan Foster from *Lady Oracle*, whose faked suicide metaphorically renders fame itself a species of living death. Taking gender into account, I see the deathly spectre of fame in Atwood's works as a tricky ideological negotiation of female celebrity. As a woman possessing a power that many observers have found threatening, no matter how unstable its status, Atwood needs both to acknowledge and to devalue cultural celebrity. She needs, as sociologist Pierre Bourdieu might have said, to see fame both as "authentic" cultural power and as destructive of cultural value.

This contradictory valuation of celebrity is fraught in turn by the complex negotiations of fame that take place in the national context. Canadian celebrity is a messy, contradictory affair. The drastically polarized responses to Atwood's fame have been well documented in the media and in academic studies like those of Caroline Rosenthal, a German Atwood scholar. Imagine her surprise when she conducted a survey about responses to Atwood's work from far and wide and discovered that the most lukewarm or even hostile critical comments came from Canada. She wrote:

> Very few Canadian scholars praised Atwood's work but rather felt that they had to put her achievements and success into perspective. Most of them seemed to be annoyed that Canadian literature is often identified with Atwood internationally, and that in most countries her fame has not promoted the study of other Canadian authors. (Rosenthal 49–50)

As Rosenthal concluded, Atwood is "proudly referred to as a superstar, on the one hand, and who is rejected for being one on the other" (43). To literary Canadians, this is no surprise; we have known about the harshly polarized responses to Atwood's persona for some decades. What has been less recognized, however, is that such a situation is explicable in terms of the concept of celebrity itself. Richard Dyer suggested years ago that rather than representing stable ideas, stars may represent values that are perceived to be under threat or at issue. David Marshall, looking more closely at this idea, suggests several of these possible ideological debates or contradictions that find expression through the star. The one that I think is most applicable to this case concerns the conflict between individuals and collectivities. Marshall argues that one power of celebrity, in his words, is its "capacity to house conceptions of individuality and simultaneously to embody or help embody 'collective configurations' of the social world" (xi–xii). The celebrity of Margaret Atwood is, if you think in these terms, a site for Canadians to negotiate individual achievement and its relation to national embodiment. Everyone taking cultural positions on Atwood can be located somewhere on that spectrum, from those who celebrate her as a cosmopolitan artist who merely happens to be Canadian, to those who feel that her success somehow validates all Canadians, to those who think that she is overrated and undeserving of a fame that could better be spread out and shared by a wider range of cultural workers.

In closing, I offer one observation about the very term "celebrity" and I make what I hope is a modest appeal. When I began to be interested in Atwood's public persona, I analyzed what I called her "iconic" status. I worked through the visual arts and the ways in which they had understood "icons," and from there I analyzed how Atwood herself had deployed the notion of iconicity in her writing. It was only gradually that I realized that the framework I really needed to engage was that of cultural celebrity. At the time, though, "iconicity" sounded more academically respectable than "celebrity." Even now, after the massive influence of the cultural studies movement in our academic institutions, we still employ a double discourse when we are talking about celebrated writers in our learned journals and in daily newspapers alike. "Icon" tends to have, as Bourdieu would say, a commanding cultural capital, whereas "celebrity" is more geared toward the realm of popular culture. In my own work on cultural celebrity, I have tried to avoid the critical, suspicious tone of many academics who write about celebrity, even those engaged in the pursuit of cultural studies here and abroad. As a term, "celebrity" seems to have something of the tawdry permanently attached to it. While recognizing the existence of the tawdry and superficial in contemporary celebrity, I want to appeal to those of us who work in literature to question the dichotomy between the tawdry-sounding "icon" and its maligned cousin, "celebrity." I suggest, instead, that we embrace an understanding of fame as an instance of what Derrida would call the "pharmakon," that which may kill or quicken. Celebrity may be a deathly spectre haunting many of Atwood's works, but it is also a condition and cause of her ability to speak globally. As Atwood herself put it with characteristically acerbic wit:

> Even now, ... some Jack or Jackess emerges with seasonal regularity to take one more crack at *moi*, the supposed Giant, in a never-ending

game of Let Us Now Blame Famous Women. You get to feel like the mechanical duck at the fun-fair shooting gallery, though no one has won the oversized panda yet, because I still seem to be quacking. (Atwood, "Survival" 55)

—McMaster University

WORKS CITED

ABC [online]: <http://www.abc.net.au/sydney/stories/s285525.htm> (accessed 16 June 2002)
ABC [online]: <http://www.abc.net.au/worldtoday/s209839.htm> (accessed 16 June 2002)
Atwood, Margaret. Cat's Eye. Toronto: McClelland & Stewart, 1998.
———. O.W. Toad Margaret Atwood Reference Site [online]: <http://www.owtoad.com/> (accessed May 4, 2005).
———. "Survival: Then and Now." *Maclean's*, July 1, 1999. 54–55.
Becker, Susanne. "Celebrity, or a Disneyland of the Soul: Margaret Atwood and the Media." In *Margaret Atwood: Works and Impact*, edited by Reingard M. Nischik, 28–40. Rochester: Camden House, 2000.
Bourdieu, Pierre. *The Field of Cultural Production: Essays on Art and Literature*. Edited and introduction by Randal Johnson. New York: Columbia University Press, 1993.
CBC [online]: <http://www.cbc.ca/news/national/magazine/atwood/> (accessed 16 June 2002)
Collison, Robert. "Margaret Atwood Takes N.Y.C." *Chatelaine*, June 1986. 64–65.
"Concrete Evidence of Fame." Photograph. Louie Palu. *Globe and Mail* (Toronto), October 20, 2001. A21.
deCordova, Richard. *Picture Personalities: The Emergence of the Star System in America*. Urbana: University of Illinois Press, 1990.
Dyer, Richard. *Stars*. 2nd ed. London: British Film Institute, 1998.
French, William. "I'm an Expert on Anorexia." *Globe and Mail* (Toronto), November 3, 1983. E1.
Gedhill, Christine, ed., *Stardom: Industry of Desire*. London: Routledge, 1991.
King, Barry. "Articulating Stardom." *Stardom: Industry of Desire*. London: Routledge, 1991. 167–182.
Liar, Liar. Dir. Tom Shadyac. Perf. Jim Carrey. Universal, 1997.
MacGregor, Roy. "Atwood's World." *Maclean's*, October 15, 1979. 64–66.
Marshall, P. David. *Celebrity and Power: Fame in Contemporary Culture*. Minneapolis: University of Minnesota Press, 1997.

Miner, Valerie. "The Many Facets of Margaret Atwood." *Chatelaine*, June 1975. 33+.

Rosenthal, Caroline. "Canonizing Atwood: Her Impact on Teaching in the US, Canada and Europe." In *Margaret Atwood: Works and Impact*, edited by Reingard M. Nischik, 41–56. Rochester: Camden House, 2000.

Ross, Val. "The Elusive Margaret Atwood." *Quill & Quire* 66, no.1 (2000):18-19.

Slinger, Helen. "Interview with Margaret Atwood." *Maclean's*, September 6, 1976. 4, 6–7.

Spicer, Nick. "Atwood Joins Greats of English Literature." *Sunday Herald* (Glasgow), November 15, 1998. D11.

Timson, Judith. "The Magnificent Margaret Atwood." *Chatelaine*, January 1981. 42+.

Yanofsky, Joel. "Celebrating the Femme Fatale." Montreal *Gazette*, September 12, 1993. F1.

Eyes Wide Shut: Atwood, Bill C-32, and the Rights of the Author[1]

RENÉE HULAN

ON NOVEMBER 22, 1996, readers opening the pages of local or national newspapers would probably have recognized the prominent public figure entering the debate around Bill C-32, the bill to amend Canadian copyright law. Headlines announced the following: "Atwood wants to crack down on photocopying" in the *Calgary Herald*; "Authors can't afford 'theft', Atwood says: Proposed exemptions in copyright legislation called unfair to writers" in the *Ottawa Citizen*; "Atwood wants compensation for authors of photocopied material" in the *Vancouver Sun*. An account written by Kevin Burns for the *National Library News* gave this summary:

> The morning after her reading at the National Library of Canada, Margaret Atwood appears at the House of Commons before the federal Heritage Committee, representing the Writers Union of Canada and the League of Canadian Poets. Her subject is copyright, and Atwood is blunt. "Writers should not be asked to subsidize libraries and schools," she warns. "Reproducing intellectual property without permission from its owner amounts to theft." (20)

The debate surrounding Bill C-32, in which private and public interests were clearly in competition, presented an occasion for exploring the relationship between literature and society in Canada. Margaret Atwood's role in the debate around Bill C-32 and her published statements concerning the writer's role in society, considered within the context of published responses of her presentation to the committee, highlight her prominence as a public intellectual and raise crucial issues in contemporary Canadian social life.

Appearing before the Standing Committee on Canadian Heritage on November 21, 1996, and on behalf of the Writers Union of Canada (WUC) and the League of Canadian Poets, Atwood championed the rights of authors to control the dissemination of their work in the face of widespread photocopying by targeting exceptions for public institutions:

> In conclusion, I want to emphasize that writers are small business people and our copyrights are often our only real assets. Exceptions to copyright are an expropriation of our property against our will. If copyrights were cars, this would be car theft. (4)

The executive director of the WUC, Penny Dickens, and the Union's legal counsel, Marian Hebb, were also present and fielded many of the committee members' questions afterward. The Standing Committee had heard from sixty-five groups and received 190 briefs during its deliberations, and the WUC was one of the last. For Atwood and other writers, the issues at stake in the debate around Bill C-32 were of great concern; the WUC made specific recommendations to enhance licensing—especially of electronic technology—to prevent book dumping, and to extend copyright protection to seventy years. These issues of author's rights, as Atwood repeated to the committee, were about money, and money could be a matter of life and death, of *survival*. As Rosemary Sullivan tells it, Atwood had initially been persuaded of Canada's need for a writers' union by stories like that of Gwethalyn Graham, who, despite publishing success, died in poverty.[2] It was on behalf of authors who, according to reports from Statistics Canada for 1994, made on average CA$ 15,000 that Atwood went to Ottawa. Appealing to nationalist sentiment, Atwood argued that in order for Canada to have a "flourishing literature," the rights of authors needed to be protected. By limiting revenues from some copies and refusing to extend copyright protection, the government would be endangering the ability of writers to provide for themselves and their families, thus threatening the survival of Canadian writers and writing.

At first glance, the presentation seemed a typical response from the public figure and private writer, for it was not the first time Margaret Atwood had given her voice and name to a cause. As one of Canada's most recognizable citizens and activists, and probably Canada's most famous author, Atwood is known for supporting the causes she believes in. It is a role—regardless of her stated suspicion of roles and their models—that she has embraced, and this role conforms with her published views on the writer's role as witness to society.[3] Citing Yeats' admonishment to poets to "cast a cold eye," she views witnessing as the writer's imperative: "The eye is cold because it is clear, and it is clear because its owner must look: he must look at everything. Then she must record" (*ND* 121).[4] Atwood critics and biographers have argued that her success provokes jealousy and her politics, opposition; at the very least, her public persona inspires strong feeling. If she has been one of the few literary covergirls, she has also had to guard her privacy by creating "the mysterious multifaceted Margaret Atwood" (qtd. in Becker 31), the double and multiple selves who come out to play in Nathalie Cooke's "Lions, Tigers, and Pussycats." Atwood's thoughts on the role of the writer in society are part of this public persona, or personae, crafted over five decades of writing.

In *Negotiating with the Dead*, Atwood continues to fashion personae by reclaiming her biography, retelling well-known stories, deflating gossip, anecdote, and supposition, and scrupulously revisiting the most often-cited details: the Bohemian Embassy, the aunts, the walk across the football field, the exiled parents, the northern campsites, and even *The Red Shoes*. In its form and content, *Negotiating with the Dead* distinguishes between the private person bewildered by the public persona, using images of domestic life to refer to the self that is not "the author." The private person is a "dab hand at cookies" (35), or "turning out a nicely browned loaf of oatmeal-and-molasses bread" (36), and a cosy "knitter of sweaters" (35). These images, presented as glimpses of private life, are also allusive and literary. The "nicely browned loaf," for instance, calls to mind Susanna Moodie's "maiden loaf" in *Roughing it in the Bush*, a book whose importance for Atwood is well known. Moodie writes that she could have borne the harshest criticism of her writing better than the failure of that loaf. As Misao Dean shows, in this scene and elsewhere, subordinating authorship to domestic life grants the nineteenth-century woman writer legitimacy. For Atwood, the two roles indicate the author's double identity. Atwood also uses literary allusions as examples, often at the point of concluding an argument, and while she offers her own anecdotes, most are well-known, well-crafted literary stories in themselves. Like the first-person in her essays and interviews, the public role of spokesperson appears to unify selves in one authentic self, a witness or observer of the society. The audience listens because the eyewitness, whether voyeur or truth teller, survivor or fake, makes us believe that the story is true. But asking the real Atwood—or any writer for that matter—to step up is an interpretive dead end. If the Author is always constructed, then, as Foucault asks, why does it matter who is speaking?

Foucault's analysis of authorship traced the Romantic notion of the writer as solitary genius to the control and commodification of discourse in the eighteenth century. Indeed, at that time, the Statute of Anne (1709) responded to the newly lucrative publishing industry by giving authors the sole right to print books not already in print. The general principles underlying copyright have not changed, nor have the arguments to extend copyright protection to accommodate technological change: writers must be adequately compensated for their labour both in accordance with natural rights and for the benefit of society. Creativity is believed to be stimulated by protecting the livelihood of writers, and since creativity is seen to have social benefits, it is in the best interest of society to protect the rights of the author. The United States Copyright Act of 1790 and *le décret des 13–19 janvier 1791* in France also defined the rights of the author as serving both public and private interests with the state legislating an appropriate balance.[5] These principles remain influential in today's global legislation on copyright, and the influence of the literary construction of the Author on legal interpretation of copyright is a study in itself.[6] In this discussion of copyright, Foucault's historical argument situating the Author as a function of codified property relations is often cited, yet the implications of his theoretical argument for the Romantic view of authorship has not displaced its position. By demonstrating the function of the Author, Foucault shifted the focus from the creative act of the solitary individual, which he presented as a construction, to the creation of meaning in the intellectual commons. Though copyright legislation acknowledges the existence of such a commons, it legitimates the Romantic view of what an author is by granting the Author rights that are conceived in individual terms.

As her famous response to William Wigle shows, Atwood has always been keenly aware of what's in a name.[7] In *Negotiating with the Dead*, she warns readers against thinking that they have a handle on the author "with a capital A," the person who "does the writing and becomes a name, divorced from the body but attached to the body of work" (62) and who, as she says, is always "double," always changed from the one who did the writing in the first place, though this, she adds, is both evasive and true (37). As Rosemary Sullivan observes, from early in her career, Atwood "was dismissive of the Romantic fantasy of the bohemian artist … She had a different model: the Victorian man or woman of letters (like Dickens or George Eliot) who was an active participant in society and lived by his or her work" (308). In the copyright debate, Atwood's implied (double) author conformed to this model in terms of the writer's social function while also retaining the Romantic view of the Author as the origin of creativity.

In most newspaper accounts of the copyright debate, the constructed Atwood was not a witness, secret agent, or double author but a celebrity engaged in a sharply pitched battle between individual or corporate copyright holders and public institutions. Coverage in the *Toronto Star* was typical, leading with the sentence that described Atwood as the "recent winner of the Giller Prize—Canada's richest—for her latest novel *Alias Grace*," and highlighting her statement that reproducing work without permission is theft. In general, the coverage displayed the "heat and lightening" Atwood is so used to taking (Atwood, MT 3). Perhaps the harshest article was one printed in the *Edmonton Journal* entitled "Photocopier Criminals Beware" which began, "Canadian novelist Margaret Atwood marched into the country's battle over copyright law last week, both lips blazing" (Sass F1). From this familiar image of Atwood as *femme fatale*, the medusa or sorceress ready to pounce, the article goes on to portray her as just plain greedy:

> Gung-ho all-or-nothing folks like Atwood defy common sense and muddy the already muddied waters by demanding every penny from every kid who had to write a report on *The Handmaid's Tale* and copied the book jacket in the library. Goodness knows how much she'd want if the kid memorized one of her poems. (F1)

By treating Atwood as if she was speaking only on her own behalf and by failing to refer to the presence of Dickens and Hebb, this article, like so many others, unhelpfully personalized the public position.

Few newspapers failed to mention awards and other marks of Atwood's success in the opening paragraph. Even the most balanced account of the hearing, published in the *Globe and Mail* and reprinted in the Halifax *Chronicle-Herald* paraphrased, "Award-winning fiction writer Margaret Atwood says copying an author's work without permission or payment is theft" (C2). Although this article presented more information than most, the effect of the paraphrase was a much more strident position, one that seemed naive and simplistic, even petulant. None of the coverage attempted to understand Atwood's position in historical context; none connected her presentation to her thoughts about what she has since called the "cog eat cog" world of publishing (Atwood, ND 66). In their stories, the privately owned corporate print media focused on the individual author—Atwood—construing her position as serving private and personal interests, and constructing the writer as both private entrepreneur and Romantic cliché: the solitary genius, the drowned poet, the madwoman.

Even though her appearance at the committee created a flurry of media activity on Parliament Hill, what the papers made of the story did not help the writers' cause. By characterizing Atwood as an award-winning and bestselling author, they positioned her as an exception to the rule of her argument, and by printing the most pointed comments made during the presentation, they made her sound shrill. This despite the fact that, during the hearing, she had engaged in light banter with the committee members and had stated clearly that her concerns did not apply directly to her own work, or to novels generally, but to writers such as freelance journalists who stood to lose the most if the bill was not amended. Even so, the print journalists were not terribly sympathetic—or informed.

In contrast, discussions within professional associations, such as the one in the Canadian Libraries Association's (CLA) newsletter, *Feliciter*, offered the in-depth and sustained critique of the proposed copyright amendments that was lacking in commercial media. The CLA supported the draft bill, and fought hard for the exceptions that the WUC opposed. Standing before the committee, Dr. Marianne Scott, the National Librarian, argued on behalf of public interest that authors' rights should not be allowed to outweigh the rights of public-lending institutions. Penny Dickens had argued that Bill C-32 would cause "writers to subsidize the education and library sectors to a greater degree than that of other taxpayers" (Atwood, "Presentation"11). Barbara Clubb, head librarian and CEO of the Ottawa Public Library, responded by pointing out that libraries support and subsidize writers. Clubb wrote that it was a "tragedy" that the two groups found themselves at odds when "public libraries are negotiating with CanCopy to allocate even more money for authors out of our beleaguered budgets" (B7). Despite Susan Riley's observation that "one of the ironies of this debate is that it pits two groups that are usually allies against one another: writers and public libraries" (qtd. in Burns 20), the commercial media did little to pursue the story and relegated the arguments of users' groups to "Letters to the Editor." In one such letter to the *Vancouver Sun*, Paul Whitney, the chief librarian of the Burnaby Public Library, expressed "dismay that Atwood and [the WUC] have chosen to attack legislation that represents a reasonable balance between the interests of writers and the broader public good" (C2). Since taxpayers support both libraries and authors through direct grants and other indirect spending, Whitney concluded that the real target of the amendments would be the Canadian public. In a letter to *Quill & Quire*, Robert Kasher, a writer and "sales representative to the library market," wrote that he was "utterly appalled and deeply embarrassed by Margaret Atwood's presentation on libraries and copyright," concluding that

> she sounded more like a corporate lawyer from Disney in hot pursuit of Chinese software pirates than the socially aware author I've heard she is ... I doubt Margaret Atwood minds all the free publicity and advertising her books get in libraries in the form of placement, posters, and readings. (4)

What was perhaps most shocking to these observers was that the WUC, whose primary interest was writers writing, did not seem equally concerned about readers reading.

Several spokespeople for public institutions argued that the attempt to extend property rights beyond production and exchange to reception and circulation would encroach on the public domain by limiting public access.[8] Although the librarians and other representatives did not argue against the compensation of creators, they did object to paying twice—first by buying books and acquiring other sorts of material, paying fees for library use of books, and paying for licensing agreements; second by preserving or making books available to users. They feared the impact this would have on access. As a series of presentations to the committee illustrated, the writers' proposed amendments would make research more difficult and the preservation of documents more time-consuming and costly. While librarians searched for copyright holders, original documents were crumbling, incurring even greater financial costs to shrinking budgets. Writers argued that safeguarding their individual property rights would protect Canadian culture, but the pressure on library budgets caused by removing exceptions would actually limit the funds generated for licensing agreements and acquisitions. As academic organizations such as the Canadian Association of University Teachers (CAUT) joined the CLA in its opposition, several groups stressed the bill's implications for the preservation and advancement of knowledge, especially involving archival materials. Increased costs for scholars and professional researchers would put pressure on research funds, and could be prohibitive for unfunded students and amateurs, like genealogists. J.R. Miller, then president of the Canadian Historical Association, specifically mentioned genealogists in a letter to the editor of the *Globe and Mail*, and concluded with the following:

> Under the new legislation it will be illegal to make a single photocopy of a complete unpublished document for a researcher for research purposes ... Together these provisions will impede and render far more expensive archival research into Canadian historical topics. (A16)

Librarians and academics alike emphasized how extending copyright protection and removing exceptions for library research could determine *how* readers would access documents as well as *who* would read them.

Upon closer examination of the presentation transcript, it becomes clear that the WUC was not prepared to consider the implications its proposals would have for research. At the hearing of the WUC, Beth Phinney (MP for Hamilton Mountain) had access for researchers in mind when she asked if the Union would be in favour of making an exception for those making a single copy of an unpublished work. Hebb replied that such instances are "covered" by existing procedures in the archives, and Dickens added that

> access used to be a problem. That's been dealt with through the collectives. Now it's money. If the writers don't receive money from the use of their work, they will not be able to write. That's the bottom line. Copyright legislation is supposed to assist the copyright holders. (Atwood, "Presentation" 11)

Although seeming to acknowledge a social benefit of copyright, Dickens did not emphasize how that benefit serves the public good. Phinney also wondered why the WUC had queried the definition of perceptual disability and was told that the Union was concerned the exception might be broadened to persons with mental disabilities. Throughout this rather low point in the writers' argument, the issue of payment was obscured by an attempt to assess the merits of exceptions for certain types of individuals, and the effect of the new legislation on research was set aside. The WUC did not seek to balance the rights of the public with those of the individual but instead reiterated the position that there should be no exceptions whatsoever.

When asked by Jim Abbott (MP for Kootenay East) to comment on the issue of access in the public interest, Atwood replied:

> You can get a book out of the library or buy a book in the bookstore with no problem. We have these copying collectives. It's not limiting access any more than it's limiting access to toothpaste. You go into the drugstore, get your tube of toothpaste and pay your $1.50. (7)

Asked about the specific instance of access for genealogists engaged in research, Atwood responded:

> I don't quite see the problem. What we're talking about is the right to reproduce. If a genealogist goes to a library or goes to the archives, they can usually forage and rummage away to their heart's content, unless the material has been put aside by the person who has died so it cannot be opened for eighty years or fifty years … What we're talking about is the right to publish, not the right to research. There is a difference. (8)

When MP Phinney took up the issue, asking about researchers specifically, Atwood added:

> This happens to me all the time. I have unpublished material in the archives. If people want to do research on it, they go to the archives. The library phones me to ask whether they can make a copy. I say sure. And if I were dead, my executor would say sure. Or maybe I would; I can come back. (10)

This rather casual reply belies the complexity of permission granting, as any researcher knows. Indeed, Atwood's responses referred specifically to permission, not the cost of doing the research or circulating and preserving documents. The concern did not regard the theft of intellectual property by means of plagiarism, only the mechanical reproduction of that property for any purpose.

After Atwood's opening remarks, Dickens and Hebb narrowed the focus from the public interest to private interests, presenting a singular view of the public good, one achieved by allowing writers to participate freely in the market economy. In this economy, writers would earn their living, own their own property—whether intellectual or material—pass that property on to their heirs, and control the wealth generated from it, meagre though it may be. The only role of government in this economy is to ensure that everyone is free to do all these things; yet, ironically, without the state's legislation to protect creators, writers would be left to survive in a free market.

Working with limited definitions of "creators" as journalists and published creative writers, and "users" as anyone looking for a "free lunch," the WUC reasoned that individual acts of copying, taken together, added up to a form of publishing. Educational institutions were identified as prime culprits, and the existence of collectives was cited as a reason to remove all exceptions. Anticipating the problems this would create, Mauril Bélanger (MP for Ottawa-Vanier) asked if removing exceptions would require making membership in collectives mandatory. Atwood replied, "We still believe in free will. We're old-fashioned" (12). Although Bélanger balked a little, he did not press the issue further, unfortunately. How libraries would deal with those who did not join collectives, what sort of liability this would entail without some exceptions, was never addressed at the hearing. Would a library be able to make a single copy for preservation or for research purposes in such a case? If not, and if failure to join a collective could potentially limit access, the policy would be coercive. The public interest, including the effect on costs incurred by public libraries and archives, was eventually subordinated to the copyright holders' interest.

The Standing Committee on Canadian Heritage pushed through amendments in mid-December, and, as Vic Parsons predicted in his report for Canadian Press, the hastily drafted amendments led to aggressive lobbying on both sides through the spring of 1997. In "An Open Letter to Jean Chrétien" published in the Montreal *Gazette* on March 6, 1997, and in the April edition of *Quill & Quire*, thirty-one signatories, including Atwood, Timothy Findley, Michel Tremblay, and Alice Munro, called on the government to reconsider by appealing to nationalist sentiment: "A country's creators are the lifeblood of its culture. Do not rob us and future generations of writers of our ability to survive doing what we do—reflecting Canadian realities to Canadians and to the world" (3). Bernard Katz, chairman of the Copyright Task Group for the Ontario Library Association, warned that the "sudden shift to the side of copyright owners at the eleventh hour represent[ed] a betrayal of the previous policy" (A20). Bill C-32 received a final reading on March 25 and royal assent on April 25, 1997. In the same month, *Quill & Quire* reported that Atwood had donated a letter obtained while researching *Alias Grace* to the Richmond Hill Public Library. The letter was so fragile that a copy of it would have to be displayed (Land 13).

Most of these amendments took the form of additional language that shifted the balance in favour of copyright owners. For example, in Clause 30, which allowed the copying of short passages from literary collections for use in educational institutions, if only a maximum of two passages from a single author was reproduced and the source acknowledged, there was an additional requirement that "the name of the author, if given in the source, is mentioned" (House of Commons of Canada 34). Since acknowledgement is standard ethical practice in academic work, this addition was not a true limitation, yet it exemplifies the shifting balance. Other clauses favouring the user, such as those allowing multiple copying by persons with perceptual disabilities, were removed. A new section on archival materials (30.2) was added, giving copyright owners the right to prohibit any and all copying of papers deposited. Works already deposited in archives and whose copyright owner remained unknown were grandfathered by this clause, applying it to future acquisitions only. In each case, limitations were placed on access. But what those representing users objected to most was the inclusion of collectives in the definition of "commercially available," an amendment that, they argued, effectively eliminated all other exceptions (Morton 14).

The WUC had won the battle over exceptions, but groups like the CLA and CAUT pointed out that "less than half of what is copied in Canadian libraries is written by Canadians," leaving libraries to pay creators in other countries, mostly the United States, for uses that would be exempt in their countries (15). It was even more deeply ironic that this appeal for protection for Canadian writers and individual free speech served to promote values of liberal individualism, private ownership, and a free market economy, the same ideology that informs cuts to public funding. By referring to writers as small businesses, emphasizing the exchange value of intellectual property to individuals, and downplaying the social value of copyright protection, the WUC advocated a strong view of intellectual property that stood to serve the privatization of knowledge. If the serious issues at stake in the debate over Bill C-32 were left to a competition of private interests, it has also been left to the courts to restore balance as copyright law continues to be interpreted and challenged. In March 2004, defenders of public access scored a victory when the Supreme Court upheld an appeal by the Law Society of Upper Canada ruling that the exception for a single copy made for purposes of research and study held as a form of fair dealing.[9] In this case, the issues were given a cold, clear eye while in the public hearings and media coverage, the debate had been waged blindly.

—St. Mary's University

ACKNOWLEDGMENTS

Funding from the SSHRC supported the research for this article. Many thanks to my two research assistants, Megan Clare and Stefanie Winters, who located documents cited in this paper.

NOTES
1. This paper was presented on World Book and Copyright Day, a day created by the United Nations Educational, Scientific and Cultural Organization to celebrate books and to encourage people to read them.
2. Graham's bestselling novel *Earth and High Heaven* earned CA$ 450,000. However, "because an author's income was then regarded as 'unearned,' and 1945 was the highest taxation year ever, [Graham] was left with $10,500 by the government. The government made a settlement in Equity, as they put it, for about $30,000. She died in poverty" (Sullivan 302).
3. Ironically, as Frank Davey notes in *Post-National Arguments*, women engaged in social or political action are "parodically portrayed" in Atwood's fiction (223), and Susanne Becker points out that Atwood usually takes "an ironic view of her own celebrity in her essays and fiction"(29).
4. Atwood's record of service includes being a founding member of the WUC as well as a past vice-president (1979) and past president (1981–1982), founder and past president of PEN Canada (1984–1986), member of Amnesty International, supporter of the Civil Liberties Association of Canada, and an outspoken critic of public policy on issues ranging from conservation to free speech, NAFTA to copyright. Both Rosemary Sullivan and Nathalie Cooke in their respective biographies describe the enormous energy and effort she and Graeme Gibson contribute as citizens and as a family on behalf of a variety of causes.
5. As Gillian Davies explains in *Copyright and the Public Interest*, from these three traditions, copyright evolved as a means of satisfying justice and fairness according to natural law, protecting rights to remuneration for labour, stimulating creativity, and safeguarding social usefulness (10–13). To underline its public function, for example, she reveals that Article 6 of the French statute enjoined authors to deposit two copies of a work in the Bibliothèque Nationale or forfeit the right to pursue damages for copyright infringement (186).
6. For a discussion of the continued influence of the Romantic idea of authorship on the legal interpretation of copyright, see Peter Jaszi. Looking at cases in United States legislation, Jaszi cites this idea as the most serious impediment to fair use analysis in which "originality" and "style" have been cited as reasons for limiting use (see 50–51; see note 71).
7. For accounts of the action taken against Wigle and *Northern Journey*, see Cooke (216–218) and Rosenberg (157).
8. Other professional groups who submitted briefs arguing on behalf of the public included the following: the Association of Universities and Colleges of Canada, the CAUT, the Association of Canadian Community Colleges, the Canadian Teachers' Federation, the CHA; the Canadian Association of

Research Libraries, the Association of Canadian Archivists, l'Association des archivistes de Québec, among others.

9. Four publishing companies, CCH Canadian Ltd., Thomson Canada Ltd., Thomson Professional Publishing, and Canada Law Book Inc., had complained that the Law Society of Upper Canada's (LSUC) custom copyright service under its "Access to the Law Policy" constituted an infringement of copyright. At issue was the applicability of copyright to the contents of the publications which included legal material in the public domain but also the case summaries, headnotes, indices, and compilations of legal decisions provided by the publisher. In *CCH Canadian Ltd v Law Society of Upper Canada*, the chief justice agreed that these contents were original works protected by copyright but concluded that the LSUC had not infringed upon copyright because it had provided photocopies exclusively for the purpose of research. The Court also denied the cross-appeal of the plaintiffs by concluding that, because fax transmissions are not a form of communication with the public, the LSUC had not sold the publishers' works by providing faxed copies.

WORKS CITED

"An Open Letter to Jean Chrétien." *Quill & Quire* 63, no. 4 (1997): 2–3.

"Arts Ink Atwood speaks out against exemptions from copyright royalties." *Globe and Mail* (Toronto), November 23, 1996. C2.

Atwood, Margaret. *Moving Targets: Writing with Intent 1982–2004*. Toronto: Anansi, 2004.

———. *Negotiating with the Dead*. Cambridge: Cambridge University Press, 2002.

———. "Presentation to the Standing Committee on Canadian Heritage." November 21, 1996 [online]: <http://www.parl.gc.ca/committees352/heri/evidence/39_96-11-21/heri39_blk101.html> (accessed July 17, 2003).

Becker, Susanne. "Celebrity, or a Disneyland of the Soul: Margaret Atwood and the Media." In *Margaret Atwood: Works and Impact*, edited by Reingard M. Nischik, 28–40. Rochester: Camden House, 2000.

Burns, Kevin. "Triple Bill: A Hard Act to Follow." *National Library News* 29, no. 2 (1997): 19–20.

"Cars or Copies—it's all theft, says Atwood." *The Record* (Waterloo), November 22, 1996. F6.

CCH Canadian Ltd v Law Society of Upper Canada [2004] 1 S.C.R. 339, 2004 S.C.C. 13. [online]: <http://www.canlii.org/ca/cas/scc/2004/2004scc13.html> (accessed September 24, 2004).

Clubb, Barbara H. "Tragedy that librarians and writers are pitted against each other." *Ottawa Citizen*, November 30, 1996. B7.

Cooke, Nathalie. "Lions, Tigers, and Pussycats: Margaret Atwood (Auto)-Biographically." In *Margaret Atwood: Works and Impact*, edited by Reingard M. Nischik, 15–27. Rochester: Camden House, 2000.

———. *Margaret Atwood: A Biography*. Montreal: ECW, 1998.

"Copyright laws need changing but Atwood's rhetoric isn't helping." *Edmonton Journal*, November 30, 1996. W7.

Davey, Frank. *Post-National Arguments: The Politics of the Anglophone-Canadian Novel since 1967*. Theory/Culture Series. Toronto: University of Toronto Press, 1993.

Davies, Gillian. *Copyright and the Public Interest*. Vol. 14, *Studies in Industrial Property and Copyright Law*. Munich: Max Planck Institute, 1994.

Dean, Misao. *Practising Femininity: Domestic Realism and the Performance of Gender in Early Canadian Fiction*. Toronto: University of Toronto Press, 1998.

Ede, Lisa, and Andrea Lunsford. *Singular Texts/Plural Authors: Perspectives on Collaborative Writing*. Carbondale: South Illinois University Press, 1990.

Foucault, Michel. "What is an Author?" In *Language, Counter-Memory, Practice: Selected Essays and Interviews*, edited by Donald F. Bouchard. Translated by Donald F. Bouchard and Sherry Simon, 113–38. Ithaca: Cornell University Press, 1977.

Guly, Christopher. "Coalition Fights for Readers' Rights: Senators should address inequities in a copyright bill that favours writers, group says." *Globe and Mail* (Toronto), March 26, 1997. C3.

Harrison, Karen. "President's Message: When the Going Gets Tough." *Feliciter*, January 1997, 6–7.

House of Commons of Canada. *Bill C-32: An Act to Amend the Copyright Act*, 2d sess., 35th Parliament, 1996–1997 (as passed by the House of Commons, March 20, 1997).

Jaszi, Peter. "On the Author Effect: Contemporary Copyright and Collective Creativity." In *The Construction of Authorship: Textual Appropriation in Law and Literature*, edited by Martha Woodmansee and Peter Jaszi, 29–56. Durham, NC: Duke University Press, 1994.

Kasher, Robert. "Personal Copying Okay." Letter. *Quill & Quire* 63, no. 3 (1997): 4.

Katz, Bernard. "Copyright." Letter. *Globe and Mail* (Toronto), March 13, 1997. A20.

Land, Mary. "Atwood Donates Letter to Library." *Quill & Quire* 63, no. 4 (1997): 13.

Miller, J.R. "Copyright Legislation." Letter. *Globe and Mail* (Toronto), November 6, 1996. A16.

Morton, Elizabeth. "CLA Opposes Amended Copyright Bill." *Feliciter*, April 1997, 14–15.

"Ottawa in a bind over copyright law." *Toronto Star*, December 8, 1996. B2.

Parsons, Vic. "Amendments Made to Canada's Copyright Bill No Quick Fix." *Chronicle-Herald* (Halifax), January 1, 1997. B8.

Riley, Susan. "Atwood wants crackdown on photocopying." *Calgary Herald*, November 22, 1996. D9.

———. "Atwood rips into copyright legislation." *Edmonton Journal*, November 22, 1996. C3.

———. "Authors can't afford 'theft,' Atwood says: Proposed exemptions in copyright legislation called unfair to writers." *Ottawa Citizen*, November 22, 1996. A6.

Rosenberg, Jerome. *Margaret Atwood*. Twayne's World Authors Series, edited by Robert Lecker, 740. Boston: Twayne, 1984.

Sass, Bill. "Photocopier criminals beware." *Edmonton Journal*, November 26, 1996. F1.

Sullivan, Rosemary. *The Red Shoes: Margaret Atwood Starting Out*. Toronto: HarperCollins, 1998.

Whitney, Paul. "Countering Atwood's Rhetoric." Letter. *Vancouver Sun*, November 30, 1996. C2.

"Writers face grave injustice: Copyright changes would reduce what they earn when work is reproduced." *Montreal Gazette*, March 6, 1997. B3.

"Writers press Chrétien: 31 oppose copyright changes." *Toronto Star*, March 5, 1997. D2.

"Les talents de la voisine":[1]
Margaret Atwood and Quebec

EVA-MARIE KRÖLLER

IN 2000, THIRTY-FOUR years after its original publication, Margaret Atwood's *The Circle Game* was published in French translation as *Le cercle vicieux*, and *Le Devoir*'s literary reporter Caroline Montpetit marked the occasion with an essay and interview entitled "Margaret Atwood, prêtresse, sorcière et écrivaine," epithets to which is added the distinction of "[l']ambassadrice de la littérature canadienne" ("Margaret Atwood" A1). The standard opening description of the author's physical appearance does not shy away from superlatives either: "Ses cheveux bouclés, foncés, encadrent toujours un visage aux traits fins, anguleux, un regard d'un bleu perçant, insaisissable, inimitable, et sans doute inoubliable."

The reporter's enthusiasm appears to have become *Le Devoir*'s typical response to Atwood: she is variously "la matriarche des lettres canadiennes" (Montpetit, "25ᵉ salon" B10), "la grande dame de la littérature canadienne" (Guay D5), "l'auteure canadienne à succès" (Chouinard, "Lectures" D1), one of the "célébrissime" (Lamontagne D10), one whose radio conversation with Victor-Lévy Beaulieu resembles "un échange entre Virginia Wolfe [sic] et Marcel Proust" (des Rivières B11). She is listed alongside Quebecois authors and artists, often as the only Anglo-Canadian writer, as if she existed in a class of her own (see "Pour se tenir"; "En bref"; Chouinard, "Lectures"; Tremblay). Not infrequently, lavish coverage of her work goes hand in hand with the admission that Anglo-Canadian writing remains little known in Quebec. Thus, a special dossier of the quarterly *Le Québec français*, designed to familiarize readers (especially teachers of French) with Canadian writing in English, introduces various contemporary Anglo-Canadian authors, but features no fewer than five photos of Atwood who is omnipresent in the essays as well.

Le cercle vicieux is not the only work by Atwood to have appeared with some considerable delay in French translation in Quebec: for example, l'Hexagone's edition "En tous lieux" issued *Politique de pouvoir* (*Power Politics*) in 1995, twenty-five years after the English original. The book appeared simultaneously with l'édition de la pleine lune's *La troisième main*, the translation of *Good Bones*, which had been published only three years before. These gaps in making available translations of earlier works, in tandem with almost instantaneous translation of virtually anything written by Atwood during the nineties and beyond, suggest that her celebrity status in Quebec is relatively recent. Indeed, early commentators on her work often allude to the absence of translations that would allow francophone readers to familiarize themselves with it (Houle 18; Pelletier 13).

Judging by coverage in *Le Devoir*, the decisive moment was the enthusiastic reception of *Captive*, the translation of *Alias Grace*, in both Quebec and France, although *The Handmaid's Tale* and *The Robber Bride* had earlier caused "[d]es vagues de popularité" in France (Chouinard, "Atwood" D1). Atwood was received "comme une star" in France in 1998 when *Captive* appeared, and her status there was further confirmed by the inclusion of *The Handmaid's Tale* in the texts required for the *agrégation* at French universities (Dolbec B9). The publication, in 2005, of *Le dernier homme* (Laffont), the translation of *Oryx and Crake*, was accompanied by a "grand entretien" in *Le Magazine littéraire* (Paris), celebrating Atwood in superlatives as "une figure majeure de la littérature anglo-saxonne," "une intellectuelle engagée," and "une grande dame des lettres canadiennes" (Huy 93) in an issue of the magazine that also revisited the fame of Stendhal. Enthusiastic reception in France, as we shall repeatedly see below, does not guarantee enthusiastic reception in Quebec and vice versa, but in this case the verdict was unanimous: Atwood was indeed "une star." In its turn, Radio-Canada included *La servante écarlate* among the five books featured on the 2004 *Le combat des livres*, a literary *Survivor* show and francophone equivalent to the CBC's *Canada Reads*.[2]

In part, the development of Quebec's response to Atwood reflects her growing international reputation, which made it simply impossible to aver, as could still be done in 1984 and 1987, that together with most Anglo-Canadian writers, she was a "[r]omancière méconnue" or "pratiquement inconnue" in Quebec ("Romancière" D4; Gagnon E1). However, even if Anglo-Canadian writing has long been widely ignored in Quebec, American literature has not, and during the eighties Atwood was already a household name in the United States. As Caroline Rosenthal has impressively documented, Atwood has frequently found herself mistaken for an American writer or she has even been deliberately adopted as one. If Quebec did not accept her as such, there must have been additional factors to cause the delay.

Above all, Quebec's complex relationship and occasional difficulties with Margaret Atwood are a sort of *mise en abyme* for the traditional tensions between the Anglo-Canadian and Quebecois cultures. The author has energetically involved herself in questions of Canadian nationalism and Quebec separatism, and interviews with her seem to have been timed to obtain her views on national crises such as the failed Meech Lake Accord and the 1995 referendum, or on the ramifications of the Free Trade Agreements for both anglophone and francophone Canadian culture (Rioux A1; des Rivières B11; Saletti D7; Laurin D8; Voisard, "Écrivaine" C5). To sum up her profile, one such interview is headlined "Écrivaine préoccupée par la politique" (Voisard). Her interviewers are quick to point out parallels between the contents of books like *Bodily Harm* and political events like the October Crisis (Pelletier 13). They also link the title of volumes like *Two-Headed Poems* to the "bicéphalisme" of the so-called founding nations (Pelletier 13), or note her absence at a writers' festival in France in 1996 because she did not want to "accréditer l'idée d'un Québec séparé à quelques mois du référendum" (Rioux A1). Commentators have been preoccupied with the competition between English and French and the questions of power associated with language. As a result, they have been wary of her insistence on speaking French in these interviews despite the fact that, as one of them notes, her fluency is "toute relative" (Saletti D1); they have been bothered by the Parisian translations of her work that flood the francophone market at the expense of translations from Quebec, and they have objected to the sometimes dubious French into which Parisian publishers have translated the Canadianisms of her work (Voisard, "La servante" D6).

Moreover, Atwood's popularity in the Americas and in Europe has encroached even on areas where Quebecois authors have traditionally been able to rely on linguistic and cultural loyalties largely undisturbed by anglophone competition. Atwood's phenomenal stature as "l'écrivaine la plus connue à l'étranger" (Montpetit, "Margaret Atwood" A1) has been compounded by what is perceived as the overwhelming success of Anglo-Canadian writing over the past decade. "[L]a percée littéraire canadienne-anglaise" (Rioux A1) is aided by the defection of highly successful writers of francophone background into the English-speaking camp—among them Yann Martel, Aimée Laberge, and Michel Basilières—and by the transgression into francophone prerogatives of writers perceived as anglophones, as witnessed in the controversy over Nancy Huston's Governor General's Award in 1993 (Buzzetti B8).[3]

There have been attempts to establish reasons for the discrepancy between the success of the two literatures and to find ways to address the imbalance (Leith F1; Aubin 52). There has also been retaliation: anger at the French media for ignoring authors from Quebec ("En bref"), amusement at the large contingents of English-speaking writers in Paris with their "magnifique accent lorsqu'ils parlent français" (Rioux A1) and *Schadenfreude* when, for once, the equation seems to be reversed and English Canada must show its "produits" on the Quebec stand at an international book-fair in Mexico because it hasn't been granted a display of its own (Montpetit, "25ᵉ salon" B8). The "internationalization" of Canadian literature clearly comes at a price, and a closer look at Atwood's reception in Quebec over the years reveals how worries about cultural autonomy hover even behind Quebec's current enthusiasm for her work. At the same time, reading through dozens of interviews and articles from the last thirty years is also a worthwhile endeavour because some of Atwood's francophone readers are alert to aspects of her work that rarely occur to their anglophone counterparts precisely because the cultural sensitivities they bring to the task are so different. Because its coverage of literary matters has been consistently serious and wide-ranging, I rely mostly on *Le Devoir*, but I also cite occasional items from *Le Soleil* and *La Presse*, and other publications.

An interview with Margaret Atwood can be an exercise in which stereotyping (of Atwood as Anglo-Canadian, author, woman, public intellectual) is difficult to separate from the auto-stereotyping of the interviewer and the readership for which he or she speaks. The process often begins with close attention to Atwood's personal appearance. Few public women in

Canada, except perhaps Adrienne Clarkson, have been the target of such close and often impertinent scrutiny of their looks and mannerisms, and it would be inappropriate to suggest that this attention is specific to the Quebecois media. What is specific, however, is the cultural subtext of some of these comments. Early interviews do their best to situate Atwood in an intellectual and artistic milieu familiar to francophone readers, and they make her look petite, artless, and *farouche,* as is expected of women prodigies following in the footsteps of Françoise Sagan and walking alongside Marie-Claire Blais. Journalists describe Atwood's casual appearance ("[l]es cheveux relevés un peu n'importe comment" [Petrowski 38]) as charming, and they note with approval her lack of the "artifices et ... tics" that characterize other celebrity authors ("Margaret Atwood: De l'ignorance des puissants"). Interviewers see in her a Parisian bohemian *manqué,* an impression that Atwood does little to discourage and a role in which she has parodied herself (in the comic strip "Portrait of the Artist as a Young Cipher," for example).[4] She is described as a delicate figurine ("avec son visage de médaillon élizabéthain" [Pelletier] 13), a mermaid ("ses yeux outremer" [Pelletier]13), or a mischievous young woman who "rit comme une enfant" ("Margaret Atwood: De l'ignorance des puissants").

However, nine years after Petrowski's approving assessment of Atwood's youthful demeanour, the tune has changed. Lysiane Gagnon all but takes a magnifying glass to forty-seven-year-old Atwood and finds her fashion sense wanting: "[c]ette petite femme qui n'a l'air de rien" (E1) looks dowdy, slight, and self-effacing in the modest hotel where her Montreal editor has put her up. A second look convinces Gagnon that "[v]ue de près, elle est jolie" and would even be "ravissante si elle s'arrangeait mieux." The author is still a figurine or perhaps now a more utilitarian object such as a teacup, one that survives being tapped for soundness: " On pense à de la porcelaine, fragile, presque transparente, mais de bonne qualité." As if Atwood's bemused observation that her work has now created a research industry of its own, including studies of "le ton, les inflexions de ma voix quand je fais des lectures publiques," did not apply to her, Gagnon continues that Atwood's lack of facial expression is disconcerting but that, luckily, "elle bouge des mains." The underlying assumption appears to be that the middle-aged "auteur à succès" (E1) owes it to her fans to be elegant, effectively made up, and imposing in appearance as well as intellect—along the lines of Julia Kristeva, perhaps. If, in the earlier examples, Atwood's growing fame is fitted into (and thus controlled by) a model in which she competes, reassuringly, with francophone authors, Gagnon's observations diminish the author's now even greater status by criticizing her in the one area in which she is considered to fall short: her appearance. (Atwood's self-mockery in her contribution to *Mortification: Writers' Stories of Their Public Shame* suggests that she is prepared for what may be in store for her and her interviewers when she reaches her so-called "third age" [see Robertson].)

Comments on the quality of the author's French often complete the picture, but the register switches here from a determination to judge her appearance by predetermined aesthetic standards to criticism of her ability to communicate convincingly with Quebecois readers one-on-one. At least one early interview indicates that Atwood spoke English throughout and that her responses have been translated (Houle 18). In another, the young woman in a flowery dress who laughs "comme une enfant" also speaks like one, interspersing her laborious French with English expressions that the interviewer finds herself obliged to translate ("Margaret Atwood: De l'ignorance des puissants"). Faulty pronunciation may be the reason why Atwood describes herself as living near Toronto "avec mon mari [...] et mon *fils*" (Petrowski, emphasis added), but one interviewer notes with approval the author's courteous fear "de commettre des impairs" (Atwood cites a few famous howlers, committed by Winston Churchill and J.F. Kennedy, to illustrate what she too might be capable of), assuring her that she speaks French "fort correctement" (Voisard, "Écrivaine" C5).[5]

Once Parisian publishers began to commission translations of Atwood's work as a matter of course, often employing star translators for the task, Quebec critics paid less attention to Atwood's own ability to speak French than to the quality of translations done by people who, it was felt, were insufficiently familiar with the Canadian context of Atwood's work. Although Réginald Martel's acidic review of Marlyse Piccand's translation of *Lady Oracle* proves that work done in Quebec does not receive automatic approval, other critics make a point of favouring the homegrown product.[6] Anne-Marie Voisard, for example, compares *La servante écarlate* by "[l]a Française Sylviane Rué," who does not know the difference between "Muguet des bois" and "Muguet sauvage," with *Meurtre dans la nuit* by "la Québécoise Hélène Filion," who writes in a language "qui reflète notre culture et celle de l'auteure" (Voisard, "La servante" D6). Filion herself points out that Parisian translators have transformed a "motel" into an "auberge de campagne," although she finds Atwood's own observation that Grasset changed the Northern woods in *Surfacing* into a kind of Bois de Boulogne "un peu forcée" (qtd. in Gagnon E1).

As is typical of Atwood's approach to her métier, she concerns herself with the cultural politics and economic consequences of translation, and she notes that translations prepared in Quebec are difficult to sell in France, and vice versa. A Parisian publisher has access to a greater market than one from Quebec, and a Parisian publisher will normally employ a Parisian translator. (It is not apparent from the material I have read how Atwood decides which books are to go to a publisher and translator from Quebec and which ones to France, and whether she is motivated in her decisions by the precarious situation of Quebec publishing.) Scrupulous attention to the quality of Atwood's French and that of her translators does not, incidentally, stop francophone journalists from, in their turn, committing numerous errors in spelling the names of Anglo-Canadian authors, ranging from Marvis Gallant, Timothy Finley, and Hugh McLellan to Russel Banks, Alice Munroe, and Mordechai Richler.

Atwood's radio dialogue with Victor-Lévy Beaulieu in 1996, published as *Deux sollicitudes* and *Two Solicitudes* in 1996 and 1998 respectively, aptly encapsulates some of the preoccupations and paradoxes I have surveyed above. Commentators do find polite fault with Atwood's spoken French and welcome the printed version because "les zones d'ombre de la communication que sont les hésitations et les reprises n'y paraissent plus" (Saletti D7), and in apparent retaliation for any remaining linguistic shortcomings, the English translation misspells the names of several Anglo-Canadian authors. Above all, however, this remarkable exercise—at twelve recorded hours of conversation broadcast in half-hour segments this was no "*fast food* culturel" (des Rivières D11)—shows that Atwood is accepted as a public intellectual with powerful influence. This acceptance, and the realization that such figures are rare in English Canada (Vuong-Riddick 16), may account for the very different reading in Quebec of *Survival: A Thematic Guide to Canadian Literature* from the one this famously controversial book has received elsewhere in Canada. *Survival*, which features a substantial section on writing from Quebec, was published in translation by Boréal as late as 1987 under the title of *Essai sur la littérature canadienne*.[7]

The book received a puzzled review by Lori Saint-Martin, who wondered whether its publishers seriously considered the two literatures not to have changed since 1972, but going through the francophone press on Atwood with some care reveals that the book was well known in its English version before 1987 and that the original continues to be referred to even after the publication of the translation (Houle 18; "Margaret Atwood: De l'ignorance des puissants"; Pelletier 13; Saletti D7; Montpetit, "De l'histoire" 3). Few of the critics who mention the book bother to take issue with Atwood's reading of Quebec writing, selective as it is. This, I suggest, is because francophone critics read *Survival* as an existentialist manifesto rather than as a literary handbook. A particularly remarkable item, Louis Cornellier's "Éloge des perdants," cites *Survival* along with Hubert Aquin on the subject of "[c]et art de la défaite" (A6). "Ils avaient raison," Cornellier writes, "mais il aurait fallu aller plus loin et dire que nulle âme éveillée n'y échappe." (Naim Kattan's reading of *Survival* represents an important early recognition that it would be "futile, voire injuste, de réagir à *Survival* comme si c'était un essai de critique littéraire," instead of reading it as "un manifeste du nationalisme canadien-anglais [107]," but francophone critics do not seem to have been overly concerned with the Anglo-Canadian nationalism of the book either.)

As the titles indicate, the *Sollicitudes/Solicitudes* dialogue is a particularly elaborate and high-profile instance of the periodic efforts of Canada's two "solitudes" to connect with each other, but Saletti's excellent feature points out that the program was not merely convened as an emergency response to the 1995 referendum. Beaulieu had previously conducted radio interviews with veteran writers Roger Lemelin and Gratien Gélinas, and generally speaking Beaulieu is well known for his "manière d'interpeller les autres écrivains et de dialoguer avec eux par le moyen d'essais-fictions": Beaulieu's *Monsieur Melville* trilogy is probably his masterpiece in the genre. The contextual richness provided by Beaulieu's literary and other interests exceeds the rationales that have been offered for other "pairings" of Atwood with francophone authors, although these duos have been popular enough to find institutional expression in the "Margaret Atwood–Gabrielle Roy Chair in Canadian Studies and Culture" sponsored by Foreign Affairs Canada (FAC) at the Universidad Nacional Autónoma de México since 2002. Francophone criticism has obsessively repeated the notion of the two solitudes in its coverage of Atwood's oeuvre (Rioux A1;

Saletti D7; Montpetit, "Margaret Atwood" A1; Pelletier 13; Ladouceur 67; Desmeules 74), but the typical efforts to overcome the distance have been ambivalent remedies for "solitude" at best: the main aspect that is generally being drawn out in order to establish similarity between a francophone author and Atwood concerns the effectiveness with which each writer conveys isolation and solitude. As subjects, isolation and solitude answer to a mythopoeic understanding of Canadian culture popular in the sixties and seventies that all but obliterates distinctiveness, literary, and otherwise.[8]

As early as 1970, *Ellipse* (1969–, a publication devoted to publishing translations of literature in the two official Canadian languages) issued a dossier on Atwood and Michèle Lalonde, with translations of Atwood's work provided by a Who's Who in Quebec's literary scene: Gilles Marcotte, Guy Robert, Richard Giguère, Roch Carrier, Jacques Brault, in addition to Atwood herself, who together with Charles Pachter produced translations of "Axiom" and "Midwinter, Presolstice." The volume was sufficiently seminal to Atwood's reception in Quebec to be cited in Alain Houle's 1976 feature on Atwood's work and again in Patricia Godbout's essay in *Le Québec français* twenty-four years later. Elsewhere in *Ellipse*'s special issue, Atwood's work is compared to that of the two other authors with whom she is most frequently linked, Marie-Claire Blais and Anne Hébert.[9] Published in 2000, the year of Hébert's death, Desmeules' essay claims that Atwood and Hébert share "une seule et même solitude." In the same year Montpetit asserts that Atwood "se reconnaît en cette femme isolée [Hébert]" and that she has made of Blais "son modèle"("Margaret Atwood" A1). These assessments virtually duplicate the comments in *Ellipse*'s 1970 *cahier* that Blais and Atwood both have a taste for the macabre derived from "le même univers canadien" (Marshall 81), that Lalonde and Atwood share "la même aliénation dans un pays démésuré," and that Hébert and Atwood dwell on the same "lieux imaginaires" ("Avant-propos" 4–5).

There are readings that go beyond mythopoeic similarities. For example, Vuong-Riddick's observation that Atwood was in a better position to appreciate Blais's *Un joualonais, sa joualonie* than critics from Quebec because she was not sidelined by the same preoccupations bears investigating, as does the fact that Vuong-Riddick herself does not fit neatly into the traditional Canadian "bicéphalisme"[10] and so was perhaps alert to aspects of Atwood's writing to which neither anglophone nor francophone critics have paid equal attention. In this manner, Vuong-Riddick's observations outline one way in which the one-on-one pairings have become difficult to maintain. Another emerges from the "Avant-propos" to the 1970 *Ellipse cahier* which avers that "Michèle Lalonde et Margaret Atwood disent chacune à leur manière la même aliénation dans un pays démésuré *qui ne compte que des immigrants*" (4, emphasis added). The dialogue between Atwood and Beaulieu, complex as it is, appears to proceed from the same assumption. When Atwood insists, without much success, that Beaulieu address the question of Aboriginal land claims should Quebec decide to secede, neither author acknowledges that no Aboriginal author has been included in their conversation who might have had a thing or two to say about the subject.

Atwood may now be accepted in Quebec as an author who exists in a class of her own, but her work raises questions that concern the entire situation of writing from Canada, many of them heightened or new as a result of its internationalization. Christian Rioux called the resulting challenges "la quadrature du cercle" when the 1996 *Les belles étrangères* festival in France featured a large delegation of Anglo-Canadian writers, all apologetic because their colleagues from Quebec were not included "pour cause de multiculturalisme doctrinaire": "[C]omment inviter les Québécois dans un festival consacré à la littérature en langue étrangère?" Such situations have, however, become the rule rather than the exception, and Canada's presence at literary festivals often elicits similar "quadratures," including the suggestion that "[l]es Québécois sont les Latinos du nord" but also that they encounter less prejudice in Mexico than "une Canadienne connue comme Alice Munroe [sic]" because she is "perçue comme étant américaine au Méxique" (Montpetit, "25ᵉ salon" B8). Atwood has her own ideas on how to deal with such confusions of cultural identity and not all of them meet with the approval of her francophone colleagues. In spite of this, she has consistently used her stature to ensure that such situations are not lost in official rhetoric but are addressed in all their practical and philosophical implications.

—University of British Columbia

NOTES

1. I borrow my title from Réginald Martel.
2. Atwood's book competed against Yann Martel, *L'Histoire de Pi*; Gaétan Soucy, *La petite fille qui aimait trop les allumettes;* Jacques Godbout, *Une histoire américaine*; Gil Courtemanche, *Un dimanche à la piscine à Kigali*. Eleven listeners wrote in to "defend" *La servante écarlate*, while Soucy, Martel, and the winner Courtemanche received support from thirty-one, thirty-four, and thirty-six listeners respectively, and Godbout from three. It bears noting that Martel's book too is a translation, and that Courtemanche's novel became a worldwide success only when it appeared in English (Patricia Claxton's translation, largely financed with a grant from the Quebec government, won the Governor General's Award [Aubin 52]). In a controversial decision, Hubert Aquin's *Prochain épisode* (in a new translation by Sheila Fischman) won the 2003 *Canada Reads* contest. My thanks to Laura Moss for pointing out the inclusion of Atwood's book in *Le combat des livres*.
3. Quebec publishers L'Hexagone, VLB, XYZ, Pierre Tisseyre, and La Courte échelle protested the Governor General's Award given to Nancy Huston in 1993 for *Cantique des plaines*, her own French version of *Plainsong*. The publishers wrote, "Nous considérons que les membres du jury ont erré en accordant ce prix à une oeuvre non admissible et que ce choix porte un préjudice grave aux auteurs francophones du Canada" (qtd. in Buzzetti B8). Apparently in order to avoid a similar controversy, the Canada Council for the Arts disqualified Huston's novel *The Mark of the Angel*, her own English version of *L'empreinte des anges*, in 1999, though the book had been admissible in the French category the year before. Huston responded that the reason for this decision was "de toute évidence, le conflit entre les deux communautés linguistiques que composent le Canada" (qtd. in Buzzetti B8), an assessment vehemently denied by the Council.
4. Shortly after Antonine Maillet received the Prix Goncourt for *Pélagie-la-charrette*, Grasset published Atwood's *Surfacing* in French, using as a publicity slogan the line that "le Canada anglais a aussi son grand écrivain." A feature in *Les nouvelles littéraires* (Paris) characterizes Atwood's style as "plus 'français'" than Maillet's, and explains that this is a "paradoxe qu'expliquent notre prétendu goût de la mesure et notre crainte des excès." Using the trope of colonial writing fertilizing the tired culture of the mother country, the critic sees Maillet's exuberant fiction as shaking up French writing in ways that Atwood's does not (Garcin 7).
5. During the debate over the Meech Lake Accord, Atwood proved that she paid close attention to the political purchase of correct translation. Here, she defends herself against the suggestion that she had "jeté un pavé dans la mare

québécoise": "J'ai dit que le mot 'distinct' était mal traduit en anglais. J'ai simplement dit la vérité. En anglais, le mot a une connotation de supériorité. On doit, on devrait traduire le mot 'distinct' par le mot anglais 'différent.' C'est tout ce que j'ai dit" (Laurin D8).

6. My own edition of *Lady Oracle*, published in 1997 by Éditions Autrement Littératures in Paris, still lists Marlyse Piccand as the translator but changes the notation from "de l'américain" to "traduit de l'anglais" and adds that the "traduction française" has been "revue et corrigée par Sylvie Perron." The meaning of "traduction française" is ambiguous and could be read to mean "translation to meet metropolitan standards," in addition to indicating that errors noted by reviewers of the L'Etincelle edition have been corrected.

7. Montpetit describes this period at Boréal as one when the publisher began to open "sur le monde." She includes the translation of Anglo-Canadian authors such as Atwood and Michael Ondaatje among the endeavours that illustrate this development. Pascal Assathiany, who helped initiate Boréal's new direction, appears to be a key figure in ensuring that Quebec writing has a place in the world market. He was responsible for obtaining the Government of Quebec grant that made translation of Courtemanche's *Un dimanche à la piscine à Kigali* and therefore publication by Knopf Canada possible (see note 2 above) (Montpetit, "De l'histoire" 3). At the 2002 Festival America des littératures d'Amérique du Nord in France he, along with Boréal author Monique Proulx, protested against the lack of interest shown by French readers and critics in writing from Quebec (see "En bref").

8. I do not have the space to survey recent critical work in comparative Canadian literature that addresses some of the larger methodological questions involved. See "La littérature québécoise sous le regard de l'autre" and "Francophone/Anglophone."

9. Most of the authors with whom Atwood's work has been paired also appear in *Survival*, which based its selections on available translations, so that Atwood herself has reinforced these comparisons. The more recent pairings with Hébert deserve separate study. In several instances it almost seems as if Atwood's liking for Hébert's work is used to help rehabilitate an author whom "plusieurs avaient jugée durement" for her exile and refusal to involve herself in Quebec's politics (Montpetit, "Margaret Atwood"A1). See also the special issue on Anglo-Canadian writing of *Le Québec français*, which features both an essay comparing Atwood and Hébert as well as two items written in homage to Hébert who had recently passed away.

10. Poet and critic Vuong-Riddick was born in Hanoi and educated in Paris before emigrating to Canada in 1969. She taught French literature at the Université de Montréal, McGill University, and the University of Victoria. Using a practice resembling Nancy Huston's, she wrote her volume of poetry *Two Shores/Deux rives* first in English, then "recreated" it in French.

WORKS CITED

Atwood, Margaret. *Lady Oracle*. [1976] Translated by Marlyse Piccand. French translation reviewed and corrected by Sylvie Perron. Paris: Éditions Autrement Littératures, 1997.

Atwood, Margaret, and Victor-Lévy Beaulieu. *Deux sollicitudes: entretiens*. Trois-Pistoles: Éditions Trois-Pistoles, 1996.

———. *Two Solicitudes: Conversations*. Translated by Phyllis Aronoff and Howard Scott. Toronto: McClelland & Stewart, 1998.

Aubin, Benoît. "Voilà, a hit novel!" *Maclean's*, December 8, 2003. 52.

"Avant-propos." *Ellipse* 3 (Spring 1970): 4–5.

Buzzetti, Hélène. "Le prix du gouverneur général: oui en français, non en anglais." *Le Devoir* (Montreal), September 3, 1999. B8.

Chouinard, Marie-Andrée. "Atwood Margaret: forte personnalité." *Le Devoir* (Montreal), April 25, 1998. D1.

———. "Lectures d'été." *Le Devoir* (Montreal), June 20, 1998. D1.

Cornellier, Louis. "Eloge des perdants." *Le Devoir* (Montreal), September 2, 1998. A6.

Desmeules, Georges. "Anne Hébert et Margaret Atwood: une seule et même solitude." *Le Québec français*, no. 117 (Spring 2000): 74–76.

des Rivières, Paul. "De Toronto à Trois-Pistoles." *Le Devoir* (Montreal), January 26, 1996. B11.

Dolbec, Michel. "Margaret Atwood est reçu comme une star en France." *Le Devoir* (Montreal), November 19, 1998. B9.

"En bref: la France dénoncée." *Le Devoir* (Montreal), October 22, 2002. B8.

"Francophone/Anglophone." Edited by Réjean Beaudoin and André Lamontagne. Special issue of *Canadian Literature*, no. 175 (Winter 2002).

Gagnon, Lysiane. "Margaret Atwood, la grande plume de l'autre Canada." *La Presse* (Montreal), June 6, 1987. E1, E4.

Garcin, Jérôme. "Antonine en deça, Margaret au-delà." *Les nouvelles littéraires* no. 2626 (9–16 March 1978): 7.

Godbout, Patricia. "La poésie canadienne-anglaise vue de face et de profil." *Le Québec français*, no. 117 (2000): 84–86.

Guay, Hervé. "Entrevue avec Margaret Atwood." *Le Devoir* (Montreal), February 2, 2002. D5.

Houle, Alain. "Avec Margaret Atwood, écrivain du 'gros bon sens.'" *Le Devoir* (Montreal), December 18, 1976. 18.

Huy, Min Tran. "Les mondes perdus de Margaret Atwood." *Le Magazine littéraire* (Paris), no. 441 (April 2005): 93–97.

Kattan, Naim. *Écrivains des Amériques*. vol. 2: *Le Canada anglais*. Montreal: HMH, 1972.

Ladouceur, Louise. "Solitudes rompues." *Le Québec français*, no. 117 (Spring 2000): 67.

Lamontagne, Marie-André. "Littérature étrangère: un périple sans fin." *Le Devoir* (Montreal), August 25, 2001. D10.

Laurin, Danielle. "Atwood repart en guerre." *Le Devoir* (Montreal), June 17, 1995. D8.

Leith, Linda. "Vie littéraire: étonnants Canadiens." *Le Devoir* (Montreal), October 26–27, 2002. F1.

"La littérature québécoise sous le regard de l'autre." Edited by Réjean Beaudoin, André Lamontagne, and Annette Hayward. Special issue of *Voix et images* 72 (Spring 1999).

"Margaret Atwood: De l'ignorance des puissants." *Le Devoir* (Montreal), June 28, 1980. 13.

Marshall, Tom. "Les animaux de son pays: notes sur la poésie de Margaret Atwood." *Ellipse*, no. 3 (Spring 1970): 81-86.

Martel, Réginald. "Les talents de la voisine." *La Presse* (Montreal), August 18, 1980. B3.

Moisan, Clément. *Comparaison et raison: essais sur l'histoire et l'institution des littératures, canadienne et québécoise.* La Salle, Quebec: Hurtubise HMH, 1986.

———. *L'Age de la littérature canadienne: essai.* Montreal: HMH, 1969.

Montpetit, Caroline. "De l'histoire à la littérature: une porte d'entrée sur la scène internationale." *Le Devoir* (Montreal). Special issue: *"Les 40 ans de Boréal."* May 31, 2003. 3.

———. "Foire internationale du livre de Guadalajara—Tergiversations diplomatiques: Le Canada s'étonne de la place qu'occupera le Québec en 2003." *Le Devoir* (Montreal), December 3, 2002. B8.

———. "Margaret Atwood, prêtresse, sorcière et écrivaine." *Le Devoir* (Montreal), March 28, 2000. A1.

———. "25ᵉ salon de livre de Montreal." *Le Devoir* (Montreal), October 30, 2002. B10.

Pelletier, Mario. "Margaret Atwood: par delà les solitudes." *Le Devoir* (Montreal), January 9, 1982. 13.

Petrowski, Nathalie. "Une heure avec Margaret Atwood." *Le Devoir* (Montreal), April 8, 1978. 38.

"Pour se tenir au chaud." *Le Devoir* (Montreal), October 29, 2002. B7.

Rioux, Christian. "Paris découvre l'autre solitude: La France consacre un festival à la littérature du Canada anglais." *Le Devoir* (Montreal), May 8, 1996. A1.

Robertson, Robin, ed. "Margaret Atwood." *Mortification: Writers' Stories of Their Public Shame.* London: HarperCollins-Fourth Estate, 2003. 1–4.

"Romancière méconnue." *Le Soleil* (Quebec), February 4, 1987. D4.

Rosenthal, Caroline. "Canonizing Atwood: Her Impact on Teaching in the US, Canada, and Europe." In *Margaret Atwood: Works and Impact*, edited by Reingard M. Nischik. Rochester: Camden House, 2000. 41–56.

Saint-Martin, Lori. "L'échec et la survie selon Atwood." *Le Devoir* (Montreal), April 9, 1988. D4.

Saletti, Robert. "La rencontre des écritures." *Le Devoir* (Montreal), November 23, 1996. D7.

Tremblay, Odile. "La mort d'Hermès." *Le Devoir* (Montreal), August 10–11, 2002. C6.

Voisard, Anne-Marie. "Écrivaine préoccupée par la politique: Margaret Atwood: un regard lucide posé sur le monde." *Le Soleil* (Quebec), May 23, 1987. C5.

———. "'La servante écarlate' de Margaret Atwood: à lire, malgré la difficulté." *Le Soleil* (Quebec), February 3, 1988. D6.

Vuong-Riddick, Thuong. "Un aspect méconnu de Margaret Atwood." *Le Devoir* (Montreal), August 27, 1983. 16.

P.K. Page and Margaret Atwood: Continuity in Canadian Writing

SANDRA DJWA

A LITTLE OVER two decades ago Margaret Atwood gave a witty but poignant talk at the 1983 "Women and Words" conference in Vancouver, explaining just how difficult it was for her to become a poet in the early sixties. As she said, if you were a respectable academic, as she then considered herself, you did not write poetry or fiction because the only acceptable writers were dead. Then, too, if you were a woman, "combining marriage and art was a risky business" and, finally, there was the "Canadian complication":

> Could you be a female, a writer, be good at it, get published, not commit suicide, and be a Canadian too? ... Canadian writers were ... not at all well known, but if you dug around you could find them, and many of the best ones were women. ... About this time I was reading P.K. Page, Margaret Avison. ... Jay Macpherson ... It was comforting as well as exciting to read these writers ... It was ... like a laying on of hands, a feeling that you could do it because, look, it could be done. (Atwood, "If You Can't Say Something Nice" 17)

Atwood has always been generous in acknowledging her predecessors and she often cites P.K. Page as a poet whom she read and respected early in her career. A quick reading of Atwood's first two books of poetry reveals echoes of Page's diction, suggesting continuity in English-Canadian writing. For example, the genealogy of angels in Page's poem "Images of Angels" (*The Metal and the Flower* 36–39) can be compared with Atwood's "A Messenger," (*CG* 13) or Page's poem "Man With One Small Hand" (*MF* 46) can be compared with Atwood's "Man With a Hook" (*CG* 26). The phrase "the person you call I" from Page's poem "If It Were You" (*As Ten as Twenty* 14–17) is echoed in Atwood's line "The Thing that calls itself/I" from the poem "A Sibyl" (*CG* 49). Furthermore, as several critics have noted, we hear the diction of Page's poem, "Permanent Tourists," (*MF* 28–29) in Atwood's line "perennial watchers,/tourists of another kind" from "Some Objects of Wood and Stone" (*CG* 59–60). This poetic continuity runs the gamut from conscious and unconscious imitation—the kind of verse a young poet might write when apprenticing herself to a senior poet to learn the craft—to what might be seen as affinity: a predilection for similar subjects and techniques.

To generalize, both Page and Atwood are poets who write prose, frequently from the "I-eye" perspective. Both are fascinated by metamorphosis; both write about male/female relationships; both use map and landscape imagery; both present landscape as the human body, or vice-versa. Both writers occasionally surprise us with a flash of sardonic wit. They also characteristically shift planes and dimensions, moving easily from the real to the surreal. In this essay I will compare several poems by Page and Atwood with similar titles and subjects and also suggest some continuity in their prose writings. Many of the Page poems that Atwood particularly liked appeared in her first books of poetry, *Unit of Five* (1944), *As Ten as Twenty* (1946) and *The Metal and the Flower* (1954): the latter two books were read by Atwood, circa 1960–1961, when she was house-sitting for Jay Macpherson, then a faculty member at the University of Toronto. Atwood echoes Page in her first books of poetry, *The Circle Game* (1966) and *The Animals in That Country* (1968), in the novel *Surfacing* (1972), and in a short story from *Wilderness Tips* (1991).

Atwood first met Page in Victoria, British Columbia, in the spring of 1969 when she was reading at the University of Victoria and had come to visit Page at her home on Exeter in Oak Bay. Shortly after this visit, Atwood wrote to Page, saying how much she enjoyed her visit because she had "some sense of parts of [my] mind being a shared area as I do with Jay M[acpherson]—but a different part—with Jay it's myths transformed to images, with you, images transformed to myths" (Atwood, Letter 1969). By this distinction, Atwood is saying that Macpherson, in a poem like "Mary in Egypt," begins by identifying the myth in her title but transforms the story to contemporary images. Page, in poems like "Photos of a Salt Mine," usually does the reverse, working from an image, or a series of images, to imply a larger structure (*MF* 12–13).

Atwood's recognition of an affinity with both Page and Macpherson points us toward one aspect of Page's poetic structure that the younger poet may have found helpful. Page, since– the early forties, had been experimenting with some of T.S. Eliot's ideas about the use of the "objective correlative," an image, or a series of images, which carries the emotion the poet wishes to express in a given poem but that is not directly linked to the perceiving poet. Often, this chain of imagery has mythic overtones. For example, in "The Event" from *The Metal and the Flower*, Page's subject is the myth of the apocalypse but she does not directly indicate this. Instead, she says:

> The lion and bear will waken up
> ravenous after sleep
> and lilies then will be their bread,
> archangels their white meat. (11)

Atwood has casually remarked that when she first read Page's work as a student at Victoria University, University of Toronto in the early sixties, some of her poems "blew the top of my head off" (introductory remarks at the reception in honour of Mimmo Paladino/P.K. Page). In 1961 Atwood published a poem called "Event," which reflects both the subject and title of Page's poem:

> The old apocalypse rouses itself
> Within my world of skull;
> I feel a sounding in my head
> That heralds this world's fall (3)

Unlike Page, Atwood specifically identifies the myth of apocalypse that informs her poem. This identification suggests that she might be working toward the distinction she later draws between Page and Macpherson, that is, trying out the differences between poetry that is structured through myth (Macpherson) and poetry structured through image (Page). Atwood continued to use both myth and image as a structural strategy in her own writing. However, she later remarked, "[Most often] I start out with an image and the book develops around it" (Brans 308). Page's poetry may have helped point her in this direction although, as Atwood points out, "writers take as 'influences' things that resonate with their already-established inner direction" (Atwood, Letter 1992).

In 1970 Atwood sent Page a copy of *The Journals of Susanna Moodie*, inscribed "with admiration," and two years later Page and Atwood undertook a joint poetry reading tour to Lethbridge, Alberta, and Prince George, British Columbia. We know a little about this trip because Page wrote to a friend giving her impressions of Atwood:

> She is ... only [thirty-two] and astonishingly on top of things. Very cool indeed. Very funny. And very generous. She was the star of this reading circuit but she began each reading by saying how much she admired my work and how when she first began reading some of my poems were and still are among her favorite poems. Very sweet of her. No need for her to say it. (Page, Letter 1972)

The following year Atwood took on the task of introducing Page to a new generation of readers by editing a paperback collection of Page's prose that included both *The Sun and the Moon* and a group of short stories. By spring 1973, Page had sent Atwood a copy of *The Sun and the Moon* in its original 1944 publication and Atwood replied, saying: "[It is] one of the weirdest books I've read for some time [for]...the light it casts on male-female roles, among other things" (Atwood, Letter to P.K. Page 1973).[1] When describing the projected edition to the editors at Anansi Press, Atwood wrote of Page, "Her mode is not realism but a kind of odd Gothic romance, with elements of the distinctly bizarre. I think she's at her worst when doing just plain folks, at her best with things like the foot coming through the ceiling; & the end of *The Sun & the Moon* I find totally chilling" (Atwood, Letter to Jim Polk and Shirley Gibson).

A year later, Atwood edited Page's *Poems: Selected and New*. She took her task as editor very seriously and produced a new collection of Page's poetry, drawing upon magazine publications as well as earlier books of poetry. Justifying this process to her editor, Shirley Gibson, at Anansi, Atwood pointed out that Page emerged as a "much more socially-oriented, much angrier poet" and added "the poems on women and love, as well as the ones on social conditions, madness, ... are of particular interest now." She saw Page as "a supreme artificer, an expert technician; her verbal dexterity and the gorgeousness of her textures have received ample attention. The danger has been to see her *only* as that, and I believe this collection rescues her from this fate" (Atwood, Letter to Jim Polk and Shirley Gibson). Because Atwood presents Page's poems chronologically—early poems of social protest like "Bank Strike" form the first section of the book—succeeding poems are read through a filter of social protest, another concern shared by both writers.

Both poets are known for their psychological portraits. Section Two of *Poems: Selected and New* groups together a number of psychological poems beginning with "The Landlady," a poem that may be compared with another by Atwood of the same title. Page gives us a portrait of an intrusive landlady and the psychological effect of her actions on tenants who desperately attempt to guard their privacy. They click their doors "like shutters on her camera eye," but the landlady continues to invade their rooms and their psychic space in images that are iterative and overpowering. Page writes:

> [She] knows them better than their closest friends:
> their cupboards and the secrets of their drawers,
> their books, their private mail, their photographs
> are theirs and hers. (*ATT* 35–36)

One of the most arresting images in this poem is that of the landlady's "camera eye," all-seeing, invasive, destructive: this is a metaphor familiar to readers of Atwood's work, one that she uses to great effect in novels like *The Edible Woman*[2] and *Surfacing*, as well as in poems like "Camera": "Camera man/how can I love your glass eye?" (*CG* 45).

I see Atwood's poem "The Landlady" as a conscious reworking of Page's poem, a finger exercise. We are presented with the same kind of landlady— "She is everywhere, intrusive"—who cannot be kept out of the narrator's room or psyche. The speaker, the tenant, again recognizes that "Nothing is mine." But changing social mores have gutted the landlady's power. She can now be dismissed with humour, and Atwood does just that in her first line: "This is the *lair* of the landlady."

> She is everywhere, intrusive as the smells
> that bulge in under my doorsill;
> she presides over my meagre eating,
> generates the light for eyestrain.
>
> From her I rent my time:
> she slams
> my days like doors.
> Nothing is mine. ... (*ATC* 14)

This poem—with its slamming doors—parallels Page's poem. But Atwood inflates the landlady's overpowering qualities with a pun that projects them onto the landscape—"I find myself walking/always over a vast face/which is the land-/lady's."[3] However, in the last line of this poem, the landlady is deflated to the pig that the poet thinks she is: "solid as bacon." Here Atwood is having a little fun by manipulating a series of images triggered by Page's poem, but her own tone is closer to caricature, prefiguring her later work as a social satirist.

Another comparison can be made between Atwood's poem "This is a Photograph of Me" and Page's "Photograph." What is most interesting in these poems is the matter-of-fact combination of a normal landscape with the bizarre and the surreal. Page's poem begins:

> They are all beneath the sea in this photograph—
> Not dead surely, merely a little muted
> Those two lovers lying apart and stiff ... (*UF* 51–52)[4]

The lovers are framed by the photograph, depicted as going about the ordinary routine of beach life, but their image is refracted as through a glass bowl. We understand, although we are not told explicitly, that something has gone awry with their relationship: "all their paraphernalia a pretence ... while overhead the swimmers level waves." The conclusion of this poem startles us as we recognize, once again, that the normal activity detailed in the poem has actually taken place in a surreal location under water.

Atwood's twinning poem, "This is a Photograph of Me" is the first—and surprising—in *The Circle Game* (1966), a book with a number of poems about male/female relationships gone awry. When comparing the two poems, we notice that the action is also framed by the photograph but that Atwood's style is more fluid and personal: "This is a Photograph of *Me*" (emphasis added). Nonetheless, the structure of Atwood's poem parallels Page's poem in terms of matter-of-fact observation and tone. Similar also is the allusion to refraction: "The image of water/on light is a distortion." The narrator's insistence on the normal accentuates our shock when we encounter the following lines:

> (The photograph was taken the day after I drowned).
>
> I am in the lake, in the center
> of the picture, just under the surface. (*CG* 11)

Again, the locale is under water; there is the added fillip of listening to the dead speak.[5] This poem serves the same function in Atwood's *The Circle Game* as does Page's "Personal Landscape," the first poem in her book *As Ten as Twenty*; that is, it introduces a landscape interpenetrated with the human—in this case, with a woman's body, a metaphor central to the early poetry and prose of both Page and Atwood.

We might also look at the Atwood poem "you fit into me" from which the title of the University of Ottawa symposium "The Open Eye" was derived, and compare it with Page's "Element," a prize-winning poem from *Poetry* (Chicago), later printed in *As Ten as Twenty*.[6] The poem begins with an implied female speaker who feels "my face has the terrible shine of fish/ caught and swung on a line under the sun." What she wants is to sink back into the comfortable darkness of water, the only element in which the speaker feels comfortable. The glare of daylight makes her as conspicuous

> as dime flipped or gull on fire or fish
> silently hurt—its mouth alive with metal. (*ATT* 32)

It is the startling conclusion of this poem, the woman as fish on a line, "its mouth alive with metal," that leads us into Atwood's poem "you fit into me."

In this poem, the central metaphor is again the fishhook but the *frisson* of the poem is brutal surprise. The shock of the imagery is cumulative—building up to the last line where the poem suddenly reverses to an image of an open (shall we say trusting?) eye impaled on a fishhook: "a fish hook/ an open eye" (*CG* 1). Atwood's declaration is a rejection of the victim state, yet the striking, final metaphor is almost identical to that of Page's poem.

As a last indication of continuity, we might first look at Page's use of metaphor in *The Sun and the Moon,* which evokes the Daphne myth, and Atwood's use of similar themes, characters, and metaphors in her short story "Death By Landscape" in *Wilderness Tips* (1991) and in her earlier novel *Surfacing* (1972). Page's novella *The Sun and the Moon* (1944) was originally published under the pseudonym of Judith Cape. The protagonist, Kristin, born during an eclipse of the moon, has a strange "empathetic" ability that allows her to enter into other human beings and inanimate objects. She falls in love with a successful artist named Karl who possesses some of the qualities associated with the sun; thus, in this allegorical romance he has the potential to eclipse Kristin's moon. Her moon power ultimately proves dominant; nonetheless, at one point in their relationship, she recognizes that she is "drowned" in his being. Kristin then describes herself as surfacing in relation to her lover:

> "I felt it happening and fought against it but the waters of his being closed over me quickly," she said. "I was drowned in him. And this morning, ... I came to the surface, I emerged from the sea and reclaimed myself." (111)

Terrified that her strange power will destroy the man she loves, Kristin bonds with the inanimate; Page's metaphors describe the young woman literally becoming a tree: "The wind was like a mad creature tearing at her branches .... [Kristin] knew only an instinctive desire to stay standing, ... to dig her roots into the earth (120)." The conclusion of this tale (which Atwood found "totally chilling") focuses upon the natural landscape:

> The sun and a small wind broke the surface of the lake to glinting sword blades. On the far side, where the trees marched, unchecked, right down to the water's edge, there the lake was a shifting pattern of scarlet, vermilion and burnt orange. (137)

Page presents her images without commentary: nonetheless, they effectively coalesce into myth. We, as readers, insert Kristin into the treed landscape of the final paragraph of the novella.

When Atwood edited *The Sun and the Moon* in 1973, she wrote a preface, pointing out that one of the qualities of the romance, which she identified as the genre of the tale, is the supernatural. In her own later tale, "Death By Landscape" from *Wilderness Tips* (1991), Atwood tells a similar story with larger dimensions. A young woman, Lucy, mysteriously disappears into the northern landscape during a camping trip, leaving behind her friend, Lois. Years later, Lois contemplates Group of Seven paintings:

> Who knows how many trees there were on the cliff just before Lucy disappeared. Who counted? Maybe there was one more, afterwards ...
>
> [Lois] looks at the paintings ... Every one of them is a picture of Lucy. You can't see her exactly, but she's there ... In the yellow autumn woods she's behind the tree that cannot be seen because of the other trees, over beside the blue sliver of pond. (145–46)

Again, there is no explicit reference to the Daphne myth but the images of Atwood's tale carry this resonance. But given that Atwood edited *The Sun and the Moon* almost twenty years before she wrote "Death By Landscape," it is reasonable to suggest that similarities in this tale indicate literary continuity between two generations of Canadian women writers.[7]

Atwood's second novel, *Surfacing* (1972), also suggests connections with Page's prose. This book, at one level a serious study of a young woman's individuation, is also highly parodic,[8] alluding to a number of Canadian historical events, novels, and poems (Djwa, "Here I Am" 170). Two allusions in *Surfacing*—"I lie down, keeping the moon on my left hand and the absent sun on my right" (161)—together with a description of the face of Joe, the narrator's lover, as "shadowed" as in an eclipse of the sun at a climactic moment in the novel, can be read to suggest that Atwood's female narrator as moon is eclipsing Joe's power: "The forest condensed in him, it was noon, the sun was behind his head; his face was invisible, the sun's rays coming out from a centre of darkness, my shadow" (147).[9] These lines suggest Atwood had read *The Sun and the Moon* prior to publishing *Surfacing*.

I link both novels in this discussion because of verbal and thematic similarities, especially surfacing and transformation. *Surfacing*, like *The Sun and the Moon*, is about male/female relationships, about a woman's fear of being "drowned" in the past, in her own psyche, as well as by the men in her life. She recovers, in part, through a ritual cleansing and metamorphosis. Finally, she becomes tree-like and "surfaces" through the ground:[10]

> I'm ice-clear, transparent, my bones and the child ... showing through the green webs of my flesh ... the trees are like this too, they shimmer ...
>
> I lean against a tree, I am a tree leaning...
>
> I am not an animal or a tree, I am the thing in which the trees and animals move and grow, I am a place
>
> I have to get up, I get up. Through the ground, break surface. (181)

Here, as in the conclusion of Page's *The Sun and the Moon,* Atwood's female protagonist has become part of the landscape.

Was Page, then, another of the various fictional and poetic voices—Canadian and otherwise—to be found in the highly parodic *Surfacing,* a novel that includes intertextual allusions to a large number of Canadian writings (Djwa, "Here I Am" 171)? Probably. Do we also conclude that Page and Atwood may have derived some of their poetic images from similar sources, ultimately perhaps, from Carl Jung's collective unconscious? Quite possibly. And can we argue for continuity between P. K. Page's writing and that of Margaret Atwood? I think so. Thus, I revisit Atwood's remarks on Page, Macpherson, and Avison, cited at the beginning of this essay: "It was comforting as well as exciting to read these writers ... It was ... like a laying on of hands, a feeling that you could do it because, look, it could be done."

—Simon Fraser University

ACKNOWLEDGMENT

Thank you to Margaret Atwood, P.K. Page, and the estate of Florence Bird for their permission to use the quotes below.

NOTES

1. Two articles offer helpful readings of this novel: Constance Rooke's "P.K. Page: The Chameleon and the Centre," *Malahat Review*, no. 45 (1978): 169–95 and Rosemary Sullivan's "A Size Larger than Seeing: The Poetry of P.K. Page," *Canadian Literature*, no. 79 (1978): 32–42. Atwood also writes on *The Sun and the Moon* in "Canadian Monsters: Some Aspects of the Supernatural in Canadian Fiction," in *Second Words: Selected Critical Prose*, edited by Margasret Atwood , 238–40 (Boston: Beacon Press, 1982).
2. See *The Edible Woman* in which the glass eye of the camera paralyzes.
3. Thank you to David Jarraway of the University of Ottawa for drawing my attention to the deeper implications of this metaphor.
4. This poem, which first appeared in *Preview* in 1943, was reprinted in *Unit of Five* in 1944. It was not selected for any of Page's own published books until Atwood chose it for *Poems: Selected and New* in 1974.
5. I have suggested elsewhere, in "Back to the Primal," in *The Art of Margaret Atwood* that the theme of the drowned poet also evokes Milton Wilson's article "Klein's Drowned Poet: Canadian Variations on an Old Theme," an article Atwood knew. Wilson observes that at the end of Klein's poem, the poet-photographer "has resurrected his own drowned body" and "the last picture to be developed under water is that single-camera view (14–15)."
6. Critic A.J.M. Smith thought so highly of this poem that when he chose a selection of Page's poetry for *The Oxford Book of Canadian Verse* in 1967, he placed "Element" first. In 1982 when Atwood edited *The New Oxford Book of Canadian Verse in English*, she omitted Smith's choice of "Element," and changed the selection of Page's poetry to include some of her own favourites, such as "Stories of Snow," "Photos of a Salt Mine," and "The Snowman." She also added some new poems, thus bringing the Page selection up to date (179–88).
7. Both Kristin and Karl are spelled with a K in the original 1944 publication, perhaps emphasizing their similarity. However, Carl is spelled with a C in the 1973 Atwood edition. Similarly, in Atwood's story "Death By Landscape" the two friends, Lois and Lucy, are associated by alliteration (*WT* 119–46).
8. Atwood remarks in an early interview with Linda Sandler that some of her writing is "closer to caricature than to satire" (Sandler 24).
9. Solar eclipses occur when the moon moves between the sun and the earth, and the moon's shadow falls upon the earth's surface. The sun appears to be blocked by the moon, yet its rays create a halo. In this case, the protagonist's shadow, like the moon's shadow, blocks the face of Joe, rendering him invisible, yet with a halo.

10. This suggests her rejection of the victim state both in *Surfacing* and *Survival:* "This above all, to refuse to be a victim" (*Surfacing* 191).

WORKS CITED

Atwood, Margaret. Introductory remarks at the reception in honour of Mimmo Paladino/P.K. Page. Toronto: Italian Cultural Institute, 1998.

———. *The Animals in That Country*. Toronto: Oxford University Press, 1968.

———. "Canadian Monsters: Some Aspects of the Supernatural in Canadian Fiction." In *Second Words: Selected Critical Prose*, edited by Margaret Atwood. 238–40. Boston: Beacon Press, 1982.

———. *The Circle Game*. Toronto: Contact Press, 1966.

———. *The Edible Woman*. Toronto: McClelland & Stewart, 1969.

———. "Event." *The Sheet*, Vol. 3. Toronto: Bohemian Embassy, 1961.

———. "If You Can't Say Something Nice, Don't Say Anything at All." In *Language in Her Eye: Views on Writing and Gender by Canadian Women Writing in English*, edited by Sarah Sheard, Libby Scheier, and Eleanor Wachtel. 15-25. Toronto: Coach House Press, 1990.

———. Letter to P. K. Page. April 2, 1969. MG30 D311 14-1 1976-83.

———. Letter to P. K. Page. April 20, 1973. MG30 D311 12-3 1972-5.

———. Letter to Jim Polk and Shirley Gibson circa fall 1973. University of Toronto Archive.

———. Letter to Sandra Djwa. December 6, 1992. Private collection.

———. Letter to Shirley Gibson. December 13, 1973. MG30 D311 12-3 1972-5.

———, ed. *The New Oxford Book of Canadian Verse in English*. Toronto: Oxford University Press, 1982.

———. *Surfacing*. Toronto: McClelland & Stewart, 1972.

———. *Wilderness Tips*. Toronto: McClelland & Stewart, 1991.

Brans, Jo. "Using What You're Given: An Interview with Margaret Atwood." *Southwest Review* 68, no. 4 (1983): 301–15.

Djwa, Sandra. "Back to the Primal." In *Various Atwoods: Essays on the Later Poems, Short Fiction, and Novels*, edited by Lorraine M. York. 13–46. Toronto: House of Anansi Press, 1995.

———. "'Here I Am': Atwood, Paper Houses, and a Parodic Tradition." *Essays on Canadian Writing*, no. 71 (2000): 169–85.

Hambleton, Ronald, ed. *Unit of Five: Louis Dudek, Ronald Hambleton, P.K. Page, Raymond Souster, James Wreford*. Toronto: Ryerson Press, 1944.

Page, P.K. *As Ten as Twenty*. Toronto: Ryerson Press, 1946.

———. Letter to Florence Bird. November 7, 1972.

———. *The Metal and the Flower*. Toronto: McClelland & Stewart, 1954.

———. *The Sun and the Moon, and Other Fictions.* Edited by Margaret Atwood. Toronto: House of Anansi, 1973.

Rooke, Constance. "P.K. Page: The Chameleon and the Centre." *Malahat Review*, no. 45 (1978): 169–95.

Sandler, Linda. "Interview with Margaret Atwood." *Malahat Review*, no. 41 (1977): 7–27.

Sullivan, Rosemary. "A Size Larger than Seeing: The Poetry of P.K. Page." *Canadian Literature*, no. 79 (1978): 32–42.

Wilson, Milton. "Klein's Drowned Poet: Canadian Variations on an Old Theme." *Canadian Literature*, no. 6 (1960): 5–17.

Negotiations with the Living Archive

ROBERT MCGILL

> Perhaps I should leave this trunk and its contents to a university, or else to a library. It would at least be appreciated there, in a ghoulish way. There are more than a few scholars who'd like to get their claws into all this waste paper. *Material,* they'd call it—their name for loot.
> —Iris Chase Griffen, in *The Blind Assassin* (286)

THE IMPULSE TO archive is a common one. Whether in filing cabinets, photo albums, or chest freezers, inevitably all of us catalogue and preserve items in our possession. Restrictions of time and space mean that we also have to make decisions about what to keep and what to throw away, but for some people the options are more complex than that. In the case of an author like Margaret Atwood, not only is there a constant accumulation of manuscripts, letters, research notes, and other documents but there are also people interested in viewing them. Consequently, both logistical and conceptual quandaries arise: for instance, how might an author permit access to texts while preserving privacy and safeguarding her own interests? How can order be established and maintained? One response—a response made by Atwood herself—is the creation of a living archive. I call it "living" because it is an archive inaugurated by the person whose name it takes, a person who contributes to it with some frequency during her lifetime. The archive is also living in the sense that it exists in the public domain, where it takes on a life of its own as it is encountered by an audience that expects it to speak back. What the archive says and how, in speaking, it affects the relationship between authors and critics are questions requiring further consideration.

The Margaret Atwood Collection at the University of Toronto's Thomas Fisher Rare Book Library speaks first in terms of its chronological scope and physical proportions, which testify to the longevity and productivity of Atwood's writing career, as well as to a prolonged critical interest in her work. Atwood's first donation of materials to the Fisher occurred in 1970, the major accession was in 1981, and she continues to add to the collection regularly. At last count, it consisted of some forty-two boxes measuring fifty metres in length, making it the second largest author archive at the Fisher, after the Earle Birney Papers, while its 300 users a year make it by far the most visited one.[1] The archive's sheer size, along with the willingness of the Fisher librarians to accord such space to it, declares the presence of a "major" author. Accordingly, the archive is a monument to Atwood's reputation as much as it is a resource in the study of her work.

With regard to this latter end, scholars can expect to find in the Atwood Collection a large amount of manuscript material in a variety of literary forms, as well as visual art and correspondence with agents, publishers, and writers. In other words, as the finding aid states, "[t]he focus of the collection is almost completely on Atwood's literary work," and one will not find in the archive any telephone bills, love letters, shopping lists, or items of clothing. The content of the archive, as well as the classification of that content, bespeaks an attempt to circumscribe the orientation of academic inquiry, even as the archive ostensibly encourages and engenders critical interest in Atwood. If, as Michel Foucault conceives of it, the archive is not simply a collection of documents but "the law of what can be said" (*Archaeology* 129), the Margaret Atwood Collection—while not quite so sweeping in its shape or powers as Foucault's discursive object of study—is susceptible to the sorts of questions that Foucault asks: for example, how does the archive delimit the types of critical discourse that we utilize? Where does it begin and end?

A fundamental conflict in the living archive lies in the apparently contradictory tasks with which it is charged: first, to lift the veil on a writer's life, to facilitate the work of critics, and second, to keep critics at a distance, to construct a boundary between them and the author, between the public and the private. For the author to negotiate between these tasks she must enact multiple strategies of editing, selecting, and shaping. While a dead writer whose personal archives have been posthumously appropriated need not have decided what to suppress and what to relinquish into the public domain, a living writer must make conscious choices. Accordingly, as Paul Voss and Marta Werner observe, the archive does not simply offer up materials to the public gaze; it also "preserves and reserves, protects and patrols, regulates and represses" (1).

On one hand, it preserves legal and financial interests with regard to intellectual property. For instance, the Margaret Atwood Collection features eight boxes of Atwood's script for a movie version of *Cat's Eye*, but the finding aid notes that Atwood has restricted access until such time as a film of the novel is made. On the other hand, the archive preserves a degree of privacy. In a secure environment like the Fisher Library, an author can control access to the archive without having to deal directly with every graduate student engaged in research. Critics who might otherwise write to Margaret Atwood herself with questions about, say, her manner of composition can instead bypass the author and view manuscripts directly. However, although the archive might presume to effect a barrier between the public "literary" work and a private life, it also calls the stability of that barrier into question. The Atwood Collection, for one, includes undergraduate essays as well as a school operetta. To present these as "public" works alongside Atwood's published texts is implicitly to insist on their relevance to her development as a writer, but this expansion of the Atwood canon also threatens to create an archive that functions as a Pandora's box in reverse, swallowing up all texts into the public world. Despite the archive's ostensible focus on literary production, it stretches toward totalization, extending as far as possible into the active life of the author and—with the archive's yearly growth—staying nearly contemporaneous with that life.

Moreover, as I have already observed, scholars may still attempt readings of the archive that exhibit a more intimate biographical curiosity than a writer like Margaret Atwood might prefer, and it is not guaranteed that they will be satisfied by the range of materials it offers. As Jacques Derrida has observed in *Archive Fever*, some people will always be interested in crossing the line between the public and the private, regardless of where that line is drawn. In fact, the archive, by drawing a line at all, might be seen as courting this very sort of curiosity. Derrida writes:

> [B]eyond every possible and necessary inquiry, we will always wonder what ... every "careful concealer" may have wanted to keep secret. We will wonder what we may have kept of his unconditional right to secrecy, while at the same time burning with the desire to know, to make known, and to archive the very thing he concealed forever. ... We will always wonder what, in this *mal d'archive*, he may have burned. (101)

This scholarly search for knowledge has even been described in terms of rights. For instance, Mary Rubio's meditation on editing Lucy Maud Montgomery's letters leads her to wonder about the need to balance "the individual's 'right to privacy' against the public's 'right to information' about the life of one of Canada's most influential authors" (67). However, it is by no means self-evident that the public does have any kind of right to information about a writer's life, even a life as famous as Montgomery's or Atwood's. The only certainty is that a *desire* for information exists, and the archive is a pragmatic means of addressing that desire, if not of sating it.

For a writer to offer any text—archival or otherwise—under her authorial name to an audience is to sacrifice the text to interpretation beyond her control, and to approach the edge of a slippery slope that might carry the person herself careening after the text into the public domain. The authorial ambivalence that can result is painfully clear in a book such as Dave Eggers's recent autobiography *A Heartbreaking Work of Staggering Genius*, which begins with Eggers presenting a proliferation of exegetical paratexts, as though to maintain as much hermeneutic control over his book as possible, and which ends with Eggers offering himself up to his readers like an ecstatic martyr—"what do you want how much do you want because I am willing ... I want it fast and right through me" (437)—knowing that inevitably he must relinquish his grip over his life story and surrender it to an audience's interpretation.

The living archive is similarly fraught as an attempt to install a life within text. While its strictures and exclusions can impinge to some degree on the scope and tenor of academic inquiry into its contents, it is more difficult to govern the interpretations that critics impose on the archive's contents. Not only does the inclusion of manuscripts and letters make the archive ripe for genetic criticism, but virtually every line of critical investigation can find some foothold, whether it be new historicist, feminist, or biographical. In an era when the distinction between literary and non-literary texts has been challenged, archival documents—and perhaps the archive as a whole—are often being read in much the same way that one might read a poem or novel. And in the case of the Atwood Collection, the librarians responsible for cataloguing decisions have further abetted this dissolution of textual hierarchies by organizing items according to genre, so that a manuscript of an unfinished novel is in the same category as one nominated for the Booker Prize.

However, clearly manuscripts and letters do not always function identically with their published counterparts. From one point of view, her archival texts are the materials that Margaret Atwood has cast off. To adopt Julia Kristeva's term, they are texts that Atwood has abjected, in order to define herself—or, at least, to define her published and putatively final texts—in contrast with those texts that she has placed outside herself and classified as "other." Published books gain their status and value partly in opposition to these archival materials, which appear as preparatory to or ancillary to literature by its conventional definition; to appropriate Wittgenstein's metaphor for philosophy, archival materials are the ladder that Atwood has kicked away once she has produced books to be sold in stores. From this perspective—quasi-formalist for its celebration of the well-wrought urn of a single, autonomous, published text, and genetically teleological in its belief that a chain of texts constitutes a progression to some ultimately valuable product—research into the living archive risks appearing redundant, if not unseemly, as though such study were only a more hygienic alternative to rooting through Margaret Atwood's recycling bins.

But then, materials in the living archive have their own value conferred on them by the very fact that they have been archived. Such an action declares them worth preserving and, implicitly, worth studying. In this sense, they are marked as being of psychological interest because they have been only partially abjected. Within the archive they are not completely "other" to Atwood at all but rather fall into the penumbra of the published texts and accordingly are within the circle of a larger, less clearly defined oeuvre. In this sense, one might identify in the process of archivization something of a redemptive function. Consider, for instance, Box 80, Folder 1 of the Atwood Collection, which contains the holograph and typescript of an unfinished short story called "Dancing in Circles." The archive's finding aid contains a supplementary note by Margaret Atwood about "Dancing in Circles" in which she speculates that she must have become discouraged with the story and put it aside. Taken together, the story and the note raise the question of whether a text can be somehow rehabilitated by being placed in the archive. In the same sense, Janet Malcolm observes that one gives value to unsent letters by keeping them:

> By saving the letter, we are in some sense "sending" it after all. We are not relinquishing our idea or dismissing it as foolish or unworthy…; on the contrary, we are giving it an extra vote of confidence. We are, in effect, saying that our idea is too precious to be entrusted to the gaze of the actual addressee, who may not grasp its worth, so we "send" it to his equivalent in fantasy. (173)

In the case of Atwood's choice to preserve "Dancing in Circles," the "addressee" may be not only Atwood's potential audience but also Atwood herself as writer, and the judgment is that she is not able to make something of the manuscript. Accordingly, to place it in the archive is a compromise: there, it is no longer a candidate for completion, but it finds inclusion as a text worth reading—by scholars, if not by the general public. Indeed, the archivization of such materials allows an author both to repudiate a text—it is "only" a rough draft—and simultaneously authorize it.

Of course, part of the redemptive value that a text like "Dancing in Circles" accumulates in the Atwood Collection is a function of the fact that the collection is a living archive, since the author herself has made the decisions of inclusion and exclusion. Consequently, there is always the possibility that one might read the archive with an intentionalist eye as an enormous act of autobiography. In this scenario, each constituent of the archive has a role in a larger signifying textual matrix; each alters the way we read the whole. To explore this possibility further, I want to consider one particular part of "Dancing in Circles." It appears at the end of the manuscript, after a series of pages with handwritten notes on them. It is a single, yellow sheet. And on both sides it is completely blank.

When I first came upon the blank page I had just been reading *Tristram Shandy*, so of course the thing seemed redolent with meaning. Aside from signalling the manuscript's incompleteness, the page was a reminder of the open endedness of the archive itself, with its promise of further accessions, further inscriptions. The page might also serve to remind critics of their role in creating and circulating meaning from Margaret Atwood's texts. It alludes to as-yet-unwritten scholarly elucidations. One might even see the page as signalling the symbiotic relationship between author and academic, as an invitation for critics to write themselves into the archive. And perhaps the blank page is a warning, reminding us that the archive has gaps and silences, that even in fifty metres of boxes, it does not tell all. As Atwood herself has written in her prose poem "The Page": "Beneath the page is a story. Beneath the page is everything that has ever happened" (*MD* 78). This blank yellow page may even be a pointed sign of resistance on Atwood's part, a sign of her refusal to confess in front of an audience and appear fully complicit in the archival process.[2]

Clearly one blank page can resonate strongly for a critic ready to find resonance. It can come alive and speak. And at the same time, there is the lurking possibility that this page is a mistake, that it was not supposed to be in the archive at all. As Voss and Werner write, "The archive's dream of perfect order is disturbed by the nightmare of its random, heterogeneous, and often unruly contents" (2). Yet once this piece of paper has been admitted into the collection, it is difficult to fathom removing it. If I were to rip it, or steal it, I would be disrupting the order of things in some way. And still, I doubt I would have many takers if I were to offer the blank page for auction on its own. Its value and its meaning are dependent on its presence within the larger text of the archive, as a part of an ongoing act of authorial self-expression, however coded or indirect that expression might be in comparison with a memoir.

Nevertheless, a view of the blank page as constituent of a gargantuan and sustained autobiographical production depends upon an individualist conception of the archive that is not quite descriptively adequate. When one considers the living archive's existence as a communal venture—librarians make final cataloguing decisions and act as security guards of the work, while scholars choose how to use and interpret the materials on offer—the archive seems more like an act of biography than of autobiography. Moreover, Atwood's own role in shaping the archive is hardly that of a traditional autobiographer. For instance, beyond the evident design leading to the presentation of only those materials relating to the "literary work," it would be difficult to identify in the archive any overarching figure in the carpet as one might expect from a traditional autobiography.

One obvious figure, however, is Atwood herself. Given the communal aspect not only of archival creation but also of many materials within the collection, it is no small function of the archive to discipline its diverse contents by setting them together under the rubric of a single authorial name—a name that, as Foucault observes, establishes "a relationship of homogeneity, filiation, [and] authentification" between texts ("Author" 982). After all, not every text in the Atwood Collection is by Margaret Atwood. For instance, there are letters and articles by other people, and at least one of Margaret Atwood's manuscripts is written on the back of mimeographed notes for someone else's entomology lab. Other individuals who make appearances in the collection are given due credit in the finding aid and, in the case of correspondence, there are viewing restrictions in order to accommodate the interests of the parties involved. These restrictions remind us that to attach a single author's name to an archive—as with a book—is a conventional catachresis with attendant strategies of acknowledgement and elision.

The authorial name is further reductive in its presentation of a seemingly static and concrete object of study, as the living archive framed by that name mediates between author and critic by presenting a textual monument for interrogation. Like all authors, Margaret Atwood depends on being yoked to her authorial doppelgänger, not only for material and legal reasons but to maintain some manner of ontological connection to the text. Given the fact that, as Atwood herself has noted, authors continually find themselves changing from the person they were when they wrote a particular book (*ND* 39), in a key sense an author's static text retains a proximity to its creator that the living, changing author cannot maintain herself. Like autobiography, the archive exteriorizes the author's life in a record, an abjection that effectively doubles the author, installing a more or less fixed textual self that is to some extent independent of the living person. The archive transforms the diachronic formation of a life lived into a synchronic, textual figure identified by the authorial name—the figure who, in critical writing, is always quoted in the present tense, regardless of the date of the publication from which the words are taken. Margaret Atwood, the person, becomes removed from the Margaret Atwood Collection, and in her place is an alter ego, the Author, who appears not from behind archival texts but through them. This alter ego is all the more attractive to critics because, while it may change over time, growing as the author contributes more and more texts to the archive, it will not die.

In this light, the archive seems less something abjected from the author—and thus defined as not-her—than something that has come precisely to be identified with her. The assembled record is apparently motivated by the absent author, but it also itself produces an Author to be scrutinized. The archive arranges a chaotic and disparate range of materials into a single, homogeneous text under the auspices of a single authorial name, reifying and delineating a textual corpus that substitutes for the living body, making autobiography both a pretext and effect of bibliography.

Accordingly, while the archive might seem to represent a link in a quasi-platonic chain leading to the original, authentic life of the artist, in fact the process is more complex than that. Like all authors, Margaret Atwood is constantly hailed as someone who is not quite herself, a subject existing in text as much as in a biological body. It is a phenomenon that Atwood herself—or a past Atwood, at least, in the 1970s—evoked through her character Joan Foster in the novel *Lady Oracle*, herself a writer:

> [I]t was as if someone with my name were out there in the real world, impersonating me, saying things I'd never said but which appeared in the newspapers, doing things for which I had to take the consequences: my dark twin, my funhouse-mirror reflection. She was taller than I was, more beautiful, more threatening. She wanted to kill me and take my place, and by the time she did this no one would notice the difference. (250–51)

And as another, more recent Margaret Atwood has observed in *Negotiating with the Dead*, this spectral, authorial self transforms the living person in turn. Referring to Borges, Atwood has asserted, "The writer writes himself into his work—which contains an element of posturing and artificiality—and the more he does this, the more he loses what might be called his authentic self" (121). Because so much of a writer's life is spent writing, it is difficult to separate life from text. The archive is not so much a record of the artist's life as a portion of that life, a fact that must be further complicated now by Atwood's awareness as she writes that her manuscripts will one day be archived.

Given Atwood's own penchant for dualities, it's tempting to identify Atwood-the-author and Atwood-the-person as the two distinct co-existing entities. However, such a binary is too reductive, given the sense of conflation that Atwood has described. One might more accurately talk of one

Atwood with many incarnations: the one who has written each of the novels appearing under her name, the one who writes now, and the one whose views we can synthesize from a survey of her texts, to name but a few. She's also an embodied human being in the world, as well as a reified body of texts. A strict taxonomy here would be impossible, for each of these Atwoods overlaps, shifts, and can never be precisely located. To admit as much is not to confess to a critical failure but, rather, to identify a necessary conceptual web that generates meaning and that cannot be unpicked, lest the different Atwoods become detached and cease their dialogue with each other. This dynamic, reciprocal relationship between author and text means that the question of what is appropriate to the public archive and what is not becomes difficult. Given that shopping lists and telephone bills play a part in constituting the life of Margaret Atwood, are they not also somehow relevant to her literary texts and the study of them? If they are, it seems hard to imagine that the archive could ever be capacious enough to attain descriptive adequacy in accounting for what the finding aid calls the "literary work."

At this point we should recall the story of King Sadim, the backwards cousin of King Midas, who decided that in the interests of posterity, whatever he touched would be archived, so that he never wore the same clothes twice, never drank more than once from the same glass. Instead, everything was deposited into the Sadim Archive. In the king's later years, he decided that it would be better to archive not only what he touched but what he set eyes on. Houses, animals, whole villages were carefully uprooted, catalogued, and deposited. The king's archivist, needless to say, had to remain always behind his back, lest she in turn be put into the collection. The edifice housing the Sadim archive grew bigger and bigger, until at last the whole kingdom was contained under its roof. That accomplished, things returned to pretty much the way they had been before.

The story of this king reminds us that no matter how comprehensive, the archive is a rather provisional and ill-bordered thing, and that its walls are more permeable than we might think, but that it is a necessary fiction of discreteness that permits us to think in terms of stable, individual subjects of study. The story might also be read as an allegory of the future, as we move toward a world in which notions of materiality and publication, so central to the archive as currently conceived, become passé. Derrida has said that email alone is "transforming the entire public and private space of humanity" (17). The materials in the Atwood archive are only a tiny sample of what may become available to literary critics in the future, as our daily communications, routines, and even mental processes are increasingly encoded electronically with video cameras, cellphones, PDAs, and the Internet. Given such a scenario, we can expect to find archival and bibliographical notions in need of revision. Where is the "original" manuscript of an email? Where does an email exist at all? How far will copyright be extended in an age when speech and print become blurred? We may even find ourselves facing a challenge to concepts as fundamental as individuality. Already it is becoming an exercise in science rather than science fiction to imagine a day in which discrete human subjectivity evaporates as technology gives us the ability to share each other's sensations and thoughts. In such a milieu the desire for privacy, and for the kinds of boundaries that the living archive seeks to establish, may well increase, not diminish, as the maintenance of such boundaries becomes more difficult and thus more valuable.

Of course, neither Margaret Atwood nor anyone else is quite at this stage yet. Atwood has a website, but she does not keep a blog, she has no webcams set up in her house or attached to her forehead, and, as far as I know, she hasn't yet signed on to star in *Celebrity Survivor*. Still, the living archive gestures toward a future in which everything is simultaneously experienced and recorded, so that it becomes more challenging, and perhaps more futile, to distinguish the person whose life is being archived from the archive itself. As the archive becomes a mode of living, the living body of the author, already neatly excised from the loop of text and criticism, may be increasingly excised from life itself.

—University of Toronto

NOTES

1. My thanks to Jennifer Toews at the Thomas Fisher Rare Book Library for these figures.
2. For the suggestion of this last possibility, and for the reference to "The Page," I owe respective debts to two interlocutors at the "Margaret Atwood: The Open Eye" symposium.

WORKS CITED

Atwood, Margaret. *Lady Oracle*. Toronto: McClelland & Stewart, 1976.

———. *Murder in the Dark*. [1984]. London: Virago, 1994.

———. *Negotiating with the Dead: A Writer on Writing*. New York: Cambridge University Press, 2002.

Derrida, Jacques. *Archive Fever: A Freudian Impression*. Translated by Eric Prenowitz. Chicago: University of Chicago Press, 1996.

Eggers, Dave. *A Heartbreaking Work of Staggering Genius*. 2nd ed. London: Picador, 2001.

Foucault, Michel. *The Archaeology of Knowledge*. Translated by A.M. Sheridan Smith. London: Routledge, 2000.

———. "What Is an Author?" In *The Critical Tradition: Classic Texts and Contemporary Trends*, edited by David H. Richter, 978–87. Boston: Bedford, 1989.

Kristeva, Julia. *Powers of Horror: An Essay on Abjection*. New York: Columbia University Press, 1982.

Malcolm, Janet. *The Silent Woman: Sylvia Plath and Ted Hughes*. 1st paperback edition. London: Picador, 1994.

Rubio, Mary. "'A Dusting Off': An Anecdotal Account of Editing the L.M. Montgomery Journals." In *Working in Women's Archives: Researching Women's Private Literature and Archival Documents*, edited by Helen M. Buss and Marlene Kadar, 51–78. Waterloo: Wilfrid Laurier University Press, 2001.

Voss, P.L., and M.L. Werner. "Toward a Poetics of the Archive." *Studies in the Literary Imagination* 32, no.1 (1999): 1–9.

Writing History, from *The Journals of Susanna Moodie* to *The Blind Assassin*

CORAL ANN HOWELLS

AS ANTONIA FREMONT remarked in *The Robber Bride* (1993), "All history is written backwards" (109), and the impulse behind this essay is likewise retrospective. Though my main focus will be on *The Robber Bride, Alias Grace* (1996), and *The Blind Assassin* (2000), which arguably constitute Atwood's trilogy about Anglo-Canadian history from the 1840s to the millennium when *The Blind Assassin* was published, I shall also be looking back to *The Journals of Susanna Moodie* (1970). The apparent gap of twenty-five years between that early poetic sequence that focuses on a figure from Canadian colonial history and *Alias Grace*, her first explicitly historical novel, raises several interesting questions: Is there any evidence in Atwood's fiction over that twenty-five year period for that "strong historical sense" that critics of her poetry remarked on from the mid-1970s to the mid-1990s (Woodcock 95; Nicholson 15)? Why should Canadian historical subjects resurface in her novels of the 1990s? And do these later novels mark an evolution in Atwood's thinking about history and her narrative strategies for writing history? I would suggest that *Susanna Moodie* and these three novels represent the end points in Atwood's sustained inquiry into questions of Canadian identity and stories of nationhood—though over the period since *Susanna Moodie* was written the discourse of the nation has shifted and debates around historical narrative have destabilized the traditional claims of history to be an authoritative and objective account of the past.

We could argue that Atwood has always had a historicizing consciousness, though this dimension of her fiction has been occluded by critical interest in more topical social and literary concerns, like her feminism and the power politics of gender relations, environmental issues, and her postmodern narrative experiments. However, a brief retrospective glance confirms the historical continuum in Atwood's fiction. We might think about *Surfacing (1972)* and its interest in Amerindian prehistory, "now all drowned," or *Life Before Man (1979)* with Lesje's Lost World fantasies and the dinosaur skeletons in the Royal Ontario Museum. In *Lady Oracle* (1976) Joan Foster's costume gothics are inspired by her fascination with nineteenth-century British historical romances and her delight in the shabby remains of dead fashion displayed in the stalls on Portobello Road:

> I pawed through it, swam in it, memorized it—a jade snuffbox, an enamelled perfume bottle, piece after piece, exact and elaborate—to fix and make plausible the nebulous emotions of my costumed heroines, like diamonds on a sea of dough. (159)

In *Bodily Harm* (1981) Atwood focuses on Caribbean colonial history and its post-colonial consequences, while *The Handmaid's Tale* (1985) is based on seventeenth-century American colonial history, which has disturbing implications for some Canadians: "Those nagging Puritans really are my ancestors" (Ingersoll 223). With *Cat's Eye* (1998) Atwood moves into Canada's recent colonial history of the 1940s and 1950s with its story of Anglo-Scottish dominance ("Empire Bloomers") and its postwar European refugees like Mrs. Finestein and Josef Hrbik.

However, her return to explicitly Canadian historical topics comes with the publication of *Wilderness Tips* (1991) with its named Canadian referents in several stories: "Age of Lead" (referring to the disastrous Franklin Expedition), "Death By Landscape" (referring to the Group of Seven painters), and the title story with its references to Richardson's *Wacousta* and the English-Canadian tradition of wilderness writing. It is that story that contains the telling phrase "a slippage in the bedrock" of Anglo-Canadian hegemony and heritage narratives, as if Atwood senses the paradigm shift in Canada's stories of nationhood within the context of the new official rhetoric of multiculturalism, the resurgence of the First Nations, and the separatist movement in Quebec. That collection that marks a point of crisis in Canada's stories of nationhood was published the same year that Atwood gave her Clarendon lectures at Oxford called *Strange Things: The Malevolent North in Canadian Literature*, where she took a retrospective look at Canadian history and myth before an international audience, in an updated version of *Survival*, twenty years on. Atwood speculated on the old question of what is specific about Canadian culture and literature and on one new question: How might history be looked at differently in the 1990s?

Atwood's novels of the 1990s represent her response to the debates over historiography that have been going on since the late 1950s between historians, cultural theorists, and literary critics, and that form an indispensable component in what we have come to recognize as the postmodern condition, best summarized by Jean-Francois Lyotard as a distrust of the "grand narratives" of history, religion, and nation, or, as the historian Laurence Stone (294) phrased the changes in his discipline, "a shift away from macro- to micro-history."[1] Perhaps the key figure for historical novelists has been the controversial American historiographer Hayden White, whose *Metahistory* (1973) and subsequent essays have undermined history's claims to represent the objective truth about the past. The major feature to be highlighted is the way that traditional history both occludes the historian's mediating presence and the fact that his (usually "his") account is a verbal reconstruction of events already in the past, so that history's "reality effect" makes us forget the distance between the account and the events that are being written about. White has insistently drawn attention to the subjective quality of any historical narrative, emphasizing narrative perspective and verbal fabrication:

> In general there has been a reluctance to consider historical narratives as what they most manifestly are—verbal fictions, the contents of which are as much invented as found and the forms of which have more in common with their counterparts in literature than they have with those in the sciences. (White, "The Historical Text" 222)

It is in this context of postmodern scepticism that Atwood's historical novels are situated, though her novels directly address specific issues raised by the cultural and ideological shifts that have altered the terms of debate about Canadian nationhood during the 1990s, as she argues from history itself the need to refigure colonial history and heritage myths.

In her lecture on *Canadian* historical fiction, *In Search of Alias Grace*, Atwood pointed out how figures from the Canadian past were used by writers as points of reference for the Canadian present (21), but the 1990s is a different present from the cultural nationalism of the late 1960s and 1970s out of which *The Journals of Susanna Moodie* (1970) came. Nevertheless, the appeal of historical figures and the legends around them remains strong, as Atwood explained in her Clarendon lectures, for they hold a curious fascination both for those who tell them and for those who hear them: they are handed down and reworked, and storytellers come back to them time and time again, approaching them from various angles and discovering new and different meanings each time the story, or a part of it, is given a fresh incarnation (*Strange Things* 11).[2]

Susanna Moodie is, as Rosemary Sullivan called her, "a Canadian archetype" who provides Atwood with a "way of exploring the moral and psychological problems of the colonial situation" (106). The poems in *Journals* show Atwood as mythographer rather than historian, for a historical figure is imaginatively transformed in a dream and the voice of "Atwood's Moodie," as Al Purdy (39) called her, is that "other voice" that only Atwood can hear running underneath Moodie's nineteenth-century prose, characteristic of that "inescapable doubleness of vision" that Atwood sees as symptomatic of the Canadian psyche: "What struck me most about this personality was the way in which it reflects many of the obsessions still with us" (*JSM* 62). The *Journals* are poetic autobiography and poetry works through metaphors and metamorphoses, in which nothing is static and nothing goes away. Atwood comes at the end by a process George Woodcock describes as a "kind of transference" (95) to a late twentieth-century celebration of Moodie's ghostly voice declaring, "I have my ways of getting through" (*JSM* 60), that duplicitous female storyteller's voice that will recur in the 1990s novels. But the speaking "I" is always multiple, and there is an interesting slippage too between Moodie as mythic figure and Moodie who already speaks with the voice of a postmodern historian:

> One of the
> things I found out by being
> there, and after:
> That history (that list

of ballooning wishes, flukes,
bent times, plunges and mistakes
clutched like parachutes)
Is rolling itself up in your head
at one end and unrolling at the other (35 JSM)

Susanna Moodie's comments on the 1837 Rebellion sound very much like Tony on wars in *The Robber Bride* and look ahead to *Alias Grace*, in the sense that history is made out of contingencies, and that events, like wars, have no finite ends, nor do they become more understandable over time; in fact, they become less understandable and their significance shifts. The image of the scroll rolling up as if to mark a completed event, but at the same time unrolling out into uncertainties, suggests the double movement of memory over time, and Moodie recodes the events of 1837 as if viewed through a telescope, where the soldiers appear as grotesques in a child's drawing, strongly suggesting that these war games have been reduced to insignificance. Atwood comments on this shifting interpretation in her afterword: "Ironically, Susanna later admitted that the rebellion was probably a good thing for Canada (63)."

It is to the resonances of Canadian history and its multiple interpretations that Atwood returns with her novels of the 1990s, but now the cultural and literary context has changed, for the old narratives about Canadian identity and heritage are obviously in need of revision and the debates around historiography have induced a general scepticism about the legitimating narratives of history: "Don't ever ask for the true story" as the voice in Atwood's poem "True Stories" advises (11). Maybe history is merely a narrative mode for explaining the past and by no means offers a comprehensive reconstruction, a point increasingly emphasized with the advent of feminism and multiculturalism, which has drawn attention to marginalized histories formerly suppressed as insignificant. All of these factors contribute to what Linda Hutcheon (herself very influenced by Hayden White) calls "historiographic metafiction" (61–77) to describe the new genre of postmodern Canadian historical novels of the late 1970s and since. Atwood explores the implications of this postmodern shift toward what Hayden White calls "the inexpungable relativity in every representation of historical phenomena" (White, "Historical Emplotment" 375), for as a novelist she is fascinated by the different forms that historical narratives might take.

Though we probably would not think of *The Robber Bride* primarily as a historical novel but, rather, focus on gender politics or issues related to ethnicity, multiculturalism, and estrangement (Rao 112–19; Howells, "The Robber Bride" 88–101), when we recontextualize it in relation to the two novels that come after it, we can see how it is the first of Atwood's postmodern explorations into ways of writing Canadian history. It's even written on a chronicle model, divided into ten-year periods from the 1960s to the 1980s, for this is contemporary Canadian history set in Toronto since the Second World War up until 1990–1991. That city itself is located in an international context, and the novel stretches back in a long historical perspective via Tony's study of wars. Atwood gives us both macro- and micro-history here, where the story of individuals is set within the wider thematic imperatives of history. This is, like *Alias Grace* and *The Blind Assassin*, history as *herstory*, where three women's life stories are mediated through the figure of Zenia, the Other Woman, who blurs the borders between history and myth. She reflects these women's private histories back to them in exaggerated or distorted form, like a magic mirror that makes visible something that is "secretly familiar but which has become alienated through repression," as Freud reminds us in his essay on "The Uncanny" (345). As a postwar refugee, Zenia bears layers of European history, which she brings to Canada. As a drug addict, a sufferer from cancer and from AIDS, she represents the phobic underside of late twentieth-century Western history in which Canada is inevitably implicated.

However, it is Tony as medieval military historian who spells out the changes that have taken place in her discipline, voicing her doubts from the first page with her deconstructive approach to history: "*Pick any strand and snip, and history comes unravelled.*" She reconstructs the past from the facts available to her, though fully aware that history is full of gaps and that historical facts might be made into very different kinds of story. She is clearly a follower of Hayden White's Generic Emplotment theory, in which he suggests that the choice of the plot structure is the historian's and not inherent in the events themselves; and Tony sounds exactly like White in his *Metahistory* when she assumes the authority to tell Zenia's story in *The Robber Bride*:

> So now Zenia is History.
> No: now Zenia is gone. She is lost and gone forever. She's a scattering of dust, blown on the wind like spores; she's an invisible cloud of

> viruses, a few molecules, dispersing. She will only be history if Tony chooses to shape her into history. At the moment she is formless, a broken mosaic; the fragments of her are in Tony's hands, because she is dead, and all of the dead are in the hands of the living. (461)

History serves as verbal artefact and explanatory device, and above all as a way of remembering: Atwood signals the importance of private and collective memory here, in a novel that sets out to give a more realistic appraisal of the otherness and sense of unbelonging that is concealed within constructions of contemporary Canadian identities. Bhabha writes "The other is never outside or beyond us; it emerges forcefully… when we *think* we speak most intimately and indigenously between ourselves" (4).

Yet, despite her doubts, Tony still believes in the value of history, as an act of defiance and an attempt to make sense and order out of the past: "These histories may be ragged and threadbare, patched together from worthless leftovers, but to her they are also flags … glimpsed here and there through the trees, on the mountain roads, among the ruins, on the long march into chaos" (Atwood, 462). Atwood too still believes in the value of history. Interestingly she gives us hints on how to read all her historical novels, with Tony's metafictional comments on history, then with her public lecture *In Search of Alias Grace*, and later with her Cambridge lectures *Negotiating with the Dead* just prior to the publication of *The Blind Assassin*.

Turning to *Alias Grace*, Atwood's first explicitly historical novel, we note that she chooses a subject and a character out of the same period of colonial history as Susanna Moodie, but why turn away from tales of wilderness and settlement, choosing instead a rather murky double murder and a historical character like Grace Marks, who remains an enigma? Atwood explains why when she says that she wished to know what was behind the reassuring accounts of Canadian history she was taught in school: "The lure of the Canadian past, for writers of my generation, has been partly the lure of the unmentionable—the mysterious, the buried, the forgotten, the discarded, the taboo" (*Search* 19). Atwood tells Canadian history as a haunted Gothic tale, for the past lurks like an uncanny Other behind the present. We might even see Grace as the Other Woman to Susanna Moodie, for there are strong connections here—most remarkably in the title of the first chapter, "Jagged Edge," which is taken from one of the Moodie poems ("The Planters"), and Susanna Moodie is quoted and demythologized in the later novel; she is even accused of being a Gothic storyteller herself, fascinated by Grace as a female criminal and possibly a madwoman!

In her investigation into one of the more notorious narratives of colonial history, Atwood does her research, as she says in her afterword and acknowledgements and also in her lecture. She goes to the historical records only to find that they are incomplete and also contradictory, which opens up the space for fiction. Atwood worked by a set of rules: when there was a solid fact, she did not alter it, but where there were gaps, she felt free to invent, so that "*Alias Grace* is very much a novel, rather than a documentary" (*Search* 35). This is a novel that illustrates the impossibility of getting the facts of the past straight. What remains of it is a collection of stories about Grace Marks as "a celebrated murderess. Or that is what has been written down" as Grace remarks (*AG* 25), and from this fragmentary evidence Atwood, like any historiographer, constructs the pattern of her narrative. It is a mark of the postmodern storyteller's self-consciousness that quilt making should feature so insistently in this novel, as both a woman's everyday activity and as a metafictional analogy. The quilt block motifs at the head of every section are visible reminders that patterns are being constructed, though these separate blocks have to be assembled to form the larger pattern of the whole quilt (Rogerson 19–21; Ingersoll 391–92). Grace is not allowed to do the final assembling process at the house of the prison governor's wife, but only at the end when she designs her own quilt. The novel structure itself is analogous to a patchwork quilt, as several recent critics have discussed, in that everyone's versions of Grace Marks's story are included, though just as Grace warns that her own finished quilt will have some surprises and deceptions in it, so Atwood in her final assemblage of the narrative blocks leaves the riddle of Grace's guilt or innocence unsolved, acknowledging that the story is no more accessible over a hundred years later than it was at the time: "But I have to conclude that, although there undoubtedly was a truth—somebody did kill Nancy Montgomery—truth is sometimes unknowable, at least by us" (*Search* 37).

Atwood writes history here using a number of different scripts. We can read it as detective story, as Victorian Gothic melodrama full of secrets and sex and violence, and of course as fictive autobiography, and the novel's power derives from the fact that this is a woman's oral narrative, stimulated by the game of hide-and-seek that Grace plays with the young American psychiatric doctor Simon Jordan. Grace's oral narrative is supplemented by her interior monologue, which is much closer to the inchoate nature of memory than the story that she pieces together for Dr. Jordan in a manner that is not only analogous to her quilt making but also to Tony's making of Zenia into history from story fragments. Grace claims to be suffering from traumatic memory loss, but we do not know if it's true any more than Simon Jordan does. (Grace may have been criminally insane or a split personality or a hysteric, all popular mid-nineteenth-century diagnoses, or she may even have been innocent—though Atwood's narrative in no way confirms that.) However, there is a real sense of terror when Grace alone in her cell at night comes close to remembering what happened on the day of the murders:

> When you are in the middle of a story it isn't a story at all, but only a confusion … It's only afterwards that it becomes anything like a story at all
>
> When you are telling it to yourself or to someone else. (*AG* 245–246)

This passage may refer to the confusion of traumatic memory, but it also sounds like the arguments of contemporary historiographers: "We do not *live* stories, even if we give our lives meaning by retrospectively casting them in the form of stories. So too with nations or whole cultures" (White, "Historical Text" 245). Conversely, we might see a nation's history as sharing many of the characteristics of traumatic memory.

Of course Atwood is writing a very contemporary novel, as she reminds us (*Search* 37) when she highlights the unreliability of private and collective memory. It is Grace's forgetting that is the crucial element here, for it is via her memory loss that Atwood makes the crossing from personal history to national history, where "forgetting … is a crucial factor in the creation of a nation" (Bhabha 11). Atwood is referring to dimensions of amnesia in Canada's official history, like the 1837 Rebellion, which happened only seven years before the double murder case. Grace as the marginalized Other (like Zenia) becomes the screen on to which dimensions of national amnesia deemed necessary in the biography of a nation or an individual are projected (Howells, "The Robber Bride" 37–39). As Tony asks of Zenia, so we can ask of Grace, "Are we in any way like her?" (Atwood, RB 470)

The problems of history do not go away though they may be transformed as they are mediated through retellings over time, as Atwood has indicated:

> The past no longer belongs only to those who lived in it; the past belongs to those who claim it, and are willing to explore it, and to infuse it with meaning for those alive today. The past belongs to us, because we are the ones who need it. (*Search* 39)

That passage spells out the uses of history while also taking us straight into *The Blind Assassin*, which fills in the period between *Alias Grace* and *The Robber Bride*, from the 1870s onward, and focuses on Iris's heyday in the 1930s and 1940s up until the Second World War. Iris does not die until 1999, so this novel is both a retrospective view of some of Canada's major crises in the twentieth century and also a memorial to the end of an era. There is a much wider social and historical perspective here than in *Alias Grace*, partly because Iris lived so long but mainly because she belonged to the old Ontario Establishment in which family history and national history were closely intertwined, and one of the questions the novel asks is: What is the difference between private memoirs and public memorials? Or do they both tell socially convenient lies? Again, this is history as herstory, but this time in the different form of an old woman's handwritten memoir, where life writing becomes a kind of ghost writing in Iris's prolonged series of negotiations with the dead. In her Empson lectures Atwood spotlighted the motivations behind Iris's memoir writing (though we did not realize it at the time): "All writing of the narrative kind, and perhaps all writing, is motivated, deep down, by a fear and fascination with mortality" (*ND* 156). Atwood explodes the orthodoxies of the memoir form here with those two interpolated stories—Laura's novel and the science fiction fable—where the secrets in Iris's own life peep out in strange correspondences with the narrative of Laura's novel. This is the most complexly structured of all Atwood's historical novels, presenting a multi-dimensional narrative that erodes the boundaries between fact and fiction, as apparently competing stories offer different perspectives on Canadian history. Iris's memoir is her reconstruction of a private history, highlighting nothing so much as the subjective dimensions of retrospective narrative. William Wordsworth has famously described such memorializing as "emotion recollected in tranquillity," but

Iris's memoir works in exactly opposite ways. There is no tranquillity in her recollections: "My bones ... ache like history: things long done with, that still reverberate as pain" (*BA* 70), and writing for her is a kind of bleeding to death: everything spills out onto the page. Memory plays tricks with its repressions and distortions, but nothing goes away, as she discovers: "You can never get away from where you've been" (485). But Iris's memoir offers a very limited view of history, constrained as it is by her gender and social class, and it is through the two other narratives (which Iris disowns till very near the end) that a wider view is represented. "Laura's" novel glances at dimensions of immigrant and working-class history in Toronto during the 1930s and 1940s, which Iris could never have articulated in her own voice, while the fable of the blind assassin and the tongueless virgin offers a savagely Marxist social critique of the same period, plus an unexpected dimension that blurs the boundary between history and myth. "He" draws satiric parallels between contemporary social practices and the Code of Hammurabi, for example, while his fabled city of Sakiel-Norn, now reduced to a "pile of stones," comes directly out of the Bible, as Atwood reminded one interviewer (Reynolds 20). Nothing has been forgotten here, but much has been deliberately hidden. And what will Iris's granddaughter Sabrina find when she comes back from India and opens the locked steamer trunk of her inheritance? What she will find in it is her grandmother's uncanny memoir (provided that all those handwritten pages did not blow away, as Frank Davey disturbingly suggested at the Ottawa "Margaret Atwood: The Open Eye" symposium), plus multiple copies of Laura's novel in its first and later editions, Laura's coded notebooks, and the mysterious mutilated photograph—the tangled evidence of two sisters' lives and times.

Iris claims to be offering Sabrina the truth about her family history as a way to free her from false narratives of origin and identity: "*I offer the truth, I say. I'm the last one who can*" (Atwood, *BA* 536). Certainly there is no other witness to dispute her version of the past, for everyone else is dead, and the historian has total authority at last, "for the dead are in the hands of the living," as Tony remarked in *The Robber Bride* (461). Iris is now in the position of the historian; though given her frequent sleights of hand in the course of her narrative, we could not entirely depend on her account:

> I didn't think of what I was doing as writing—just writing down. What I remembered, and also what I imagined, which is also the

> truth. I thought of myself as recording. A bodiless hand, scrawling across a wall.
>
> I wanted a memorial. That was how it began. For Alex, but also for myself. (AG 626)

When we consider the moral ambiguity around memoirs and memorials for Iris, there is something truly sinister in her description of her work as "a left-handed book" (627).

The materials in the trunk really offer no definitive interpretation of her family's or the nation's history but, rather, a destabilization of the truth claims of historical writing in a postmodern context, in which different stories about the past are told from different perspectives. There are so many forms in which history is recorded—a handwritten memoir, a published novel, an oral tale told during a love affair, newspaper reports and obituaries—that history appears to be nothing but a set of competing narratives. As Hayden White commented, "Our knowledge of the past may increase incrementally, but our understanding of it does not" (White, "Historical Text" 223).

Iris's memoir is profoundly biased by her own narrative perspective, but, as this novel has demonstrated, that is the condition of historiography and we need to note how Atwood has characterized history here. It is not her own definition or a postmodern one but a nineteenth-century definition derived from Guy de Maupassant: "*L'histoire, cette vieille dame exaltée et menteuse*", in which history is represented as an overexcited, lying old woman. That quotation is used twice (by two men, neither of whom have much respect for women): once when the Chase sisters' abusive schoolmaster refers to written history (Atwood, BA 199) and again in Iris's dream when Alex's ghost accuses historical process itself of being a destructive force (573). History consists of violence and traumatic events, and the telling of history is always deceptive. (And of course "histoire" means both "history" and "story"). It is interesting in the context of an old woman's memoir that Atwood should choose this quotation, emphasizing that history (like truth) is in the feminine gender in French, for its associations with duplicity inevitably rub off on Iris. By the end, she becomes an allegorical if not a mythic figure, speaking with the voice of history herself.

So, I shall end with Iris's uncanny voice speaking from beyond the grave—she too has her "ways of getting through." (Atwood, *JSM* 60) Radical doubts have been cast on narratives of heritage and identity by her left-handed narrative, here at the end of Atwood's trilogy, which reveals the breadth and scepticism of Atwood's views on Canadian history, acknowledging that telling history is a way of forging links with a past that may be already forged.

—Reading University

NOTES

1. For comprehensive accounts of the history and narrative debate see Geoffrey Roberts (2001,10–38), and Marc Colavincenzo (2003, xiii–xxii).
2. I was directed to this passage by Mary K. Kirtz's essay in Wilson (56–7). However, I view Atwood's revisions of history more positively than Kirtz; Kirtz sees them as a response to a nation under threat, whereas I see them as opening a way to new figurings of history and identity.

WORKS CITED

Atwood, Margaret. *Alias Grace*. London: Virago, 1997.
———. *The Blind Assassin*. London: Virago, 2001.
———. *In Search of Alias Grace*. Ottawa: University of Ottawa Press, 1997.
———. *The Journals of Susanna Moodie*. Toronto: Oxford University Press, 1970.
———. *Lady Oracle*. London: Virago, 1993
———. *Negotiating with the Dead*. London: Virago, 2003.
———. *The Robber Bride*. London: Virago, 1994.
———. *Strange Things: The Malevolent North in Canadian Literature*. Oxford: Clarendon, 1995.
———. *True Stories*. Don Mills, ON: Oxford University Press, 1981.
———. *Wilderness Tips*. London: Virago, 1992.
Bhabha, Homi K., ed. *Nation and Narration*. London and New York: Routledge, 1990.
Colavincenzo, Marc. *Trading Magic for Fact, Fact for Magic: Myth and Mythologizing in Postmodern Canadian Historical Fiction*. Amsterdam and New York: Rodopi, 2003.
Freud, Sigmund. "The Uncanny." Vol. 14, *Penguin Freud Library*. London: Penguin, 1990. 335–76.
Howells, Coral. *Contemporary Canadian Women Novelists: Refiguring Identities*. New York: Palgrave Macmillan, 2003.

———. "*The Robber Bride*; or Who Is a True Canadian?" In *Margaret Atwood's Textual Assassinations: Recent Poetry and Fiction*, edited by Sharon R. Wilson. Columbus: Ohio State University Press, 2003. 88–101.

Hutcheon, Linda. *The Canadian Postmodern: A Study of Contemporary English-Canadian Fiction*. Toronto: Oxford University Press, 1988.

Ingersoll, Earl G. "Engendering Metafiction: Textuality and Closure in *Alias Grace*." *American Review of Canadian Studies* (Autumn 2001): 385–401.

———, ed. *Margaret Atwood: Conversations*. London: Virago, 1992.

Kirtz, Mary K. "(Dis)unified Field Theories: The Clarendon Lectures Seen through (a) *Cat's Eye*." In *Margaret Atwood's Textual Assassinations: Recent Poetry and Fiction*, edited by Sharon R. Wilson. Columbus: Ohio State University Press, 2003. 54–73.

Nicholson, Colin, ed. *Margaret Atwood: Writing and Subjectivity*. London: Macmillan, 1994.

Purdy, Al. "Atwood's Moodie." In *Critical Essays on Margaret Atwood*, edited by Judith McCombs. Boston: G.K. Hall, 1988. 39–45.

Rao, Eleanora. *Heart of a Stranger: Contemporary Women Writers and the Metaphor of Exile*. Naples: Liguori Editore, 2002.

Reynolds, Margaret, and Jonathan Noakes. *Margaret Atwood: The Essential Guide*. London: Vintage, 2002.

Roberts, Geoffrey. "History and Narrative Debate, 1960–2000." In Roberts (ed.), 2001. 10–38.

Rogerson, Margaret. "Reading the Patchworks in *Alias Grace*." *Journal of Commonwealth Literature* 33. no.1 (1998): 5–22.

Stone, Laurence. "The Revival of Narrative: Reflections on a New Old History." In *The History and Narrative Reader*, edited by Geoffrey Roberts. London and New York: Routledge, 2001. 281–98.

Sullivan, Rosemary. "Breaking the Circle." In *Critical Essays on Margaret Atwood*, edited by Judith McCombs. Boston: G.K. Hall, 1988. 104–14.

White, Hayden. "The Historical Text as Literary Artifact." In *The History and Narrative Reader*, edited by Geoffrey Roberts. London and New York: Routledge, 2001. 221–42.

———. "Historical Emplotment and the Problem of Truth." In *The History and Narrative Reader*, edited by Geoffrey Roberts. London and New York: Routledge, 2001. 375–89.

Wilson, Sharon R., ed. *Margaret Atwood's Textual Assassinations: Recent Poetry and Fiction*. Columbus: Ohio State University Press, 2003.

Woodcock, George. "Margaret Atwood: Poet as Novelist." In *Critical Essays on Margaret Atwood*, edited by Judith McCombs. Boston: G.K. Hall, 1988. 90–104.

Atwood and the "Autobiographical Pact"
—*for Reingard Nischik*

SHERRILL GRACE

THIS IS A PHOTOGRAPH OF ME

. . . .

The photograph was taken
the day after I drowned.

. . . .

but if you look long enough,
eventually
you will be able to see me. (Atwood, *CG* 11)

IT IS NO surprise, surely, for anyone familiar with Margaret Atwood's work to be reminded of her pervasive use of first-person pronouns. "I" and "me" are everywhere in her work from the earliest poems (of which "This is a photograph of me" is still one of the finest, most haunting examples) through her fiction, from *The Edible Woman* to *The Blind Assassin*. Offred's "I" asserts itself insistently throughout *The Handmaid's Tale*; Grace Marks comes to life through the first person in *Alias Grace*; and Susanna Moodie is Susanna Moodie because of her (I mean, Atwood's) journals: "I am a word/in a foreign language" (*JSM* 11), she tells us, but also "I am the old woman/sitting across from you on the bus" (61). And, of course, along with these pronouns—"I" and "me"—comes that other one: "you." I/you go hand in hand; we/you are always being addressed by Atwood's many "I's."

My purpose here is not to speculate on who this "I" or "you" *really* are. That is the biographer's challenge. In any case, these pronouns are ambiguous and I like their ambiguity. I want to focus on the I/you conjunction, on what a theorist of autobiography like Philippe Lejeune calls the "autobiographical pact," on how Atwood uses this pact and on why, in her hands, it is so effective. But first a caveat: Despite over thirty-five years of sophisticated study (and basic common sense), we still need to remind ourselves that the various forms of life writing we classify as "autobiography," and "biography" for that matter, are always creative acts, recreative processes, *fictions*. It is all too easy to fall into the trap of thinking that autobiography and biography give us Truth, the inside scoop, the real person, that facts are fixed, authentic markers of reality, and that the life story can, should, be *believed*. It is easy because auto/biography makes these claims for itself. It claims referentiality to a pre-existing, external reality, to truth, accuracy, and authenticity, and it makes these claims in many ways but, most importantly, through the use of those pronouns "I," "me," "you," and through the autobiographical pact.

In his discussion of the "autobiographical pact," Lejeune argues that autobiography works because we, its readers, agree to accept the fundamental identity of the author's name with the first-person narrator who is also the character (*le personnage*) in the story.[1] Moreover, we also agree to believe that this individual really exists outside the covers of the text, that we can meet this selfsame person over tea or out walking the dog or in a lineup at the Green Machine. Such are the seductions (as Mary Rhiel and David Suchoff call them) of auto/biography that *we* (or at least those readers who are deceived by the pact) become outraged to discover that, for example, Margaret Atwood does not have red hair and was never fat. Surely the theory of auto/biography has taught us to understand that all life stories are artistic recreations, possibly very deceptive, inevitably unreliable, and hugely manipulative, even when they are classified as memoir, testimony, or diary. The trick comes in knowing how to read these texts and in learning how to tell the difference between types of fictionality and degrees of referentiality. And when the writer is as skilled an artist as Atwood, as superb a ventriloquist, then the knowing and learning are a challenge.

Before I turn to examples of the autobiographical pact with its "I/you" in Atwood's writing, I want to summarize five assumptions that I make about auto/biography, all of which are based on my reading of key theorists. First, I see a continuum, not absolute distinctions, between testimony at one end of the truth and reality scale and first-person novels at the other; second, I believe that we are trained (conditioned, if you prefer) to accept, believe, or take for granted that when we read (or hear) a first-person voice we are getting the straight goods—hence our confusion or outrage if we discover we have been lied to; third, I am convinced (see also Gilmore; Rhiel and Suchoff) that we live in an auto/biographical age—from "reality TV" to serious theatre and documentary film, to the revival of portraiture and self-portraits, from the re-presencing of the body and the return of the author, to the obsessive production of life-writing texts and the privileging of auto/biography in book stores; fourth, I am convinced that biography and autobiography are inextricably related to each other and to other genres, including theory and scholarly discourse; and last, I am convinced by theorists such as John Paul Eakin, Susanna Egan, Leigh Gilmore, Sidonie Smith, and Julia Watson (to name a few) that relationality (self-representation through an other) is fundamental to the construction of identity in all modes of auto/biography, that the *process* of articulating *self* is dialogic, and that underpinning all such representations (including Paul de Man's concept of apostrophe as the impetus behind the specular structure of autobiography) is some version of Lejeune's pact.[2]

In his original 1975 discussion of the "autobiographical pact" from *Le pacte autobiographique,* Lejeune made a number of crucial observations and comparisons to buttress his argument that the pact was the defining characteristic of autobiography and that it differed from what he called the "pacte romanesque" (29). Whereas in first-person (or autobiographical) fiction the reader should understand the narrator and the character to be fictive and not identical with the name of the author, in autobiography the "nom du personnage = nom de l'auteur. Ce seul fait exclut la possibilité de la fiction" (30). He went on, after examining many examples from French literature, to conclude that autobiography was defined as "un mode de lecture autant qu'un type d'écriture, c'est un *effet contractuel* historiquement variable" (45). When he revisited this concept in his 1989 essay, "The Autobiographical Pact (bis)," he allowed greater latitude for the reader's understanding of the pact and the writer's manipulation of it; on this occasion he suggested that "any text governed by an autobiographical pact"

(124) is autobiography, and he concluded that "in spite of the fact that autobiography is impossible, this in no way prevents it from existing" (131). Upon reflection, Lejeune allowed that, for the reader, autobiography exists when we are asked to believe it does, when certain indicators provided by a text (and thus by the author) elicit this response from a reader.

Atwood, of course, has always known this and has long counted on the power of the autobiographical pact to seduce us, as have many writers before her. At the same time she has carefully guarded her biography, even from her biographers (see Cooke and Sullivan), and has often given us potted and playful versions of her life story. One such version of her life appeared in her "Personal Statement" conclusion to her 1976 essay "On Being a Woman Writer." Another particularly playful example is her 1977 comic strip autobiography called "Portrait of the Artist as a Young Cipher" (see Fig. 1).[3] My personal favourite appears in an early Atwood essay called "Witches" from *Second Words*, but she recently published a potted version in her mock interview for the "Personal History" page of the *Globe and Mail* called "I left Ottawa in a packsack."

But she has not always been merely playful. Many times her autobiographical comments are revealing (please note I am not saying *true*, although they may be that too). I am thinking here especially of her explanation of how she discovered Susanna Moodie and came to write *The Journals of Susanna Moodie* (see 62–64) and of the talk she gave to the 2004 symposium, "Margaret Atwood: The Open Eye," when she gave an illustrated PowerPoint version of her autobiography, as if to remind her audience that this was *her* story to tell.

Sherrill Grace 125

Margaret Atwood, "Portrait of the Artist as a Young Cipher" (1977)

But the work I want to focus on here is *Negotiating with the Dead: A Writer on Writing* (2002). This volume began as the 2000 Empson lectures at Cambridge University; therefore, in one sense, the first-person voice in the published book is inevitable. On the actual occasion she was speaking in her own voice and *in propria persona* about her own life as a writer. It was a classic autobiographical moment with an undeniable, embodied pact. The real Margaret Atwood stood up and told her audience how she became a writer and why. Along the way she made a number of observations about biographers and about writers as the subject of biographies: "Is the writer," she asked, Shelley's "unacknowledged legislator of the world ... or is he one of Carlyle's blimp-like Great Men, or is he the snivelling neurotic wreck and ineffectual weenie so beloved of his contemporary biographers?" (xviii). In the prologue to the book, she describes her first chapter as "the most autobiographical" (xxv), which in a factual sense it is; however, the facts she presents in this chapter are only the entrance, the gateway into a far more profound and interesting life story. She assures us that she cannot locate what biographers love to describe—"some determining moment in early life that predicts the course of the future artist or scientist or politician" (15)—and she gives up the search, leaving us with the image of herself "back in 1961, twenty-one years old, biting my fingers and just beginning to realize what I'd got myself into" (25).

In the rest of *Negotiating with the Dead*, I would argue that what she in fact gives us is an autobiography of her imagination—not *the* autobiography necessarily but an autobiographical story complete with an autobiographical pact in which I am asked to take her hand, trust her words, and believe her confession. *Negotiating with the Dead* is highly confessional, intensely personal, and personally *for me* moving because I too am a writer of sorts, I too have a story, and I too dare to think my story might be told and that someone (my children?) will be interested enough to listen. Moreover, I have been interested in Margaret Atwood for a very long time; she has become part of my autobiography.

But there are many other reasons besides these personal ones that lead me to describe this book as an autobiography. At many points she comments on biography, autobiography, testimony, diaries, and letters, and she tells us that she keeps "a journal of sorts" (*ND* 129). Her reason is Beckettian: like Krapp with his tape recorder she has trouble remembering her former selves. Not surprisingly, she is acutely aware of the power of such autobiographical materials: "There is something magical about such real-life documents. The fact that they have survived, have reached our hands, seems like the delivery of an unexpected treasure; or else like a resurrection" (128). She is also aware of the role of the eye/I-witness, the one who bears witness, who gives testimony, and that such witnessing implies truth: "The power of such narratives is immense, especially when combined with artistic power. ... Real life's jagged extremes mixed with verbal artistry are a potent and sometimes explosive combination" (118). At other points in this book, she reflects on the ironies of autobiographical writing, on the ethics of truth claims, and on the fundamental "duplicity" of all writing. This duplicity, as she calls it, arises from the simple fact that the name on the title page and the "I" in the story never are the author or, if we must insist on Lejeune's pact and say that they are one and the same, then none of them is the person of the writer. To drive home this point Atwood returns to concepts she has explored from the start: doubles and duality. The writer, she insists, is Jekyll and Hyde, he/she is "two": "All writers are double, for the simple reason that you can never actually meet the author of the book you have just read" (37). And there are, she explains, two Atwoods, the one who writes whom we can know through her writing and that other Atwood, her double, whom we can never know, who has already disappeared around a corner to go to that Green Machine or into the kitchen to bake "oatmeal-and-molasses bread":

> Who was I then? My evil twin or slippery double, perhaps. I am after all a writer, so it would follow as the day the night that I must have a slippery double—or at best a mildly dysfunctional one—stashed away somewhere. I've read more than one review of books with our joint surname on them that would go far toward suggesting that this other person—the one credited with authorship—is certainly not me. She could never be imagined—for instance—turning
> out a nicely browned loaf of oatmeal-and-molasses bread, whereas I ... but that's another story. (36)

Atwood's concluding message on writing and on the autobiographical impulse in *Negotiating with the Dead* is what gives the volume its title. Writing, she insists, is "a reaction to the fear of death" (157). If I were to attempt a biographical reading of Atwood's work, this is where I would begin—with this comment, this essay, this self-consciously autobiographical book. In answer to her own question about why writing above all other art forms should be so closely linked "with anxiety about one's own personal extinction," she replies, because "it survives its own performance" (158). The dead want to talk and writers know how to listen; good writers also know how to make us listen and believe the truth of what they say. They know how to seduce us with the siren song of "I" and "you." They know how to set the imagination-hold trap of the autobiographical pact, never more so than when they are writing fiction.

Negotiating with the Dead tells us a lot about the writer Atwood, her voice, her desires, her motivations, her imagination, and thus about the self that matters most to *us*, the "we," "you" who are literature specialists. I will go a step further and say that in *Negotiating with the Dead*, especially in the final chapter, she tells us how to go about reading her work, where to locate her motivation *as a writer*, and what to identify as her persistent themes. This book provides us with clues, instructions, and guidelines for understanding "Margaret Atwood." In this book she performs an "autobiographics" of herself as writer, or, to rephrase Leigh Gilmore's concept of autobiographics, she gives us a method—an autobiographics—of reading and coming to terms with the importance of writing and reading.[4] But let me explain briefly what I mean.

Although some secret about that other Margaret Atwood's off-page life may be revealed here—has she always been fascinated by negotiation with the dead because of a personal experience? Is she obsessed with mortality because of some near-death scare in early childhood? Was that image in *Surfacing* of the drowning brother in fact her own near drowning? (In that autobiographical piece for the "Personal History" column of the *Globe and Mail* she describes her brother teaching her to swim by taking her out over her head and then just letting go!)—I am far from sure that it matters very much. What matters is that so much of her poetry, fiction, and nonfiction deals with the dead because, as she reminds us, "*all* writing of the narrative kind, and perhaps all writing, is motivated deep down, by a fear of and fascination with mortality—by a desire to make the risky trip to the Underworld, and to bring something or someone back from the dead" (*ND* 156).

From *Double Persephone* (1961) on, Atwood the writer has made this trip. Her narrators come back from the grave, or from near-death experiences, to tell us important things, or to plead with us for remembrance, or to warn us, or simply to play games—deadly serious games about staging deaths (especially drownings) that will scare us: *Surfacing, Lady Oracle, Bodily Harm, The Handmaid's Tale, The Robber Bride, Alias Grace, The Blind Assassin*, and so many of the stories (for example, "Death By Landscape"). The same is true of the poetry. *The Journals of Susanna Moodie* represents not only Atwood's personal journey to the underworld (a poetic autobiographics) but our collective, national journey, a mythic tale of origins for Canada, and an answer *avant la lettre* to Ted Chamberlain's recent question: "If this is your land, where are your stories?"[5] But this process of negotiation with the dead is everywhere in the poems, nowhere more personally and privately than in *Morning in the Burned House*, from its opening poem:

> You come back into the room
> where you've been living
> all along.... (3)

to its final poem:

> I can't see my own arms and legs
> or know if this is a trap or blessing,
> finding myself back here, where everything
>
> in this house has long been over,
> kettle and mirror, spoon and bowl,
> including my own body,
>
> including the body I had then,
> including the body I have now
> as I sit at this morning table, alone and happy,
> . . . .
>
> holding my cindery, non-existent,
> radiant flesh. Incandescent. (127)

I have just described *The Journals of Susanna Moodie* as inscribing Atwood's personal journey as poet—a poetic autobiographics—that has a wider, national application. After living with and loving this volume of poetry for thirty-four years, I am convinced that it has achieved the status of a Canadian autobiography in that "Moodie" performs herself, *outliving both her historical presence and her present creator*, to re-create herself in a dramatic process of autobiographics that represents the country. Moodie's life story (in Atwood's hands) is our story, a "people's history" long before the CBC caught on to the idea. Moreover, Atwood's "Moodie" keeps coming back from the dead to tell us who we are today, how to recognize ourselves, and how—maybe—to survive. On one level, sadly, judging by *Oryx and Crake* and the signs of global warming in the Arctic, we have not been paying attention. On another, however, we have. The *Journals* itself, with Atwood's illustrations, has never gone out of print, and it was published in 1980 as a limited edition *livre d'artistes* with serigraphs by Charles Pachter, a volume, in its own turn, reprinted in 1997.[6] These "journals" have become iconic—made "Moodie" a national icon—and they have succeeded in telling our story because of the extraordinary beauty and skill with which Atwood uses the autobiographical pact—the "I/you," the concept of journals, the photograph of Moodie, and so on. It is precisely this pact that leads readers (like generations of my students) who encounter the poems for the first time—just now, for us—to believe they were written by Susanna Moodie. Such readers are then either reassured or puzzled by the afterword, but they continue to believe that "Susanna Moodie" *is* Margaret Atwood either because they accept Atwood's story about being a student who discovered Moodie's books and recreated them, or because they insist that if Atwood dreamed the poems then the story in the journals must be hers.

In all her work Atwood has been profoundly auto/biographical and if we have missed this I believe it is because we have been looking for the wrong story, expecting autobiography to be something it is not. Perhaps it is easier now to look for the right story because we have better theoretical tools or because she herself has become more overt about the process. If I am correct in reading *Negotiating with the Dead* as an autobiography about the autobiographics of being a writer and as a fine guide to reading that writer's imagination, then she has finally given us the keys to her story—if we dare to follow her into that dangerous realm of doubles, the dead, Persephone, and the Underworld. We must also remember that the autobiography she gives us is not one thing, homogenous. It runs the gamut from self-performance to the creation of others' auto/biographies, and some of those *others* did once exist. The "I" she uses is multiple, sometimes her own embodied I/eye, sometimes a completely invented "I," and often what Paul de Man calls the "specular" "I" that always employs "the figure of prosopopeia, the fiction of an apostrophe to an absent, deceased, or voiceless entity [*you*], which posits the possibility of the latter's reply and confers upon it the power of speech" (75–76). Atwood's "I" invites "you" to speak by first enjoining "you" to listen.

Why has she always written this way? Perhaps because she is not a high modernist determined to erase the personal in favour of some illusion of godlike Joycean neutrality. Perhaps because the "I" voice feels right to her, and most certainly because she has always understood the capacity of the autobiographical pact to call up "you," whether living or dead. Unlike de Man, I believe that apostrophe functions *within* autobiography to activate this pact; it is because of apostrophe—the address to the dead or absent one *and to the* reader—you—that the pact is so effective as a narrative strategy, whether we are reading a self-proclaimed life story or a fiction. But let me give Atwood in *The Blind Assassin* (or should I say Iris, or Laura?) the closing questions ... and answers:

> Why is it we want so badly to memorialize ourselves? Even while we're still alive. We wish to assert our existence, like dogs peeing on fire hydrants. We put on display our framed photographs, our parchment diplomas, our silver-plated cups; we monogram our linen, we carve our names on trees, we scrawl them on washroom walls. It's all the same impulse. What do we hope from it? Applause, envy, respect? Or simply attention, of any kind we can get?
>
> At the very least we want a witness. We can't stand the idea of our own voices falling silent finally, like a radio running down. (*BA* 95)

—University of British Columbia

NOTES

1. In *Le pacte autobiographique* (23–24), Lejeune defines autobiography as follows: "L'autobiographie (récit racontant le vie de l'auteur) suppose qu'il y ait *identité de nom* entre l'auteur (tel qu'il figure, par son nom, sur la couverture), le narrateur du récit et le personnage dont on parle. C'est là un critère très simple, qui définit même temps que l'autobiographie tous les autres genres de la littérature intime (journal, autoportrait, essai)."
2. De Man dismisses attempts to elevate autobiography to the category of a genre because, he insists, autobiography is "always slightly disreputable and self-indulgent" (67–68). Instead of a genre or a mode of writing, he describes autobiography in terms of "a figure of reading or of understanding" (70) and the figure that operates in autobiography is, he argues, "prosopopoeia" (75).
3. My thanks to Reingard Nischik for bringing this cartoon to my attention and for her interesting analysis of "inverse poetics" in *Murder in the Dark*. Speaking of Atwood's use of the first-person singular in "Autobiography," Nischik comments that this fragment, for all that it resembles autobiography, is in fact "a fragmentary epiphanic [text] that undermines the sequence of events encountered in traditional autobiographies" (7). I am tempted to call this fragment an anti-autobiography-as-autobiographics; see note 4.
4. Gilmore coins the term "autobiographics" to describe "those elements that ... mark a location in a text where self-invention, self-discovery, and self-representation emerge within the technologies of autobiography" (42) (legal, literary, ecclesiastical, etc.) to resist and contradict such traditional (and she argues, masculinist) technologies. Autobiographics is as much a reading practice as it is a description of self-representation, and it operates in many non-hegemonic discourses. I find Atwood's strategy in *Negotiating with the Dead* to be precisely this kind of self-invention—one that confounds our accepted notions of what constitutes truth claims about identity insofar as identity is defined by Western philosophy to be contained, self-consistent, stable, and knowable.
5. By linking Atwood's *Journals* to Chamberlain's argument I am not suggesting that the *Journals* inscribes a colonialist counter-story to displace indigenous stories. The process of belonging that the poems imagine for "Moodie" is far more complex, ambiguous, and double-sided than any mere assertion of dominance.
6. When the *Journals* was first published it included a cover design by Atwood and several of her collages within a volume that resembled, in its oblong shape, the kind of expedition journal carried by explorers; this text remains in print. The 1980 *livre d'artistes* is quite a different entity. For this limited edition of 120 copies, Pachter hand-set the text and created thirty-seven serigraphs that respond to the poems, rather than simply illustrating them. This edition, like

the 1997 reprint, is a collaborative work by two artists, one verbal, and the other visual. The size, cost, and aesthetic beauty of the original *livre d'artistes* make it a rare collector's item; the 1997 reprint with an introduction by David Staines and a memoir by Pachter shift the emphasis considerably. As Pachter declares in the reprint, the volume "is nothing if not my homage to the writer, poet, and friend whose genius has been a sustained source of inspiration for my imagination" (xxiii). In other words, this volume mythologizes Atwood as much as—maybe more than—Moodie.

WORKS CITED

Atwood, Margaret. *The Circle Game*. Toronto: Anansi, 1966.

———. "Death By Landscape." *Wilderness Tips*. Toronto: McClelland & Stewart, 1991. 107–129.

———. "I left Ottawa in a packsack." *Globe and Mail* (Toronto), February 7, 2004 R14.

———. *The Journals of Susanna Moodie*. Toronto: Oxford University Press, 1970.

———. *Morning in the Burned House*. Toronto: McClelland & Stewart, 1995.

———. *Negotiating with the Dead*. Cambridge: Cambridge University Press, 2002.

———. *Second Words: Selected Critical Prose*. Toronto: Anansi, 1982.

Atwood, Margaret, and Charles Pachter. *The Journals of Susanna Moodie*. [1980]. Toronto: Macfarlane Walter & Ross, 1997.

Chamberlain, J. Edward. *If This Is Your Land, Where Are Your Stories? Finding Common Ground*. Toronto: Knopf, 2003.

Cooke, Nathalie. *Margaret Atwood: A Biography*. Toronto: ECW Press, 1998.

de Man, Paul. "Autobiography as De-Facement." *The Rhetoric of Romanticism*. New York: Colombia University Press, 1984. 67–81.

Eakin, Paul John. *How Our Lives Become Stories: Making Selves*. Ithaca and London: Cornell University Press, 1999.

Egan, Susanna. *Mirror Talk: Genres of Crisis in Contemporary Autobiography*. Chapel Hill: University of North Carolina Press, 1999.

Gilmore, Leigh. *Autobiographics: A Feminist Theory of Women's Autobiography*. Ithaca and London: Cornell University Press, 1994.

Lejeune, Philippe. *Le pacte autobiographique*. Paris: Éditions du Seuil, 1975.

———. "The Autobiographical Pact (bis)." In *On Autobiography*, edited by Paul John Eakin. Translated by Katherine Leary, 119–37. Minneapolis: University of Minnesota Press, 1989.

Nischik, Reingard M. "*Murder in the Dark*: Margaret Atwood's Inverse Poetics of Intertextual Minuteness." In *Margaret Atwood's Textual Assassinations: Recent Poetry and Fiction*, edited by Sharon R. Wilson, 1–17. Columbus: Ohio State

University Press, 2003.

Rhiel, Mary, and David Suchoff, eds. *The Seductions of Biography*. New York and London: Routledge, 1996.

Smith, Sidonie, and Julia Watson. *Reading Autobiography: A Guide for Interpreting Life Narratives*. Minneapolis: University of Minnesota Press, 2001.

Sullivan, Rosemary. *The Red Shoes: Margaret Atwood Starting Out*. Toronto: HarperFlamingo, 1998.

EARLIER NOVELS

"Saying Boo to Colonialism": *Surfacing,* Tom Thomson, and the National Ghost

CYNTHIA SUGARS

Every culture has its exemplary dead people. ...
(Atwood, "True North" 146)

IN A 1972 interview with Graeme Gibson, Margaret Atwood became impatient with the endless round of predictable questions about the plot elements of *Surfacing*: "All the things that you've been talking about are really just the jam on the sandwich, because the interesting thing in that book is the ghost. ... [T]he other stuff in there, it's quite true, but it is a condition; it isn't what the book is about" ("Dissecting" 17). But what kind of a ghost story is it? Eli Mandel states that "*Surfacing* presents itself as political and social criticism disguised as ghost story" ("Atwood" 139). Can we, then, call it a national ghost story ... or a post-colonial one? What would these mean?

The construction of an ancestral ghost is key to providing symbolic legitimation for colonial settler descendants. If *Surfacing* describes a symbolic shedding and regaining of an ancestral father, it also stages the narrator's quest for origination (both physically, via the birth metaphor, and abstractly, via language/national identity), a trajectory that is contained in the very metaphor of "surfacing" itself. This is epitomized, perhaps, in the narrator's identification of her father's drowned corpse as her lost fetus. The fetus represents not only that of her aborted baby but also herself, since it is after discovering her father's body that she finds the picture of herself in her mother's womb (143–44). In more ways than one, the novel might be said to stage a fantasy of (re)invention.

Yet as a metaphor, "surfacing" also implies concealment, and therefore points to hidden depths, particularly when it is a drowned corpse that has brought one to the point of surfacing in the first place. Jodey Castricano observes that, paradoxically, it is death that brings us face to face with origination, for "death tells us there is no meaning outside memory" (3). In *Surfacing* the narrator's psychic journey produces this realization—both on the level of the individual and the community—for it parallels "interpersonal familial haunting" with "haunting [as] a phenomenon affecting entire generations" (Castricano 140). A woman in search of herself (her lost past/her parents/her aborted baby) is paralleled by a nation in search of its identity (Canada versus the United States; English Canada versus Quebec; modernization versus the environment; settler versus Aboriginal; male versus female), and both quests are figured in terms of a need for an absent—but ultimately authenticating—progenitor/father.[1] The novel might thus be read as a narrative about the limits of origins, even as it seeks to forge these origins and locate them in the landscape. In other words, the narrator's experience of parental loss is merged with the national absence of an authenticating archetype. To the extent that object loss is figured in the psychoanalytic sense as an "originary" internalized other, what Freud describes as "the shadow of the object [fallen] upon the ego" (258), a ghost becomes the perfect figure for this presence as absence. If the *narrator* is searching for her "lost" parents, and is thereby fixing on an originary moment, the *narrative* is searching for an authenticating mythology. The metaphor of absence thus takes on archetypal proportions, as the narrator (and author) seeks a form of the *genius loci* (an indigenous spirit or ghost) of the Canadian landscape. What I will argue in this essay is that, in *Surfacing*, Atwood pursues these effects via the invocation of the legendary ghost of Tom Thomson, a ghost that has a fetishized presence in the national imaginary, and which, like the classic fetish object, in fact embodies the very absence of an authentic Canadian ghost.

In his 1977 essay "Atwood Gothic," Eli Mandel asks, "Who are the ghosts of *Surfacing*?.... A mother, a father, a lost child, Indians, the animals" (140). It is true, as Rosemary Sullivan observes, that the narrator of *Surfacing* is "a woman possessed by ghosts ... whom she will have to confront and reclaim" (288), though Sullivan also identifies the ghost that appears at the end of the novel as a "nature god" (288). According to Atwood, the novel's protagonist "is obsessed with finding the ghosts, but once she's found them she is released from that obsession" ("A Question" 43). In the interview I cited above, following Atwood's attempt to set him on the right course, Gibson blurted out, "She sees her own ghost, doesn't she?" ("Dissecting" 18).

More precisely, the narrator sees her own projection of a ghost, a projection that occurs on a metatextual as well as a narrative level. One of the compelling elements of *Surfacing* is the way a tale of personal psychic loss is mapped alongside a narrative of national identificatory absence. If the narrator of the novel must confront the ghosts of her forgotten personal past—namely the ghosts of her parents and of her aborted baby—her quest is mapped alongside an equally unsettling recognition of the absence of an authentic national zeitgeist or spirit. In effect, anything that should be easily identifiable as indigenous (or that should satisfy the need for belonging and validity) is always already foreign in this novel (as is encapsulated in the famous line from the novel: "home ground, foreign territory" [11]). Canadians behave as Americans. Quebeckers are familiar but also foreign. Feminists are also chauvinists. Apparent nature lovers are aggressive consumers. Mothers are murderers. Memories are lies. And Aboriginals are forgotten.

Atwood has said of *Surfacing* that it emerged "out of pressures that are oppressively Canadian" ("Ich Über Mich" 2). More specifically, she notes how her essay "Nationalism, Limbo, and the Canadian Club" immediately preceded her eventual rewriting of *Surfacing* (*SW* 20). The need to recoup or conjure up an authenticating and defining Canadian spirit in a period marked by residual colonial attitudes toward Canadian culture was a challenge Atwood tackled head-on in many of her writings of the sixties and seventies:

> I think that my fascination with forgetting and remembering the past had something to do with the way I had learned, or not learned, or had to dig up, the history of my own country. Canada, like most ex-colonial countries, and most new-world ones, suffered from bouts of collective amnesia. ... The central push of the narrative in *Surfacing*

is the speaker's discovery of her own forgotten past. ("Self-Discovery" 8–9)

"Saying Boo to Colonialism," she wrote in her 1973 response to Robin Mathews, "will [not] make it go away" ("Mathews" 149). Instead, one had to answer the ghost of colonialism in like kind: by conjuring a sufficiently authentic ghost, and perhaps a self-ironizing one, that could "talk back" to a long history of transgenerational haunting, by which I mean "that manifestation of the voices of one generation in the unconscious of another" (Castricano 16).[2] Interestingly, Atwood saw evidence of this colonial mindset in Canadians' sense that their culture lacked an interest in the supernatural. In her 1977 essay "Canadian Monsters," she notes that Canadian literature is not usually associated with "magic and monsters" (98), but affirms that there has in fact been an extensive "calling up of ghosts" in a cultural-national "search for reassurance" (100). The presence of ghosts becomes an index of national self-recognition: "We want to be sure that the ancestors, ghosts, and skeletons really are there" (100).

If a national culture can, as Earle Birney so evocatively identified it, be haunted by a perceived "lack of ghosts," how does a purportedly post-colonial ghost story like *Surfacing* meet this lack (and listen to the ghosts), both at the time of composition and today? Atwood has famously described *Surfacing* as a "psychological ghost story" ("Dissecting" 43), and literary critics, most memorably Eli Mandel, have variously written about the ways she post-colonializes the genre of the gothic in this novel. As Mandel put it, "Ghost stories [are] the structural principle of the Canadian character" in Atwood's work ("Atwood's" 63). Given the many contemporary reconsiderations of Canadian post-coloniality, this might be a good moment to reappraise the significance of *Surfacing* as a post-colonial ghost story, particularly given what I see to be the novel's invocation of that most emblematic of Canadian spirits, the ghost of Tom Thomson.

In *Surfacing* Atwood was hard pressed to conjure up a *genius loci*—written, as it was, at the very time when any such authenticating spirit of Canadian culture seemed palpably elusive. What resulted was a kind of composite: a conflation of the ghost of the drowned father in a lake in Quebec with the spirit of one of the nation's most infamous ghosts, that of Tom Thomson, who, in 1917, died a death strikingly similar to the narrator's father, in Canoe Lake in Algonquin Park. Furthermore, the details of the father's misadventure echo very closely those outlined by the groundbreaking and controversial account of Tom Thomson's fate in William Little's 1970 *The Tom Thomson Mystery*, a book that was published while Atwood was working on the final drafts of the novel.[3] In *Surfacing* the narrator has been called to investigate the unexpected disappearance of her father, "a voluntary recluse" who has been staying alone in a cabin on the lake (11). Like Thomson's, the possibility of his death seems unlikely, since he was known to be an excellent swimmer, an expert woodsman, an ingenious fisherman, and an able canoeist. "I can't accept it," the narrator states, "he knew too much, he was too careful" (46). Like the novel's father (and Atwood's own father), Thomson was also an avid naturalist, specializing particularly in entomology (Murray 15–18). The father has also been engaged in a series of drawings, not landscape drawings per se but his own attempt to speak to the ghosts of the landscape by reproducing and deciphering the Aboriginal rock wall paintings (the real-life counterparts apparently being those on Inscription Rock in Ontario's Agawa Bay) that were painted to conjure the local spirits of the lake (102).

When the narrator finally discovers her father, it is by accident. She dives beneath the water and sees his corpse, "a dark oval trailing limbs" (142), floating disembodied some distance below. His death mirrors Thomson's closely: he has apparently died accidentally, though, like Thomson, he has a "skull fracture" (157), suggesting the possibility that he might not have died of drowning after all. Just as a fishing line was found entangled around Thomson's leg (Little 57), the camera strap of the narrator's father has become entwined around his neck. Speculation has it that Thomson might have been murdered and hidden under the water's surface "by binding the leg with a fishing line and weighting the body with a large stone," for, as Little asks in his book, "What else could have held the body under the water for eight days?"(159). Similarly, the weight of the camera has held the narrator's father underwater: "'He had a camera around his neck,'" David tells the narrator, "'they think the weight kept him down or he would've been found sooner'" (157). Also like Thomson, the father's body is found in a state of advanced decomposition, so he is at first difficult to identify; in both cases, a close friend (Paul in *Surfacing*; Mark Robinson for Thomson) identifies the body by its clothing (*Surfacing* 157; Little 75–76).

In *Surfacing* there is also a suspicious "American" in the picture who wants to buy up the property (94–95), a man named Malmstrom (93) whose "name sounded German" (94). He, along with the other American in the book, Evans, is rendered even more suspect when he admits to having had his eye on her father's property for some time: "I've taken the liberty, when no one seemed to be here, of having a stroll around" (94), and David later suggests that the man is a front man for a C.I.A. take-over. Later the narrator poses this suspicion herself: "Perhaps the C.I.A. had done away with him to get the land, Mr. Malmstrom was not quite plausible" (101). This figure echoes William Little's proposal that Thomson was murdered by the German-American cottager, Martin Bletcher, a proposition that had been in circulation well before the publication of *Surfacing*.[4] Indeed, the narrator's speculations about the cause of her father's death—"accident or suicide or murder" (49)—mirror the various possibilities that have been bandied about for Thomson's death.[5] Some days later, at the end of the novel, the Father's bloated body is discovered accidentally by some campers/fishermen, as was also true in the case of Thomson (Little 54), and this "surfacing" concludes the narrator's wilderness adventure. Connected to all of this are the supposed "real-life" sightings of Thomson's ghost on Canoe Lake in Algonquin Park: "The painter drowned in Canoe Lake," writes John Robert Colombo in *Mysterious Canada*, "and it is said that on certain mornings, through the mist rising from this lake, one may discern his spectral form forever canoeing its nervous waters" (120). The legend soon became standard fare among the young campers at the Taylor Statten Camps and tourists in Algonquin Park (Addison 79).[6]

What is particularly interesting in the case of *Surfacing* is the ways the various drafts of the novel in the Thomas Fisher Rare Book Library suggest that, between 1965 and 1972, Atwood was gradually making the Tom Thomson intertext (and hence the iconographic one) more explicit. At some point, it appears that she found it desirable to authenticate the story by overlayering her fictional ghost with a real-life Canadian *genius loci*. A very early draft of *Surfacing*, dating from 1965, contains a brief narrative of a pair of sisters (reminiscent of Atwood's short story "Wilderness Tips") who revisit their family cabin.[7] There is no drowned father, but instead the focus is on the main character's obsession with change and her sense of complicity in the deterioration of the landscape of her past—hence the title of the piece, "The Transfigured Landscape." While this theme is also evident in the final version of *Surfacing*, the source of the haunting in this early draft is the human presence in the wilderness, the intrusion of tourists, the encroachment of civilization. What haunts the main character is the realization that her experience of the wilderness cannot remain her own psychic property; it cannot remain pristine, and she herself is part of the problem. When she is on one of her woodland walks she notices the scrape of blue paint on a rock and is shocked:

> Someone else had been here before me. Someone else comes here. ... It was not the darkness of the woods that frightened her. It was the possibility of a human form stepping suddenly from the green penetrable screen of leaves, a thing with a mind & a voice emerging from the mindless & voiceless forest. (Box 21, Folder #14, page 17)[8]

By the early 1970s, Atwood had added the narrative of the missing father, but the Thomson intertext was built up in the course of further revisions. In these drafts the present-day version of *Surfacing*, as we now know it, is apparent, but the father's work on the Indian paintings is yet to be added. At the same time, Atwood was debating between making the brother or the father the Thomson figure. In an early version of chapters seven and eight, there occurs a description of the brother's supposed drowning, which was subsequently cut from the later version: "I steer us close to the steep island, the one off the point that the trail goes to, the one near which my brother finally drowned later; they found the canoe floating upside down, then him with his feet tangled in the fishing line" (Box 21, Folder 3). This, of course, echoes the precise details of Thomson's "drowning": his canoe was found adrift and upside down (Little 52) and his left leg was entwined with fishing line (57–58). However, this passage had to be cut since it is, instead, the narrator's father who will be made to suffer a fate similar to Thomson's. In these drafts from 1970/1971, the Thomson allusions are steadily being woven into the text. In the draft of chapter nineteen, the scene in which the men announce the discovery of the father's body, Atwood has inserted by hand the details of the American tourists finding the body, the unidentifiable corpse, the skull fracture, and the camera strap entangled around the father's neck and weighting the body down (Box 21, Folder 11). Inserted, as well, is the detail of her father wanting to be buried near the lake, a case that Thomson's friends made for him as well: "He'd want to be buried around here" (157).[9]

It appears, then, that Atwood's final revisions to the novel's ghost story were in part influenced by William Little's "uncovering" of the Thomson murder, and, like Little, she chose to turn her novel into a kind of detective story. In a handwritten insert included on the back of one of the pages of the second draft, immediately following the passage cited above, is the passage from chapter nineteen: "Convincing details, if he could invent I could invent also, I'd read enough murder mysteries" (157). The "details" might refer, as well, to those that Atwood herself has scattered throughout her novel. Tom Thomson's body, then, surfaces in the interstices of this novel only to function as a metaphor for the tantalizing functioning of narrative generally, thus highlighting the narrative's working as what Gayatri Spivak terms "a structure of concealment" (lxxv). Paradoxically, a ghost, like a weighted-down corpse, serves a similar function: it suggests a deflection, or displacement, of something else.

While the Thomson intertext might seem a rather small detail in what is an extremely complex and carefully interwoven narrative, it is important to recall Atwood's insistence on the novel's status as both a ghost story and a nationalist intervention. The choice of Thomson as a ghostly intertext in this novel is therefore apt, for his legend provided an already available, and increasingly infamous, Canadian *genius loci*. Yet what is it about Thomson that renders him the perfect figure for this tale of national/personal haunting?—a sort of "ghost-of-a-ghost," as Jonathan Kertzer puts it (38), but this time as a ghost who is animating the more easily identifiable ghost of the narrator's father?

To answer this, we might consider three questions. What is it that would be seen to constitute an adequately national ghost in Canada in the late 1960s/early 1970s (and perhaps, even, today)? What has Thomson come to represent for Canadian culture at large, and how does Atwood's novel incorporate this ghost? More important, how does the appeal to the ghost of Thomson problematize the novel's implicit nation-forging goal?

The inscription composed by J.E.H. MacDonald on the cairn built on the hill of Thomson's original gravesite offers some clues to these questions:

> To the memory of Tom Thomson, Artist, Woodsman and Guide, who was drowned in Canoe Lake, July 8th, 1917. He lived humbly but passionately with the wild. It made him brother to all untamed

things in nature. It drew him apart and revealed itself wonderfully to him. It sent him out from the woods only to show these revelations and it took him to itself at last. (qtd. in Robson, 8)

This figuration of Thomson as a kind of wilderness man has become standard fare in portrayals of the artist. Indeed, his persona as a "brother to all untamed things in nature" has, in some instances, become more significant than his work as a painter (a parallel we see in the similar and pervasive tendency to construct Margaret Atwood herself as a creature of the wilderness). The accounts of Tom Thomson echo, to some degree, the more notorious case of Grey Owl, the difference being that "Thomson's character was largely projected onto him after his death" (qtd. in Gessell 2002, J9). According to Gessell and others, Thomson was an urban son who transformed himself into a wilderness child: "Thomson's wilderness affair only began in 1912 and ended with his death five years later" (J8). The legend developed with the help of his celebrants (namely the members of the Group of Seven), who wrote repeated encomiums in the wake of his unexpected but, at the same time, symbolically appropriate death. For many, he is the prototypical Canadian. Ottelyn Addison refers to his "typically Canadian spirit" (76). Joan Murray argues that Thomson "satisfies a secret desire on the part of our national psyche" (7). Arthur Lismer described him as "a true Canadian savage ... the manifestation of the Canadian character" (qtd. in Gessell, J1). To Little, he is a "native son" (109).

More important, however, Thomson is figured as the interpreter of this wilderness expressly because he has become an integral part of it. Like the people in Atwood's poem "The Settlers," he now constitutes the marrow of the land, and rests there to welcome and guide future visitors. "Without Thomson the north country seems a desolation of bush and rock," Addison writes. "He was the guide, the interpreter, and we the guests partaking of his hospitality" (75). Moreover, Thomson is regarded as a kind of transcendental signifier, and is seen to offer contact with the Canadian sublime. According to Albert Robson, Thomson "was a mirror of the wilderness" who "interpreted intrinsic truths with unerring accuracy" (3, 4). Because he was taken into the land—or, as J.E.H. MacDonald expresses it in the inscription, "it took him to itself at last"—he has become *of* the land and the land has become his.[10] Thomson's tale is that of the making of an authentic Canadian; he is the Canadian settler *par excellence*, the post-colonial wilderness guide. He is our interpreter of Canada. He teaches us to *be* Canadian.

This figuration of Thomson as a kind of *genius loci* echoes perfectly Kertzer's exploration of this phenomenon in *Worrying the Nation* (1998). According to Kertzer, the Romantic notion of national culture fuses spirit, language, and place (5)—the very fusing that we see in Atwood's "survival" motif as representative of Canadian literature, not to mention many other conceptualizations of the national-cultural spirit. The national spirit, he argues, is seen to emerge from the wilderness and attain self-consciousness through art (38). If a national literature is to combine spirit and place, the two of these combine in the figure of the *genius loci* (40): both the guardian spirit of the place (Thomson) and/or the spiritual double of a person (the narrator's father). But in a colonial context, this quest for the *genius loci* is always compromised, since a transplanted culture has difficulty becoming a "native" culture. The *genius loci* is dependent on making a transplanted literature become native, in which case, how local is it? One solution is to turn to Native mythology, which many Canadian writers and artists have done (and which Atwood obliquely points toward by invoking Native spirits in the novel). But since this is largely an unconvincing process for those of settler heritage (what Goldie [1989] terms the "impossible necessity" of going Native [13]), what else can one do but turn to the *indigenized settler* as a figure of authenticating Canadianness?

Even more than Susanna Moodie, Thomson satisfied this need for Atwood, in part because the reinvention of Thomson had already been accomplished. Thomson, writes Joan Murray, was figured after his death as "a kind of woodland god" (95), a "spirit of the north" (95–96). For Paul Gessell, he was also "a reincarnated *voyageur*" (J1). His authentically Canadian death—what Atwood, in her essay "True North," describes as a death by landscape, a phrase that forms the title of her short story about Algonquin Park and the Group of Seven—is in part what contributes to this effect. For herein lies the paradox: in order to be validated as a ghost, you must have been first subjected to the murderous intent of a wilderness that responds to you as an invader. If "death by landscape" is a figure for the settler-invader's experience of psychic unsettlement in the New World, it is also that which renders one's position here authentic. Judith McCombs writes of such deaths as the archetypal settler experience. On one hand, early settlers were "panicked, threatened, crazed, and quite literally killed by the North American Wilderness" (43); on the other, Atwood's Moodie, like Thomson, "crosses over into the wilderness and becomes its voice" (46). To be swallowed up by the landscape is to become *of here*. It is to be legitimated. In her poem "Procedures for Underground," Atwood conjures this dual nature of an authenticating national ghost: to be engulfed within the landscape is to be murdered as an intruder; to become the haunter of the landscape following this death is to authenticate the culture that imposed itself on the landscape. Thus the poem "The Settlers" concludes with an image of the dead colonists who now *are* the land, and who open their hands in nurturing welcome to the future generations of settler children (95). You need to die in order to *live on*, one might say. This, of course, is the trajectory relayed by Atwood for Susanna Moodie, but it is also that which authenticates Thomson, as well as that which informs the *Surfacing* narrator's progression, for she all but simulates a death by landscape (like Joan in *Lady Oracle*) by effectively starving herself and going back to nature.[11]

As Wayland Drew perceptively put it in his own wilderness novel from this period, *The Wabeno Feast*, Tom Thomson "was killed because he was too good a survivor" (140). If survival is the motif of the settler-invader, then in order to be legitimized in this place, in order for the "invader" epithet to be lobbed off, one must be securely murdered and resurrected (much like Moodie in Atwood's poem sequence). Death yields true belonging, death by landscape even more so, and drowning even more than that. Thus, in 1960, Milton Wilson could write of the drowned poet as a "Canadian archetype" (Djwa, "Where" 17),[12] while Atwood herself, in explaining her own obsession with drownings in her writings, stated to Geoff Hancock: "[I]f you have your choice about how people die in natural accidents in Canada, it's most likely to be by drowning" ("Margaret" 273).

This notion of the inherent threat of the landscape was articulated by numerous early Canadian writers and is of course central to Atwood's thesis in *Survival*; Northrop Frye in his 1965 conclusion to the *Literary History of Canada* famously outlines this as well. However, it is in his 1940 essay "Canadian and Colonial Painting" that Frye anticipates Birney's notion of being haunted by a lack of ghosts. Frye identified a paradox, whereby the very vacancy of the New World landscape is precisely what constitutes its haunting effect:

> [A] large tract of vacant land may well affect the people living near it.... Explorers, tormented by a sense of the unreality of the unseen, are first; pioneers and traders follow. But the land is still not imaginatively absorbed, and the incubus moves on to haunt the artists. (199)

Yet there is further confusion in Frye's account that is perhaps emblematic of Canadian hauntings. For Frye, there is both nothing (vacancy) and something (incubus) that haunts the settler psyche from a perceived "outside." As a materialization of the vacancy, the incubus is an embodied absence, a ghost of a ghost. Ultimately, Frye cannot decide what the Canadian landscape/psyche (the two become fused in his account, as in Atwood's) is haunted by.[13] He articulates the classic settler post-colonial predicament: an anxiety about the incompletion of settlement, which leaves the Canadian artist at once haunted and haunting. Focusing on this spectral "incubus" as it appears in Tom Thomson's paintings, Frye describes the "imaginative instability" of Thomson's vision, "the emotional unrest and dissatisfaction one feels about a country which has not been lived in" (200). As might be expected given the rhetorical presumption of perceiving the land as unoccupied, Frye is describing a process of projection. In effect, the country is seen to eke out its revenge for Thomson's (and "our") incomplete occupation of the land; when the country was through with Thomson, Frye writes, "she scattered his bones in the wilderness" (201).

The influence of Frye's landscape metaphysics is hard to miss in Atwood's work, and it is no coincidence that her original title for *Surfacing* was "Where Is Here?" an allusion to Frye's 1965 conclusion to the *Literary History of Canada*. Atwood expressly stated that *Surfacing* aimed to conjure the gothic ambivalence that was peculiar to both the Canadian landscape and the settler psyche. In her presentation at the Shastri Institute in the late 1980s, she outlined the genesis of *Surfacing*, a novel that she felt was trying to put Canada on the literary map:

> I know already that this is going to be a ghost story. Why? Because the setting I'm using lends itself to, or suggests, such stories.... Tales of obsession, of hallucination—there's even a word for going crazy in the Boreal forests—"bushed," it's called—are however particularly at home there. The landscape I've been describing is a haunting one. ("Self-Discovery" 6)

However, if Frye's projection of a "demonic or ghost world" onto the inadequately incorporated landscape emerges from "guilt feelings" (Watson, 95) associated with a not-so-repressed history of colonial settlement and conquest, Thomson's haunting effect is rather different. Less an incubus who lurks in the wilderness, the sightings of Thomson's ghost on Canoe Lake have an aura of wish fulfillment and desire. We *want* to encounter Thomson's ghost. He is peaceful, going about his business, evoking a longed for "oneness with the landscape in question" (Atwood, "True North" 146). In this case, the haunting effect is a reassuring one, for his presence in the landscape assures us of our potential incorporation of/by that landscape too. Likewise, in *Surfacing*, the incubus in the landscape is fused with a guardian spirit, since once conjured the ghosts of the narrator's parents are both threatening and guiding, just as the paradox of a "post-colonial" haunting is to be both reassured and threatened by the ghosts.

Thomson's ghost (and Atwood's invocation of it) emerges to fill in for Canada's notorious lack of ghosts not as a "symbolic debt" (Castricano 23) but as a fetishized supplement (both there and not there), a validation of a lack. Thus, Joan Murray concludes her study of Thomson by articulating the constitutive effect of his haunting: "We will have to put up with him looking over our shoulders to give us a few pointers whenever we decide to design our culture anew" (103). Likewise, in her comments on *Surfacing*'s ghosts, Atwood, like Frye, could state that our landscape *is* clearly populated by ghosts: "It is difficult to walk through these forests without starting to think that someone, or something, is watching you" ("Self-Discovery" 6–7). In her short story "Death By Landscape," that "someone" is the American girl, Lucy, who dies a "death by landscape" (presumably a drowning, possibly a suicide, maybe a murder) in the Canadian bush and is immortalized as the eyes looking out through the Group of Seven's paintings. The ghosts, therefore, are not the Native spirits spying on the European intruders, as one might expect, but rather those Europeans who have been assimilated into the landscape and become native spirits. Atwood stated this explicitly in the course of discussing *Surfacing* with Gibson:

> Everybody has gods or a god, and it's what you pay attention to or what you worship. And they can be imported ones or they can be intrinsic ones, indigenous ones, and what we have done in this country is to use imported gods like imported everything else. And if you import a god from somewhere else, it's fake; it's like importing

> your culture from somewhere else. The only good, authentic thing is something that comes out of the place where you are. ("Dissecting" 19)

Atwood's words echo what theorists of settler-invader post-colonialism have long been demonstrating: that the construction of local, ancestral ghosts helps to provide symbolic legitimation for settler cultures. However, such ghosts are condemned to be ambivalent, illusory. In this case, an apparent absence of a national identity is fleshed out via the notorious remains of the absent, but fetishized, presence of an ancestral national father figure, the dead Tom Thomson. Yet there is a problem with this, since the father's ghost is also figured as a displacement of the original Aboriginal spirits.[14] When the narrator sees his corpse underwater, she clambers onto the cliff-side to leave his ghost an offering (*Surfacing* 145), and she later prepares a food sacrifice for the dead with the scraps from one of their meals (155). In these moments the father's ghost becomes explicitly fused with the Aboriginal ones, as, in a sense, it already has via his following the trail of the Aboriginal wall paintings: "He had been here and long before him the original ones, the first explorers" (126). The identification of Aboriginals as "first explorers" initiates an identification and slippage between first inhabitants and subsequent invaders, which in effect renders the two in a single legitimating genealogical line. Later, when the narrator sees the ghost standing outside the garden fence, the father's metamorphosis into a kind of Aboriginal spirit is complete: "I see now that although it isn't my father it is what my father has become" (187).

Once again, the narrative is struggling to articulate an adequate mythology. If the metaphor of absence acquires particular resonance in this text, Thomson's story is perfectly suited to this paradox because it encodes an inherent uncertainty: whether, ultimately, Thomson is to be celebrated as Native or Settler. By his very malleability Thomson is able to embody the ambivalence of Canadian post-colonial identity: he is at once a national cultural hero, a wilderness guide, an honorary Native, an archetypal settler, a voyageur, a ghost in the landscape, a native son. He embodies various national desires for indigenization. He is an ancestral figure who fuses both settler and indigene, and thereby solves the dilemma of how to construct a *genius loci* in a new world. However, like the myth of Thomson itself, the novel finally can't decide if it wants to celebrate "going settler" or "going native"—which is true, as well, on the level of the narrator's own "wilderness" experience-cum-vision quest in the book. Whose ghosts does she see, after all? Which ghosts catalyze her vision? Those of her parents, or of the Aboriginal gods? Or is it the slip from *settler-invader* to *settler* that is being enacted in this sleight of hand, as perhaps is enacted in all of the Grey Owl, wilderness-guide, cottage-culture, boy-scout play that so pervasively informs our culture? As Scott Watson observes in his insightful meditation on Canadian landscape painting:

> It would be straining credibility to imagine that the construction of the Tom Thomson type out of Indians and coureur-de-bois was some sort of meaningful recognition of First Nations' history, polity, and presence in the north. The construction of Thomson involved forgetfulness. (102)

The same might be said of *Surfacing* (not to mention *Survival*). Traces of Natives remain, yet, outside of the meagre blueberry-picking episode in the novel (85–86), their displacement receives little consideration.[15] Himani Bannerji describes the narrator in *Surfacing* as a politically correct, yet nevertheless compromised, settler (296–97), and there is something to this accusation. If the figures in the rock paintings are symbols of the Ojibway Manitous that once guarded over the lakes, they have been displaced: now it is the narrator's father as Tom Thomson who is the *genius loci* of the place.

Ghosts, for Atwood, emblematize something integral to the Canadian national psyche. Indeed, what occurs in *Surfacing* is a curious form of substitution—whereby one lack, when substituted with another, creates the illusion of substantiality. Kertzer writes of this in terms of the ways Canada is haunted by a "palpable absence" (38), an absence that is materialized, on command, via the resurrection ("surfacing") of Thomson's ghost. According to Robert Kroetsch, the narrator of *Surfacing* "locates our story by not finding it" (68), another version of our lack of ghosts. This is epitomized, perhaps, in the ambivalence of the Thomson story itself. Thomson has been described by Frye as a haunted man, whose melancholy was "the result of an incomplete absorption or possession of the land" (Watson 99). That Thomson was in a sense killed by the landscape that gave him symbolic being (like the narrator's father in the novel) at once authenticates and jeopardizes his iconic status. Moreover, Thomson's ambivalence as a Canadian post-colonial icon (since he is both Native and settler at once) is echoed in the status of the narrator herself. In other words, the settler fantasy enacted in *Surfacing* circles around the quest for a man who, like Atwood, was himself mythologized as the prototypical pioneer. While Natives constitute a prominent absence in Atwood's narrative, the novel skirts around this guilty absence via the figure of Thomson, who stands in as an indigenized settler. The novel thus inadvertently becomes a narrative about the limits of origins, even as it seeks to forge these origins and locate them in the national and geographical landscape. In effect, *Surfacing* forces one to pose a critical post-colonial question: Is there a difference between going settler and going native, and if Canada's national ghosts must necessarily incorporate both processes, is their post-coloniality compromised?

Gerry Turcotte has written of our need to "gothicize" literary study, by which he means that we should welcome those moments of unsettlement "where our own solid ground is shown to be both substantial and insubstantial, simultaneously" (163). Atwood's use of Tom Thomson enables a reflection on one such moment of compromised (un)settlement. Literary critics have variously written about the ways Atwood post-colonializes the genre of the gothic in this novel. However, as an example of post-colonial gothic, the novel offers not only a meditation on post-colonial guilt, nor solely a resurgence of the repressed past in the present (cf. Botting 1), but also an expression of post-colonial *desire* (desire in the sense of the impossible quest for the Real of identity/memory), a desire for post-colonial legitimation. It may indeed be, as Kertzer has it, that a ghost haunts "all efforts to define ... 'our' literature" (38). As Slavoj Zizek puts it, "The master signifier that guarantees the community's consistency is a signifier whose signified is an enigma for the members themselves. ... what binds the group together is ultimately their shared *ignorance*" (58). Joan Murray states that Thomson "represents our longings, not our realities" (qtd. in Gessell, J1). Yet what does his conjuring in Atwood's national ghost story signify? If burying one's dead is a means of establishing oneself in the land, does *Surfacing* stage an exhuming or an implanting? For the narrator, it would seem to involve both. On a metatextual level, this is a story about the paradoxical desire for ghosts. As Atwood states in her essay "Negotiating with the Dead," "dead bodies can talk if you know how to listen to them, and they *want* to talk" (163).

—University of Ottawa

NOTES

1. While I realize that the ghost of the narrator's mother is also an important presence in the novel, the storyline is focused on the quest for a lost father and the tracing of the father's final moments. The mother's ghost provides the narrator with the gift of conception, literally a view of her own conception as depicted in the drawing of the baby in the womb. The father's ghost, however, points the narrator to her symbolic origination, and hence exemplifies a desire for transcendent signification.
2. Sandra Djwa has provided a detailed account of some of these "voices" in her analysis of the parodic intertexts of *Surfacing*. According to Djwa, one way that Atwood's novel attempts to overcome "the view that Canada lacked a culture" was by itself embodying a Canadian literary tradition ("Here" 172–73). "[T]he medium of Atwood's novel is the message," Djwa writes, "it incorporates allusions that [point] to the whole tradition of the Canadian search for political identity and its literary articulation" (173). This might be yet another sense in which the novel enacts a kind of reinvention of Canadian selfhood.
3. Sherrill Grace argues that Little's book "marks a major turning point ... in the invention of Thomson" (62) since it introduced the theory that Thomson was murdered. Subsequent accounts of the Thomson story, as Grace demonstrates, were influenced by Little's account. Grace's book was published after I submitted this essay for this collection, so I have not incorporated it into my argument. However, her account of the "invention" of the Thomson legend following his death concurs with my description of Thomson's national significance here.
4. In a letter to me dated July 19, 2004, Atwood asserted that she was indeed aware of the rumours circulating about Thomson's "murder" at this time. Since William Little's account, the mystery of Thomson's death has sparked even further controversy. In a June 9, 2002 article in the *Ottawa Citizen*, Roy MacGregor provides another version. MacGregor was told by Daphne Crombie, a friend of Annie Fraser, both of whom were at Canoe Lake the year Thomson died, that Thomson was killed in a drunken argument with his friend Shannon Fraser. The two men were arguing about a debt Fraser owed Thomson, and when Fraser struck his friend, Thomson fell down and hit his head on the fire grate. Together, Fraser and his wife, Annie, disposed of the body by weighting it down with fishing line and dropping it in the lake.
5. It was rumoured that Thomson might have committed suicide because his woman friend, Winnifred Trainor, had become pregnant and was pressuring him to marry her (MacGregor C8).
6. In her late teens and early twenties, Atwood worked at a number of summer camps in Ontario, including Camp Hurontario and Camp White Pines, which would have made her well aware of the legend of Thomson's ghost.

7. See the Margaret Atwood Papers, accession 200, box 21, folder 14. Other citations from the various drafts of *Surfacing* in the Thomas Fisher Rare Book Library are identified in parentheses in the text.
8. Curiously, in these early drafts the main character's son, who is also present on the trip, is periodically named "Tom," and in each case Atwood has carefully scratched out the name and changed it to "David."
9. According to MacGregor's sources, Thomson remains buried at Canoe Lake even though his family had arranged to have the body disinterred and moved to the family plot in Leith, Ontario. Jimmy Stringer told MacGregor that "there were in fact three different gravesites: the original grave at Canoe Lake, the Thomson family plot at Leith, and a third, unknown, site just beyond the original grave on the hill overlooking Canoe Lake. Thomson's wild friends at the lake, knowing the undertaker was coming to remove the body from where they felt it should lie forever, decided to move him to a second, hastily dug grave just before the undertaker, H.W. Churchill, arrived" (C8).
10. Atwood mentions these lines in "True North": "I remember a documentary on Tom Thomson that ended, rather ominously, with the statement that the north had taken him to herself. This was, of course, pathetic fallacy gone to seed, but it was also a comment on our distrust of the natural world, a distrust that remains despite our protests" (146).
11. She also metaphorically fuses with the landscape toward the end of the novel, in part through an imagined process of reverse evolution, in part by fantasizing herself as *becoming* the land: "I am the thing in which the trees and animals move and grow" (181).
12. I am citing Sandra Djwa's interpretation of Wilson's account in her article "The Where of Here." Wilson's suggestion that the "drowned poet in Canadian poetry" is usually "anonymous or international" (6) underscores his own variation on the Canadian lack of ghosts: "Maybe for a Canadian poet to be elegized as drowned, he should … not be dead at all"(5). Canadian drownings, while pervasive, are nevertheless in search of an indigenous prototype, an absence in our literature that Wilson describes as a drowned poet in search of an elegy (5).
13. This is echoed in Atwood's *The Journals of Susanna Moodie,* which describes Moodie's psychic introjection of and invasion by the landscape/wilderness: "I was frightened/by their eyes (green or/amber) glowing out from inside me"(27). Moodie is both gazer and gazed upon, both haunter and haunted. If she is threatened by this invasion in the knowledge that she is "not completed," she also wants something from these ghosts: "There was something they almost taught me/I came away not having learned."

14. There is an interesting parallel to this scene in Moodie's *Roughing It in the Bush*. Even though Moodie is told by the Yankee driver that "'there are no ghosts in Canada'" (267), there is, in fact, an Aboriginal ghost that is described in the text. Moodie tells the story of Susan Moore, a young "squaw" whose "father had been drowned during a sudden hurricane, which swamped his canoe on Stony Lake" (292). This drowning results in a curse: "The soul of an Indian that has been drowned is reckoned accursed, and he is never permitted to join his tribe on the happy hunting-grounds, but his spirit haunts the lake or river in which he lost his life. His body is buried on some lonely island, which the Indians never pass without leaving a small portion [of] food, tobacco, or ammunition, to supply his wants" (293). The father in *Surfacing* is a conflation: both a drowned and haunting "native" whose spirit must be appeased and an ancestral, guiding spirit. In both cases, he is indigenized by virtue of his incorporation into the wilderness.
15. The description of the Natives in the novel echoes their role in the text. They glide silently into view, then disappear "as though they had never been there" (*Surfacing* 86).

WORKS CITED

Addison, Ottelyn, with Elizabeth Harwood. *Tom Thomson: The Algonquin Years*. Toronto: Ryerson, 1969.

Atwood, Margaret. "Canadian Monsters: Some Aspects of the Supernatural in Canadian Fiction." In *The Canadian Imagination: Dimensions of a Literary Culture*, edited by David Staines, 97–122. Cambridge: Harvard University Press, 1977.

———. "Death By Landscape." *Wilderness Tips*. London: Virago, 1992. 109–129.

———. "Dissecting the Way a Writer Works." Interview with Graeme Gibson. 1972/1973. In *Margaret Atwood: Conversations*, edited by Earl G. Ingersoll, 3–19. Willowdale, ON: Ontario Review Press, 1990.

———. Letter to author [email]. July 19, 2004.

———. "Ich Über Mich." [1978/1979]. Margaret Atwood Papers, accession 200, Box 56, Folder 34. Thomas Fisher Rare Book Library. University of Toronto.

———. *The Journals of Susanna Moodie*. Toronto: Oxford University Press, 1970.

———. "Margaret Atwood." Interview with Geoff Hancock. 1986. In *Canadian Writers at Work*, edited by Geoff Hancock 256–87. Toronto: Oxford, University Press, 1987.

———. "Mathews and Misrepresentation." *Second Words: Selected Critical Prose*. Toronto: Anansi, 1982. 129–50.

———. "Nationalism, Limbo, and the Canadian Club." [1971]. *Second Words: Selected Critical Prose*. Toronto: Anansi, 1982. 83–89.

———. *Negotiating with the Dead: A Writer on Writing.* Cambridge: Cambridge University Press, 2002.

———. "Procedures for Underground." *Procedures for Underground.* Toronto: Oxford University Press, 1970. 24–25.

———. "A Question of Metamorphosis." Interview with Linda Sandler. 1976/1977. In *Margaret Atwood: Conversations*, edited by Earl G. Ingersoll, 40–57. Willowdale, ON: Ontario Review Press, 1990.

———. *Second Words: Selected Critical Prose.* Toronto: Anansi.

———. "Self-Discovery Through Integration with One's Past." 1988. Margaret Atwood Papers, Accession 200, Box 148, Folder 28. Thomas Fisher Rare Book Library. University of Toronto.

———. "The Settlers." *The Circle Game.* [1966]. Toronto: Anansi, 1978. 94–95.

———. *Surfacing.* [1972]. Toronto: McClelland & Stewart, 1994.

———. *Survival: A Thematic Guide to Canadian Literature.* Toronto: Anansi, 1972.

———. "The Transfigured Landscape." Margaret Atwood Papers, Accession 200, Box 21, Folder 14.

———. "True North." *Saturday Night*, January 1987. 141–48.

———. "Wilderness Tips." *Wilderness Tips.* London: Virago, 1992. 197–221.

Bannerji, Himani. "Geography Lessons: On Being an Insider/Outsider to the Canadian Nation." In *Unhomely States: Theorizing English-Canadian Postcolonialism*, edited by Cynthia Sugars, 289–300. Peterborough, ON: Broadview, 2004.

Botting, Fred. *Gothic.* The New Critical Idiom Series. London: Routledge, 1996.

Castricano, Jodey. *Cryptomimesis: The Gothic and Jacques Derrida's Ghost Writing.* Montreal: McGill-Queen's University Press, 2001.

Colombo, John Robert. *Mysterious Canada: Strange Sights, Extraordinary Events, and Peculiar Places.* Toronto: Doubleday, 1988.

Djwa, Sandra. "'Here I Am': Atwood, Paper Houses, and a Parodic Tradition." *Essays on Canadian Writing*, no. 71 (2000): 169–85.

———. "The Where of Here: Margaret Atwood and a Canadian Tradition." In *The Art of Margaret Atwood: Essays in Criticism*, edited by Arnold Davidson and Cathy Davidson, 15–34. Toronto: Anansi, 1981.

Drew, Wayland. *The Wabeno Feast.* [1973]. Toronto: Anansi, 2001.

Freud, Sigmund. "Mourning and Melancholia." In *On Metapsychology: The Theory of Psychoanalysis.* Vol. 2, *The Pelican Freud Library*, edited by Angela Richards. Translated by James Strachey, 251–268. Harmondsworth: Penguin, 1984.

Frye, Northrop. "Canadian and Colonial Painting." [1940]. In *The Bush Garden: Essays on the Canadian Imagination.* Toronto: Anansi, 1971, 199–202.

———. Conclusion. *Literary History of Canada: Canadian Literature in English*, edited by Carl F. Klinck, 821–49. Toronto: University of Toronto Press, 1965.

Gessell, Paul. "The Man, the Myth, the Icon: The Legend of Tom Thomson Was Spread by His Fellow Artists." *Globe and Mail* (Toronto), June 1, 2002. J1, J8–J9.

Goldie, Terry. *Fear and Temptation: The Image of the Indigene in Canadian, Australian, and New Zealand Literatures.* Montreal: McGill-Queen's University Press, 1989.

Grace, Sherrill. *Inventing Tom Thomson: From Biographical Fictions to Fictional Autobiographies and Reproductions.* Montreal: McGill-Queen's University Press, 2004.

Kertzer, Jonathan. *Worrying the Nation: Imagining a National Literature in English Canada.* Toronto: University of Toronto Press, 1998.

Kroetsch, Robert. "Disunity as Unity: A Canadian Strategy." In *Unhomely States: Theorizing English-Canadian Postcolonialism*, edited by Cynthia Sugars, 61–70. Peterborough, ON: Broadview, 2004.

Little, William T. *The Tom Thomson Mystery.* Toronto: McGraw-Hill Ryerson, 1970.

MacGregor, Roy. "Death on Canoe Lake." *Ottawa Citizen*, June 9, 2002. C8–C9.

Mandel, Eli. "Atwood Gothic." *Another Time.* Erin, ON: Press Porcepic, 1977. 137–45.

———. "Atwood's Poetic Politics." In *Margaret Atwood: Language, Text, and System*, edited by Sherrill Grace and Lorraine Weir, 53–66. Vancouver: University of British Columbia Press, 1983.

McCombs, Judith. "Atwood's Haunted Sequences: *The Circle Game, The Journals of Susanna Moodie*, and *Power Politics*." In *The Art of Margaret Atwood: Essays in Criticism*, edited by Arnold Davidson and Cathy Davidson, 35–54. Toronto: Anansi, 1981.

Moodie, Susanna. *Roughing It in the Bush; Or, Life in Canada.* [1852]. Toronto: McClelland & Stewart, 1989.

Murray, Joan. *Tom Thomson: Design for a Canadian Hero.* Toronto: Dundurn, 1998.

Robson, Albert H. *Tom Thomson.* Toronto: Ryerson, 1937.

Spivak, Gayatri. "Translator's Preface." In *Of Grammatology*, edited by Jacques Derrida. Translated by Gayatri Spivak, ix–lxxxvii. Baltimore: Johns Hopkins University Press, 1976.

Sullivan, Rosemary. *The Red Shoes: Margaret Atwood Starting Out.* Toronto: HarperFlamingo, 1998.

Turcotte, Gerry. "Compr(om)ising Post/colonialisms: Postcolonial Pedagogy and the Uncanny Space of Possibility." In *Home-Work: Postcolonialism, Pedagogy, and Canadian Literature*, edited by Cynthia Sugars, 151–65. Ottawa: University of Ottawa Press, 2004.

Watson, Scott. "Race, Wilderness, Territory and the Origins of Modern Canadian Landscape Painting." In *Semiotext(e): Canadas*, edited by Jordan Zinovich, 93–104. Peterborough, ON: Marginal Editions, 1994.

Wilson, Milton. "Klein's Drowned Poet: Canadian Variations on an Old Theme." *Canadian Literature*, no. 6 (1960): 5–17.

Zizek, Slavoj. "The Real of Sexual Difference." In *Reading Seminar XX: Lacan's Major Work on Love, Knowledge, and Feminine Sexuality*, edited by Suzanne Barnard and Bruce Fink, 57–75. Albany: State University of New York Press, 2002.

A Silhouette of Madness: Reading Atwood's *Surfacing*

TINA TRIGG

WITH THE POSSIBLE exception of the more recent *Alias Grace* (1996), which complexifies, subverts, and directly challenges the reader's ability to determine the psychological state of Grace Marks with any degree of certainty, *Surfacing* (1972) is the novel with which Atwood's readers are most familiar as a representation of madness. And *Surfacing* is, in many ways, the paradigmatic Atwood novel on madness, representing the narrator's response to her dissociated state that is figured in her namelessness and that includes an increasing recognition of her extreme condition of alienation. The novel's seemingly prototypical representation of madness has garnered impressive amounts of critical attention to date. Much of this attention is directed to analysis of the narrator's psychological states, her physical enactments thereof, and the variable interpretations not only of this process of apparent disintegration but also of the implied meaning of the novel's typically indeterminate conclusion. The ambivalence of this conclusion is often obscured in the criticism that "reads" the narrator's positioning with unwavering certainty, essentially interpreting it as a cathartic, perhaps even redemptive, experience.

Regardless of the overt theoretical approach, every critic who considers madness arguably (if unwittingly) inhabits the role of psychological analyst and consequently positions the narrator as analysand; in other words, the narrator becomes the patient awaiting the critic's "expert" diagnosis. In this fashion, the critic as reader always already privileges herself or himself as the normative measure and uses language to substantiate that ideological stance. Notably, even if the critic self-consciously acknowledges his or her subjective position, as is increasingly the case in our postmodern era, this awareness may mitigate the authoritative stance but it cannot eliminate it. The critic's role is to analyze; hence, his or her position is inexorably a privileged one. Since the critic *becomes* the analyst, this stance problematizes every critical reader's position—no less in *Surfacing* than in *Alias Grace*. In fact, the reader's facile positioning and subsequent dismissal of the narrator as a mad figure is precisely what Atwood's works implicitly criticize. The more "sophisticated and certain" the so-called "diagnoses" or psychological labels are, the more pointed Atwood's elbow becomes as she nudges us in the ribs—either with complicitous recognition of our tendency to categorize and then to dismiss, or with a more authoritative, perhaps teacherly, jab to "pay attention" to the power politics at work in our reading experiences. Similarly, Atwood subverts any attempt by readers to avoid psychological categorization by resorting to the more generic term "madness"; therein lies no refuge for readers from culpability. In short, Atwood complicates the analytical process by highlighting the roles of its participants (reader, characters, author) and their respective complicity in all constructs of normality or madness attained through the acts of interpretation.

As a representation of madness, *Surfacing* contains the elements to enable insightful, if somewhat predictable, psychological readings. One can invoke Freudian interpretations of the narrator's search for the father (and the mother), archetypal readings of the various motifs (perhaps most obviously of water), or, more broadly, studies of the conscious and unconscious elements of the psyche—and these as Freudian, Jungian, or Lacanian trinities. In all of these readings, Atwood's novel provides ample evidence: the unnamed narrator wrestles with her unconscious (in dreams), the irrational (in visions and hallucinations), the wilderness, her own repressed memories and false reconstructions, a legacy of madness represented by her father's bush madness, the mind-body schism represented by her repression of feeling, and the self-other schism represented in her tenuous relationships with her travelling companions. The narrator's extreme emotional, social, and psychological alienation and apparent normality are juxtaposed with her recognition and criticism of her companions—specifically of the constructions of normality, which they blithely regard as reality. Ultimately, Atwood's narrator withdraws from them into her inner journey, which takes outward form in a symbolic dive into the lake, leading to the discovery of her father's corpse and the dive into her psychological depths.

However, rather than enumerate the particulars of this progression—which have been insightfully explicated by numerous scholars since the 1970s including Frank Davey, Sherrill Grace, and John Moss—I should like to work from that foundation to focus on the latter portion of the novel and to problematize the interpretation of its conclusion in the broader context of madness. In particular, the narrator's abrupt abandonment of the trappings of civilization, an act exemplified by taking on an "animal" form, is suggestive as a position of social removal that is most strikingly akin to madness in its silence.

While her external actions—discarding clothing and shelter, scavenging for food, and leaving her droppings on the ground—simulate the stereotypical behaviour of a "wild man," the narrator posits herself as a distinctly gendered figure: a woman in danger of being misunderstood, secretly disposed of and forcibly silenced by the power of social hegemony. These misgivings are neither paranoia nor exaggeration but, rather, perceptions that align the fictional character with social and historical realities. Michel Foucault argues that, historically, as societal structures changed, the mad were edged out of contact with the masses; it was "so difficult ... to determine the place madness was to occupy ... [or] to situate madness in a social sphere that was being restructured" (240). Consequently, those in power instituted asylums under the guise of offering appropriate medical attention to those individuals categorized by the masses as "mad," but in reality to contain them; this era was deceptively termed "that happy age when madness was fully recognized" (241). Such cant, however, hints at the questionable motivations shadowing this practice of segregation, motivations that Atwood's narrator implicitly understands as being mediated by this historical threat that continues to be a social reality in the contemporary era. The recognition of madness is decidedly not a "happy" one for those who fall under its stigma; perhaps more accurately, it may be described as a form of stress relief for the masses who are thereby absolved of the complicating, difficult presence of the Other. To argue for madness being "fully recognized" is ironic and hyperbolic—both in this diachronic reading and most certainly in Atwood's novels. Ultimately, madness is negatively defined by absence; from the "normal" perspective, madness is what we are not and so the mad should be removed from social agency (lest they ruin our "happy age"). Significantly, madness is not the same as comic relief, so society neither welcomes nor tolerates its aberrations; they are merely intrusions.

In Foucault's historical rendering, then, institutionalization was a convenience and madness, a condition arbitrarily determined by the ruling social class. Contemporary psychologist Jane M. Ussher maintains that this condition remains unchanged:

> [B]ehaviour which is at odds with that of the ruling élite will be deemed "mad." This can act to stigmatize particular social groups, such as women, blacks or the poor—or those deemed outside, the "alienists." Yet what each society deems to be alienists differs, as is illustrated by cross-cultural analysis. ... Outsiders and aliens maintain the cohesion of social groups and play an important part in defining the identity of the in-group, defining what is normal behaviour. The "Other" is needed to define the "One." Through defining what is mad, we denote what is sane, what is "normal," a process carried out by psychiatrists, and other social control experts, who negotiate reality on behalf of the rest of society. (138)

Thus Ussher highlights the significant role of dichotomous thinking and negative definition in the social construction of normality and protection of tenuous notions of selfhood—an endangered species in our contemporary era. *Surfacing* demonstrates the outworkings of just this perspective and its problematic nature. Perhaps more tellingly, if ironically, Ussher also identifies this defensive, reflexive reasoning with a psychological and emotional cause: "[I]n fact, it is the fear of the fall into madness which determines our need to position the mad person as being fundamentally different from ourselves" (138). More broadly, she argues that "by making groups out as different, as deviant, as mad, we can affirm our own normality, or even ascertain what it is. Thus the boundaries between 'normal' and 'abnormal' are an important part of the maintenance of society itself, of sanity and order" (140). As Foucault also observes, identification of madness and consequently of normality is a social control mechanism, and those in power prescribe the definitions along with the supposed solutions (240–41).

Notably, *Surfacing* affirms this direct correlation of the label of madness with fear and with the consequent physical segregation from social agency. Atwood's narrator, having separated herself from the masses (represented not only by the city but also by her companions), describes the source of her fear. She identifies "the real danger now" as "the hospital or the zoo, where we are put, species and individual, when we can no longer cope" (190). This diachronic understanding highlights the difference of her position; the danger she fears is neither internal dissolution nor external manifestation of her difference—that is, neither of losing her mind nor of "acting crazy"—but, rather, the external imposition of control and containment. The narrator's fear is of the physical institutionalization that inevitably results from a particular interpretation of her psychological capacities by others. This interpretation is based on evidence provided by her actions and, more significantly, by the absence of language. In short, she fears the social ramifications of a diagnosis of madness. Neither is it incidental that the narrator equates the human and the animal as objects of spectacle in either "the hospital or the zoo," if one recalls the fascination with Newgate and the spectacle of the mad figure; consequently, she describes herself as "neither animal nor human." Intriguingly, Atwood's narrator denies being the masses or the animal, leaving her to occupy the position of the individual human Other. Nonetheless, she refuses the label of madness and, in fact, exhibits the "normal" reaction by affirming her fear of this label.

By manifesting this fear of madness, the narrator of *Surfacing* thus occupies a paradoxically inclusive position. As the views of Foucault and Ussher suggest, she *can* be posited as the norm: the individual who represents the masses' fear of madness. Yet, ironically, at the very moment she acknowledges this fear, Atwood's narrator already occupies the role of the Other, for in every respect, she *is* the stereotypical madwoman. In fact, the narrator physically and discursively becomes a striking revision of Ophelia, whom Atwood identifies as one of "the great-grandmothers of almost every poetic and theatrical and operatic madwoman of the nineteenth century"—the other being Lady Macbeth (see "Ophelia"). Perhaps unsurprisingly, then, Atwood's narrator consciously identifies her own subject position in a clear allusion to this "grand dame" by musing, "This was the stereotype, straws in the hair, talking nonsense or not talking at all" (*Surfacing* 190). Yet through this dual representation of the narrator as both normal and mad, Atwood also questions the viability of this Ophelia model as a definition of madness. Thus, more broadly, Atwood draws attention to the physical and the linguistic associations of madness in society and in literary representations both historical and contemporary.

The narrator further argues that she is not mad but is "only a natural woman," one who is mistakenly assumed to be unable to cope with social demands, unwritten rules, and expectations, one who is in danger of being taken away and locked up. The misunderstanding is perpetrated by the tenuous but powerful "they" of Western society, the amorphous representatives who, the narrator argues,

> would never believe it's only ... a state of nature, they think of that as a tanned body on a beach with washed hair waving like scarves; not this, face dirt-caked and streaked, skin grimed and scabby, hair like a frayed bathmat stuck with leaves and twigs. A new kind of centerfold. (190)

She is scornful of this superficial society, but in attempting to distance herself from "them," the narrator lapses into conceptualizing herself as part of a binary: us versus them, where "they" clearly hold the power to determine "normality." Yet Atwood's novel also overturns this dichotomy, for the narrator's discursive shift into binary thinking is part of what shackles her. The normality determined through such binaries is overtly artificial, a construct that oversimplifies, airbrushing out any and all imperfections until reality is that constructed image that obscures human complexity, hiding the dirt, the wounds, the pain, and even the humour in life. Moreover, for the narrator, that airbrushed image is implicitly a gendered one from which she seeks freedom but, at this point, to which she remains psychologically bound by positioning herself as a helpless victim—a binary that is also a construct the narrator allows to define her. While she resists physical enclosure (180), she remains discursively trapped.

This linguistic positioning mirrors the narrator's dual psychological position: she fears and rejects but also inhabits and speaks from the binary position of the Other. In *Madness in Literature*, Lillian Feder suggestively remarks that "the prototypical mad man or woman is analogous to the wild man" (3). Thus the narrator's pseudo-animalistic state is actually linked with wildness and, by extension, with madness. Feder's remarks also imply the converse; if wildness *is* madness, then normality *is* civilization—that airbrushed superficial construct that the narrator rejects. She does so consciously, maintaining, "I tried for all those years to be civilized but I'm not and I'm through pretending" (168). The narrator's overt rejection of civilization, then, is also an implicit rejection of normality—at least in the sense it is societally defined. This "no man's land," to borrow Gilbert and Gubar's usage of the term, indeed becomes "the war of the words" as Atwood's narrator wrestles with her social, psychological, and discursive positions.

In addition to the emotional isolation and physical segregation from her companions, the narrator purposely negates herself from discourse, initially and provocatively suggesting the limitations of linguistic determinants and of language's power to contain. Her view—"Language divides us into fragments, I wanted to be whole" (*Surfacing* 146)—sharply contrasts with the normative view, a position the narrator understands and (ironically) articulates clearly. Despite her understanding, the narrator attempts to distance herself from this view by using the third-person possessive to situate the interpretation: "To have someone to speak to and words that can be understood: their definition of sanity" (190). Such fissures are precisely where some critics posit empowering readings of madness, arguments of "superior sanity" or of expressions of protest through withdrawal. Barbara Hill Rigney, for example, argues that Atwood's narrator achieves a supranatural female condition: "to the protagonist belongs the ultimate sanity: the knowledge that woman can descend, and return—sane, whole, victorious" (115). Rigney exemplifies feminist readings of Atwood that romanticize madness, positioning the narrator as one who must "break down before she can break through."

Such a glorified reading of madness can be traced, albeit in a different form, to Gilbert and Gubar's *The Madwoman in the Attic*, in which, to grossly simplify this seminal feminist work, anger finds a voice in madness. Certainly, this line of argumentation has appeal, redeeming a dire situation by providing meaning for suffering, the means of articulation for intense emotion, and power for the powerless. Such a reading seems to provide a redemptive possibility that even encompasses both genders, for while Gilbert and Gubar focus on the mad*woman* character in fiction, the authors do extend their assessment of madness to include both genders; they claim that "the mad character ... [as] a figure of rage" is one not to be ignored but that "her (or his) fury must be acknowledged not only by the angelic protagonist to whom s/he is opposed, but, significantly, *by the reader as well*" (78). The reader-character-author triad that Atwood invokes seems to coincide with this feminist reading of madness as empowerment, yet the question of voice remains problematic.

Marta Caminero-Santangelo's recent study, *The Madwoman Can't Speak: Or Why Insanity is Not Subversive*, outlines the extent of this interpretation's appeal while also indicating its inherent difficulty: "In its most extreme form, this interpretive model reads madness, whenever it appears in women's texts, as a willed choice and a preferable alternative to sanity for women" (1). Extrapolating this view to that extreme position that romanticizes madness as "a preferable alternative for women" is undeniably dangerous and misleading for the very reader that Gilbert and Gubar also recognize as inescapably involved in the acts of interpreting and constructing madness. Caminero-Santangelo emphasizes that madness is distinctly not an avenue of freedom but one of self-delusion and even further restriction, where

> insanity is the final surrender to [dominant] discourses, precisely because it is characterized by the (dis)ability to produce meaning—that is, to produce representations recognizable within society. ... As an illusion of power that masks powerlessness, madness is thus the final removal of the madwoman from any field of agency. ... Madness is not rage or even hate but hopelessness. (11–12, 17)

In this view, the voice given to the madwoman by Gilbert and Gubar is actually a scream of silence because it remains unintelligible to the society that made it a desperate response to a constructed binary position in the first place; madness is not a "willed choice" or "preferable alternative" but an anguished, unarticulated voicing of frustration and dislocation that society largely dismisses or ignores.

In *Surfacing*, Atwood's narrator simultaneously rejects, critiques, and inhabits the role of madwoman, thereby demonstrating its futility. Even in the moment she enacts that role, the narrator derides the stereotype of the madwoman: "shoulders huddled over into a crouch, eyes staring blue as ice from the deep sockets; the lips move by themselves. ... talking nonsense or not talking at all" (190). However, the moment of purposeful discursive withdrawal neither lasts nor liberates her but proves to be untenable. Even as the narrator sardonically considers her own position as "[a] new kind of centrefold," her impulse is to vocalize a response: "I laugh, and a noise comes out like something being killed: a mouse, a bird?" Her voice is symbolically strangled, sounding not "natural" but distorted, dire.

While the narrator sustains her withdrawal from language, relying on sound as utterance but avoiding language itself, tellingly, she finds neither liberation nor cathartic release in this spontaneous articulation—the only sound that shatters her withdrawal into silence. Instead, Atwood positions her narrator at a crux; the animalistic, perhaps piercing, sound of her own unrecognizable voice reveals something "being killed," silenced, forcibly, just as she feared. This time, however, she is both the perpetrator and the victim, the oppressor and the oppressed. The earlier laughter of the wild woman, which irrepressibly "extrudes" (184), is the sound of pending defeat. Not only does the narrator's hysterical laughter position her as a stereotypical madwoman but, a short time later, what may have seemed a brave rejection of social constructs can no longer be vocalized. All that remains is noise—the noise "like something being killed." There are no facile dichotomies of "us and them" behind which the narrator can hide, not even a master language that exerts insidious ideological control, for she has stepped outside of linguistic articulation at this point. The narrator's removal from language thus distinctly marks her as a madwoman by removing her from a position of agency and placing her instead in "powerlessness" and "hopelessness." She is, in effect, institutionalized and so her greatest fear is realized—not by the actions of "them" but herself. In this sense, the Other *is* the norm; the one becomes the masses; the binary of "us versus them" is transformed into an equation. She who fears madness *becomes* the madwoman.

Surfacing sustains such a reading, for the strangled outcry immediately spurs the narrator to action. She is jolted out of silence back into agency and into survival mode:

> This above all, to refuse to be a victim. Unless I can do that I can do nothing. I have to recant, give up the old belief that I am powerless and because of it nothing I can do will ever hurt anyone. A lie which was always more disastrous than the truth would have been. (191)

Significantly, the narrator relates this self-preservation specifically to discourse and seems to recognize that removal from discourse is necessarily a removal from agency—symbolically a retreat into the undefined and as yet untenable: "The word games, the winning and the losing games are finished; at the moment there are no others but they will have to be invented" (191). Atwood's narrator realizes that she *must* use language; rejection is not an option, though *how* to use the linguistic fragments remains to be discovered.

That said, as is typical of Atwood's novels, the narrator remains poised for action at the conclusion but couched in ambiguity. While she admits that "withdrawing is no longer possible and the alternative is death," awkwardly dresses again, and claims to "re-enter [her] own time" (191), she remains ambivalent and even suspiciously hesitant about re-engaging with reality. In response to her lover, Joe, who returns and calls for her, the narrator is ominously silent, weighing her alternatives while acknowledging the need for discourse. In one of Atwood's subtly ironic gender inversions, the female narrator concedes, "If I go with him we will have to talk. ... For us it's necessary, the intercession of words" (192). This awareness notwithstanding, the narrator does not immediately opt for agency. She wavers but withholds herself: "I tense forward, towards the demands and questions, though my feet do not move yet. ... His voice is annoyed: he won't wait much longer. But right now he waits" (192). The discursive world of constructed normality, reality, and communication that the relationship with Joe represents starkly contrasts the narrator's isolated retreat into nature, where she serenely notes, "The lake is quiet, the trees surround me, asking and giving nothing" (192). While she is "tens[ing] forward" and assuring herself that she "can trust him [Joe]" (192), Atwood clearly leaves the narrator hovering on the edge of the forest, straddling the two worlds in silence, thereby leaving the readers to determine the course of action.

Ultimately, *Surfacing* manages to undermine readers' confidence in our own interpretation of the character through the reading experience itself. Assumptions are shattered by this unpredictable figure, leaving readers tensed on the edge of certainty. Our reading is complicated by discovering the narrator's unreliability, questioning her sanity, and, finally, being confronted with an unstable figure wavering on the edge of normality and sharing our fears of madness. Thus, Atwood strategically complicates any attempt to step into the role of analyst, for the expert is no longer readily distinguishable from the Other. Viewing madness as distanced and easily identifiable is a misleading construct that Atwood nudges us to recognize through this complex physical and discursive representation of the narrator. This awareness of the elusive nature of madness and of our own fears exposes normality as a shifting contingency, a limited and tenuous construct, a silhouette of madness within which we, as Atwood's readers, can and do exist only by turning a blind eye.

—King's University College

WORKS CITED

Atwood, Margaret. "Ophelia Has a Lot to Answer For." Stratford Festival Lecture. September 1997. Margaret Atwood reference site. [online]: <http://www.owtoad.com/ophelia.html> (accessed October 15, 2003).

———. *Surfacing*. [1972]. New Canadian Library ed. Toronto: McClelland & Stewart, 1994.

Caminero-Santangelo, Marta. *The Madwoman Can't Speak: Or Why Insanity is Not Subversive*. Reading Women Writing Series. Ithaca, NY: Cornell University Press, 1998.

Feder, Lillian. *Madness in Literature*. Princeton, NJ: Princeton University Press, 1980.

Foucault, Michel. *Madness and Civilization: A History of Insanity in the Age of Reason*. [1965]. Translated by Richard Howard. New York: Vintage, 1988.

Gilbert, Sandra M., and Susan Gubar. *The Madwoman in the Attic: The Woman Writer and the Nineteenth-Century Literary Imagination*. New Haven, CT: Yale University Press, 1979.

———. *No Man's Land: The Place of the Woman Writer in the Twentieth Century*. Vol. 1, *The War of the Words*. New Haven, CT: Yale University Press, 1988.

Rigney, Barbara H. *Madness and Sexual Politics in the Feminist Novel: Studies in Brontë, Woolf, Lessing, and Atwood*. Madison: University of Wisconsin Press, 1978.

Ussher, Jane M. *Women's Madness: Misogyny or Mental Illness?* Amherst: University of Massachusetts Press, 1992.

"It looked at me with its mashed eye": Animal and Human Suffering in *Surfacing*

JANICE FIAMENGO

ON THE OPENING page of *Survival*, Margaret Atwood reports that the first Canadian books she read as a child were "heart-wrenching stories of animals caged, trapped, and tormented" (29), stories in Charles G.D. Roberts's *Kings in Exile* and Ernest Thompson Seton's *Wild Animals I Have Known*. She devotes a whole chapter of *Survival* to stories of animal suffering, finding in the elegiac genre an illuminating window into the Canadian psyche. Unlike British literature, in which animals are "Englishmen in furry zippered suits" (73), or American literature, in which the focus is the hunter and his quest, Canadian animal stories "are about animals *being* killed, as felt emotionally from inside the fur and feathers" (74). According to this now-familiar argument, the concern in Canadian literature for "doomed and slaughtered animals" (76) signifies the national concern with cultural survival, the fear that Canada is in danger of extinction. Significant to my discussion is that Atwood considers and then firmly rejects a reading of animals *as animals* in these texts in favour of a symbolic reading of the colonial predicament. She notes that the preoccupation with animal death and extinction might be seen as "national guilt: Canada after all was founded on the fur trade" (a reference that recurs in *Surfacing*). But such a reading would be, in her view, "mistaken" (79). Instead, it is "much more likely that Canadians themselves feel threatened and nearly extinct as a nation ... and that their identification with animals is the expression of a deep-seated cultural fear" (79).

With this statement, Atwood to some extent pre-empts and invalidates the argument of this essay, which is that in *Surfacing* (the novel she wrote just prior to *Survival*, and which helped to crystallize her *Survival* thesis), dead animals signify dead animals, and national guilt for their slaughter is a real issue. Atwood the artist tells a more complex story than Atwood the critic, which is why *Surfacing* continues to provoke and repay critical scrutiny. In a novel full of ghosts, animals are prominent among the dead who will not stay buried, and their suffering and death evoke a ferocious narrative melancholy that exceeds the cultural anxiety with which it is associated. (When the narrator thinks of her country being sold to the Americans, she reflects that "the people were sold along with the land and the animals" [132], suggesting the interconnection between the colonial predicament and animal death.) Reading *Surfacing* in light of Atwood's comments on animals in *Survival*, I will argue that the narrator's identification with animals is, ultimately, not an expression of her own fear (or not only—she is, after all, a narrator who lives according to the principle "if it hurts, invent a different pain"[13]) but a recognition of and longing for connection with non-human animals.[1] Only when she recognizes animals as more than symbols for human values or situations does she move toward the human integrity she is seeking.

Surfacing is not, of course, an animal story per se.[2] Animals are not its central characters, and many critics have usefully clarified its generic associations with myth (Campbell; Davidson and Davidson; Grace), fairy tale (Baer), folk tale (Godard), grail romance (Thomas), and Aboriginal vision quest (Guédon; Ross) to name only the predominant patterns that anchor this story of a young woman's search for herself. Yet the novel announces an affiliation with this diverse and flexible genre by alluding to a number of Canadian and other animal tales. On the second page of the novel, the narrator reflects on the sense of grievance she detects in her lover, Joe. She speculates that "secretly he would like them to set up a kind of park for him, like a bird sanctuary. Beautiful Joe" (8). *Beautiful Joe* is the name of the first Canadian best-seller, Margaret Marshall Saunders's prize-winning tale, published in 1894 to instruct children about the humane treatment of farm and pet animals.[3] Later in the novel, the narrator, who is a commercial artist, reflects on the collection of *Quebec Folk Tales* she is illustrating, and wonders why there is no *loup-garou* story in the collection. The *loup-garou* is the werewolf story, a tale of a human being transformed into an animal, often a wolf, because of sin. At another point, the narrator remembers a fairy tale about a king who learned to speak to animals, and wonders what story animals would tell if they could actually talk.[4] It would be, she thinks, an "accusation, lament, an outcry of rage" (130). Atwood evokes these animal stories as key reference points for her novel, which also, in part, articulates an "outcry of rage" and stresses the need for human beings to redefine their conception of and relationship to animals. In one of the narrator's final visions, she watches a fish jump from the lake and sees it transform before her eyes:

From the lake a fish jumps

An idea of a fish jumps

A fish jumps, carved wooden fish with dots painted on the sides, no, antlered fish thing drawn in red on cliffstone, protecting spirit. It hangs in the air suspended, flesh turned to icon, he has changed again, returned to the water. How many shapes can he take.

I watch it for an hour or so; then it drops and softens, the circles widen, it becomes an ordinary fish again. (187)

The description suggests her recognition, at the climax of her mystical journey, that the creature is at once an idea, a representation, a totem, and—finally and most importantly—itself.

This vision is achieved with difficulty. The narrator's initial journey into the wilderness, rather than bringing communion with nature and animal life, provokes a melancholic recognition of loss, both real and symbolic, and a numbed sense of inevitable doom. According to Akira Lippit, this sense of loss in relation to animals is one of the key expressions of modernity, of a world in which human beings, in separating themselves from animals through technology, recognize and perpetuate their (paradoxical) dehumanization. As if writing back to the fiction of Roberts and Seton, in which the wilderness path is a "potent emancipator" (Roberts, *Kindred* 26) leading to the understanding that "we and the beasts are kin" (Seton 11), Atwood makes clear that entering the bush and encountering animal life are not enough to re-establish a connection with the insects, fish, toads, frogs, herons, jays, owls, rabbits, beaver, deer, and bear that populate it; everywhere, evidence of human predation marks the separation of a technology-worshipping society, with its "dead elm skeletons ... cuttings dynamited in pink and grey granite" (9), from its animal kin. Wrenched out of any natural connection with animal being, her own and others, the heroine must undergo a complex psychological and spiritual reorientation in order to regain it.

In guiding readers to recognize animals not only as symbols for human experiences or actors in a human drama, the novel provides a number of examples of what Atwood has defined, in *Survival*, as "American" animal stories—the type in which "the hunter wishes to match himself against [animals], conquer them by killing them, and assimilate their magic qualities" (74). When Bill Malmstrom, from the Detroit branch of the Wildlife Protection Association of America, approaches the narrator with the offer of buying her father's property, he explains how the members would use the retreat to "meditate and observe ... the beauties of Nature. And maybe do a little hunting and fishing" (94). Malmstrom's formulation, though crude, is an accurate representation of many "American" hunting stories, including a number by Seton, in which the hunter connects with animal nature by killing it.[5] *Random Samples*, David and Joe's film project, is mainly composed of pictures of dead animals—fish guts, the heron—and their devastated habitat, alongside of which Anna is instructed to arrange herself as one more object of conquest. Upon arriving at the lake, David is exhilarated at the thought of hooking "one of them smart fish" and Anna teases him by calling him "a great white hunter" (29), perhaps a reference to Moby Dick, a touchstone novel in Atwood's account of the American attitude to animals. The white whale in that novel is not really a whale but a symbol for something Ahab hopes to acquire by killing it.

In contrast, the suffering, hunted animal, as a being in itself rather than a symbol, assumes a central role in *Surfacing*, both thematically and structurally. As many readers have noted, the discovery of the dead heron is second in importance only to the discovery of the narrator's dead father as a turning point in the narrative; both discoveries reveal a truth the narrator must face in order to escape from her "paper house" (144) of lies, a truth that involves taking responsibility for the suffering of an other. In order to orchestrate this realization, the novel employs animal images and metaphors in nearly every key scene, creating a haunting threnody that signifies the return of the repressed. And in a novel concerned with cultural annihilation, traumatic memory, and the willed forgetting of historical and personal violence, we are led first to dismiss and then to remember a comment by David early on in the narrative when he asks his companions: "Do you realize that this country is founded on the bodies of dead animals? Dead fish, dead seals, and historically dead beavers, the beaver is to this country what the black man is to the United States" (39–40).

David is an unreliable spokesperson for Atwood's ideas, yet two key moments in the novel suggest the need to take seriously the slaughter of animals as an element in the national unconscious. The first such moment involves the dead and decaying blue heron, which has been killed and tied to a tree with a nylon rope. As a sign of human dominion, it seems to the narrator to represent the American way of death, and her comparison of it to a "lynch victim" (116) parallels David's evocation of American slavery as the economic foundation and repressed truth of the nation. Announcing "It looked at me with its mashed eye" (115), the narrator experiences a shock of identification as she looks back at the bird. As Atwood explains in *Survival*, it is a moment of self-recognition for the narrator who, in the classic Canadian pattern, recognizes her own suffering in the dead bird, retracing the process of its death with outraged empathy. She sees herself and the heron as co-innocents, tortured and destroyed by the Americans, a murderous "them" distanced from the narrator. Realizing that violence is made possible by a process of dis-identification in which the subject projects onto an other a loathed, disavowed part of the self, the narrator wonders, "what part of them the heron was, that they needed so much to kill it" (119). She has not yet recognized that she too has displaced her own capacity for violence onto the conveniently faceless, blankly evil, Americans.

Much hinges on this subsequent recognition, for when she next sees the heron, after the encounter with the Americans in the canoe, who turn out to be Canadians, the shock of self-recognition is worse, as she can no longer identify *with* the heron against its murderers. The "look" from the "mashed eye" now accuses her. Now she feels "a sickening complicity, sticky as glue, blood on my hands, as though I had been there and watched without saying No or doing anything to stop it" (130). No longer co-victim but now guilty conspirator, she recognizes her complicity in violence and understands that as a human being she has inherited a relation to animals of destructive predation. Even as a child, "it was in us too, it was innate" (132). Her emotional numbness and self-protective sense of disassociation crumble from this moment in the narrative onward, as Atwood takes her narrator beyond the territory charted in *Survival*.

In *Survival*, Atwood accounts for the look exchanged between hunter and animal, "a recurring moment in Canadian literature" (80), by focusing on the human projection of his suffering on to the animal, but the narrator's recognition is more complicated than that. As John Berger explains, the look from an animal is often a particularly charged one for human beings precisely because it is both familiar and alien. It is not a call to identify but a summons to recognize the other across a "narrow abyss" (3), to renounce the anthropomorphizing gaze that turns an other into an image of the self. Perhaps the fact that the heron is dead signals the impossibility of finding the confirmation of innocence sought by the narrator: the "mashed eye" invites her to recognize a pain apart from her own.

The larger ethical and spiritual issues associated with this recognition are emphasized in a second, related scene. As she prepares for her pivotal dive into the lake, the narrator reflects on the slaughter of the heron in the context of her modern culture of death. She thinks of the heron's body as it flies as a "blue grey cross" in the sky, and the body of the heron "hanging wrecked from the tree" (*Surfacing* 140) as an image of crucifixion, an unacknowledged sacrifice that, because it is unrecognized, "redeems no one" (*Survival* 77). "The animals die that we may live," she concludes, stating that "anything that suffers and dies instead of us is Christ" (*Surfacing* 140). Human beings fail to recognize their debt to animals and fail to give thanks. Seeing the animals as analogous to Christ, she sees human beings as sinners who "refuse to worship" (*Surfacing* 140), and the result is a living hell. Worshipping only our own power, we produce a culture of death without resurrection and guilt without absolution. A society that kills without honouring what it relies on for life, the narrator recognizes, will be a culture that destroys itself along with everything it touches.

These moments of realization are not only thematically central in the novel but also formally significant, marking a shift in the text's presentation of animal imagery. In roughly the first half of the novel, references to animals occur in a series of metaphors, in which the suffering of animals illuminates human experience. After the discovery of the dead heron, however, the emphasis shifts toward animals as literal subjects of violence and suffering, representing at the level of language what the narrator painfully discovers on the island.

The metaphor of species extinction, for example, is used flippantly for an effect of sardonic humour. At the beginning of the novel, the narrator describes her lover, Joe, as looking "like the buffalo on the U.S. nickel ... with the defiant but insane look of a species once dominant, now threatened with extinction" (8). The buffalo, a symbol for the defeat of nature by technological power, points up Joe's extravagant self-pity. The threat of extinction is evoked again as the narrator thinks about the effect of logging on the island, which has left behind massive saw-cut stumps, remnants of the giant trees that will never be allowed to grow again, now "killed as soon as they're valuable" and thus "scarce as whales" (46); in this simile, whales are an iconic signifier of loss. Animal experimentation is another major metaphor. In one example, the narrator remembers being so bored in the "cage" of her desk at school that she used to poke at herself with pen nibs and compass points; she compares her situation to that of a rat in a cage, remarking that "they've discovered rats prefer any sensation to none" (111), a reference that glances obliquely at the pain and imprisonment of test animals. In a false memory of childbirth, the narrator objects to women's treatment as animals during labour, comparing women both to dead animals butchered for meat and to live animals subject to scientific testing: "They stick needles into you so you won't hear anything, you might as well be a dead pig, your legs are up in a metal frame, they bend over you, technicians, mechanics, butchers, students clumsy or sniggering, practising on your body" (80). The grotesque, Gothic charge of such a comparison seems to exceed the angry objection to the medicalization of childbirth.

By far the most frequent metaphors are of animals wounded, hunted, and tortured for sport. When David and Joe manage to cut down a dead tree for firewood and insist on filming it for *Random Samples*, the narrator highlights their self-love by comparing them to trophy hunters: "In the end they stuck the axe in the log, after several tries, and took turns shooting each other standing beside it, arms folded and one foot on it as if it was a lion or a rhinoceros" (81). The mock-heroic comparison to big-game hunting highlights the ineptitude of David and Joe's conquest of the wilderness. When the narrator refuses Joe's marriage proposal and is embarrassed by his vulnerability, she feels sorry and resentfully guilty, "as though I'd stepped on a small animal by accident" (88). Worrying over the disintegration of their relationship, she falls back on one of her father's favourite maxims, providing a literalist gloss: "There's more than one way to skin a cat, my father used to say; it bothered me, I didn't see why they would want to skin a cat even one way" (92). Perhaps most memorably, the sound of Anna reaching sexual climax with David is described as "pure pain, clear as water, an animal's at the moment the trap closes" (82). In many of these examples, the vehicle of the comparison tends to overwhelm the subject with its emphatic, lurid violence. We are likely to be struck as much by the animal's cry in the trap as by Anna's pain, as much by the pity of animal death as by Joe's inarticulate misery. Atwood's strategy of representation makes the suffering animal absent, because it is not literally evoked, but also eerily present as a repressed but insistent reality.

In a novel in which the significance of the narrator's dive into the lake is precisely its revelation of the abortion's repressed but insistent reality, these frequent references to animal death and suffering deserve attention. As we come to see the narrative as a text of trauma revealing to the wary reader what the narrator cannot name directly, we recognize animal torture and death as equally urgent truths demanding recognition. We notice that repressed memories of the abortion reveal themselves through linguistic slips in the narrator's fake cover story, as when she refers to divorce, with a surgical metaphor, as "an amputation" (42) and laments the "section of my own life, sliced off" (48): she refers to her abandoned child, "taken away from me, exported, deported" (48) in words that rhyme with *aborted*, and she reflects on having "allowed myself to be cut in two" (108), a homonym for "cut into." Her language consistently points us toward a truth concealed, in the way that Freudian slips supposedly reveal the truth of the unconscious. In a similar way, the text's conscious narrative of human pain is consistently disturbed by evidence of animal torture. Just as the shock of seeing her father's dead body initiates a memory of abortion, the shock of confronting the heron's gaze, its "mashed eye" prohibiting further evasion or false comfort, causes repressed images of animal pain to erupt into consciousness.[6]

After the discovery of the heron, the violence of animal abuse, torture, and murder comes dramatically to the fore in the narrative. For example, on the evening after seeing the heron, the narrator feels discomfort while fishing and describes it in excessively violent language, calling it a "violation" committed for "sport or amusement or pleasure" and expressing repugnance at her friends for "admiring David's murder, cadaver" (120). From absent referents, animals have become the literal subjects of violence. Meeting the Americans who turn out to be Canadians, the narrator remembers the stories she has heard about their characteristic behaviour, of how "they got drunk and chased loons in their powerboats for fun, backtracking on the loon as it dived, not giving it a chance to fly, until it drowned or got chopped up in the propeller blades" (122). Remembering the suffering of the small creatures her brother kept in his wilderness laboratory, she accuses herself of complicity: "because of my fear, they were killed" (131). As a result, she is tormented by guilt and self-loathing, unable to rid herself of memories of leeches crawling, maimed, out of the fire (132) or of the heron hanging with its wings fallen: "In my head when I closed my eyes the shape of the heron dangled" (118). So moved is she by the horror of her realization that she longs for "a machine that could make them [the Americans] vanish" so that there would "be more room for the animals" (154). All human beings, she realizes, have blood on their hands.

In addition to foregrounding the reality of animal suffering, the novel also highlights, through metaphorical linkages, how the destruction of animal life makes possible the destruction of human life. As the narrator notes, "Anything we could do to the animals we could do to each other: we practised on them first" (121). Her pregnancy and abortion are both associated with animal imagery, as when the narrator describes her idea of an unborn baby "look[ing] out through the walls of the mother's stomach, like a frog in a jar" (32) and then remembers her aborted fetus "in a bottle curled up, staring out at me like a cat pickled" (143). But reflecting that she never saw the fetus, she realizes the bottle was her own invention, "a remnant of the trapped and decaying animals" (143) her brother had collected. Animal imagery repeatedly signals the emotional and ethical linkages between the murder of animals and of unborn children, as when the narrator reflects on her lover's rationale for her abortion: "He said it wasn't a person, only an animal. I should have seen that was no different, it was hiding in me as if in a burrow and instead of granting it sanctuary I let them catch it" (144–45). In this startling statement of correspondence, the narrative raises unsettling questions about the relationship between various forms of murder routinely discounted by Western culture. Abortion and animal slaughter, the novel implies, require the same operation of the mind—the making of a sentient being into an *it* in order to kill it—that accompanies other human atrocities such as war, colonial violence, and misogyny. If Atwood's novel is a feminist critique of the destructive and hateful aspects of North American society, it is also a critique of feminism and its implication in that culture.

The narrator's response to her realization that all human beings, including herself, are "Americans" in their relation to animals leads her to renounce membership in the human race altogether. Unable to accept the atrocious guilt of "being a witness" (82), she attempts in the final section of the novel to become an animal or animal-spirit, rejecting history and society (176), discarding her clothing (177), foraging for food (180), digging herself a lair (178), and waiting for her fur to grow (177): a number of readers (Baer; Godard) have speculated that she becomes the wolf whose absence she had noted in the fairy tales she was illustrating. She imagines birthing her child alone, breaking the umbilical cord with her teeth, licking the baby clean like a cat (162). As Baer has noted, she imagines her developing fetus as a divine animal too, a creature "covered with shining fur, a god" (162). She renounces language, perhaps partially in recognition that non-language sounds, especially cries of pain and pleasure, murmurs and sighs, link human beings with animals in shared bodily experiences. As she moves more deeply into her mystical journey, she is accepted by a loon as part of the landscape, and has visions of her mother as a jay and her father as a wolf. These references in the last part of the novel signify the narrator's rejection of what she believes to be the prison of rationality that separates her from nature and makes her a killer. Her desire is to experience the mystery of animal otherness.

Hints of that desire have surfaced earlier in the novel: in the sense of "unbearable" (123) failure associated with her mother's doomed attempt at flight, perhaps the most humanizing and poignant of the narrator's memories of her otherwise rather distant mother; in the narrator's fascination with the complex biology of the animals she had to dissect in school, which she associated with saints' pictures, enchanting and awesome, "the detached heart still gulping slowly like an adam's apple, no martyr's letters on it" (120); in her father's preference for animals with their consistent and predictable behaviour (59) over human beings; even in her brother's gruesome nature collection itself. Everyone in her family, it seems, has been affected by their experience in the bush, which has brought them glimpses of an animal world separate from human reality and inaccessible to human understanding; they have recognized in it some defence against the machine-like civilization to which all are bound.

Ultimately, the narrator draws back from the path of transformation, recognizing that for her it would lead to madness and death, accepting the complicity of being human. But the longing that this experience embodies—and the guilty horror that precipitated it—speak to the novel's preoccupation with the vexed dynamic of human and animal at the heart of human self-definition. Just before she decides to "re-enter [her] own time" (191), the narrator has a vision of her father-as-wolf, an ambiguous encounter that defies a conclusive interpretation. Yet her observation that "it tells me it has nothing to tell me, only the fact of itself" (187)—an elusive non-message—might provide a partial answer to the narrator's desire for "other choices" (189) than those of killer and victim, indifference or identification. How does one encounter a being with "nothing to tell"? How does one engage with one for whom language is irrelevant? At the very end of the novel, there is a similar statement about the natural world in the moment at which the narrator is poised to respond to Joe's call, with the lake and the trees "asking and giving nothing" (192). The phrase is often interpreted to mean that nature has nothing for her and she must return with Joe to the city—but such is surely not the case. I suggest that these two parallel statements announce the novel's final vision of animal significance, which is "only the fact of itself," awesome and unnecessary.

From her earliest years, the narrator has tried in different ways to "immerse [herself] in the other language" (158), to imagine animal being. As a child, she drew people-shaped bunnies who lived in eggs and ate ice-cream cones (91). As a youngster, she believed her mother could talk to animals, with special power over jays and bears. When she fished as a child, she would offer a vague prayer, "*Please be caught*," in order to believe "they had chosen to die and forgiven me in advance" (64). She is attracted to Aboriginal religion not least because it has a concept of the animal as "the soul of an ancestor or the child of a god" (128), worthy of reverence and rituals of obedience. By the end of the novel, she is watching the fish leap from the lake, undergoing a series of transformations that leaves it, finally, "an ordinary fish again" (187). Perhaps learning to live with animals in a non-predatory relationship involves the difficult understanding that they are not anthropomorphic projections, or metaphors, or symbols, or even gods—but beings whom we cannot know and cannot do without, creatures valuable in themselves outside of anything they might "give" or "tell" us. The description of the fish as image, symbol, and icon does not prohibit metaphor, suggesting that representation is both necessary and valuable ("for us it's necessary, the intercession of words" [192]), but it asserts the importance of attempting to see across the "narrow abyss" (Berger 3) to the thing itself.

In *Survival* Atwood argued that "seeing yourself as a victimized animal ... can become the *need* to see yourself as a victimized animal" (81). What she does not say, and what *Surfacing* demonstrates, is that this need can also blind one to the real animals in one's midst. Now more than ever, *Surfacing* alerts us to the urgency of facing Canada's ongoing history of environmental waste, blindness, and rapacity, to accept that this is a country "founded on the bodies of dead animals," in which cultural survival may be inextricable from animal survival. Atwood offers no program for animal or national liberation in this disturbing novel, but her attention to the issue demonstrates the ethical complexity of her feminist and nationalist project.

—University of Ottawa

NOTES

1. Considering that *Surfacing* has been the subject of extensive critical study and varied interpretations, I am surprised that so few scholars have discussed its attention to animal life. See Kathleen Vogt and George Woodcock for insightful, but very brief, discussions. Many more have analyzed the novel's ecological vision generally: Coral Ann Howells, for example, reads the novel as a healing journey into a redemptive wilderness and Ronald Hatch finds it a portrait of despoliated nature that attacks Canadian wilderness myths.
2. See Marian Scholtmeijer for a discussion of the traditional animal story as a genre combining the beast fable and natural history sketch (94–99).
3. See Sandra Djwa for a discussion of this and other allusions as part of a system of "respectful parody" (170).
4. Peter Klovan discusses Richard Wagner's "Siegfried" as one example of such a tale.
5. In Seton's "Lobo," for example, the narrator has a moment of compunction, experiencing a flicker of fellow feeling, as his gaze meets that of the cunning wolf he has finally captured in multiple traps (39–41).

6. According to Carol J. Adams in her study of feminist-vegetarian critical practice, North American culture "generally accepts animals' oppression and finds nothing ethically or politically disturbing about the exploitation of animals for the benefit of people. Hence our language is structured to convey this acceptance" (66). When references to animals appear in metaphors for human pain, that use of language naturalizes, elides, and makes invisible their suffering, murder, and dismemberment. When a woman in labour is said to be treated "like a dead pig," as Adams explains, "the death experience of animals acts to illustrate the lived experience of [human beings]," with the animal as an "absent referent" (42). It is a process by which "the material reality of violence" is rendered in "controlled and controllable ... metaphors" (43). Adams argues that shifting away from this use of metaphor could be a crucial linguistic tool in reorienting ourselves toward awareness of animal suffering.

WORKS CITED

Adams, Carol J. *The Sexual Politics of Meat: A Feminist-Vegetarian Critical Theory.* New York: Continuum, 1991.

Atwood, Margaret. *Surfacing.* [1972]. New Canadian Library ed. Toronto: McClelland & Stewart, 1994.

———. *Survival: A Thematic Guide to Canadian Literature.* Toronto: Anansi, 1972.

Baer, Elizabeth R. "Pilgrimage Inward: Quest and Fairy Tale motifs in *Surfacing*." In *Margaret Atwood: Vision and Forms*, edited by Kathryn VanSpanckeren and Jan Garden Castro, 24–34. Carbondale: Southern Illinois University Press, 1988.

Berger, John. *About Looking.* New York: Pantheon, 1980.

Campbell, Josie P. "The Woman as Hero in Margaret Atwood's *Surfacing*." *Mosaic* 11, no. 3 (1978): 17–28.

Davidson, Arnold E., and Cathy N. Davidson. "The Anatomy of Margaret Atwood's *Surfacing*." *ARIEL* 10, no. 3 (1979): 38–54.

Djwa, Sandra. "'Here I am': Atwood, Paper Houses, and a Parodic Tradition." *Essays on Canadian Writing*, no. 71 (2000): 169–78.

Godard, Barbara. "Tales Within Tales: Margaret Atwood's Folk Narratives." *Canadian Literature*, no. 109 (1986): 57–86.

Grace, Sherrill. "In Search of Demeter: The Lost, Silent Mother in *Surfacing*." In *Margaret Atwood: Vision and Forms*, edited by Kathryn VanSpanckeren and Jan Garden Castro, 35–47. Carbondale: Southern Illinois University Press, 1988.

Guédon, Marie-Francoise. "Surfacing: Amerindian Themes and Shamanism." In *Margaret Atwood: Language, Text, and System*, edited by Sherrill Grace and Lorraine Weir, 91–111. Vancouver: University of British Columbia Press, 1983.

Hatch, Ronald B. "Margaret Atwood, the Land, and Ecology." In *Margaret Atwood: Works and Impact*, edited by Reingard M. Nischik, 180–201. Rochester: Camden, 2000.

Howells, Coral. *Margaret Atwood*. London: Macmillan, 1996.

Klovan, Peter. "'They Are Out of Reach Now': The Family Motif in Margaret Atwood's *Surfacing*." *Essays on Canadian Writing*, no. 33 (1986): 1–24.

Lippit, Akira. *Electric Animal: Toward a Rhetoric of Wildlife*. Minneapolis: University of Minnesota Press, 2000.

Roberts, Charles G.D. *Kindred of the Wild*. Boston: Page, 1902.

———. *Kings in Exile*. New York: Macmillan, 1910.

Ross, Catherine S. "Nancy Drew as Shaman: Atwood's *Surfacing*." *Canadian Literature*, no. 84 (1980): 7–17.

Saunders, Margaret M. *Beautiful Joe*. [1894]. Owen Sound: Ginger Press, 1995.

Seton, Ernest T. *Wild Animals I Have Known*. [1898]. Mineola, NY: Dover, 2000.

Scholtmeijer, Marian. *Animal Victims in Modern Fiction: From Sanctity to Sacrifice*. Toronto: University of Toronto Press, 1993.

Thomas, Sue. "Mythic Reconception and the Mother/Daughter Relationship in Margaret Atwood's *Surfacing*." *ARIEL* 19, no. 2 (1988): 73–85.

VanSpanckeren, Kathryn, and Jan Garden Castro, eds. *Margaret Atwood: Vision and Forms*. Carbondale: Southern Illinois University Press, 1988.

Vogt, Kathleen. "Real and Imaginary Animals in the Poetry of Margaret Atwood." In *Margaret Atwood: Vision and Forms*, edited by Kathryn VanSpanckeren and Jan Garden Castro, 163–182. Carbondale: Southern Illinois University Press, 1988.

Woodcock, George. "Transformation Mask for Margaret Atwood." *Malahat Review*, no. 41 (1977): 52–56.

Having It Both Ways? Romance, Realism, and Irony in *Lady Oracle*'s Adulterous Affairs

TOBI KOZAKEWICH

FROM THE TRIANGLE comprising Marian McAlpine, Peter, and Duncan in her first published novel *The Edible Woman* to those in her last, *Oryx and Crake* (Jimmy's mother, father, and Ramona; Jimmy, Oryx, and Crake), Margaret Atwood has consistently returned to the trope of the adulterous triangle. Given W.H. New's claim that Atwood stands alongside Michael Ondaatje as the foremost Canadian writer of the 1980s and 1990s (303), it is fitting that her oeuvre reflects the increasing interest in adultery that English-Canadian letters as a whole displays in the twentieth century. Atwood's unique prominence in Canadian literary culture makes it even more appropriate that her interrogations of adultery differ from those of such contemporaries as Mordecai Richler and Ondaatje himself, in whose works adulterous affairs are equally ubiquitous. For while in Ondaatje's novels adultery repeatedly appears as a site of romantic tragedy, and while in Richler's it functions as a site of juridical (prohibitive) discourse, in Atwood's novels, a character's negotiation of the love triangle repeatedly represents her analogous negotiation between conflicting identities—a negotiation that often involves a struggle to establish herself as an articulate creative artist.[1]

Nowhere is Atwood more overt in mapping these simultaneous negotiations than in her 1976 novel, *Lady Oracle*.[2] Joan Delacourt Foster's oscillation between the role of bumbling domestic she plays with her husband,

Arthur, and that of carefree artist she plays with the Royal Porcupine, duplicates and thereby reinforces the ways literature occupies and demarcates the site of (her) particular cultural struggles. More specifically, in the tensions between and imbrications of its romantic, realistic, and ironic treatments of the love triangle, Atwood's third novel clarifies the interrelation of gender and genre (i.e., romance), pointing, in the process, to the relation between sexual dynamics and cultural production. Ultimately, its focus on romance, both as a literary genre and as a sociological phenomenon, means that *Lady Oracle* cannot only elucidate the battles waged on what Pierre Bourdieu calls the "field of cultural production" but also insist on the interrelation between that cultural field and the broader social context of which it is a part.

The novel performs the work of highlighting the ways gender and genre illuminate the ideological aspects of cultural production most clearly in its account of "Lady Oracle," Joan Foster's fictitious book of poetry. The production and reception of Joan's most autonomous creative work correspond closely to the processes that Bourdieu suggests characterize the field of cultural production, contesting, at the same time, Bourdieu's view that "the cultural field possesses a relative autonomy with respect to its economic and political determinations" (Johnson 15). In stressing, as Bourdieu does, the subordinate or dominated position that the cultural field occupies within the field of power, *Lady Oracle* construes the latter and its impact as being essentially phallocentric.

The production of Joan's work is clearly a collective action, involving editors, publishers, critics, and a media audience, in addition to Joan herself; indeed, the literary circus that Atwood here creates has be interpreted as a "farcical sham" that "pok[es] fun at Canada's literary establishment" (MacLean 181). Perhaps it is, but this joke has a dark side: with the singular exception of Joan, all the players in this cultural field are men. From the publishers, John Morton and Doug Sturgess, to the editor, Colin Harper, to media pundits like Barry Finkle, and self-professed art *aficionados* like the Royal Porcupine, it is a collectivity of men—and sexist men at that—who interpellate the artifact of Joan's manuscript as a work of art. Inevitably, while doing so, these men assert not only the legitimacy of "Lady Oracle," but also their own "claim to the right to talk about it and judge it" (Bourdieu 36). So jealously do they guard their cultural authority that they eventually exile Joan from the field of cultural production altogether; Barry Finkle, the host of the television program *Afternoon Hot Spot*, for example, makes so much of Joan's gender that she has very little air time of her own, and Joan's publishers, Morton and Sturgess, insists that she not "worry [her] pretty little head" about anything (240), as they take upon themselves even the naming of her book.

The way Morton and Sturgess decide upon the title, "Lady Oracle," is symbolic of their more general assertion of power and cultural authority. Rather than giving Joan time to participate in the process of naming her work, the publishers come up with a title off the cuff. Although they refer to Joan's manuscript while doing so, and even borrow one of her phrases, they modify her words to suit their purposes, thereby obscuring the manuscript's original emphasis. In her poem, Joan refers not to a lady oracle but to a *"blank lady   oracle/of blood"* (240). A visible caesura divides lady from oracle, with the result that the subsequent phrases qualify rather than complete the original "blank lady." Sturgess and Morton miss the point. Never considering that the silence of the blank space on the page is both symbolically and syntactically necessary, they write over the blankness of Joan's lady, filling her mystery with their own syntax. This glossing over the unspoken or unknown facilitates their assertion of unequivocal dominance in the field of cultural production and foregrounds the constructedness of that production, for the meaning that Sturgess and Morton attach to Joan's book is of *their* making. In other words, by emphasizing the processes of the cultural production of the poem "Lady Oracle," the novel *Lady Oracle* points to the distance that can divide the initial artefact from its manifestation as a cultural production, a distance that in this instance is clearly increased and reinforced by a male-dominated field of power.

The fact that this phallocentric bias carries over from the field of cultural production to the larger field of power in which it is situated becomes evident when Joan attempts to take the potentially subversive aspects of romance off the page in order to apply them to sexual relations in her actual life. While she originally sees in romance and in her transposition of its conventions onto her daily life only their liberating potential, she subsequently comes to realize that these actually reinforce male dominance in the material world, if not also in the cultural field.

Writing at a time when feminist critics like Germaine Greer were dismissing romance as "dope for dupes," Joan (like her "real-life" counterpart Margaret Atwood) anticipates the recuperative work regarding the genre that later feminists would perform.³ Joan identifies, for example, the benefits that the escapist nature of such literature offers to readers:

> "Escape wasn't a luxury for them," she insists; "it was a necessity. They had to get it somehow. And when they were too tired to invent escapes of their own, mine were available for them at the corner drugstore, neatly packaged like the other pain-killers." (33)

Joan characterizes romance as a corrective for unsatisfactory marriages: most simply, it takes women out of the torpor of their daily lives; still more subversively, it introduces a third party into the conventional marital dyad, offering up, as Stevi Jackson suggests, the "classic romance" hero as a source of the emotional "nurturance" female readers "lack [...] in their relationships with men" (55). Indeed, in mentally refuting Arthur's dismissal of romance as "worse than trash" (32), Joan goes as far as to assert that the "vision of a better world" that she presents in her costume gothics is "just as realistic" as that articulated in Arthur's own "god-damned theories and ideologies," which, she says, "made me puke" (34). In this claim that romance is as "realistic"—or "romantic"—as Arthur's socialist rhetoric, Joan starts undermining, if not shifting, the field on which her principle critic stands.

A problem arises, however, when Joan tries to up the ante by applying her cultural views to her marital life. Although Joan challenges the heteronormative structure of her marriage by embarking on an affair with the Royal Porcupine, its failure either to provide her with the escape she seeks or to satisfy her need for nurturance curtails the effectiveness of the protest it might otherwise register.⁴ Before meeting the Royal Porcupine, Joan keeps the peace by moderating her expectations of her husband, Arthur. Unlike other wives, who want "the earth to move" as well as "help with the dishes," Joan keeps her sense of romantic and companionate love separate, with Arthur in their apartment, and with the "cloaked, sinuous .... strangers in their castles and mansions, where they belonged" (229). Eventually, however, she feels a need to reconcile these two aspects of her desire in an affair that is at once passionate and companionate. She thus falls for the be-caped and be-caned Royal Porcupine, who entices her back to his place—not under the pretense of a nightcap but under the exigency of her helping him smuggle home a dead dog that he wants to preserve for a future "con-create" poem (255).

Even though the lovers meet at a launch of Joan's "Lady Oracle," the Royal Porcupine asserts from the start a cultural superiority over Joan. He dismisses her book as being merely a "publishing success" and asks her what it's like "to be a successful bad writer" (254). As an unappreciated and impoverished player in the field of restricted cultural production (very restricted, given the finite number of dead animals he's able to use at any given time), the Royal Porcupine commands an aura of mystery and bohemianism that appeals to Joan until it is obscured behind the Royal Porcupine's egocentric flaunting of his dominance in the field of power as well as in the field of cultural production. What follows is an inverse relation: as the Royal Porcupine increases the field of his power, he inadvertently decreases his sexual appeal, a fact symbolized by the emergence of his alter ego, Chuck Brewer. Indeed, it is not so much that the Royal Porcupine *has* an alter ego as that he *is* the alter ego of a rather banal commercial artist, who is, in Joan's words, "gray and multi-dimensional and complicated like everyone else" (286). Worse still, Chuck is obtuse where he should be sensitive, and controlling where he should be compliant (after all, a romance hero should command an extraordinary ability to anticipate and respond to the heroine's every desire in addition to displaying conventional masculine prowess). But Joan does not see Chuck as a failed hero. Rather, in the wake of her disappointing affair, Joan starts to reconsider the sexual and power dynamics of romance as a literary genre as well as a sociological phenomenon.

Joan comes to recognize the phallocentric nature of both the field of cultural production and the field of power that provides its broader social context. She remains incapable, however, of restructuring the gendered power relations that govern those fields, in large part because she has internalized them. According to Bourdieu's notion of the "habitus," this process of internalization is inevitable, as are its residual effects in Joan's post-disillusionment life. As Randal Johnson explains, the "habitus" is "a set of dispositions" resulting from "a long process of inculcation, beginning in early childhood, which becomes a 'second sense' or a second nature" (5). For Joan, the "second sense" involves a recognition of limited options, especially for women, as her struggle to complete "Stalked by Love," the (unpublished) Gothic romance that is supposed to finance her new life in Terremoto, suggests. But although Joan becomes ever more aware of the limiting nature of the habitus, she does not recognize its own constructedness.

Joan's difficulty in bringing "Stalked by Love" to a satisfactory conclusion derives from her increasing resistance to romantic conventions that, among other things, pit women against each other, as virgin and whore, and offer up a man as the only means of escaping that antagonist dynamic. Moreover, in her reluctance to transform that male character from a morally ambiguous villain to a redeemed hero, Joan indicates the extent to which she has grown beyond the point of believing a strong man will—or even can—rescue her from herself and provide her with the coherent identity for which she strives. Her resistance finds expression in the story she writes, as Felicia develops from a femme fatale into a remorseful and wronged woman, whose flaming red hair and general physiognomy bear, it must be noted, a striking resemblance to Joan's own. Yet Joan initially rejects this narrative turn, breaking off writing and pronouncing definitive judgment:

> ... It was all wrong.
>
> Sympathy for Felicia was out of the question, it was against the rules, it would foul up the plot completely. I was experienced enough to know that. If she'd only been a mistress instead of a wife, her life could have been spared; as it was, she had to die. In my books all wives were eventually mad or dead or both. But what had she ever done to deserve it? How could I sacrifice her for the sake of Charlotte? I was getting tired of Charlotte, with her intact virtue and her tidy ways. Wearing her was like wearing a hair shirt, she made me itchy, I wanted her to fall into a mud puddle, have menstrual cramps, sweat, burp, fart. Even her terrors were too pure, her faceless murderers, her corridors, her mazes and forbidden doors. (339–40)

The tension that Joan here describes illustrates the extent to which her creative capacities are limited by the habitus that influences her epistemology—by what she calls her "experience." Similarly, her frustration at being unable to write, or to believe in, the story she wishes to write reveals the extent to which she is trapped in a self-perpetuating system—a system that extends beyond the parameters of romance to include the acts of creation that could potentially modify the genre. In other words, the problem here transcends the limitations of romance and points, once again, to the gendered prescriptions that characterize the entire field of cultural production.

Although Joan moves toward an understanding of the operative power structures of the fields she inhabits, she does not apprehend the ways she reinforces these structures in her own life and writing. In both these areas, Joan's actions are influenced by a habitus—a set of dispositions—that is not natural or inevitable but, rather, is simply structured to appear as if it were. Joan, however, doesn't recognize the constructedness of the habitus. She is consequently unable to reposition herself in either the field of cultural production or that of power. In order to recuperate Felicia as a central character in "Stalked by Love," for example, Joan simply writes Charlotte out of the narrative, inserting Felicia in her place as conventional heroine and reducing Redmond to a type of pure evil. She then repeats her strategy of transposing the dynamics of her Gothic romances onto her material life, misconstruing the newspaper reporter who pursues her as a captor or murderer who is plotting an end to her new life. For Joan, at the end of the novel as at the beginning, the only position available to women is that of victim.

Thus we arrive at the chief irony of *Lady Oracle*: after all its foregrounding of the contructedness of cultural production, the arbitrariness of power, and the inculcation of dispositions, the novel refuses to take the next step. Instead, it reaffirms the relevance—the rightness—of the very structures it initially resists. Ultimately, *Lady Oracle*, like *Northanger Abbey*, which it resembles, implies not that the protagonist is wrong when she reads the world around her according to the conventions of romance but, rather, that she is right in doing so: while the newspaper reporter at the end of the novel is not literally a Gothic villain, he is a figure of control, making possible (and inevitable) Joan's return to Toronto, the city from which she fled in an attempt to protect herself from the persecution of the various men around her. In reaffirming the relevance of Gothic romance to Joan's material world, the novel obscures the extent to which Joan herself is complicit with the power structures that entrap her.

Even before writing "Lady Oracle," the work that most explicitly complicates her identity as a woman and a wife, Joan is aware of a split in her personality: as Louisa K. Delacourt, she creates countless fictitious affairs with happy endings; as Joan Foster, she struggles to transpose the conventions of romance onto her daily life. However, the prescriptive habitus she naturalizes and carries within herself precludes her from commanding genuine power in either of these fields. *Lady Oracle* thus suggests that despite her attempts to have autonomy and authority in the fields of both cultural production and power, Joan remains unable to change the systems that govern her material and creative worlds. More broadly, the novel raises the question of whether the same might be said of Atwood herself.

—University of Ottawa

NOTES

1. See, for example, *Surfacing*, where the protagonist struggles to recognize her present love life as different from her past one; *The Handmaid's Tale*, where, through her memories of her pre-Gilead life, Offred ironically defines herself against the role of handmaid she is required to play as she documents her present situation; *The Robber Bride*, where Roz, Charis, and Tony, learn to articulate their shared hurt—even if only to themselves—after Zenia resurfaces; or *The Blind Assassin*, where Iris Chase Griffen exposes her husband's brutal infidelity and her own more necessary one in the inset novel purportedly written by Iris's sister, Laura.
2. For other interpretations of the way *Lady Oracle* presents the merging of Joan's creative and personal life as a vital step in the integration of her multiple selves see, for example, Sybil Korff Vincent, "The Mirror and the Cameo: Margaret Atwood's Comic/Gothic Novel, *Lady Oracle*"; Carol L. Beran's "George, Leda, and Poured Concrete Balcony: A Study of Three Aspects of the Evolution of 'Lady Oracle'"; and Ann Parsons's "The Self-Inventing Self: Women Who Lie and Pose in the Fiction of Margaret Atwood."
3. See, for example, *Romance Revisited*, edited by Lynne Pearce and Jackie Stacey.
4. In this respect, Joan's affair repeats previous patterns in her life: as Sue Ann Johnston points out, Joan's reactionary attempt to escape from her mother's hold results in her carrying her mother "around [her] neck like a rotting albatross" (*LO* 226); and, as J. Brooks Bouson (1993) observes, while "through its focus on female obesity, ... *Lady Oracle* rebels against the social discipline and

male control of the female body.... it also depicts the unregulated and undisciplined female body as a grotesque spectacle" (69).

WORKS CITED

Atwood, Margaret. *The Blind Assassin*. Toronto: McClelland & Stewart, 2000.

———. *The Handmaid's Tale*. Boston: Houghton Mifflin, 1986.

———. *Lady Oracle*. [1976]. Toronto: McClelland & Stewart, 1998.

———. *Oryx and Crake*. [2003]. Toronto: Random House, 2004.

———. *The Robber Bride*. [1993]. Toronto: Random House, 1999.

———. *Surfacing*. [1972]. Toronto: McClelland & Stewart, 1994.

Beran, Carol L. "George, Leda, and a Poured Concrete Balcony: A Study of Three Aspects of the Evolution of 'Lady Oracle.'" *Canadian Literature*, no. 112 (1987): 18–28.

Bourdieu, Pierre. *Distinction: A Social Critique of the Judgement of Taste*. Translated by Richard Nice. Cambridge, MA: Harvard University Press, 1984.

———. *The Field of Cultural Production: Essays on Art and Literature*. Edited by Randal Johnson. New York: Columbia University Press, 1993. 29–73.

Bouson, J. Brooks. *Brutal Choreographies: Oppositional Strategies and Narrative Design in the Novels of Margaret Atwood*. Amherst: University of Massachussetts Press, 1993.

Jackson, Stevi. "Women and Heterosexual Love: Complicity, Resistance and Change." In *Romance Revisited*, edited by Lynne Pearce and Jackie Stacey, 49–62. London: Lawrence & Wishart, 1995.

Johnson, Randal. Introduction. *The Field of Cultural Production: Essays on Art and Literature*. By Pierre Bourdieu. New York: Columbia University Press, 1993. 1–25.

Johnston, Sue A. "The Daughter as Escape Artist." *Atlantis* 9, no. 2 (1984): 10–22.

MacLean, Susan. "*Lady Oracle*: The Art of Reality and the Reality of Art." *Journal of Canadian Fiction*, nos. 28–29 (1980): 179–97.

New, W.H. *A History of Canadian Literature*. 2nd ed. Montreal: McGill-Queen's University Press, 2003.

Parsons, Ann. "The Self-Inventing Self: Women Who Lie and Pose in the Fiction of Margaret Atwood." In *Gender Studies: New Directions in Feminist Criticism*, edited by Judith Spector, 97–109. Bowling Green, OH: Bowling Green State University Popular Press, 1986.

Pearce, Lynne, and Jackie Stacey. *Romance Revisited*. London: Lawrence & Wishart, 1995.

Vincent, Sybil K. "The Mirror and the Cameo: Margaret Atwood's Comic/Gothic Novel, *Lady Oracle*." In *The Female Gothic*, edited by Juliann E. Fleena, 155–63. Montreal: Eden Press, 1983.

How Can a Feminist Read *The Handmaid's Tale?* A Study of Offred's Narrative

TAE YAMAMOTO

WHILE *THE HANDMAID'S TALE* has been hailed as "a feminist *1984*," the responses of feminist critics and scholars to all aspects of the novel have not been unanimously positive. In particular, the way that Offred, in falling in love with Nick, seems to niche herself so meekly into a banal romance plot has elicited various evaluations and interpretations, even prompting one critic to argue that the novel's sexual politics are not feminist but nationalist, with the relationship of Offred and Nick symbolizing "ways of 'making do'" in view of Canada's "missionary position under Uncle Sam" (Tomc 91). Critics who take the love plot at face value depict love as a subversive power fighting against the totalitarian regime.[1] Others, such as Gayle Greene and Madonne Miner, argue that the novel's portrait of love is highly qualified, and regret that the novel does not offer any alternative vision (Greene 14–15; Miner 166–67).[2]

I agree with Greene and Miner that the novel's view of love is highly ambivalent, but I would like to offer a slightly different interpretation of the novel's treatment of the love plot in this paper. Offred's account of "the religion of love" is not just a way of circumventing a sad condition but may be seen to pertain to the deep insights of recent gender theory into the role of language in constituting desire and love. Atwood's novel does not aim at offering a decisive solution: it offers a critical anatomy of our condition, informed by her keen awareness of the way a human subject operates in a given linguistic community. It is from these insights that we shall benefit and draw strength for further critical thinking.

Recent theories of gender argue that because we live in the net of language, we cannot conceptualize "Body" or "Sex" unless they are mediated and refracted through language. In *Surfacing* Atwood already grappled with the problem concerning language and human perception. The protagonist realizes that words, with their classifying/differentiating functions, lead us to objectify, manipulate, and finally kill other humans and animals. Her initial reaction is to abandon language and flee, but she decides to go back to human society, acknowledging that we have to use words as long as we live as human beings.[3] More than a decade later, *The Handmaid's Tale* explores how a living subject interacts with the master narrative. Each of us lives in a linguistic community weaving our life stories, and no individual story can exist without referring to the master story prevalent in the community. The stories we weave are imitations or repetitions of the master story, yet those stories in turn help constitute the prevalent discourse in society. For the consideration of this relation of subject and language, few literary texts seem to be more relevant than Offred's self-reflexive narrative in this novel.

To examine the role of narrative or storytelling in *The Handmaid's Tale*, it is helpful first to compare it to *1984*. Both show a deep interest in the relationship of language, or the "story," and the construction of the human subject. In the Oceania of *1984*, Newspeak is invented in order to narrow the range of people's thought, and historical records are perpetually rewritten so that people live in the present in which the Party is always right. What the novel makes clear here is that, without language to communicate one's thoughts or chronological perspective, it is impossible to delineate one's identity as a human subject. In such a situation, Winston keeps a diary, not only because he can fix his thoughts and memories in it but also because it is a "story" that assumes a potential reader. When he starts to write, what he cares about is to whom he is addressing his writing. Even though it may not actually be read by anyone, a writer needs to be assured that what he/she writes can be understood or shared by someone, for that is what makes one a human being.[2]

The handmaids in Gilead are put in a similar situation. Any form of writing (or reading) is forbidden to them. As Offred says, what she needs is perspective, but it is denied them, both physically and chronologically. Symbolically, the only mirror available to Offred is a convex one in which she sees her "face squashed against a wall, everything a huge foreground" (143). Little information of what is happening inside or outside Gilead is given, and she is forced to "live in the moment"(143), thus disabled from forming a self-image in a broader physical/chronological context.[4] Offred's storytelling is the equivalent of Winston's diary in such a state. It is a means by which she can stay a human being, and she also insists that the story is addressed to someone: "You don't tell a story only to yourself. There's always someone else" (40), she says; "I tell you, therefore you are" (268).

There are, however, two characteristics that make Offred's narrative different from that of *1984*. One is the role of the past. The recovery of Winston's lost memory constitutes much of the plot of that novel, but in *The Handmaid's Tale* Offred remembers the pre-Gilead days well. Yearning for the life in the past, she recounts the doctrines and regulations of Gilead in a highly critical tone. Sometimes, however, she finds herself looking at the customs and lifestyles of pre-Gilead from a viewpoint affiliated with Gilead. Seen through Offred's acclimatized eyes, for example, the fashions of pre-Gilead—and of ourselves—seem alien, and are shown to be strange or ridiculous. This reciprocal gaze between the present and the past gives the novel a twofold function. It is a cautionary tale in which the reader, watching the extrapolated, exaggerated horrors of the near future, is warned against any potential for those evils in our own time. It also functions as a satire on our own society, in which our own habits and lifestyles are de-familiarized and criticized through being observed from the viewpoint of an outsider.

The other characteristic that differentiates Atwood's dystopia from Orwell's is its self-reflexivity, emphasized in Offred's statement "All of it is a reconstruction" (134) and in other metafictional asides. One critic thinks that this aspect makes it difficult to valorize the authenticity of her tale, because it is not as "synchronic" as the reader first imagines it to be (Stein 274). In this book, however, the line between the "authentic," "synchronic" narrative and the reconstructed narrative is blurred from the first. Quite early in the book, Offred says:

> I would like to believe this is a story I'm telling. I need to believe it. I must believe it. ...

> It isn't a story I'm telling.
> It's also a story I'm telling, in my head, as I go along. (39)

This passage can be read as a metafictional statement on the nature of storytelling. Offred wishes that what is happening to her now were a story (a fiction/lie), but she has to admit that it is a reality not fiction. Nevertheless, that reality is experienced inevitably as a "story," for no experience can exist for a living subject without being mediated by language. All the phenomena one encounters and the data one receives are processed through "the grid of perception," the software given by one's culture/linguistic community, whose output is an "experience." To put it another way, when you "experience" something, or recall that experience later, the processed data are always organized and reconstructed into a story, comprehensible to you and to others.

Yet we cannot make these stories out of a void; we are using plots or ready-made storylines, which are given by our culture or by our linguistic community.[6] This is where social power intervenes; it is what the regime of Gilead tries to do is, so to speak, to permutate the entire set of processing software, plots, and storylines passable in its society, through the control of words, customs, and ceremonies, to inculcate their view on sex and reproduction into people's minds.

This indoctrination works well with characters like Janine, who ascribes giving birth to "unbabies" to her "sin." As Offred says, "People will do anything rather than admit that their lives have no meaning . . . No plot" (215). Janine clutches at Gilead's doctrine, giving her life a plot of "sin and punishment," because she would not be able to bear the sordid reality of her life otherwise.

Offred refuses to acquiesce to this state and tries to keep a distance from what Gilead teaches her. Throughout most of her narrative, this critical distance is maintained, and the reader assumes that the points of view of the narrative consciousness and of the implied author are approximately the same. There are some moments, however, when the narrative shows that Offred's perceptions are somehow assimilated into Gileadean culture. When she says that her belly aches when she sees a child's funeral, or when she enters into a trance with other handmaids during the birth rite, there seems to be little distance between her consciousness and the Gileadean sense of values.

This kind of identification as shown by these small slips occurs with the codes and views pre-Gilead life, too. Offred thinks that she is the kind of person who is not prone to follow any doctrine, but sometimes, for example, when she thinks of love and sex, the old clichés and stock phrases prevalent in pre-Gilead slip in. The most interesting example is the description of her first encounter with Nick:

> It's so good, to be touched by someone, to be felt so greedily, to feel so greedy. Luke, you'd know, you'd understand. It's you here, in another body.
> Bullshit. (99)

She dramatizes this encounter in her head using the romance of "forbidden love" and the myth of "irrepressible desire," and retracts this version in the next moment. Thus we can see, within the reflective first-person narrative of Offred, small transactions going on between her and prevalent discourses, either of Gilead or pre-Gilead. When the narrator is conscious of, and critical of, prevalent social discourses, there seems to be little distance between the narrative consciousness and the implied author; when the narrator is unaware that she is under the sway of predominant social discourses, the distance seems to become greater. This distance must be carefully gauged if we are to investigate what kind of position the novel takes as a feminist critique.

Meanwhile, it must be added that saying the above does not mean the narrative of this novel deals only with the transaction of Offred's consciousness and prevalent social discourses. On the contrary, her narrative is permeated by a sense of the materiality of her body. The uniqueness of this novel lies in that we can see, in Offred's narrative, how the ideas of body and sex, defined and constructed by society, work itself out through her material body. In her narrative, Offred carefully observes how her own body has come to feel different to herself, how the physical difference affects her actions and her way of thinking. Sometimes resisting and sometimes acquiescing, Offred is affected by the definitions and meanings given to her body; her thought inevitably reflects her changed body, and she acts in however limited ways, thus reacting to this change and forging her story.

What, then, does the novel say about the sexual politics of Gilead and of our society, and what does reading her story teach us?

Lois Feuer says that what makes *The Handmaid's Tale* different from *1984* is the emphasis on "the primacy of the individual human spirit" (Feuer 87–88). One is led to ask, however, how "individual" the desire and feelings of humans are. In this novel, we see that even sexual desire is controlled or heightened by social power. The Commander tells Offred that the regime of Gilead built up their system because they wanted to "create" desire: "You know what they were complaining about the most? Inability to feel. Men were turning off on sex, even. They were turning off on marriage" (210). It is the general idea that power represses spontaneous sexual desire, and that the liberation of sex can be a revolutionary force. The regime of Gilead knows, however, that repression and inhibition produce or heighten desire and so ingeniously manipulate them.[7] Offred herself knows "it's amazing what denial can do" (154), and maliciously uses her body, constituting what little power she has, on young guardians.

Yet, though the proprietors of the regime imagine themselves to be able to control the desire and sexual behaviour of the people, there is nothing original or perceptive in the body politics of Gilead. Enjoying sneaking out with Offred into the brothel full of high-ranking officers, the Commander justifies their behaviour, saying, "Nature demands variety for men" (237). This crude, banal view and his childish appetite for rendezvous and showing off elicit feelings of anger and contempt in Offred. What is behind their architecture and the teachings of the Aunts is nothing but a mock-Victorian, stereotypical double standard for men and women.

Offred revolts against this and raises the importance of falling in love as a counter idea. Thinking back on the "freedom" of pre-Gilead, however, Offred wonders if the love and desire she and other women felt were all that individual, either.[8] The heroines in the films she saw when she was young, "women on their own, making up their minds" (25), and the images of women on the cover of *Vogue*, suggested to women that they were "able to choose" (25); there was "an endless series of possibilities," one adventure after another, one improvement after another, one man after another (157). But Offred is aware that the autonomy and endless possibilities offered to them in those days were illusions made up by the media and the consumer culture. She becomes aware, too, that the yearning and expectation for sex and love that young girls felt, and the religion of love adult women believed in, were rooted in and encouraged by the same culture, goading women to run after these images.

This seems to be a most lucid, insightful analysis of our culture, reached by the narrator and the implied author as well. Then why, I ask, does Offred fall in love again with Nick in such a melodramatic way, after she has become aware of this situation?

This question would be answered in different ways by different groups of critics. Those who think the novel depicts love as subversive force would insist, although acknowledging the illusory nature of the religion of love, that the relationship of Offred with Nick *is* true love with the right man. Those who think the novel is critical of the love plot would argue that Offred unfortunately falls into a plot of the "right" man again. To Miner, for example, the fact that Offred resorts to Harlequin romance-type clichés in her description of her affair with Nick, or that Nick is not Mr. Right but is interchangeable with Luke or the Commander, is evidence that the novel presents Offred's love as stumbling over the same old stone (161–64). Although they do not deny the value of love, Miner and Greene regret that the novel does not offer any new feminist options.

Here, however, I would like to suggest a slightly different way to read Offred's account of their religion of love. Let us look at the following passage:

> God is love, they once said, but we reversed that, and love, like heaven, was always just around the corner. The more difficult it was to love the particular man beside us, the more we believed in Love, abstract and total. We were waiting, always, for the incarnation. That word, made flesh. (225–26)

If we follow Miner's discussion, this is the trap that could be avoided if a new option for feminists were to be discovered. But that seems not likely to be the case. After our consideration of the relation of the master narrative and the story of an individual, this passage rather seems to be elucidating the fundamental condition of human subjects.

Lacan explains how our desire is not our own but the desire of the Other which is fundamentally unattainable; similarly, Zizek describes men's love as an infinite, metonymic movement to seek for Woman with a capital W (115).[9] Although Atwood is not a direct follower of Lacan, she also seems to be talking here about Love with a capital L, which can never be attained. Here, Love with a capital L is explained as one of the master stories of our society. We live under the sway of this master story, and each of us, when we fall in love with an individual human being, lives a repetition, or version, of the master story. The experience of love in actual life is always somewhat different from the master story of Love and is, therefore, unsatisfactory; but we attribute this failure and dissatisfaction to our attitude or to having chosen the wrong partner, and continue to change men or change ourselves, metonymically. Love with a capital L, however, is a metaphor, a collective ideal, that is constructed *ex post facto*; it reveals itself only through our individual experience of love. Yet to each of us, Love with a capital L seems to have ontological existence, to be "just around the corner" (226), which should be actualized in our life some day; and the myth of Love continues to be consolidated.

This reading would explain why Offred, trying to describe her affair with Nick, falters with stock phrases and clichés and abandons them, saying it did not happen this way or that way. This is not a sign that her love was not a "true" one. It is because, whatever her experience with Nick may be like, it is a version of Love; however hard she might try to capture the experience, as she rightly says, "the way love feels is always only approximate" (263), and we have to use our stock of ready-made stories to reconstruct it. In retrospect Offred hovers between boasting of her love for its extremity and seriousness, and rationalizing it as "making a life for oneself" (271). However unsatisfactory and inconclusive it may sound, we can only grope for an approximate explanation of our experience.[10] We cannot abandon the love plot altogether, for we need to have stories to live, and it is impossible to have an original, individual story without referring to the master story.[11]

If we are to read Offred's narrative and her affair as a parable revealing the relation of the master story and the individual story, then the disappointment of some feminists at not having a more authentic feminist alternative seems to be off the mark; if Offred were to follow such a cause, it would mean taking up and following another, heroic master story. It seems also irrelevant to seek for the moral solution, say, that Offred is rescued because she finds the true love; with whom she is to be in love and if it would lead to her rescue, are matters of contingency. Glenn Deer sees a tension between Offred's narrative skill and her powerlessness as a victim (216, 225–26). I would like to paraphrase this thesis and say that the conflict embedded in this novel is the one between the acknowledgment of the discursive system in which a subject is caught and the ethical drive that strives for the agency of the individual: if we are caught in the discursive system and simply repeat the master story, where can we exert our agency, and how can we change the situation?

I do not think Atwood gives a clear answer to this question in this novel. Instead, she presents an analysis of the master story and a description of Offred's actions, whose consequences are unknown. To read Offred's narrative in this way, however, is revealing for feminists in positive ways. The book tells us, as does *Surfacing*, that "we cannot go out of our language system, but we can know what kind of system we are in." Moreover, we have Offred as our narrator, with whom we can feel empathy. Although the scope for actions is limited, she nonetheless thinks, feels, and acts in a given environment, and the outcome of her actions is unknown. On this particular fact, we should base our hope for change. And this is why, although both the autocracy and the "freer" consumerist culture are criticized in this novel, I believe Atwood prefers the latter, because the worst of these evils is to rob one of the freedom to tell one's own version of a story. While we cannot escape from the master plot, we go on telling our individual story, which signifies a slightly different repetition each time it is told, and this is where the possibility for change lies.

—Doshisha University

NOTES

1. See, for example, Barbara Ehrenreich (34), Lois Feuer (86), and Amin Malak (15). Lucy M. Freibert thinks that "Offred's real breakthrough to her courageous sexual self" comes with her affair with Nick (288).
2. Linda S. Kauffman also thinks that Atwood deconstructs the ideology of love (251).
3. In this sense, I regard *The Handmaid's Tale* to be the successor of *Surfacing* as a feminist critique that shows Atwood's deep interest in language, rather than perceiving the shift of the positions between the two books. For the analysis of the role of language in *Surfacing*, see Yamamoto "Mou Hitotsu no Gengo no Tankyu."
4. I discussed this theme elsewhere (Yamamoto, "Metafikushon" 95–100).
5. Hilde Staels connects the absence of mirrors with the loss of self-reflection and of identity (116).

6. Marta Dvorak, in her study of Atwood's use of visual images in popular culture, discusses how "the technologies of (institutionalized) discourse" construct our perception and "dictate how we see and how we value ourselves and the Other" (144).
7. See Kauffman's careful analysis of the paradox of sexual repression and her examination of the analogy and disparity between Foucauldian theory and Atwood's assertion in the novel (249–51).
8. Kauffman also says that we should be cautious against interpreting the novel "as a paean to individual freedom" (251).
9. I'm indebted here to Kazuko Takemura, who refers to Lacan and Zizek in her discussion of women's desire (111–12).
10. In other words, in reading Offred's statements, which I cite in this paragraph, I don't see a great distance between the narrative consciousness and that of the implied author.
11. This would also explain why handmaids resent Aunt Lydia's announcement at the Salvaging that they are not to be told what kinds of crime have been committed. The crimes of others show them what they might be capable of; they need models and stories to take after.

WORKS CITED

Atwood, Margaret. *The Handmaid's Tale*. [1985] New York: Ballantine, 1996.

Deer, Glenn. "Rhetorical Strategies in *The Handmaid's Tale*: Dystopia and the Paradoxes of Power." *English Studies in Canada* 18, no. 2 (1992): 215–33.

Dvorak, Marta. "What is Real/Reel? Margaret Atwood's 'Rearrangement of Shapes on a Flat Surface,' or Narrative as Collage." In *Modern Critical Interpretations: Margaret Atwood's "The Handmaid's Tale,"* edited by Harold Bloom, 141–54. Philadelphia: Chelsea House, 2000.

Ehrenreich, Barbara. "Feminism's Phantoms." *The New Republic* (March 17, 1986): 33–35.

Feuer, Lois. "The Calculus of Love and Nightmare: *The Handmaid's Tale* and the Dystopian Tradition." *Critique* 38, no. 2 (1997): 83–95.

Freibert, Lucy M. "Control and Creativity: The Politics of Risk in Margaret Atwood's *The Handmaid's Tale*." In *Critical Essays on Margaret Atwood*, edited by Judith McCombs, 280–91. Boston: Hall, 1988.

Greene, Gayle. "Choice of Evils." *The Women's Review of Books* 3, no. 10 (1986): 14–15.

Kauffman, Linda S. *Special Delivery: Epistolary Modes in Modern Fiction*. Chicago and London: University of Chicago Press, 1992.

Malak, Amin. "Margaret Atwood's *The Handmaid's Tale* and the Dystopian Tradition." *Canadian Literature*, no. 112 (1987): 9–16.

Miner, Madonne. "'Trust Me': Reading the Romance Plot in Margaret Atwood's *The Handmaid's Tale.*" *Twentieth Century Literature* 37, no. 2 (1991): 148–68.
Staels, Hilde. "Margaret Atwood's *The Handmaid's Tale*: Resistance through Narrating." In *Modern Critical Interpretations: Margaret Atwood's "The Handmaid's Tale,"* edited by Harold Bloom, 113–26. Philadelphia: Chelsea House, 2000.
Stein, Karen F. "Margaret Atwood's *The Handmaid's Tale*: Scheherazade in Dystopia." *University of Toronto Quarterly* 61, no. 2 (1991/1992): 269–79.
Takemura, Kazuko. *Ai ni Tsuite* [On Love: Identity, Desire, and Politics]. Tokyo: Iwanami, 2002. In Japanese.
Tomc, Sandra. "The Missionary Position: Feminism and Nationalism in Margaret Atwood's *The Handmaid's Tale.*" *Canadian Literature*, nos. 138–39 (1993): 73–87.
Yamamoto, Tae. "Metafikushion to Shiteno *1984* to *Frankenstein* [Reading *1984* and *Frankenstein* as metafiction]." *Doshisha Studies in English*, no. 68 (1997): 93–122. In Japanese.
———. "Mou Hitotsu no Gengo no Tankyu [In search of 'Another Language': An interpretation of Margaret Atwood's *Surfacing*]." In *Fikushion no Shoso* [Aspects of Fiction: Papers Dedicated to Professor Nobunao Matsuyama on His Seventieth Birthday]. Tokyo: Eihosha, 1999. 267–86. In Japanese.
Zizek, Slavoj. *For They Know Not What They Do: Enjoyment as a Political Factor.* 2nd ed. London: Verso, 2002.

"Lurid Yet Muted": Narrative and the Sabotage of Dissident Voice in Margaret Atwood's *Alias Grace*

JULIE GODIN

> The colours never came out clear. ... There was a misty look to them, as if they were seen through cheesecloth. They didn't make the people seem more real, rather they became ultra-real: citizens of an odd half-country, lurid yet muted, where realism was beside the point.
> —Atwood, *The Blind Assassin*

THE READER, THE scholar, and the critic know too well the moment, at the end of Margaret Atwood's *The Handmaid's Tale*, when "historical notes" intrude to operate a drastic repositioning of the narrative, which is suddenly configured as a problematic, mediated, "*soi-disant* manuscript" that has been shaped from jumbled recordings by a team of historians. Abruptly inserting a qualifying frame of temporal and intellectual distance, the text produces an editor, who addresses a gathering of colleagues to smugly declare his own adherence to a vision of ideological neutrality, and to remind his audience that "the past is a great darkness, filled with echoes" (*HT* 293). In a startling instant, our plucky handmaid, a covert agent of resistance whose elaborate confession of dissidence has detailed the workings of an immense machine of oppression, evaporates in favour of "L'histoire, cette vieille dame éxaltée et menteuse" (qtd in BA 163).

The instability of historical discourses and the problematic ways in which the ex-centric or dissident subject reaches us, embedded in structures of narration and comprehension, are assembled in Margaret Atwood's *Alias Grace*. By incorporating a "juxtaposition ... of official and authorized texts"—published histories, newspaper clippings, interviews, confessions, letters, poems—with "more overtly fictionalized" narrative segments (Cormier Michael 421), *Alias Grace* enacts a democratization of history, a version of what Jacques Rancière calls the "space of an *everything speaks*" (58). Grace is a young immigrant girl, a maid-of-all-work, a criminal, a prisoner, a patient, an experimental subject. Simultaneously, she is subaltern, assimilated, unremarkable, yet also infamous, extraordinary, deviant, as the novel assembles established explanatory scripts that would "fix" and stabilize her. Do these self-reflexive scripts or "aliases" sustain alterity, or do they instead evacuate the possibility of a dissident voice rising above the din of gathered cultural and literary constructs?

While much has been written about this novel's presentation of a disruptive, alternative "'patchwork' model for representing the past" (Cormier Michael 441),[1] I want to reconsider the text's function as a literary operation that presides over the constitution of the dissident subject, keeping in mind Rancière's (somewhat cynical) reminder that literature "suppresses and maintains at the same time, it neutralizes by its own means the condition that makes history possible and historical science impossible: the unhappy property that the human being has of being a literary animal" (52).

I. TRACING THE "INFAMOUS LIFE"

The word "alias," which in English points to a deliberate slippage or substitution of names, is used in Latin (*alius* or *alia*) to signify "another, other, different." *Alias Grace*'s celebrated patchwork structure functions not only to problematize our reception of the "echoes" that reach us as history but also to self-reflexively develop a subject who is always yet *another* thing.

Grace can be read within the novel's textured cultural landscape as a romantic figure, but also as a dissatisfied, resentful worker, a hysterical woman, a victim of spectral forces, a manipulative sinner, and a psychological or neurological anomaly.[2] The text provides an elaborate compendium of explanatory structures, and Grace, the maid-of-all-work, discloses the extent to which the cultural work of interpretation is to be anticipated and directed by a narrative apparatus that generates its own repertory for the revelation of deviance. In a kind of keepsake book gathering dominant scripts of the female ex-centric, troubled, or delinquent subject in nineteenth-century literary and popular culture, she acknowledges these constructs and the way in which she has been "picked up" by "collectors" (41) and required to provide "a right answer, which is right because it is the one they want, and you can tell by their faces whether you have guessed what it is" (40). Delivered with self-referential nods to the discursive and literary modes that are assembled in her narrative, Grace's first-person "answer" to the confessional framings of her story serves to catalogue and critique, but also to fulfill the cultural expectations that attend her self-revelation as a nineteenth-century murderess. "Wring your hands in anguish," she mimics ironically, "describe how the eyes of your victims follow you around the room, burning like red-hot coals ... confess, confess. Let me forgive and pity ... tell me all" (35).

In her detailed, elaborate narrative, then, does she not enact the workings of normalization as envisaged by Michel Foucault—a normalization that "proceeds by way of confession" (6)? John Caputo and Mark Yount remind us that Foucault's reading of institutions does not credit power relations with the abolition of the individual but, rather, with the production of subjects whose "exceedingly personal dossiers, elaborate records of ... individual life and personal history" are known, precisely because "patients are brought out of the dark chamber of the prison and endowed with the power to speak" (6).

In "The Dangerous Individual," Foucault traces what he sees as a social and institutional requirement that the accused subject provide not simply an admission of criminal acts, but "confession, self-examination, explanation of oneself, revelation of what one is" (*Politics* 126). This discourse is necessary to the extent that the accused subject is urged, pushed, if he does not "play the game":

> He is not unlike those condemned persons who have to be carried to the guillotine or the electric chair because they drag their feet. They really ought to walk a little by themselves, if indeed they want to be executed. They really ought to speak a little about themselves, if they want to be judged. (127)

For *Alias Grace*'s first-person narrator, disclosure provides the structure that contains and carries the subject inexorably: "I must go on with the story. Or the story must go on with me, carrying me inside it, along the tracks it must travel" (298).

II. A KEEPSAKE BOOK

Foucault, who, as we know, turned much of his attention to the excavation of what he called "singular lives," endeavoured to anthologize such "existences" and, in the case of his *La vie des hommes infâmes*, to create "une sorte d'herbier," (237)³ a book of preserved yet long-extinguished deviances:

> I have looked for obscure lives ... without the privileges of birth, fortune, holiness, heroism or genius; [I have wanted that there be] in their mishaps, their passions, in these loves and hatreds something grey and ordinary to the gaze that usually considers what is worthy of being told; [I have wanted] that yet they be marked by a certain ardour, that they be animated by a violence, an energy, an excess in malevolence, villainy, baseness, stubbornness or ill-fate that will have given them, in the eyes of their entourage ... a kind of awesome or pitiful greatness. (240)

In the archives of imprisonment that Foucault presents, haphazardly found documents formulate the points of contact at which these ex-centric, delinquent lives encounter the workings of a power apparatus that would enumerate, describe, and classify them. Would there be any remains of these violent and singular subjects, asks Foucault, if they had not at some point encountered and provoked the machinery of control? Do we not find in the "brief and strident" language that circulates between the forces of power and the most "inessential" lives the only monument, the only memorial that might carry word of these lives across time to us (241)?

Alias Grace is structured much in keeping with Foucault's observations of the extent to which the "singular life" is reduced to flashpoints across the grids and structures that contain and construct the subject. The novel establishes a structure by which Grace's "confessional" narrative is situated within a textual rendering of its own reception according to a series of cultural scripts: we note, for instance, a literary script of beautiful, enigmatic suffering, a popular "law and order" script of fascination and outrage, and a psychoanalytic script of hysteria. Each dominant "brief and strident" memorial to the historical subject "Grace Marks" is externally or paratextually[4] featured in an epigraph or other "keepsake," but also "internally" incorporated into a narrative homage to Victorian culture. The text thus demonstrates a further layering of discursive functions, by enacting and ironizing the application of constructs it has captured. When, for example, the novel refers to nineteenth century romance, it incorporates literary markers of the genre, even while the subject narrates her construction as an iconic reminder of romantic convention, and her own participation in proffering the stylistic and generic hallmarks of romance. "If I laughed out loud ... it would spoil their romantic notion of me," asserts Grace, who self-consciously attributes her use of overblown descriptive formulas to the influence of Sir Walter Scott. Strikingly, in recounting a moment of closeness with Mary, the fellow servant whose death will precipitate Grace's hysteric outbursts, Grace suggestively notes that Mary "wrapped [her] up in a sheet" as she made her way to the attic, and told her she "looked very comical, just like a madwoman" (132). The novel further develops the dominance of a Victorian tradition of sensation and crime novel by playing out the deployment of supernatural/spiritual open-ended discourses against scientific/legal vocabularies of expertise and closure.[5]

III. PLAYING THE PSYCHOANALYTIC GAME

One of these specialized, authoritative discourses, as I have proposed, is clinical psychoanalysis, positioned here as a framing script according to which the troubled, hysterical subject narrates "memories" and dreams proffered specifically for the barely suppressed enjoyment of her therapist. The analyst, Dr. Simon Jordan, is introduced as inhabiting a nightmare parody of classical psychoanalytic clichés. An admirer of Charcot who recalls his own (very Freudian) childhood seduction by his family's servant girl, Simon is tormented by a sullen maid named Dora,[6] whom he figures as resembling a "disappointed baby," and hostilely describes as having a mind that is "cunning, slippery and evasive. There is no way to corner her. She's a greased pig" (61). Such layered ironies should warn us against the temptation of reading the product of his "talking cure" without taking into account the mediating and distorting framing structure that shapes it. Grace's narrative reaches the reader through a play of revelations and withholdings that constitutes a therapeutic "story rich in incident ... as a sort of reward" to the analyst (247). As Grace receives validation for voicing her elaborate dreams, the libidinal economy is undeniable:

> Dr. Jordan is writing eagerly, as if his hand can scarcely keep up, and I have never seen him so animated before. It does my heart good to feel I can bring a little pleasure into a fellow-being's life, and I think to myself, I wonder what he will make of all that. (281)

Adding to this distancing mirror-within-a-mirror effect fostered by the novel, the self-revelation of this "awful and pitiful" subject is received, within the text, according to a recognition of the movement by which one "can deceive by feigning to deceive" (73). Slavoj Zizek discusses this kind of double deception as it is exemplified in popular culture, and mentions notably a scene enacted by the Marx Brothers:

> Groucho defends his client before the court of law with the following argument in favour of his insanity: "This man *looks* like an idiot and *acts* like an idiot—but this should in no way deceive you: He IS an idiot!".... By "pretending to be something," by acting as if we "were something," we assume a certain place in the inter-subjective symbolic network, and it is this external place that defines our true position. If we remain convinced, deep within ourselves, that "we are not really that," if we preserve an intimate distance toward "the social role we play," we doubly deceive ourselves ... for in the social-symbolic reality things ultimately are precisely what they pretend to be. (74)

Grace narrates the manifestations of what Dr. Jordan expects to be her "hidden" inner subjectivity, by revealing the very indicia of hysteria that he requires, and she offers for his tireless transcription every sign, every literary component of the classification with which she constantly wrestles:[7] that of a classic Victorian hysteric. Dr. Jordan states that he cannot "shake the suspicion that ... she is lying," and his response to her is structured as if she were "deceiving *by means of truth itself*" (Zizek 73): she looks and acts like a Victorian hysteric, and *that* should in no way deceive him as to her being, in fact, a Victorian hysteric. Dr. Jordan's deepest moment of anxiety occurs as he clings to the logic according to which "we effectively *become* something by *pretending we already are that*" (73). Perturbed by the spectacle of Grace's hypnosis, he "knows what he saw and heard, but he may have been shown an illusion, which he cannot prove to have been one" (407).

In this uneasy sense that the murderess has been revealed to be *alias*—another, different—(yet continues to elude this), the reader recognizes the lingering question at the heart of this novel. To paraphrase John Caputo's examination of Foucault's legacy, if there is no "message from the depths" (247), if the subject is simply produced in various modalities, and nothing but additional constructs are shown to be repressed, lost, or silenced along the way, why worry about the forms that this literary formulation of "Grace Marks" has taken? "If nothing is repressed," suggests Caputo, "then nothing is to be liberated" (248). The narrating power of the murderess, in this novel, never announces itself as a liberated, or liberating function, but is rendered instead as a framed, crowded, saturated element through which the subject can keep moving. That movement, as we see in *Alias Grace* and subsequently in *The Blind Assassin*, disturbs configurations of victimhood and oppression, and complicates our attempts to distinguish the dissident, the normalized, the clandestine, or the authorized. These texts remove the threat of sabotage and the promise of empowerment, but offer an oblique, perverse, and resilient opportunity to shift and reconfigure, to decide, as Atwood does in *Murder in the Dark* (1983), that

> if you like, you can play games with this game. You can say: the murderer is the writer, the detective is the reader, the victim is the book. Or perhaps, the murderer is the writer, the detective is the critic, and the victim is the reader. ... In any case, that's me in the dark. (30)

—University of Ottawa

NOTES

1. See Cormier Michael: "The novel's patchwork quilt design functions as ... an alternative in its ability to unsettle and move beyond authoritative (patrilineal) discourses and forms and, at the same time, conditionally authorize previously marginalized discourses and forms" (441). On reading the "patchwork" of *Alias Grace*, see also Jennifer Murray and Marie Delord.

2. Hilde Staels goes as far as to provide a case history and diagnosis ("multiple or dissociative identity disorder" [437]) for the novel's "Grace Marks": "Grace Marks has a history of repressing painful memories ... her fits of hysteria and her traumatic amnesia result from the early loss of her mother and presumably from sexual abuse by her father" (436).
3. The translation of Foucault's preface to *La vie des homes infâmes* is my own. I prefer to keep the word "herbier," which speaks to the preservation of something that was once alive.
4. Cormier Michael discusses the status of paratext in *Alias Grace* (431–32).
5. I am thinking, for example, of Wilkie Collins's *The Woman in White*, in which an eerie, fantastical, irrational element (the "appearing" woman) is transmuted into one cog in an elaborate legal problem of property rights.
6. On Dora in *Alias Grace*, see Staels (433). On the feminist and critical "cult of Dora," see Showalter (57–58).
7. For a discussion of the theatricality and variety of hysterical symptoms, see Showalter (Chap. 3). Grace does exhibit precisely the types of reactions and behaviours that would have confirmed a diagnosis: "fits," amnesia, "visual disturbances," somnambulism, suggestiveness to hypnosis.

WORKS CITED

Atwood, Margaret. *Alias Grace*. Toronto: McClelland & Stewart, 1996.

———. *The Blind Assassin*. Toronto: McClelland & Stewart, 2000.

———. *The Handmaid's Tale*. Toronto: McClelland & Stewart, 1985.

———. *Murder in the Dark*. Toronto: Coach House, 1983.

Caputo, John. "On Not Knowing Who We Are: Madness, Hermeneutics, and the Night of Truth in Foucault." In *Foucault and the Critique of Institutions*, edited by John Caputo and Mark Yount, 233–62. University Park: Pennsylvania State University Press, 1993.

Caputo, John and Mark Yount. "Institutions, Normalization, Power." In *Foucault and the Critique of Institutions*, edited by John Caputo and Mark Yount, 3–23. University Park: Pennsylvania State University Press, 1993.

Cormier Michael, Magali. "Rethinking History as a Patchwork: The Case of Atwood's *Alias Grace*." *Modern Fiction Studies* 47, no. 2 (2001): 421–47.

Delord, Marie. "A Textual Quilt: Margaret Atwood's *Alias Grace*." *Études canadiennes/Canadian Studies*, no. 46 (1999): 111–121.

Foucault, Michel. *Dits et Écrits*. Vol. 2. 1976–1988. Paris: Gallimard, 2001.

———. *Politics, Philosophy, Culture*. New York and London: Routledge, 1988.

Murray, Jennifer. "Historical Figures and Paradoxical Pattern: The Quilting Metaphor in Margaret Atwood's *Alias Grace*." *Studies in Canadian Literature/Études en littérature canadienne* 26, no.1 (2001): 65–83.

Rancière, Jacques. *The Names of History: On the Poetics of Knowledge*. Minneapolis: University Minnesota Press, 1994.

Showalter, Elaine. *Hystories: Hysterical Epidemics and Modern Media*. New York: Columbia University Press, 1997.

Staels, Hilde. "Intertexts of Margaret Atwood's *Alias Grace*." *Modern Fiction Studies* 46, no. 2 (2000): 427–50.

Zizek, Slavoj. *Looking Awry: An Introduction to Lacan through Popular Culture*. Cambridge, MA: MIT, 1991.

A Contemporary Psychologist Looks at Atwood's Construction of Personality in *Alias Grace*

REGINA M. EDMONDS

GRACE MARKS INTRIGUES and confounds us. In spite of ourselves, we are drawn in by the brutality of the murders of Nancy Montgomery and Thomas Kinnear and by the lack of clarity regarding Grace's participation in the planning and execution of these deaths. There is a certain thrill we find hard to resist in contemplating the image of a murderess. As Grace herself says:

> ... *Murderess* is a strong word to have attached to you. It has a smell to it, that word—musky and oppressive, like dead flowers in a vase. Sometimes at night I whisper it over to myself: *Murderess, Murderess*. It rustles, like a taffeta skirt across the floor. (*AG* 22–23)

But Grace also perplexes and frustrates us. How is it possible for someone to be present at a murder and recall almost nothing about it? Is Grace putting us on when she claims amnesia for significant portions of the day on which the murders occurred? Can memories of such power really be repressed and then mysteriously recalled under hypnosis? In short, is Grace guilty of murder or not? We are not alone in our fascination with these questions, as Atwood's novel, *Alias Grace*, exists to untangle this very knot.

Dr. Jordan, hired to evaluate Grace and to arrive at a decision about her complicity in the killings of Nancy Montgomery and Thomas Kinnear, is struggling in the dark. He is trying to piece together a strategy for recovering Grace's lost memories for the crucial hours when Nancy was struck with an ax and then strangled. However, as Elaine Showalter and Janet Oppenheim both point out in *The Female Malady* and *Shattered Nerves*, respectively, Dr. Jordan is doing so in 1859 without the benefit of some of the most creative thinking about amnesia, dissociation, and hysteria ever developed, since the writings of Charcot, Janet, and Freud are still at least ten years into the future.

There is no doubt that Dr. Jordan would have had an easier time fathoming Grace's psychological state had he interviewed her fifteen years after doing so. But even now, how much more do we know about the complex processes of memory, dissociation, and altered states of consciousness, as well as the impact of traumatic experience on all of these processes? The answer is, we know a great deal. In fact, sometimes the immensity of the scientific literature on this topic is overwhelming. But even with our expanded knowledge, will we be able to determine Grace's guilt or innocence, or will we end up like Dr. Jordan, fundamentally confused? Let us see.

Contemporary psychology has come a long way in understanding puzzling aspects of memory. One of the most important findings is that memories formed under conditions of trauma are different from ordinary memories in a variety of ways (see B. van der Kolk et al.). For one thing, these memories have very powerful and precise sensory components. Very often, rape victims remember the smell of the perpetrator or vivid images of some aspect of the room where the crime occurred. They may remember the roughness of the perpetrator's fingers or the colour of the shirt sleeve momentarily caught in peripheral vision. The sensations recalled by trauma victims are so intense, vivid, and unchanging that some have referred to them as flashbulb memories in the sense that they forever capture aspects of the event with amazing accuracy and sensory detail, much as a flash camera precisely freezes a moment in time. But just like a photograph, memories stored during trauma are only fragments of the situation. Other important details are often lost or inaccessible to the individual because the altered state of alertness fundamentally influences the individual's field of vision. Judith L. Herman, in her influential book *Trauma and Recovery*, captures this dual character of memories formed during trauma and discusses what she calls the "dialectic of trauma" (47) to help us understand how such memories can be paradoxically both extremely precise but also incomplete.

Memories stored during trauma also differ from ordinary memories because they lack a coherent narrative storyline. Often a trauma victim will have an especially difficult time providing a clear sense of what actually happened. Someone surviving a serious car accident might say, "There was noise. I saw her screaming; it all happened so fast. I smelled the radiator fluid; it was burning," and so forth. Here we see the predominance of the sensory images, a fragmented quality of the recall, and little ability to relate the step-by-step sequence of the events as they unfolded. Herman again provides a powerful explanation for this: "Certain violations of the social compact are too terrible to utter aloud: this is the meaning of the word *unspeakable*" (1). Lenore Terr, another expert in the treatment of trauma, reiterates this same idea and even names one of her books *Too Scared to Cry*. Likewise, Bessel A. van der Kolk, in his article, "Trauma and Memory," provides us with insight into the actual changes in the brain that underlie what he calls a "state of speechless terror" (286) by referring to brain imaging studies done with symptomatic trauma survivors. In these studies, brain scans are taken while victims are simultaneously presented with stimuli that evoke memories of their trauma. These brain scans show, as expected, increased activity in centres of the brain involved in processing emotion and sensation, but also reveal a marked decrease in activity in the section of the brain called Broca's area, the part of the brain involved in the translation of experience into speech. It seems that on a physiological level, the area of the brain most directly involved in the creation of the language necessary to describe, in a logical and orderly fashion, the sequence of events occurring during a highly traumatic experience is all but shut down, literally rendering the victim speechless.

Throughout *Alias Grace*, Atwood magnificently captures the elements unique to memories formed during trauma. For example, consider the red peonies that repeatedly appear in Grace's dreams and waking reveries; when Grace describes them, we can see them too—vivid and bright, but fragmented and associated with terror and confusion:

> It's dark as stone in this room and hot as a roasting heart; if you stare into the darkness with your eyes open you are sure to see something after a time. I hope it will not be flowers. But this is the time they grow, the red flowers, the shining red peonies which are like satin,

which are like splashes of red paint. The soil for them is emptiness, it is empty space and silence. (297)

When Grace describes her difficulty in responding to questions during her murder trial, we are provided with another fine example of speechlessness in the face of terror: "I was there in the box of the dock but I might as well have been made of cloth, stuffed, with a china head; and I was shut up inside that doll of myself, and my true voice could not get out" (295). We see this again when Grace attempts to construct a logical narrative recapturing the events occurring on the day of the murders:

When you are in the middle of a story, it isn't a story at all, but only a confusion; a dark roaring, a blindness, a wreckage of shattered glass and splintered wood; like a house in a whirlwind, or else a boat crushed by icebergs or swept over by rapids, and all aboard powerless to stop it. It's only afterwards that it becomes anything like a story at all. (298)

These examples certainly deepen our understanding of the impact of trauma upon memory formation, but how do they relate to amnesia? It would seem, from what has been said, that memories of traumatic events would be impossible to "forget," that they are indelibly burned into the memory structures of the brain. And so they are, if a person has experienced just one horrific event. But what if a person is subject to repeated acts of violence? What if this individual is captive with no means of escape? And what if this person is a child who has few resources for protection other than knowing how to hide, both literally and figuratively, and how to engage the imagination in fantasy play? How will memory be affected in this circumstance? What we find is that the research on this is becoming clearer all the time. When an individual shows profound amnesia for terrible events, it almost always occurs in someone who has been subjected to severe neglect or abuse during early childhood or who has witnessed the violent death of a parent (see Braun and Sachs; Cameron; Kluft; Putnam; Ross et al.; Vitkus; Wilbur). Children repeatedly confronted with terrifying events over which they have no control seek asylum within their own imaginations. The terrible things are not happening to them but to a dolly or a bad girl with a different name. They create places of safety and watch the events from that perspective, cut off from the bodily sensations accompanying the terrifying situation. In short, they split themselves into pieces, one part registering the events occurring in reality, another part hiding elsewhere. Most children are good at pretending and since that helps them modulate extreme feelings of fear, they use this mechanism, which psychologists call dissociation, repeatedly. The *Diagnostic and Statistical Manual,* a text used by psychologists to describe disorders, defines dissociation as "a disruption in the usually integrated functions of consciousness, memory, identity or perception of the environment" (American Psychiatric Association 477). This definition captures well what we have been describing here. Once children become skilled at dissociation, they can call up this protective state fairly easily. Eventually, dissociation may become an almost automatic response to any highly charged emotional situation that resembles the traumatizing situation in which the dissociation was learned originally.

Cosette, a character in Victor Hugo's *Les Misérables,* who has been left with neglectful and probably abusive caretakers, provides clear illustrations of dissociation. In Alain Boubil and Claude-Michel Schönberg's musical version of the story Cosette sings, "There is a castle on a cloud, I like to go there in my sleep. Aren't any floors for me to sweep, not in my castle on a cloud."[1] And when Cosette sings this, we see that castle and we understand that this form of dissociation makes sense and allows Cosette to survive and maintain hope. Thus, dissociation is not so strange after all; in fact, all of us experience it from time to time. The most common example occurs when we are driving. Often we become "lost in thought," but if a truck pulls out in front of us suddenly, our attention is once again riveted on the road. Not only can we split our attention in this way while driving but we also experience a minor form of amnesia. Often we have no clear memory of how we have got from one place to the next; no specific recall for turning right at the corner, left at the light. In other words, dissociation is almost always paired with some degree of memory distortion. When we look at the function of dissociation for traumatized children, we can see that when it is coupled with memory loss for horrific events, it is all that more potent a protective strategy. We know, from the aforementioned studies, that a large number of traumatized individuals who use dissociation become very skilled at blocking these unwanted memories from awareness by hiding them behind "amnestic barriers." We also know that children are the most skilled at dissociation and that traumatic amnesias are what van der Kolk and his colleague Rita Fisler describe as "age and dose related: the younger the age at the time of the trauma, and the more prolonged the traumatic event, the greater the likelihood of significant amnesia" (509). Herman also explores the relationship of age to the skill of forgetting, thus stating:

> Repeated trauma in adult life erodes the structure of a personality already formed, but repeated trauma in childhood forms and deforms the personality. The child trapped in an abusive environment is faced with formidable tasks of adaptation. She must find a way to preserve a sense of trust in people who are untrustworthy, safety in a situation that is unsafe, control in a situation that is terrifyingly unpredictable, power in a situation of helplessness. Unable to care for or protect herself, she must compensate for the failures of adult care and protection with the only means at her disposal, an immature system of psychological defenses.
>
> The pathological environment of childhood abuse forces the development of extraordinary capacities, both creative and destructive. It fosters the development of abnormal states of consciousness, in which the ordinary relations of body and mind, reality and imagination, knowledge and memory no longer hold. (96)

Returning once again to *Alias Grace*, we see that Atwood has developed the character of Grace in ways that are remarkably consistent with the picture of dissociation and amnesia just described. Not only has Grace suffered more loss during childhood than most of us can imagine but she also uses predictable ways of creating amnesia for these events. Grace's first profound loss comes with the death of her mother, which she witnessed as a child. Grace repeatedly flashes back to this scene and conveys to us the utter abandonment it signified. Hope Edelman, in her book *Motherless Daughters*, speaks movingly about the devastation most women experience in their childhood when they have lost their mothers, and gives us additional insight into how central Grace's loss of her mother is to her psychological development.

While Grace does not dissociate during this initial loss, she nevertheless tries to control its devastating consequences by numbing herself and showing some precursors of personality splitting. She says, "I did not cry. I felt as if it was me and not my mother that had died; and I sat as if paralyzed" (120). Linda Luecken, in her study on parental loss, shows that the impact of a parent's death can be lessened if the remaining parent is supportive and able to maintain the stability of the family, but this was clearly not the case with Grace's father, who not only neglected his children but physically abused them as well. In addition to the lack of care from her father, Grace becomes separated from her siblings not too long after the family's arrival in Canada, and eventually loses all connection to them. All of these profound losses have the predicted impact upon the formation of Grace's personality.

With subsequent losses, especially the death of Mary Whitney, her "truest and indeed the only friend" (174), Grace's defenses intensify and we begin to see the first full-blown episodes of dissociation and amnesia. As the members of the household assemble to pay their respects to Mary, the reality of her death hits Grace and she falls "to the floor in a dead faint" (179). Although Grace recalls fainting, she does not remember waking ten hours later, crying, running about, and then falling into another profound sleep. Grace tells us, "I had no memory of anything I said or did during the time I was awake, between the two long sleeps; and this worried me" (180). Once Grace develops the ability to block out her consciousness of intolerable events, her use of this defense escalates. Grace "faints" and remains "hysterical" for a long period of time after she encounters the "head-measuring doctor" (29–30), who reminds her of the abortionist responsible for Mary Whitney's death. Again, during a thunderstorm Grace has what she thinks is a "strange dream" of walking outside in the night and encountering many horrors (279–81), only to "awake" the next morning to find the hem of her nightdress wet and muddy footprints on the floor. She "faints" at her trial when the guilty verdict is read, and as we move closer to the time of the murders and their aftermath, the examples of dissociation and amnesia become too numerous to name.

Beyond the history of childhood loss, trauma, physical abuse—as well as a clear tendency to use dissociation and amnesia as defenses against consciously recalling horrific events—Grace also shows many of the other characteristics of individuals who later develop full-blown dissociative disorders—namely high levels of intelligence and creativity, along with a personality that is highly suggestible and easily hypnotized (see Braun and

Sachs; Herman; Kluft). Atwood shows us Grace's quick and imaginative mind on many occasions: Grace learns her work requirements easily and shows an interest in and good memory for biblical parables, poems, and stories she is exposed to in the various households in which she worked. At Thomas Kinnear's house, for example, Grace asks Nancy why Kinnear has a picture of a naked woman on his wall. Nancy claims it is a scene from the Bible, but Grace disagrees, considering herself something of an expert on Bible images. Finally, when Kinnear himself is consulted for a resolution of this conflict, he states that Grace is "very inquisitive for such a young person, and soon he would have the most learned maidservant in Richmond Hill" (222).

Grace's creative talents are also commented on numerous times, especially in connection with her skill as a seamstress and quilter, but we also see her imagination at work in the many daydreams and reveries she shares with us. One powerful example is found in Grace describing the sunrise from her prison cell:

> Today when I woke up there was a beautiful pink sunrise, with the mist lying over the fields like a white soft cloud of muslin, and the sun was shining through the layers of it all blurred and rosy like a peach gently on fire.
> In fact, I have no idea what kind of sunrise there was. In prison they make the windows high up, so you cannot climb out of them I suppose, also so you cannot see out of them either. (237)

Finally, we know that Grace is quite susceptible to hypnosis as she is, in fact, hypnotized by her friend Jeremiah, posing as the mesmerist, Dr. DuPont (396–403). Even before this official hypnotic session, Jeremiah tells Grace how he wishes she would join him on the road, working at fairs and doing hypnotic performances for profit. He tells her:

> You could travel with me ... You could be a medical clairvoyant: I would teach you how, instruct you in what you had to say, and put you into trances. I know by your hand that you have a talent for it: and with your hair down you would have the right look. (268)

While it is unclear exactly what characteristics of Grace's personality have led Jeremiah to view her as someone easily put into a trance, subsequent events seem to confirm his assessment of her and further support how well Atwood has designed Grace to fit the many characteristics that successfully differentiate individuals who develop dissociative reactions to repeated occurrences of trauma from those who do not.

So where are we now? We have looked at the impact of trauma on memory formation and at how dissociation and amnesia make sense as some of the only defensive strategies available for individuals (especially children) facing repeated and overwhelming trauma from which they cannot escape. But we have still not addressed the development of alternate personalities like the one we see emerging near the end of *Alias Grace*. How can a psychologist explain this?

Let's return to the score from *Les Misérables* for a moment and see if Cosette can help us again. As Cosette continues to sing, imagining her protective castle far away, she tells us, "There is a lady all in white; holds me and sings a lullaby. She's nice to see and she's soft to touch. She says, 'Cosette, I love you very much.'" Thus we see the process involved in the creation of an "alter." Here Cosette has fabricated a person who will be with her always and will comfort and soothe her. Cosette can actually hear her voice and may in time give the lady in white a name. Gradually this alter will stabilize as a living part of Cosette's experience and will become what Frank Putnam, in his book *Diagnosis and Treatment of Multiple Personality Disorder*, identifies as a "protector" personality (109). This is how multiple personality or what psychologists now call Dissociative Identity Disorder (or DID for short) begins. Individuals repeatedly confronted with overwhelming events develop these alters to serve different functions within the overall personality structure. Some exist to provide comfort, some are helpers seeking new places to hide, and of course there is what we call the "host personality," who has blocked all memory of trauma. During intensive psychotherapy, these alters emerge and report different aspects of the traumas. Almost always there is a wounded child personality who directly experienced the traumatic incidents and who holds the associated physical and emotional pain. Alters who merely observe the events also exist and dispassionately report clear details of the traumatic incidents, but do so from unusual vantage points, sometimes from high above the host, hidden among some books or toys. An alter may describe, for example, the back of a perpetrator's head (and may even comment on the bald spot forming there) as he assaults the host child on a bed, suggesting that the alter has gone to some "Castle on a Cloud" to witness the abuse from a position of relative safety. Hostile and aggressive personalities are also common, but in large measure their anger is directed at the host personality, who is seen as weak, ineffectual, and perhaps even evil, for complying with outsiders engaged in her abuse.

In the light of this knowledge, we can now describe Grace's behaviour in sophisticated psychological terms. We can say that she has not only learned how to dissociate but also how to create an alter to hold the unbearable memories that she could not otherwise endure. Grace has also learned how to construct amnestic barriers to keep the existence of her alters from conscious awareness. We now know that when Mary Whitney died and Grace ran around the house trying to escape (Atwood 179–80), an alter was in charge. We know that an alter controlled much of Grace's behaviour when she was confined to the "lunatic asylum" (403), and that on the day of the murders, when Grace spoke to the butcher and to Jamie Walsh (320), an alter was doing the talking. Most important of all, when Grace was hypnotized and a voice emerged, proudly claiming responsibility for the murders (396–403), an alter was speaking: "'The kerchief killed her. Hands held it,' says the voice. 'She had to die. The wages of sin is death. And this time the gentleman died as well, for once. Share and share alike!'" (401).

But what might contemporary psychologists say about the likelihood that such a violent alter would exist within the multiple personality organization of Grace Marks? Here the evidence is not entirely clear. Those taking a traditionally Freudian view might argue that the brutal personality uncovered within Grace Marks is quite predictable. This view holds that dissociation's function is to keep unacceptable urges, thoughts, and actions out of consciousness. For these classical psychoanalysts, alters exist primarily to act out rage and other anti-social behaviours while protecting the host's sense of morality. This view is generally in harmony with the Dr. Jekyll/Mr. Hyde scenario developed in Stevenson's story or in Thigpen and Cleckley's famous case study entitled, *The Three Faces of Eve*, in which outrageous feeling, buried deep within the person, escapes when the constraints of conscience are undermined. According to Erik Woody and Kenneth Bowers in their article, "A Frontal Assault on Dissociated Control," amnesia becomes crucial from this point of view because if the horror of one's own inner nature were permitted into awareness, the blow to the self-concept would be devastating. But while there is no doubt that most individuals diagnosed with DID do have some aggressive alters, the more current writing, presented throughout this paper, suggests that the alters come into being primarily to help an isolated and terrorized child survive. From this literature (see Pope and Brown; Waites), we get a picture of a fragile, overwhelmed, vulnerable individual relying on childlike strategies to keep the wolves at bay. Looking at the function of the alters from this perspective, violence against others seems quite unlikely. In fact, most of the studies on DID emphasize the danger inherent in severe self-abuse rather than in violence directed at others. Suicide and other forms of self-destructive behaviour are extremely common among those diagnosed with DID (see Ross et al.; Wilbur); Putnam, while also commenting on this high incidence of turning rage and despair in at the self rather than outward at others, emphasizes how this pattern is especially evident in women diagnosed with DID.

Another source of information, which also argues against the likelihood that Grace Marks has an alter capable of cold-blooded murder, is the literature on hypnosis. This research is relevant because individuals with DID and those following hypnotic suggestion both engage in behaviour for which they later have no conscious recall. What we find is that while individuals will permit themselves to follow any number of directives during a hypnotic trance, even silly and embarrassing ones, they will not engage in behaviour that is in conflict with their own moral standards. In some way that psychologists do not fully understand, we are able to monitor our behaviour even when we are not fully conscious of engaging in that particular behaviour. Ernest Hilgard, one of psychology's most highly respected investigators of hypnotic phenomena, calls this monitoring self the "hidden observer" (209).

But what does this have to do with Grace? Well, two things. First, it confirms what poor, beleaguered Dr. Jordan believed when assessing Grace's capacity for recovering her memory of the murders. Speaking about Grace and himself in the third person, he says:

> They are nearing the blank mystery, the area of erasure; they are entering the forest of amnesia, where things have lost their names. ... Anything she says now may be a clue; any gesture; any twitch. She knows; she knows. She may not know that she knows, but buried deep within her, the knowledge is there. (Atwood 291)

And he is right. Some part of Grace does know what happened. Whether Dr. Jordan's methods would have ever produced an accurate recounting of the events on the day of the murders remains a question, but most of the current psychological literature suggests that, with time, a method could be developed to release the memories held by the "hidden observer."

The second aspect of the hypnosis literature under discussion proposes the following: if the "hidden observer" assures that people will not behave in ways that violate their moral codes during hypnosis, then it makes sense that the same principle would apply to the behaviour of other unconscious actors, in this case, alters. From this point of view, it is very unlikely that Grace would allow any alter to commit murder. Grace has a very strong, almost rigid, moral code and she also expresses abhorrence for violent acts. For example, when Nancy demands that she kill a chicken for dinner, Grace cries out, saying, "Oh no, I've never done it before and don't know how; as I had an aversion to shedding the blood of any living thing" (249). In addition, Grace has no history of aggression either before or after the murders and has never lashed out at anyone who has hurt, provoked, or betrayed her, not even the guards or other prison inmates. Mary Whitney, the name of her dead friend and the alter who emerges during the session with Dr. DuPont, also has no history of violence. Throughout the novel Mary has shown more spunk and spirit than Grace, but even when the father of her child betrayed her, Mary did not act out. Instead, she subjected herself to the abortion that resulted in her death.

Those with a more psychoanalytic orientation might argue that Grace's espousal of such a rigid code of behaviour is actually a defense against the chaotic inner rage and turmoil she struggles with, given the unrelenting series of horrors she has faced. Again using the Dr. Jekyll/Mr. Hyde metaphor, these theorists might argue that Grace is full of repressed rage, which is held in check by her strict code of ethics, and that this rage would need to find expression somewhere—that somewhere being within the personality of her alter. On the other hand, those seeing individuals with DID more as wounded victims trying to cope with reality using flawed systems of information processing and childlike black-and-white moral reasoning, would predict that Grace's inner experience would not be rage as much as profound loneliness, fear, helplessness, confusion, and despair. From this point of view, hiding, running, and screaming in terror are the more predicted responses to the anticipation of another act of violence—in this case, murder.

In the end, I suppose I cannot believe that Grace could kill Nancy Montgomery, but perhaps that is just the softhearted psychotherapist in me speaking. After all, I have not seen "that conscious, even cunning look in the corner of her eye" (362). And besides, seeing Grace as primarily a disorganized trauma survivor makes for a much less interesting story! So, almost 150 years after Atwood's Dr. Jordan struggles to judge Grace's guilt or innocence, psychology cannot give us the answer. We know so much more, without knowing enough. Grace still confounds and fascinates.

—Assumption College

NOTE

1. *Les Miserables* the musical (1985) is by Alain Boubil and Claude-Michel Schönberg. The lyrics were written by Herbert Kretzmer. This particular song is called "Castle on a Cloud."

WORKS CITED

American Psychiatric Association. *Diagnostic and Statistical Manual of Mental Disorders*. 4th ed. Washington, DC: American Psychiatric Association, 1994.

Atwood, Margaret. *Alias Grace*. New York: Doubleday, 1996.

Braun, Bennett G., and Roberta G. Sachs. "The Development of Multiple Personality Disorder: Predisposing, Precipitating, and Perpetuating Factors." In *Childhood Antecedents of Multiple Personality*, edited by Richard P. Kluft, 37–64. Washington, DC: American Psychiatric Press, 1985.

Cameron, Catherine. *Resolving Childhood Trauma: A Long-term Study of Abuse Survivors*. Thousand Oaks, CA: Sage Publications, 2000.

Edelman, Hope. *Motherless Daughters: The Legacy of Loss*. Reading: Addison-Wesley, 1994.

Herman, Judith L. *Trauma and Recovery*. New York: Basic Books, 1992.

Hilgard, Ernest R. *Divided Consciousness: Multiple Controls in Human Thought and Action*. Expanded edition. New York: John Wiley & Sons, 1986.

Kluft, Richard P. "Childhood Multiple Personality Disorder: Predictors, Clinical Findings, and Treatment Results." In *Childhood Antecedents of Multiple Personality*, edited by Richard P. Kluft, 167–96. Washington, DC: American Psychiatric Press, 1985.

Luecken, Linda J. "Parental Caring and Loss During Childhood and Adult Cortisol Responses to Stress." *Psychology and Health* 15, no. 6 (2000): 841–52.

Oppenheim, Janet. *"Shattered Nerves": Doctors, Patients, and Depression in Victorian England.* New York: Oxford University Press, 1991.

Pope, Kenneth S., and Laura S. Brown. *Recovered Memories of Abuse: Assessment, Therapy and Forensics.* Washington, DC: American Psychological Association, 1996.

Putnam, Frank W. *Diagnosis and Treatment of Multiple Personality Disorder.* New York: Guilford, 1989.

Ross, Colin A., et al. "Structured Interview Data on 102 Cases of Multiple Personality Disorder from Four Centers." *American Journal of Psychiatry*, no. 147 (1990): 596–601.

Schönberg, Claude-Michel. "Castle on a Cloud," *Les Misérables.* Lyrics: Herbert Kretzmer. Director: Alain Boubil. Producer: Cameron Mackintosh, 1987.

Showalter, Elaine. *The Female Malady: Women, Madness, and English Culture, 1830–1980.* New York: Penguin Books, 1985.

Stevenson, Robert L. *The Strange Case of Dr. Jekyll and Mr. Hyde.* [1886]. New York: Franklin Watts, 1967.

Terr, Lenore. *Too Scared to Cry: Psychic Trauma in Childhood.* New York: Basic Books, 1990.

Thigpen, Corbett H., and Hervey M. Cleckley. *The Three Faces of Eve.* New York: McGraw-Hill, 1957.

van der Kolk, Bessel A. "Trauma and Memory." In *Traumatic Stress: The Effects of Overwhelming Experience on Mind, Body, and Society*, edited by Bessel A. van der Kolk, Alexander C. McFarlane, and Lars Weisaeth, 279–302. New York: Guilford, 1996.

van der Kolk, Bessel A., and Rita Fisler. "Dissociation and the Fragmentary Nature of Traumatic Memories: Overview and Exploratory Study." *Journal of Traumatic Stress*, no. 8 (1995): 505–525.

van der Kolk, Bessel A., D. Pelcovitz, S. Roth, and J.L. Herman. "Dissociation, Somatization, and Affect Dysregulation: The Complexity of Adaptation to Trauma." *American Journal of Psychiatry*, no. 153 (1996): 83–93.

Vitkus, John. *Casebook in Abnormal Psychology.* New York: McGraw-Hill, 1996. 37–52.

Waites, Elizabeth A. *Trauma and Survival: Post-traumatic and Dissociative Disorders in Women.* New York: Norton, 1993.

Wilbur, Cornelia B. "Psychoanalysis and Multiple Personality Disorder." In *Treatment of Multiple Personality Disorder*, edited by Bennett G. Braun, 133–42. Washington, DC: American Psychiatric Press, 1986.

Woody, Erik Z., and Kenneth S. Bowers. "A Frontal Assault on Dissociated Control." In *Dissociation: Clinical and Theoretical Perspectives*, edited by Steven J. Lynn and Judith W. Rhue, 52–79. New York: Guilford, 1994.

Atwood and Class: *Lady Oracle*, *Cat's Eye*, and *Alias Grace*

FRANK DAVEY

REVIEWERS OF ATWOOD'S novels in the 1970s and 1980s frequently associated her fiction with the middle class, sometimes observing that most of its characters were middle class, or at least refugees from the middle class. By the late 1980s this view had spread, along with Atwood's novels, to the United States. Here is Robert Towers in *The New York Review of Books* (April 27, 1989), reviewing *Cat's Eye*: "[Atwood] has focused her unblinking scrutiny upon the habits, the attitudes, and especially the self-deceptions of the North American—specifically, Anglo-Canadian—middle class and its bohemian offshoots during the past few decades" (50). In the 1990s Atwood appeared to complicate this reading with her servant-girl protagonist of *Alias Grace* and her labour organizer Alex Thomas of *The Blind Assassin*, although, as I will suggest below, both these characterizations contain considerable class ambiguity, and can even be read as questioning the role of class in the formation of individual subjects.

    A major problem in determining the positions that Atwood's novels take regarding class is how to interpret their configuration of the relationship between the individual and language. In my 1984 book on Atwood, I proposed that her understanding of that relationship was Lacanian and Kristevan—a proposal taken up in some detail by Shannon Hengen, Sonia Mycak, and Roxanne Fand in the 1990s. From a class point of view, the limitation of such an approach is that it tends to totalize the "symbolic order" and to invite a reading of the novels in terms of a tension between a public world of social codes and practices, including those of class, and a pre-symbolic of private and socially uncoded insights. It can lead to a view of conflict in Atwood as not between classes and ideologies but between a symbolic order and individuals who would escape its inscriptions. Vulgarized in the mass media, it can create an Atwood of romantic individualist female heroines for whom to refuse "to be a victim" may be to refuse to acknowledge one's inevitable inscription in the symbolic.

There is a lot of material in Atwood to support such an approach—material with which we are now perhaps over-familiar in *The Edible Woman*: Marian McAlpin's dropping out of subjectivity when some socially unscripted part of her psyche prompts her to opt out of the symbolic social practices of eating; *Surfacing*'s narrator finding a pre-linguistic kinship with nakedness and trees; Elaine Risley's belief in *Cat's Eye* that she refuses contemporary art fashions (and feminist fashions) and that her inspirations come from irrational sources beyond her understanding. These are characters who believe that they can stand outside of the symbolic, outside of social construction, unheeding of Althusserian hailings, and who believe that their limited interactions with socially scripted others can be done cynically, out of choice, and without illusion. The character who would withdraw—Gulliver-like—from heavily coded society is a commonplace of Atwood's fiction: Lesja in *Life Before Man* withdrawing into fantasies of dinosaur gardens; Elaine Risley withdrawing from Toronto's art scene to reclusive domestic life in Vancouver, Iris Griffen in *The Blind Assassin* withdrawing from a high-fashion Toronto to a modest cottage in a Lake Ontario village; Grace Marks refusing to be "hailed" by the codes either of working-class crudity or of those of Victorian gentility and its new psychosciences. Offred's understanding of herself in *The Handmaid's Tale* as having no social structures with which she can safely affiliate is the chosen position of Grace and many other Atwood protagonists.[1] As well there is the recurrent story of the child with the Wordsworthian childhood—in *Surfacing*, *Bluebeard's Egg*, and *Cat's Eye*—the child whose early years are spent in isolation with her parents in Northern Ontario and whose traumatic encounter with what may be the Lacanian symbolic occurs when they settle in Toronto so that she can attend school.

However, one could also take a Foucauldian approach to the novels. I am prompted here by both Judith Butler's *The Psychic Life of Power*, in which she writes that the subject is formed "in a fundamental dependency on a discourse we never chose but that, paradoxically, initiates and sustains our agency" (2) and David Simpson's extended exploration in his book *Situatedness* of the paradoxical contemporary relationship between agency and contingency, one that he describes as requiring that "the subject's self descriptions be at once abject, made by others, merged into prior formations, and at the same time bear all the marks of a recognizable agency and responsibility" (195); that is, we could read Atwood's supposedly pre-symbolic sites as also already discursively scripted—as my use of "Wordsworthian" and reference to Swift's Gulliver hint above—and thus read them as liberal-democratic sites of extreme agency in which the subject is imagined, in Althusser's understanding of that word, to be free from, or resistant to, social interpellation and inscription. Atwood's characters experiencing certain parts of their lives as being outside of social coding does not require us to believe that they are.

One reading that might then emerge is an understanding that class in much of Atwood's early fiction is a displaced sign. In *Life Before Man*, for example, it is largely displaced by ethnicity. What we read appears to be a novel in which Lesje is the only "ethnic" character in a social community of otherwise neutral or non-signifying ethnicity. Her parents and grandparents are marked by Atwood as upper-working-class—one of her grandmothers has operated a small convenience store from her front parlour, her father has operated a small shop that sells little girls' dresses; all of her family have taken in borders. However, Atwood gives this class background little emphasis, having Lesje agonize instead over her mixed ethnic "difference"—her mixed Jewish and Ukrainian families who celebrate the Christmas holidays at different times than the dominant culture, and whose ethnicities are an embarrassment to her WASP London, Ontario, boyfriend. The result is to render Lesje's class difference from the other characters relatively invisible in the novel, and to explain her desperation to "belong" (307) as a desire to be normal in terms of the cultural practices of a WASP social dominant rather than as one to rise in class.

There is a similar obscuring of class differences in *Lady Oracle*. Joan's father and mother appear to have been working-class children who rose in class through the father's becoming a doctor. Joan's maternal grandfather had been a CPR stationmaster. Her mother had "run away from home at the age of sixteen and never gone back. She'd worked at various jobs, clerking in Kresge's, waitressing" (68). Waitressing at a summer resort, she secures Joan's father by getting pregnant with Joan. His father had been a farmer's son who had sold the farm to invest successfully in a railroad, but had lost his money in the Depression: "Her maternal grandfather 'had been a stationmaster for the CPR'" (68). Joan's description of her mother's early attempts at home decorating presents the tastes of the prosperous 1950s working class, from the chesterfield of "dull pink—a nubby material shot through with silver threads" and covered in transparent plastic to the lampshades still "protected with cellophane" (70). Joan's Aunt Lou, her father's sister, attends Spiritualist meetings in a neighbourhood of semi-detached houses that look "squalid and sagging"(105). The tiny congregation is mostly "quite old, and many had chronic cough" (106). Joan's narrative, however, reads her childhood situation not as governed by class and by her mother's class ambitions but as a personal struggle with her mother over gender coding—a reading similar to that which most critics have given the book. Class issues here become displaced by feminist ones, although of course the Gothic novel through which Joan interprets her life is a narrative not only of gender politics but also of class mobility—a narrative often of wage-earning, landless governesses who can dream of becoming mistress of a manor.

Like other Atwood protagonists, Joan recurrently believes that she can step outside of social codes, whether class or gender based, or at least step outside of one set of codes and into another. Considering the link in our culture between obesity and poverty, and between middle-class respectability and the trim, manicured body, Joan's contest of wills with her mother over her weight can be viewed as a class struggle, Joan refusing the middle-class fashionability and domesticity her mother aspires to and insisting on evoking the poverty she came from. One moment in the novel is particularly clear about the associations between Joan's obesity and class. In her teens she begins looking for part-time work so she can become independent of her parents. "The only kind of jobs I was able to get were unskilled and not very pleasant. Employers as a rule didn't want to hire anyone so fat," Joan recounts.

> Thus I worked in the five-and-dime for three weeks, as a theater usher for two, a cashier in a restaurant for three, and so on ... these were often hard disagreeable jobs, like washing dishes, and I didn't stay at them long.

> My mother was baffled by these jobs. "What do you have to work for?" she asked, many times. ... She found the jobs I took degrading to her personally, which was a bonus. They must have reminded her, also, of her own early life. (96)

For *Cat's Eye* such a reading would see Elaine's childhood world as one less of apparent innocence than of apparent classlessness. Elaine's encounter with class differences when she arrives in Toronto has tended to be eclipsed in most readings of the novel by her persecution by the upper-middle-class Cordelia, and by her unhappy initiation into social conventions and practices, especially those of femininity. But when Elaine arrives in Toronto, what Atwood has her encounter are three clearly distinguished class-based practices—the working-class evangelical-church-attending Smeath family, the middle-class family of their friend Carol, and the upper-middle-class family of Elaine's persecutor, Cordelia. Atwood uses an array of shorthand signs to identify the class positions of these families. The Smeaths buy their clothing from the Eaton's catalogue and have given their daughter a name from the Bible; Mrs. Smeath's hands are "knuckly and red from the wash" (59), as Grace Marks's hands will be in *Alias Grace*. Carol's mother prefers current popular fashions, like the matching "twin-set" sweaters she and Carol both wear, and has given her daughter one of the most fashionable girls' names of the period; she wears rubber gloves when washing dishes. Only Cordelia's mother has a house with a "powder room;" she has a cleaning lady and takes painting lessons; she has given her daughters names from Shakespeare: Perdita, Miranda, and Cordelia.

Cat's Eye uses these class signs to suggest once again the possibility that one can avoid social coding. Elaine cannot locate her mother in terms of class—her mother wears practical, nondescript clothes (213), gathers bouquets of wild flowers for her table, goes ice-skating by herself, and is a potential embarrassment for Elaine no matter which of her girlfriends' families she is visiting. Her father and brother seem also untroubled by class hailings, especially when the father is doing entomological research in a forest or the brother is contemplating the determinacies of interstellar space. Elaine herself eventually leaves what she has come to see as a Toronto fraught with social politics for a quieter life in Vancouver where she can feel she is on a long "vacation" or "evasion" (15)—even though she is married to a travel agent, raising two daughters, living in a house with a fireplace and a back garden, and quietly producing her paintings.

Roxanne Rimstead has recently argued at some length that the material injustices of class in *Alias Grace* are variously displaced by what she calls "universal womanhood" (48) and by "the abstract space of psychological turmoil, discursive play, and elaborate formal design" (61). To her arguments I would add a number of observations. One is that Atwood dilutes Grace Marks's working-class identity by having her recall that her mother and Aunt Pauline were the daughters of a clergyman who both "had an education, and could embroider and play the piano" (Atwood, *AG*, 104)—the latter being abilities that mark the novel's middle-class characters such as Faith Cartwright, whom Dr. Simon Jordan eventually marries. Aunt Pauline and her husband have a comfortable income from the "general goods" store they operate; she is proud of having "two sets of dishes, one for every day and one real china for best" (104). When Grace is arrested for murder, her own enduring middle-class discretion leads her not to reveal the name of the Irish village where she was born and where Aunt Pauline still lives, because "my Aunt Pauline might still be living and I would not wish to bring disgrace upon her" (103–04).[2] Through this genealogy, Atwood comes close to not making Grace a working-class child at all but, rather, a lost middle-class child of the kind one finds in Dickens—one whose gradual displaying of intelligence and refinement is attributable to a lost birth identity.

A second observation is that, to accompany what Rimstead argues is an assertion of "universal womanhood," Atwood also offers in *Alias Grace* a class-transcending lecherous masculinity—a kind of "universal manhood," perhaps. Almost every man Grace encounters propositions her, leers at her, or lusts after her openly or unconsciously: the salesman she meets on the stagecoach to Richmond Hill, the unfortunate Mr. Kinnear, his farmhand and eventual murderer James McDermott, her lawyer Mr. MacKenzie, the jail guards who escort her on her visits to the governor's house, and Dr. Jordan. Atwood seems to take particularly mischievous delight in having Dr. Jordan, the would-be psychoanalyst, experience sudden libidinal desires for Grace without being able to understand them. Atwood also constructs many of these men as having their lusts for Grace heightened by the fact she is a purported murderess. Even Grace's husband, whom she marries when they are both in their forties, whose father had been a tenant farmer on Kinnear's property, seeks to have his passions heightened by having Grace recount "a few stories of torment and misery" (457) before he unbuttons her nightgown. The scenes remind Grace, Atwood writes, of how Dr. Jordan's "cheeks would flush" and how he would "smile like the sun" whenever she told him about her "sufferings and ... hardships" (457). That is, the aphrodisiacs of female vulnerability transcend class boundaries; male lechery varies from class to class only unimportantly, in the kinds of discourses in which it is expressed.[3]

However (and this is my third observation), Atwood also constructs Dr. Jordan as someone who—like many of her earlier characters—desires to locate himself outside of such social practices as class. He doesn't wish to be merely a man of his time and class, and frequently shows contempt for those who are. When he first sees Reverend Verringer's library, he thinks that "it is so self-consciously the right sort of library that he has an urge to set fire to it" (76). An hour or so before, while dressing for this visit, he has felt an impulsive disgust for the conventions of clothing. "Why does civilized man see fit to torture his body by cramming it into the straight-jacket of gentlemanly dress?" (73). There are echoes here of Elaine Risley's parents' impatience with codes of dress, and of the "false body" (Atwood, *Surfacing*, 178) of clothing shed by *Surfacing*'s narrator. Dr. Jordan also expresses from time to time dismay at his own reliance on social convention, as when the prison governor's attractive young daughter Lydia has expressed curiosity about witnessing a public execution and he has sententiously replied, "Women should not attend such grisly spectacles ... They pose a danger to their refined natures," but then becomes immediately "conscious of sounding pompous" (87).

Much like John Fowles in his characterization of Charles Smithson in *The French Lieutenant's Woman*, Atwood creates in Dr. Simon Jordan a character who lives at the cusp of what Foucault calls an epistemic shift (*The Order of Things* 125–65; *The Archaeology* 191–92). Fowles's character lives on the brink of Darwinian understandings of biology, Atwood's on the brink of psychoanalytical understandings of anger and sexuality. Each shift has promise for new understandings of such things as gender, poverty, and the material grounds of social practices. For each man the conflict between faintly apprehended knowledge and conservative social practice is embodied in their relationship with a woman. Their failures to act responsibly to that woman enact mildly tragic encounters between agency and contingency—encounters that gesture intertextually toward romantic figurations of lost love and missed opportunity.[4] But whereas Fowles seems to view Charles's failings as part of the condition of being—as David Simpson argues, "To be situated is indeed the condition of us all, but none of us can know the terms of our situatedness nor the degree to which those terms make possible or preclude understanding others or seeing things differently" (160)—Atwood seems to blame Jordan as an individual, to accuse him of lacking intellectual and moral courage, and to imply that if he had possessed Grace's ability to perceive beyond social practice, of whatever class, he would have been less bewildered by her or by his own sexuality; that is, Atwood's critique of society in this novel appears to call much less for systemic social change than for remarkable individuals.

The Blind Assassin, set in the Depression and concerning in part relations between a benevolent button-factory owner and his increasingly desperate employees, and a romance between one of the owner's daughters and a labour organizer, would appear to be a novel about class issues, and has often been read as such. However, again the class issues are displaced. One of the several plot surprises in this extremely clever novel is that the labour issues are red herrings, and that its focal event is a gender issue, the long-term sexual abuse of the owner's younger daughter by the much wealthier entrepreneur who has been married to Iris, the older. Moreover, none of the working-class characters have decisive roles in the action. Alex Thomas, the labour organizer, is yet another of those Atwood characters who seem to be able to exist outside of social contingencies. A First World War orphan, he has lost all records of his family, its social class, its national origin, or its ethnicity. He is a theological-college dropout, the adopted son of missionaries, and carries some middle-class attributes in his language and general knowledge, but lives without establishing a home, in a seemingly endless series of borrowed rooms and apartments. When Iris first learns of his background, she exclaims, "It must be terrible not to know who you really are," implying that he has lost his class, ethnic, national, and family identities. But he replies with an extreme statement of agency:

> "I used to think that," said Alex. "But then it came to me that who I really am is a person who doesn't need to know who he really is, in the usual sense. What does it mean, anyway—family background and so forth. People use it as an excuse for their own snobbery, or else their failings. I'm free of the temptation, that's all. I am free of all the strings. Nothing ties me down." (190)

Atwood adds humour to this scene by having his next line, "'At least you're never homesick,'" drowned out by an ongoing fireworks display, hinting that he may not be as free from contingency as he might think, but also has him continue leading a life largely detached from the other characters. Fighting in the Spanish Civil War, he is "shot at, from both sides." "Our bunch was caught in the middle. I was on the run from the good guys. What a shambles" (460).

Like many other sympathetically constructed Atwood characters, Alex is solitary, untrusting, and cynical, equally contemptuous of the middle-class characters who help shelter him and of the working-class ones who purchase his escapist tales of Assyria and Babylon. These attributes are especially similar to those of Offred, Grace Marks, Elaine Risley, Joan Foster, and of Tony Fremont in *The Robber Bride*. Alex's claim that "who I really am" has nothing to do with contingencies such as class, family, ethnicity or nationality is a claim—or perhaps a wish—about unconditioned identity that runs throughout Atwood's writing. It not only trumps thematically such considerations as class or gender affiliations but it also renders them adversarial; that is, such affiliations are depicted as dangerously and unnecessarily compromising of individual agency. The feminist art-world affiliations that Elaine treats cautiously in *Cat's Eye*, the class practices that Grace seeks to dissent from in *Alias Grace*, and the Gileadean ideologies about which Offred strives to be publicly noncommittal in *The Handmaid's Tale* are constructed by Atwood as varying more in degree than in kind. They are all presented as constraints on agency and on the liberal-democratic concept of "who I really am."

—University of Western Ontario

NOTES

1. There are a number of similarities between *The Handmaid's Tale* and *Alias Grace*, and between them and *Oryx and Crake*. Both Offred and Grace are writing or speaking from positions of incarceration and panoptical supervision; both regard their opportunities to talk with the oppressor community and to enter its living spaces as a kind of pleasure and a possible way to freedom; both are produced by their circumstances as autobiographers. Oryx lives literally in an artificial class-free pleasure dome; her sexual oppression has been so overwhelming that it appears not only to have removed her from class and from relationships with other women but also to have caused her to

view both this oppression and isolation as irremediable. Atwood emphasizes the mechanistic quality of Oryx's reply when Jimmy asks her about her rape: "'Why do you want to talk about ugly things?' she said. Her voice was silvery, like a music box. ... 'We should think only beautiful things'" (144).
2. "Disgrace" in this passage offers a resonant pun on "Grace" as well as an instructive example of the conflation of the theological and the social that can be found in the evolution of middle-class English values from at least Samuel Richardson onward (see R.H. Tawney, *Religion and the Rise of Capitalism*). Moreover, the passage points to the fact that Richardson, with his novels of cross-class sexual attraction and middle-class mores, is a major presence in *Alias Grace*, not only in the epistolary parts of its narrative but also in the moral views of Grace and in the privileged-man/abject-woman structure of their relationship.
3. Atwood creates a similar levelling of class difference in *Bodily Harm* when she constructs rural lower-middle-class Griswold and upper-middle-class Toronto as equally committed to superficiality and concealment and mistrustful of the sensuous.
4. Both Fowles and Atwood create a traditional fictional pairing of lovers at cross-purposes, setting up a reader's anticipation that—as in Austen's *Pride and Prejudice*—the novels will end in reconciliation. But while Fowles uses the failure of his lovers to critique such novelistic conventions, Atwood—by attributing the failure of her lovers to Dr. Jordan—seems to confirm the convention, and to imply that but for Jordan's naivety the story might have unfolded as expected.

WORKS CITED

Atwood, Margaret. *Alias Grace*. Toronto: McClelland & Stewart, 1996.
———. *The Blind Assassin*. New York: Doubleday, 2000.
———. *Cat's Eye*. Toronto: McClelland & Stewart, 1988.
———. *Lady Oracle*. Toronto: McClelland & Stewart, 1976.
———. *Life Before Man*. Toronto: McClelland & Stewart, 1979.
———. *Oryx and Crake*. Toronto: McClelland & Stewart, 2003.
———. *Surfacing*. Toronto: McClelland & Stewart, 1972.
Butler, Judith. *The Psychic Life of Power*. Stanford: Stanford University Press, 1997.
Foucault, Michel. *The Order of Things*. New York: Vintage, 1973.
———. *The Arhcaeology of Knowledge*. London: Tavistock, 1974.
Rimstead, Roxanne. "Working-Class Intruders: Female Domestics in *Kamouraska* and *Alias Grace*." *Canadian Literature*, no. 175 (2002): 44–65.
Simpson, David. *Situatedness*. Durham, NC: Duke University Press, 2002.
Towers, Robert. "Review of *Cat's Eye*," by Margaret Atwood. *New York Review of Books*, April 27, 1989. 50.

SHORT FICTION AND POETRY

Funny Bones Are Good Bones: Atwood and Humour

WANDA CAMPBELL

WHEN ESTELLE, THE narrator of Margaret Atwood's short story, "Rape Fantasies" tries to lighten a serious moment with humour, she is greeted with a negative response: "I swear all four of them looked at me like I was in bad taste, like I'd insulted the Virgin Mary or something. I mean, I don't see what's wrong with a little joke now and then. Life's too short, right?" (*DG* 104). What *is* wrong with a little joke now and then?

The writer, according to Atwood, "bears witness" (*SW* 348) to private and public experience, and the fact that her vision is often pessimistic is understandable, given that the century she was born into has been a dark one. As she says in "Notes Towards a Poem That Can Never be Written": "The facts of this world seen clearly/are seen through tears" (*SP* 265). And yet, there is a persistent thread of humour throughout her work that has received little attention from critics. Of over 900 entries in the MLA index related to Atwood's work, only a handful explore the comic side of her work, noting especially the "wry tone" (Smith 143) of her fiction. According to Carol L. Benton, even "scholars who have noted comic moments through Atwood's short stories and novels have often overlooked or denied the impulse toward comedy within her poetic texts" (84). And such critics as Sandra Djwa, Barbara Godard, and Elspeth Cameron, who have considered Atwood's use of parody and other potentially comic strategies, have nonetheless tended to look at the more serious or literary application of these strategies. As Godard says, "Parody is a sophisticated literary form, inviting the complicity of a highly perspicacious reader who shares the irony of recognizing difference at the heart of similarity, in order to activate its full complexity of meaning" (4). Karen F. Stein maintains that Atwood sees a connection between the roles of writer and trickster: "The trickster figure embodies contradictions, often using humour, parody and satire to expose hypocrisy and pretensions" (6). Likewise, Barbara Hill Rigney suggests that "all of Atwood's works, no matter how ultimately and seriously profound, do not neglect the aspect of humour" (14). Thus, to explore Atwood's use of humour is to illuminate some of her favourite strategies and themes and thereby gain a fuller understanding of the breadth and texture of her work.

Anyone who seeks to discuss humour in a writer's work runs into the challenge of definition. As Umberto Eco points out:

> From antiquity to Freud or Bergson, every attempt to define comic seems to be jeopardized by the fact that this is an umbrella term (referring, in a Wittgensteinian jargon, to a network of family resemblances) that gathers together a disturbing ensemble of diverse and not completely homogenous phenomena, such as humor, comedy, grotesque, parody, satire, wit and so on. (1)

Though Atwood makes use of all of these comic strategies, the most evident characteristic of Atwood's comic style is wit. Defined by the OED as "the apt association of thought and expression, calculated to surprise and delight by its unexpectedness" (8a), wit is considered to be intellectual, intolerant, and satiric, in contrast to humour that is generally seen as more sympathetic, tolerant, and warm. An excellent, if rather grim, example of Atwood's wit is the short untitled poem that was the source for "The Open Eye," the name of a major symposium on Atwood's work held in 2004:

> you fit into me
> like a hook into an eye
>
> a fish hook
> an open eye. (*SP* 111)

The only Atwood selection to be included in *The Maple Laugh Forever: An Anthology of Comic Canadian Poetry* (1981), this poem is an example of what Reingard M. Nischik calls "Atwood's 'poetics of inversion': her technique of undermining conventional thought patterns, attitudes, values, or textual norms by turning them on their heads" (6). The relatively benign though erotic opening image of a traditional fastener for clothing suddenly becomes startling and brutal when the context is changed to barbed steel inserted into a human eye, a site of vulnerability and vision.

In her displays of bold ingenuity, Atwood shows an affinity with the metaphysical poets, and in particular with John Donne, who depended on the witty and sometimes violent yoking together of apparently unconnected ideas or things to startle the reader out of complacency. Anyone who has read Atwood's poetry recognizes her talent as a word magician and her ability to surprise with a pun or a sudden ironic twist that may not be conventionally funny but that amuses nonetheless. In "Raised Eyebrows: The Comic Impulse in the Poetry of Margaret Atwood," Benton defines the comic impulse as "a poetic moment made incongruous by language, sense imagery, or any other discrepancy between what is expected and what is given" (26). The backdrop for Atwood's performance of wit is a world of the absurd and the unexpected. The unpredictable environment of Atwood's poetry often has the strange, surrealistic quality we associate with the paintings of Dali. As Robin Skelton puts it, "We become aware that while we are *accumulating* information, we are not in fact *moving*. We are like Alice on her chessboard running madly, because we want to remain in the same place long enough to understand it" (119). There is humour in the wit and satire of Atwood's poetry because we recognize familiar features in the absurd and absurdity in the familiar. Atwood herself said that "a lot of things that may seem to be satiric are quotations from real life" (Sandler 24), a claim confirmed by one of the most chilling statements in the dystopian novel *The Handmaid's Tale*: "There was little that was truly original with or indigenous to Gilead: its genius was synthesis" (289).

Other important elements of Atwood's comic style are caricature and bathos. Stein refers to Atwood as "a satirist, a caricaturist with a deeply moral vision" (5). In an interview, Atwood admits, "My writing is closer to caricature than satire—distortion rather than scathing attack—and as I say, it's largely realism" (Sandler 24). The word "caricature" derives from the Italian verb "to load," and thus concerns someone or something "loaded" with exaggerated detail. In visual caricature the face is often the focal point, and this is true of Atwood's caricature of "The Landlady" (*SP* 41). The tenant dreams of making an escape only to find herself "walking/always over a vast face/which is the land-/lady's" (*SP* 41). The landlady is the all-pervasive presence, the "raw voice," the unavoidable "bulk." Like P.K. Page's poem of the same title, this poem may well be about a real individual, though it invites a comparison with the Canadian condition of being face-to-face daily with the vast and demanding nation to the south, the elephant of Trudeau's famous quip. The closing metaphor of "The Landlady" is an excellent example of bathos, an anticlimactic descent into the common place.

> She stands there, a raucous fact,
> blocking my way:
> immutable, a slab
> of what is real,
> solid as bacon. (*SP* 42)

The related tools of hyperbole and understatement are also used to evoke irony, the "equilibrium of opposites" (Abrams 92). Atwood's metaphors are always surprising because of the startling parallels she chooses, but they are also somehow right. The logician moves from A to B to C to D; at her comic best, Atwood makes an imaginative leap from A to D, treating her audience to a chuckle while she does so. The comic effect is produced by a collision of two different frames of reference.

In "Backdrop Addresses Cowboy" (*SP* 56) we are presented with a movie set from a Western, complete with cactus. However, it is not the sheriff, the villain, or even the barmaid who speaks to the cowboy; rather, it is the backdrop, the landscape, and the horizon. The backdrop addresses the cowboy not with admiration but with condemnation for the "heroic/trail of desolation" (*SP* 56) that he leaves behind, the scattered bottles and skulls. The horizon is able to recognize the hollowness of the heroics, the cheapness and absurdity of the star-spangled myth. It is the landscape that is desecrated as the cowboy passes through "tugging a papier-mâché cactus/on wheels behind [him] on a string" (*SP* 56). The humour of the poem arises from the satiric belittling of the frontier myth and the unusual relationship suggested in the title.

Once again the poem operates on several levels. The cowboy represents the stereotypical American hero bent on glorified destruction, but also the false man-made cardboard world of the movie set that either ignores or abuses the reality of nature. The landscape could be many things: an exploited environment, a woman desecrated, or a poet ignored by a public raised on the masculine clichés of Hollywood. Atwood is able to, in some odd way, demonstrate the humour of threat. We know that each frontier holds potential for exploration or exploitation, discovery or desecration, but because we believe in our ability to choose the right thing, our tension finds relief in a smile. As Atwood puts it, "The *real* audience is the snob within, and the real accomplishment of laughter is reassurance: I am not like them. I am classier" (*SW* 178).

To enumerate the comic strategies in Atwood's work is not to suggest that they operate independently but, rather, to suggest that they are often used in combination to explore some of Atwood's favourite themes. A theme central to much of her work is that of transformation. She looks back to the influence of her entomologist father, Carl Atwood, as an explanation for her profound interest in the process of metamorphosis. Her childhood spent in the Quebec north woods while her father did his research gave her ample opportunity to observe the almost-magical transformations that take place in nature. The caterpillar-to-butterfly conversion and its reversal appear repeatedly in her work.

In addition, fairy tales rife with transformations were an essential part of Atwood's childhood reading. She once said that *Grimm's Fairy Tales* was the most influential book she ever read (Sandler 14). Metamorphosis in Atwood's work is the unexpected change perceived from an unusual perspective. The "Songs of the Transformed," as the title indicates, are dedicated to the exploration of this theme. In "Song of the Worms" harmless subterranean squiggles transform themselves into a vast and silent army of attackers. Though this allegory operates humorously on the surface, it can also be interpreted as the revolution and rebellion of any downtrodden group or minority. Perhaps it is artists who "have lived among roots and stones" and poets who "have sung but no one has listened" (*SP* 156). Perhaps it is women who "come into the open air/at night only to love" (156). Perhaps it is Canadians who "know what a boot looks like/when seen from underneath" (157). Whoever they are, when they say "Attack/you will hear nothing/at first" (157).

A related theme that frequently recurs in Atwood's work is that of mythologies ancient and new. Darkly comic revisionings of old myths include "Siren Songs" and "Helen of Troy Does Counter Dancing." But Atwood is equally interested in popular culture and the myths it creates as modern alternatives to fairy tales. Atwood has often acknowledged the importance of comic books to her childhood development: "The truth about the universe was contained in comic books traded and re-traded till their covers fell off: Batman, Blackhawk, The Human Torch, Plastic Man, Captain Marvel" (*SW* 84). Comic books offer the age-old myth of transformation in modern form.

Not everyone is aware that during the 1970s Atwood contributed a comic strip entitled "Kanadian Kultchur Komix" to *This Magazine* under the pseudonym Bart Gerrard. The heroine is, of course, Survival Woman, complete with cape and snowshoes. One theme frequently explored in the strip is the funny side of Canadian-American relations, a theme that also appears in Atwood's poem "Comic Books vs. History." The United States is the blank below the border waiting to be filled with the child's imaginative vision:

>   heroes
> lived there, we knew
> they all wore capes, bullets
> bounced off them;
> from their fists came beautiful
> orange collisions. (*SP* 102)

Twenty years later, however, the narrator of the poem actually reaches the other side, only to find the "red and silver/heroes had collapsed inside/ their rubbers suits" (*SP* 103). This narrative of realization coincides with Atwood's own experience in graduate school at Harvard. "Suddenly America was proving to be not what I had thought. It wasn't full of supermen, drum majorettes, or even kindly FDRs" (*SW* 86).

It was this new understanding of menace that led to stories like "Rape Fantasies" which, though ostensibly set in Toronto, relates to her experience of being in Cambridge, Massachusetts where, as she puts it, she "first learned urban fear" (Oates 77). After having made the distinction between actual rape and the fantasies expressed by the other women in her office, the first-person narrator Estelle offers several of her own scenarios. In each she is able to defend herself from the rapist in various ways including squirting a plastic lemon in his eye, using kung fu, sympathy for his acne, convoluted religious claims, or a shared fatal illness. Her tales, tinged with both humour and horror, share the common thread of depriving the rapist of his power by somehow revealing his weakness; her scenarios all manage to ultimately make the rapist somehow pathetic and ineffectual, whether because his zipper gets stuck or he has a terrible cold, or terrible acne, or a terrible disease. "In my rape fantasies," Estelle says, "I always end up feeling sorry for the guy, I mean there has to be something *wrong* with them" (*DG* 106). In each case, Estelle is able to defuse the situation by providing some remedy for the rapist, making him a Neo Citran or recommending her dermatologist, or simply talking. "I think it would be better if you could get a conversation going," she says. "Like how could a fellow do that to a person he's just had a long conversation with" (110). Atwood has referred to this in her essay on Canadian humour as "survival laughter, born from conditions so awful that you either have to laugh or stick your head in the oven" (*SW* 176).

Comic elements appear in many of Atwood's short stories and novels, but in none so consistently as *Lady Oracle,* which is referred to by Mordecai Richler as a "comic romp" in one of many book jacket blurbs that draw attention to the novel's humour. In addition to Joan's mother, who floats around her like some "spiritual jello" (111), we have the Royal Porcupine, hilarious parodies of costume gothics, Aunt Lou's maxims, and Atwood's own delicious descriptions: "Then I imagined my mother's face as I loomed down the aisle in white satin with this tiny foreign man slung over my arm like a purse" (*LO* 99). Rowland Smith argues that "the wry, stoic mask of the inept, attractive, alluring, dangling narrator in *Lady Oracle* covers a prolonged scream of pain" (144), but the overall impression still manages to be humorous.

There are flashes of this kind of comedy in the works that follow, but the next book that can really be described as "funny" is *Good Bones.* Here, as Linda Wagner-Martin points out, "Atwood's cynicism is more playful, less traumatic" (85). Here she fires every cannon in her comic arsenal, offering us revisions of fables such as "Little Red Hen Tells All"; Gertrude talking back to Hamlet; satiric celebrations of "Unpopular Gals" and "Stupid

Women"; five methods for "Making a Man," including the "Traditional Method," the "Gingerbread Method" ("these guys are scrumptious!"), the "Clothes Method," the "Marzipan Method" and, last but not least, the "Folk Art Method":

> You've seen these cuties in other folks' front yards, with little windmills attached to their heads. They hammer with their little hammers, saw with their little saws, or just whirl their arms around a lot when there's a stiff breeze. Why shouldn't you concoct one of these cunning fellows for your very own? (*GB* 57–58)

This is, as Sharon R. Wilson points out, "a wonderfully funny parody of creation myths" (32–33) that also offers "humourous indirect attacks on the reification of women" (Nischik 13).

In a first-person narrative entitled "My Life as a Bat," Atwood describes a system of warfare in which the man with the biggest epaulettes wins. This is laughter produced by unusual perspectives and perceptions, the seeing that revises and renews. But like *Morning in the Burned House*, Atwood's 1995 poetry collection that moves relentlessly to a final image of cindery, non-existent, radiant flesh, the vision of *Good Bones* also becomes progressively darker, ending finally with dancing lepers and good bones. Patricia Merivale argues that *Good Bones* is not a random miscellany, as some have suggested, but is like the tradition of the prose poem to which it belongs, far more carefully organized and subversive than it first appears to be:

> Such subversion of prose genres through compact parody and canny intertextuality in which an anecdotal structure is soaked in the acrid sauces of black humour has been a recipe for one branch of the oxymoronic genre of the prose poem since the time of Baudelaire. (268)

Even those critics who recognize the sophistication of what Merivale calls the "gendered metatextualities of the opening section" and "the elegiac intertextualities of the closing section" (268) still consider *Good Bones* a lesser text that offers only "weaker examples of Atwoodian strategies" (255).

Is this just another form of the negative feedback Estelle of "Rape Fantasies" receives in response to her "little" joke? Most of the examples one can draw upon to illustrate Atwood's humour are from the early years, and even *Good Bones* dates eight years before the turn of the century. Is the comic impulse being pushed to the margin rather than remaining at the centre of Atwood's work? Humour is certainly a central component of Atwood's alliterative children's books such as *Princess Prunella and the Purple Peanut* or the more recent *Rude Ramsay and the Roaring Radishes*. It is also present, though more darkly, in *Bottle*, published in England. Like *Good Bones*, this tiny book of only fifty-four pages contains a miscellany of short pieces ranging from reflections on Helen's childhood entitled "It's Not Easy Being Half-Divine," to a Pythonesque satire of the military mentality that requires a soldier to carry on, though wounded by an ever-shifting array of armaments. "Sir, they've torn my throat out./Well do the best you can" (Bottle 29). Many of these pieces are republished in *The Tent* which Atwood described "as being like a collection of licorice all-sorts, small bite-sized bits of many varieties" (Caple F1). More than half of the thirty-five pieces in this latest miscellany in the tradition of *Good Bones* have been previously published, often in support of causes Atwood holds dear, but some reviewers have been disappointed. "The relentless irony becomes wearing. Lines that are perhaps intended to be wryly comic often sound more sarcastic than funny" (Tihanyi 20), but most agree that it is an engaging if peripheral text.

Has humour disappeared from Atwood's mainstream work? *Oryx and Crake* can hardly be described as humorous, and yet, among the comments of reviewers and critics on the novel's homepage that include adjectives such as "disturbing," "chilling," and "apocalyptic," one finds descriptions such as "darkly comic," "scabrously witty," and yes, even "funny." At a public reading where she read a passage in which Snowman is faced with the challenge of describing the whys and wherefores of "toast" to those who have never experienced it, Atwood described *Oryx and Crake* as a hopeful book because "it hasn't happened yet." Humour is mentioned at several points in the novel, though primarily as a trait that is, like much else in the novel, on its way to extinction.

Snowman, the narrator, clearly values humour. It is one of the ways that he can get a reaction out of his increasingly distant mother (*OC* 32), and one of the qualities that first attracts him to Crake. "They might have something in common after all, at least the guy had a sense of humour" (74). But Jimmy soon discovers that his sense of humour does not serve him well in the compound schools "awash in brilliant genes" (174). He finds that "his talents shrank by comparison. Nor had he been given any extra points for being funny. He was less funny now, anyway: he'd lost interest in the general audience" (174). Crake's talent for irony is certainly manifested in his decision to name the simple Crakers after famous figures of Western civilization ranging from Abraham Lincoln to Simone de Beauvoir, but he has done his best to eliminate humour from his newly invented race. Snowman asks:

> "Do they make jokes?"
>
> "Not as such," said Crake. "For jokes you need a certain edge, a little malice. It took a lot of trial and error and we're still testing, but I think we've managed to do away with jokes." (306)

Though these brave new humans are "hard-wired" for singing and dreaming (352), apparently they are not hard-wired for humour. One is tempted to ask, "Where has all the laughter gone?"

In her 1974 article "What's so Funny? Notes on Canadian Humour," Atwood explains that humour is the result of a complex "triangular relationship between the person telling the joke, the person listening to it, and the person laughed at" or what she refers to as "laugher," "audience," and "laughee" (*SW* 175). The darkening direction of Atwood's work may perhaps result from changes in all three. The "laugher" is certainly not so prone to laughing any more. Atwood writes, "I'm a member of Amnesty International, and I read their monthly bulletins, which I would like to give *gratis*, a year's subscription to the next literary critic who accuses my work of being unduly pessimistic" (332).

There may also be a shift in audience. Critics seem to prefer major Atwood by which they mean "serious" Atwood. As Jimmy discovers in *Oryx and Crake*, individuals are not "given extra points for being funny" (*OC* 174) especially, one might add, if they are women. As Lisa Merrill points out, "Comedy is both an aggressive and intellectual response to human nature and experience. A cognizance of women's right to be both aggressive and intellectual is a relatively new historical phenomenon" (278). Atwood herself reminds us that "the funny bone, like other personality traits, is related to class, sex, colour, nationality and even age as well as to individual character" (*SW* 175). According to Merrill, "That which women do find funny is frequently misunderstood or devalued" (273). It may also be that "Canadian" humour does not travel well to Atwood's huge international audience, though the fact that comedians are a big Canadian export suggests otherwise.

Lastly, it may be more difficult to find a suitable "laughee" in this age of political correctness. Using the phrase that becomes the title of her 1990 essay, Atwood argued that women, who for years were told "if you can't say something nice don't say anything at all," were experiencing new kinds of silencing (25), a point humorously illustrated in the story "There was Once" published in *Good Bones*. The narrator can't get past the first three words of her story for fear of offending someone. According to Eco, "Comic is always racist; only the others, the Barbarians, are supposed to pay" (2). In the minds of some, the fact that jokes require what Crake calls "a little malice" (*OC* 306) may make them unworthy of our attention.

In her article on Canadian humour, Atwood identifies many kinds of laughter. There's the laughter of recognition and identity, the laughter of derision and distance, the laughter of survival, and the laughter of satire. Through the years she has invited us to join her in all four—the laughter that says, "I am like that," or "I am not like that," or "better to laugh than kill yourself," and the laughter that becomes a weapon against what is dangerous in the world. Perhaps Atwood's laughter has changed as the world has changed, but as many who know her have pointed out, it is one of the qualities that have allowed her to adapt and endure. In *Two Solicitudes*, Atwood asks Victor-Lévy Beaulieu, "Do you think that God has a sense of humour?" (240). When he says no, Atwood counters, "But He created man!"(241). Whether she means the male gender or all of humanity, she is deeply aware of this divine ability to imagine creatures as absurd and astounding as ourselves. Throughout her long and distinguished career, she has often made us wince but she has also made us wink. If your answer to the question "Does Atwood have a sense of humour?" is no, think again.

—Acadia University

WORKS CITED

Abrams, M.H. *A Glossary of Literary Terms*. 4th ed. New York: Holt, Rinehart & Winston, 1981.

Atwood, Margaret. *Bottle*. Hay, UK: Hay Festival Press, 2004.

———. *Good Bones*. Toronto: Coach House, 1992.

———. "If You Can't Say Something Nice, Don't Say Anything At All." In *Language in Her Eye: Views on Writing and Gender by Canadian Women Writing in English*, edited by Sarah Sheard, Libby Scheier and Eleanor Watchel, 15–25. Toronto: Coach House, 1990.

———. *Lady Oracle*. [1976]. Toronto: Seal, 1977.

———. *Morning in the Burned House*. Toronto: McClelland & Stewart, 1995.

———. *Oryx and Crake*. Toronto: McClelland & Stewart, 2003.

———. "Rape Fantasies." *Dancing Girls and Other Stories*. Toronto: McClelland & Stewart, 1977. 99–110.

———. *Second Words: Selected Critical Prose*. Toronto: Anansi, 1982.

———. *Selected Poems: 1966–1984*. Toronto: Oxford University Press, 1990.

———. *The Handmaid's Tale*. [1985]. Toronto: Seal, 1986.

———. *The Tent*. New York: Nan A Talese, 2006.

———. *Two Solicitudes: Conversations*. Translated by Phyllis Aronoff and Howard Scott. Toronto: McClelland & Stewart, 1998.

Barbour, Douglas, and Stephen Scobie, eds. *The Maple Laugh Forever: An Anthology of Comic Canadian Poetry*. Edmonton: Hurtig, 1981.

Benton, Carol L. "Reading as Rehearsal in a Communication Class: Comic Voicings in Atwood's Poetry." In *Approaches to Teaching Atwood's "The Handmaid's Tale" and Other Works*, edited by Sharon R. Wilson. 84–89. New York: MLA, 1996.

Caple, Natalee. "Writing Life: Atwood collects 'bite-sized' mini-fictions in *The Tent*." *Calgary Herald*, January 21, 2006. F1.

Eco, Umberto. "Frames of Comic Freedom." In *Carnival!* edited by T.A. Sebeok, 1–9. Berlin: Mouton, 1984.

Godard, Barbara. "Telling It Over Again: Atwood's Art of Parody." *Canadian Poetry: Studies, Documents, Reviews* (Fall/Winter 1987): 1–30.

Merivale, Patricia. "From 'Bad News' to 'Good Bones': Margaret Atwood's Gendering of Art and Elegy." In *Various Atwoods: Essays on the Later Poems, Short Fiction and Novels*, edited by Lorraine M. York, 253–70. Toronto: House of Anansi, 1995.

Merrill, Lisa. "Feminist Humor: Rebellious and Self-affirming." In *Last Laughs: Perspectives on Women and Comedy*, edited by Regina Barreca, 271–80. New York: Gordon & Breach, 1988.

Nischik, Reingard M. "Murder in the Dark: Margaret Atwood's Inverse Poetics of Intertextual Minuteness." In *Margaret Atwood's Textual Assassinations: Recent Poetry and Fiction*, edited by Sharon R. Wilson, 1-17. Columbus: Ohio State University Press, 2003.

Oates, Joyce C. "Dancing on the Edge of the Precipice: An Interview with Margaret Atwood." In *Conversations*, edited by Earl G. Ingersoll, 74–85. Princeton, NJ: Ontario Review Press, 1990.

Oryx and Crake Home Page. McClelland & Stewart. [online]: <http://www.mcclelland.com/features/oryxandcrake/praise.html> (accessed July 1, 2006).

Oxford English Dictionary Online. Second Edition, 1989. [online]: <http:dictionary.oed.com/> (accessed July 1, 2006).

Rigney, Barbara Hill. *Women Writers: Margaret Atwood.* Totowa, NJ: Barnes & Noble, 1987.

Sandler, Linda. "Interview with Margaret Atwood." *Malahat Review*, no. 41 (1977): 7–27.

Skelton, Robin. "Timeless Constructions: A Note on the Poetic Style of Margaret Atwood." *Malahat Review*, no. 41 (1977): 107–20.

Smith, Rowland. "Margaret Atwood: The Stoic Comedian." *Malahat Review*, no. 41 (1977): 134–44.

Stein, Karen F. *Margaret Atwood Revisited.* New York: Twayne, 1999.

Tihanyi, Eva. "Atwood's Dark Intent." *National Post.* January 21, 2006. WP 20.

Wagner-Martin, Linda. "'Giving Way to Bedrock': Atwood's Later Poems." In *Various Atwoods: Essays on the Later Poems, Short Fiction and Novels*, edited by Lorraine M. York, 71–88. Toronto: House of Anansi, 1995.

Wilson, Sharon R. "Fiction Flashes: Genre and Intertexts in *Good Bones*." In *Margaret Atwood's Textual Assassinations: Recent Poetry and Fiction*, edited by Sharon R. Wilson, 18–39. Columbus: Ohio State University Press, 2003.

"Back from the Dead": Journeys to the Underworld in *Wilderness Tips*

PAMELA S. BROMBERG

MARGARET ATWOOD'S RECENT essay collection on being a writer takes its name, *Negotiating with the Dead*, from the sixth and final chapter. It is here that Atwood postulates the following:

> All writing of the narrative kind, and perhaps all writing, is motivated, deep down, by a fear of and a fascination with mortality—by a desire to make the risky trip to the Underworld, and to bring something or someone back from the dead. (*ND* 156)

"[D]ead people persist in the minds of the living" and, as Atwood reminds us, storytelling is one of the chief ways in which we can visit the dead and the past (159). They draw us into conversation, even into risky journeys into the underworld, usually in quest of riches or knowledge, the chance to battle an evil monster, or in search of "the loved and the lost" (168). Contact with the dead is dangerous and storytelling is itself inescapably temporal and therefore shadowed by transience—by the running on and, finally, the running out of the clock. Paradoxically, even narrative partakes of the very mortality that motivates it. Yet reading can always bring the story back to fleeting life.

I will argue that *Wilderness Tips* is a collection of descent stories. With the exception of the final story in this volume, "Hack Wednesday," in each short story the protagonist journeys into the past for answers to questions about the present or in search of lost loves and lost selves, bringing them back to fleeting life through memory and storytelling, life that must always be "lost again" when the story ends (ND 172). Atwood warns in her essay that the dead are powerful; they "make demands" and "persist in the minds of the living" (166, 159). In "Uncles," "Death by Landscape," and "Weight," the stories of the dead have overtaken those of the living. "Uncles," for example, concludes with the terrifying fantasy of Susanna's dead father watching her childhood performance with hatred in his eyes. Haunted by the missing ending of Lucy's story of disappearance, Lois, the protagonist of "Death by Landscape," has sleepwalked through the rest of her life, unable to narrate her own life story as she compulsively searches painted landscapes for Lucy. In "Weight," remembering Molly is the nameless narrator's way of countering her "Dismemberment," a pun made both in the story and again in *Negotiating with the Dead* (149). But Molly's absence appears to have taken over the narrator's life; at the end of the story the weight of her guilt about Molly's death has brought her own life to a standstill as she plans to converse with Molly in a cemetery and "lay a wreath of invisible money on her grave" (*WT* 178). Like Lucy and Susanna, the guilt-plagued narrator has been "captured and held immobile by the past" (*ND* 178), by spectres whose own lives were cut short.

The descent into the underworld of the past often begins with fragmentary images, more like the material of dreams than coherent stories. Elaine Risley in *Cat's Eye*, for example, first accesses her past through visual images that she captures in paintings. But she needs to put those images into the narrative order of the novel's Künstlerroman plot in order to fully access her past and heal the psychic wounds of her childhood. No single short story in *Wilderness Tips* is sufficiently developed to follow its protagonist through the entire epic journey into the past. Instead, these stories present a group of protagonists at different stages of the journey to the land of the dead. Susanna has just discovered her monster and has yet to do battle with him. Lois and Molly are both lost among the shades, unable to find the way back up to the land of the living.

However, not all of the stories in *Wilderness Tips* end with their protagonists conversing with ghosts. Some converse with a present audience, demonstrating, as Atwood assures us in *Negotiating with the Dead*, that it is possible for writers to make the perilous descent into the underworld of the past to find the stories, then to return and write them down, thereby entering the realm of readers, of change, and of time as the ongoing medium for life (178–79). The protagonists of "True Trash," "The Bog Man," and "Isis in Darkness" all employ narrative art to escape the hold of the past by finding plots that give closure and leave the story with the reader. In each case they work through alternate versions of their stories, some provided by intertexts that encode culture and ideology into narrative, and end by choosing versions that enable them to leave the past behind by finding its meaning. At the end of "Isis in Darkness," Richard identifies himself as the "archaeologist," "the one who will sift through the rubble, groping for the shape of the past" (*WT* 73).

In this paper I will focus on "The Bog Man," comparing it with "The Age of Lead," a story that belongs with the first group; it ends with its protagonist Jane as "desolate: left behind, stranded" (161) by the loss of Vincent, her youth, and the risky possibilities she always refused because of her fear of "consequences." I will argue, however, that Julie, protagonist of "The Bog Man," is able to return to the land of the living through her skill as a storyteller, and who continues to revise and retell the story of her love affair with her professor, Connor.

Before discussing the two stories I would like to begin with two poems, published nearly thirty years apart, in which Atwood employs space as a metaphor for time, a trope that runs throughout her writing as well as underlying the metaphor of storytelling as a journey of descent into the past. In both poems she presents the paradox of a photograph, a static two-dimensional representation in space that preserves a moment in time, now past. The first poem is "This is a Photograph of Me," published in 1966 at the beginning of Atwood's writing career and positioned at the very beginning of the volume *Selected Poems: 1965–1975* (8). The poem's first-person speaker addresses the reader, describing in the present tense (also employed in the title) the blurred photograph of a rural landscape as a portrait of her, "taken some time ago." The reader assumes, initially, that he or she is in the presence of a living persona who is narrating a past moment. Then, in a spooky parenthetical phrase that constitutes the poem's second half, this "I" explains that the "The photograph was taken/ the day after I drowned./I am in the lake, in the center/of the picture, just under the surface." Thus, while this photograph of a landscape, which somehow captures the drowned "I," continues to exist in the present, the life it captures is gone. Yet the drowned "I" speaks, addressing the reader now, as we read. How can the dead self speak? Photographs preserve the past as a presence, but only as a two-dimensional representation of a framed and frozen moment. If we read the poem metaphorically, the past self or past moment is always "drowned" under the surface of time, absent, never to be discovered again in the present, but available through the distortions of image or language, "if you look long enough," in a kind of Derridean trace. In the poem's parenthesis, words, or voice, a story replaces the visual and spatial image. The past we access through language has depth and presence. Atwood returns to this idea repeatedly in her writing: The opening line of the retrospective novel *Cat's Eye*, for example, states, "Time is not a line but a dimension, like the dimension of space" (3).

In *Negotiating with the Dead* Atwood suggests a variety of ways in which the dead can reappear briefly to the living, including house hauntings, Halloween, and Mexico's Day of the Dead, among others. The poem "Man in a Glacier" from the 1995 collection *Morning in the Burned House* begins with a more freakish instance of the return of the dead, the exhumation of a long-dead but amazingly well-preserved body. Variations of this scenario also appear in both "The Age of Lead" and "The Bog Man." In all three works the reappearance of the dead body serves as a powerful metaphor for the paradox of the past and our desire to recapture it. In each one the preserved body emphasizes the ghoulish dimension of the desire to bring the dead back to life as well as the disembodied, purely representational status of the dead who return as images, memories, and stories. And while the exhumed body has been preserved and therefore seems static, potentially retrievable, and outside of time, it is in fact still subject to what "Man in a Glacier" calls "the icy arms of Chemistry and Physics," the entropic reality of the physical world (MBH 81–82). Furthermore, while these dead bodies are objects in the real world, living human beings must decode them, interpreting the conditions and meaning of their preservation; they must be read—according to the codes of archaeology, geology, and anthropology—before they will yield their stories.

In "Man in a Glacier" Atwood juxtaposes the discovery of the body of a man preserved in a glacier, "two thousand years old or three," with the discovery of an old box of photographic slides in the cellar that include the visual image of "my father,/alive or else preserved, younger than all/of us now, dark-haired and skinny,/in baggy trousers." The poem's first words, a command to the reader, "Now see," echo the closing line in "This is a Photograph of Me" and initiate linguistic play with the concept of vision. The reader is told to use the eye of the mind to see the two preserved men and their difference, the mortal body miraculously preserved in nature's freezer compared with "a freeze-framed simulacrum" brought to life by "a wand of light," "but there. There still." Although the unearthed body appears to live again in its presence, it is in fact as dead as the absent, ironically youthful father, whose image remains "there still," a pun articulating the paradox of its lack of bodily motion as well as its static, two-dimensional continuity.

The poem's concluding stanza moves away from the dead entirely to focus on the living. It articulates a third discovery, this one mental rather than corporeal or visual: "we opened our eyes" to find ourselves in "the icy arms of Chemistry and Physics, our/bad godmothers," an indifferent universe of space and time "we could not stop, or live backwards." The godmothers condemn the living not only to mortality but also to the curse of consciousness, the knowledge of loss that makes us pray for the "everlastingness" we cannot have. The poem is finally an elegy, not only for the dead father or the nameless "man in a glacier" but for those who remain to tell their stories, mourn their loss, and recognize their own mortality. What the reader sees in the end is that both flesh and blood, the unearthed body, and even the photographic image on the fading slide are finally subject to the physical laws of the universe; the language that brings them to light in the poem, however, exists in another realm. Only the living, with their scientific inquiry, "prayers for everlastingness," or mental vision can confer meaning upon the unearthed bodies, whether three- or two-dimensional, bringing them back to life in thought. In a final paradox, it is language, the poem itself, that creates the reader's mental image of both the photographic slide and the man in a glacier.

In *Wilderness Tips* the medium for bringing the dead back to life is narrative. In much the same way that I read the two poems as explorations of the power of language or mental vision to confer presence, I see the stories as explorations of the power of storytelling to bestow "life of a sort" on the dead (*ND* 172). Both "The Age of Lead" and "The Bog Man" include multiple stories that reflect, comment upon, and in some cases influence each other, thereby foregrounding narrative itself as a central subject. "The Age of Lead" interweaves three narratives: the life stories of a mother and a daughter, as well as a TV documentary. In "The Age of Lead" the protagonist Jane watches a television show about the discovery of the frozen corpse of John Torrington, part of the Franklin Expedition that set out in 1845 to discover the Northwest Passage. The story reveals Jane's thoughts as her attention moves back and forth from the narrative of the expedition and the death of Torrington at the age of twenty to her own parallel story about the loss of Vincent, her close friend, almost lover, who died a year earlier at the age of forty-three from a mutated virus. In the TV story, scientific analysis, as well as narrative, enable Torrington's corpse to tell its story, revealing that the entire Franklin Expedition died by lead poisoning, caused by the technological innovation of the tin cans that were supposed to help nourish them. If we read the story of the expedition as an intertextual key to Jane's narrative, then we may interpret Vincent's premature death as a precursor to *Oryx and Crake*, Atwood's environmental anti-apocalypse. This reading would locate his loss as part of an ominous 1980s trend in Toronto; "some mysterious agent, a thing like a colorless gas, scentless and invisible" seems to be killing off Jane's friends (*WT* 159), and she suspects a causal connection to environmental destruction.

But "The Age of Lead" is as much a descent story as it is a prophecy of environmental doom. Jane's memories of Vincent take her back to her own youth in the 1960s and then forward through a life not lived. Her story is, in turn, preceded by her mother's story, told to Jane as a fall story about the "*consequences*" of passion (151). In this plot, wartime romance led to unwanted pregnancy, forced marriage, and then the father's abandonment of his unwanted family.[1] The metaphor of "gravity" has shaped this plot as well as the mature, maternal body, and the arc of disappointed dreams. Jane remembers her mother "still: in terms of a pendulous, drooping, wilting motion" (151). In her mother's story Jane herself is "a consequence. She had been a mistake, she had been a war baby" (151). The powerful moral of this plot is that "love, with a capital L" causes "inevitable disaster" (152). This monitory narrative warning girls away from sex is also scripted in numerous "songs and movies," including specific intertexts such as *Gone with the Wind* and the Beau Brummels 1965 hit song "Laugh, Laugh." These interpolated texts gesture toward the power of cultural scripts to shape narrative and therefore identity. Jane's mother's life has been constituted by her metaphor of gravity, and Jane's, by the desire to flee from it. Along with Vincent, a camp, lover-substitute who protected Jane from the fearful "gravity of love," Jane "wanted a life without consequences." They sought "freedom from the world of mothers, the world of precautions, the world of burdens and fate and heavy female constraints upon the flesh" (154). They were ironists, employing wit and double meanings as defences against "the gravity of love," in both senses of the word "gravity": the weight of the mortal body and the seriousness of deep feeling.

In her quest not to follow her mother's path, not to be betrayed by the flesh—its desires and consequences—Jane has avoided love, commitment, marriage, children. But as she looks back on her life and on the death of her best friend Vincent, Jane realizes that "their mothers had finally caught up to them and been proven right. There were consequences after all; but they were the consequences to things you didn't even know you had done" (161). Jane's decision to avoid the risks and "gravity of love" has not saved Vincent from death or her from regret. Jane's story has been shaped in opposition to her mother's, but it echoes that of the Franklin expedition. The two narratives begin with dreams of escape from the constraints of the world of consequences—the noble daring of exploration and discovery in the case of the Franklin Expedition, and a "life without consequences" in the case of Jane and Vincent (154). Each story concludes with the inevitable reality of life in time, of aging bodies and death. The preserved corpses of John Torrington and the man in the glacier, the fading photographic image of a father younger than the children he has left behind, the premature death of Vincent at the age of forty-three—all of these images argue with heavy irony that eternal youth is only possible through death. The survivors of those untimely deaths are, in Jane's words, "left behind, stranded" (161), and taken by surprise by loss and the passage of time.

Julie, protagonist of "The Bog Man" is Jane's counterpart. As Arnold Davidson suggests in his essay on *Wilderness Tips*, "The Age of Lead" and "The Bog Man" can be seen as paired doubles setting forth countering versions of the stories told centrally in each (184). The two protagonists belong to the same generation that came of age in "the early sixties" (78). The retrospective stories they tell are structured as variant romance plots, though with significant differences; for example, in her youth, Julie believed in the love story that Jane and Vincent parodied and feared. Each short story also juxtaposes the protagonist's narrative journey into the underworld of the past with a story about the exhumation of a corpse, in this case a so-called bog man, sacrificed around 2,000 years ago to a fertility goddess and well preserved by the tannic acid in the Scottish peat bog where he was sunk.

However, while Jane's descent into the past is unplanned, a stream of narrative memories triggered by the television show she's watching, Julie is a practiced storyteller. She has been regaling friends with the story of her romantic affair with Connor for years, and we realize at the end that the telling of "The Bog Man" is staged as a dramatic event for an unknown audience when Julie comments, "God knows, ... what I thought I was doing" (95). "The Bog Man" both opens and closes with self-reflexive passages in which Julie silently considers the story and her crafting of it, the evolution over time of its plot and central moral as she tells it once more. The story's "physical details" remain clear to Julie, but as she moves through time and life, her vantage point continues to change and so, accordingly, does her view of the past and her understanding of Connor and of herself: "With each retelling, she feels herself more present in it" (95).

Taking Atwood's suggestion in *Negotiating with the Dead* that journeys into the underworld of the past present the opportunity to do heroic battle with monsters (*ND* 170), I read "The Bog Man" focusing on Connor's narrative transformation from the divinity of Julie's initial infatuation to the "fanged" monster who pursues her after she leaves him, to the portrait of middle-aged longing that emerges from this telling of the story. Of course, Connor's narrative metamorphoses can be read as markers in the metastory of Julie's maturing understanding of the affair, a narrative structured by metaphors of light, darkness, and vision.

In her last year of university, Julie fell in love with her archaeology professor's voice, "rich and rough-edged, persuasive and abraded, rising and falling in the darkness" (79). Connor begins for Julie as a "divinity" (92), the projection of her romantic desire for "someone to worship" (78). From her vantage point, Connor is "superhuman" and she is content to "[bask] in his light." "She did not think of him as having an existence apart from her. ... Instead, she saw him in glorious and noble isolation, a man singled out, ... like a saint in a medieval painting, surrounded by a golden atmosphere of his own" (79). The reality of Connor's life, of Connor's human body and self rather than his disembodied voice, becomes more manifest during the research trip to Scotland. There Julie sees how she and Connor are perceived by the Norwegian; she looks at the family photograph in Connor's wallet and *sees* Connor's wife; then she sees Connor's double, the sacrificial bog man. The turning point in her view of Connor takes place as Connor looks in the mirror, slaps his belly, and says, "I'm getting love-handles, ... the curse of the middle-aged" and expresses the fear that "one of these days ... you're going to run off with some young stud." At this critical moment Julie begins to see Connor as he sees himself and she realizes also "that there might be a difference between her idea of him and his own idea of himself" (88–89). As she takes in the "added weight" of Connor's reality "apart from her," especially that of his "unseen wife," Julie "no longer wants him. The divinity is going out of him, like air," and she ends the affair (89, 79, 92). In this story the gravity of reality sinks romantic desire.

What the youthful Julie has failed to recognize, however, is the role that she plays for Connor in his own parallel fantasy of eternal youth. The middle-aged man who imagines himself in love with her terrifies her. His "need" for her is frightening, even monstrous. As she cowers in the refuge of a glass telephone booth, Connor shouts his love for her:

> She is truly frightened of him now, she's whimpering with fright. He's no longer anyone she knows; he's the universal child's nightmare, the evil violent thing, fanged and monstrous, trying to get in at the door. (93)

Telling the story enables an older Julie to slay the monster by seeing truths that were unavailable to her younger self. In the last two pages of "The Bog Man," Julie recalls her successive versions of the affair with Connor. Each version in turn marks a stage in Julie's own growth and development, as well as supplying an interpretive scheme, or plot, that organizes the events of the affair and its end. At first, Julie was silent, unable to tell the story because it was too painful, confusing, and complicated. Should she read and tell it as a sexual harassment story? Or is it really a tale of self-deception on her part; this version makes her nostalgic, evoking tender longing for "her own mistaken adoration" (94). Then after she was first married and divorced, she began to tell the Connor story to other women as a male mystery story, focusing on men and their obscure behaviour. This version appears to have served as a bonding ritual influenced by the early women's movement. Now Julie is remarried (men have apparently become less mysterious) and the story has become comic entertainment, told more frequently and with emphasis on the setting and humorous details. In this version she "skims over" her "worshipping love," Connor's "once-golden aura," Connor's wife, with whom she now sympathetically identifies, and the "grief." She edits out awareness of the damage she has done to Connor, which "does not really fit into the story" (94).

At the end Julie continues to reflect upon her past, recognizing that over time the story has become more centred on her. "The story has now become a story about her own stupidity, or call it innocence" (95). The "physical details" remain vivid in her memory while the plot has evolved, telling an almost Wordsworthian story of the young student's inability to comprehend her middle-aged professor. The absent Connor has steadily dwindled from the superhuman hero constructed by adolescent romance; he "becomes flatter and more leathery, ... more dead," a bog man sacrificed on the altar of her growth. In this final version, ironically, Julie has herself moved closer toward Connor, whose identity as a middle-aged man aware of his declining body has been suspended in the timeless bog of narrative. He has remained unchanged, though increasingly less substantial, as she has continued to live and age. "By this time he is almost an anecdote and Julie is almost old" (95). She has moved from the realm of romance to "the realm of change" (*ND* 179).

Wilderness Tips closes with "Hack Wednesday," the one story in which the protagonist does not look back. It is an elegy not for the lost past but for the passing present. Marcia narrates a day in her life as she lives it, not retrospectively; she focuses not on the past but on the here and now, on her present life and on the problematic world she lives in. Marcia is sadly aware of being middle-aged and in time; for her, "time is going faster and faster" (207) and she tries to slow it down by "squirreling away bits of time—a photo here, a letter there" (214). Marcia, in contrast to so many of the other narrators in *Wilderness Tips*, is a determined realist. A columnist for the local newspaper, *The World*, she "interviews people," writing "from the particular to the general" to spotlight social issues, including "malnutrition in kindergartens, wife-beating, overcrowding in prisons, child abuse" (216). Along with her activist historian husband Eric, Marcia is a truth teller; she does not shirk from writing the "bad news" that her profit-minded newspaper may soon decide not to publish.

In this respect Marcia is Margaret Atwood's double. In *Negotiating with the Dead* Atwood poses the question of the artist's social responsibility and carefully suggests that the self-identity of the writer as an eyewitness with a cold, clear eye that "must look at everything" may combine "responsibility with artistic integrity" (*ND* 121). Indeed, the world that Marcia reports on in December 1989 is a grim and wintry place. But I would argue that "Hack Wednesday" closes the volume of stories on a note of affirmation. Notwithstanding, or perhaps because of, her clear-eyed vision of the dark and disturbing truth of the human situation, including the rapid passage of her own days, Marcia takes pleasure in the present and looks forward to the future. The story ends with a moment of benediction as she and Eric share dinner and wine by candlelight: "Marcia smiles, too, and eats and drinks, and is happy, and outside the kitchen window the wind blows and the world shifts and crumbles and rearranges itself, and time goes on" (226). As she sits eating her applesauce, "Marcia knows that the day itself is seeping away from her, that it will go and will continue to go, and will never come back" (227). The story shifts into the future tense as Marcia anticipates the arrival of her children the next day and the celebration of Christmas Day on Monday. Marcia's acute sense of the passage of time is a measure of her own love of life and her capacity to live in the present, "the realm of change" (*ND* 179) with her eyes open to the "real news" (228).

—Simmons College

NOTES

1. This is a recurrent plot in Atwood's fiction, appearing in variant forms in *Lady Oracle* and *The Robber Bride*.

WORKS CITED

Atwood, Margaret. *Cat's Eye*. New York: Doubleday, 1989.

———. *Morning in the Burned House*. Boston: Houghton Mifflin, 1995.

———. *Negotiating with the Dead: A Writer on Writing*. Cambridge: Cambridge University Press, 2002.

———. *Selected Poems: 1965–1975*. Boston: Houghton Mifflin, 1976.

———. *Wilderness Tips*. New York: Doubleday, 1996.

Davidson, Arnold E. "Negotiating *Wilderness Tips*." In *Approaches to Teaching Atwood's "The Handmaid's Tale" and Other Works*, edited by Sharon R. Wilson, Thomas B. Friedman, and Shannon Hengen, 180–86. New York: The Modern Language Association, 1996.

"*It's still you*": Aging and Identity in Atwood's Poetry

SARA JAMIESON

AS COMMENTATORS ON *Morning in the Burned House* have noted, Margaret Atwood undertakes an extended investigation of the aging self in the collection. In this respect the book continues and expands on an anticipation of old age initiated in earlier poems. In a poem from the mid-eighties, for example, entitled "Aging Female Poet on Laundry Day," the speaker takes note of bodily changes occurring in middle age, and imagines how this process will continue as she grows older:

> Whatever exists at the earth's center will get me
> sooner or later. Sooner. Than I think.
> Already it's dragging me down, already
> I become shorter, infinitesimally.
> The bones of my legs thicken—that's first—
> contract, like muscles.
> After that comes the frailty, a dry wind blowing
> inside my body,
> scouring me from within, as if I were
> a fossil, the soft parts eaten away.
> Soon I will turn to calcium. It starts with the heart. (*SP II* 129)

In Atwood's fossil image is an intriguing echo of one of Simone de Beauvoir's famously pessimistic descriptions of physical aging as a process of "petrification" (qtd. in Woodward, *Aging*, 110). While it may be possible to ambiguously read the kind of hardening that Atwood describes, her poem nonetheless plays upon a widespread cultural dread of old age: aging is figured as a kind of decomposition that metaphorically links it with death; it is associated with desiccation, frailty, and the consumption of identity; the curious image of the ossified heart suggests a physical decline accompanied by a kind of calcification of the spirit. By envisioning her transformation into a fossil, Atwood is able to place her own old age in a still-distant future by equating human aging with the slow progress of geological time. She was, after all, only in her mid-forties when this poem appeared. At the same time, however, her repetitive use of temporal markers such as "already" and "soon" communicate a fearful sense that this process is happening all too quickly. Thus, Atwood's poem both participates in and struggles against what Margaret M. Gullette insists is the "master narrative" of mid-life in Western culture, a narrative of middle age as the beginning of an accelerated, precipitous decline (159).

Scholars of aging such as de Beauvoir and Gullette, Kathleen Woodward and Sally Chivers, have all ably revealed the ways in which Western literature and culture continue to be dominated by negative views of aging as something to be feared, repressed, and, preferably, avoided, and they all have insisted on the political necessity of reimagining our own and others' aging in new and more productive ways. Woodward, for example, argues that the pervasive ageism of modern Western culture stems in part from our failure to identify ourselves sympathetically with those who are older than we are (*Aging* 59). This failure perpetuates a characterization of the old as Other, as alien, and makes it difficult for us to anticipate our own aging as anything other than a catastrophic loss of identity. Chivers too has argued that our interpretation of our own aging is bound up with the ways in which we perceive aging in others, and suggests that by "reading the signs of aging on other bodies as similar to [our] own" (17), we can avoid denigrating the old and look ahead to our own old age with feelings other than revulsion and fear. It is precisely this kind of movement from a narcissistic, fearful anticipation of old age to one that is more relational and sympathetic that I will explore in my own readings of a couple of poems from *Morning in the Burned House*. Kathryn Van Spanckeren has already traced the collection's movement from "a trickster's psychology of survival to a new mutuality" (109). This is an apt description of the narrative of aging that emerges over the course of the book. This is not to say, however, that Atwood's most optimistic imaginings of middle and late life are not still haunted by cultural fears.

Questions of aging are especially prominent in the opening sections of the book, and nowhere more so than in a poem called "Waiting." "Here it is then," the speaker says of middle age, "the dark thing you have waited for so long" (8). The poem sets up a comparison between the experience of middle age and various negative, and sometimes contradictory, ways in which our culture teaches us to anticipate it. If age does not envelope you "in a damp enfolding, like the mildew/shroud on bread," then it will "come swiftly and without sound ... like a high-speed train,/and a single blow on the head" (8). The ensuing "blackout" characterizes aging as a kind of lapse of consciousness. According to de Beauvoir, age belongs "to that category which Sartre calls the unrealizables" and is something that we may have difficulty perceiving in ourselves (291). Age is not simply a matter of how young we may feel ourselves to be, but is conferred upon us by the judgments of others. The possibility of a painful disjunction between our own and the world's estimation of our age lies at the heart of Atwood's second stanza:

> ... you thought it would hide
> in your closet, among the clothes you outgrew years ago,
> nesting in dustballs and fallen hair, shedding
> one of your fabricated skins
> after another and growing bigger,
> honing its teeth on your discarded
> cloth lives, ... (8)

Clothing is one of the most obvious indices by which society measures age-appropriateness, and, as Alison Lurie points out, disparities between age and costume are often perceived as "disgusting or even frightening" (57). Indeed, in Atwood's poem, fear is the primary affect associated with the closetful of outdated clothes that mirrors the speaker's age back to her in a manner that causes her to anticipate the reproving judgments of the world. Atwood does manage to deflate the impact of such judgments by suggesting a lack of proportion, equating age-anxiety with childhood terrors of imaginary monsters in the closet. Dismissing the fear of the clothes closet as one of several "melodramas" through which culture inculcates the fear of aging, the poem shifts into what initially seems a more realistic mode. Middle age turns out to be nothing like the speaker's imaginings: "Instead it is strangely like home" (8). Coming after the catalogue of horrors at the beginning of the poem, such familiarity might be expected to be reassuring, but this is not the case. Recognition of middle age turns out to be an eerie repetition of the moment in childhood

> when you realized for the first time
> in your life that you would be old some day, you would some day be
> as old as you are now ...
> and you would have a different body by then, an old murky one,
> a stranger's body you could not even imagine. (9–10)

The home that conceals a disturbing secret, the shocking recognition of a stranger as oneself, the surfacing of long-forgotten fears: all are characteristics of the "Uncanny," Freud's term for "that class of the frightening which leads back to what is known of old and long familiar" (220). Woodward stresses the importance of aging to the genesis of Freud's theory of the Uncanny by drawing our attention to a note in Freud's 1919 essay, in which he describes his own dismayed realization, when travelling on a train, that the "elderly gentleman" whom he at first takes to be an intruder in his compartment is in fact his own reflection in a mirror (*Aging*, 248). For Woodward, the anecdote typifies the repression of old age that she finds throughout Freudian psychoanalysis and throughout much of twentieth-century Western literature, a repression that links aging with "death, fear, [and] danger" (68). By representing the recognition of middle age as uncanny, a poem like Atwood's "Waiting" participates in this tradition of repression. Invoking Gothic horror and melodrama, the poem invites a reading of aging through generic lenses that are distancing and dehumanizing.

    An episode of uncanny doubling similarly haunts one of Atwood's earlier encounters with aging in "Five Poems for Grandmothers." In the course of this tribute to her nonagenarian maternal grandmother, the poet asks:

> Is this you, this edgy joke
> I make, are these your long fingers,
> your hair of an untidy bird,

is this your outraged
eye, this grip
that will not give up? (*SP II* 14)

The "joke" here refers ambiguously to both poem and poet. In a poem that ostensibly celebrates grandmaternal connections, at this moment the poet seems disturbed, made "edgy," by the surfacing of her grandmother's features in her own body. Literary gerontologists have stressed the importance of cross-generational relationships in enabling us to anticipate, rather than repress, the changes that we ourselves will go through as we grow older. In Atwood's sequence, however, this process is complicated by the fact that the grandmother is represented as suffering from some form of dementia that prevents her from recognizing her home or her children, and presents to the poet a frightening preview of her own possible future.

In contrast to the hereditary anxiety of "Five Poems for Grandmothers" and to the alienated self-address of "Waiting," "Shapechangers in Winter," from the final section of *Morning in the Burned House*, voices an acceptance of the middle-aged body that enables, and is enabled by, the acceptance of aging in the body of another. This acceptance in turn makes possible an anticipation of old age that betrays some trepidation, but is also marked by a confidence that is absent from the other poems I have discussed. I find it notable that this anticipation occurs not within the context of a cross-generational relationship but in a heterosexual love poem. Profound differences in the experience and social construction of male and female aging notwithstanding, this particular poem invites us to apprehend similarities through what Atwood calls our "common sense[s]" (124). In a specular, post-modern culture of mass-mediated images, in which identity is so often reduced to appearance, and a youthful appearance alone is considered pleasing, men and women alike have given voice to the feeling that as they age, their faces and bodies no longer correspond to their inner sense of self. Labelled "the mask of ageing" by social gerontologists (Featherstone and Hepworth 371), the notion of the aging body as a disguise that conceals a true identity is informed by a negative perception of aging as decline, since it figures aging as an unpromising split between an essential, internal self that does not change or develop, and an external appearance that is reviled as "disagreeable" (Gullette 146).

"Shapechangers in Winter" acknowledges that there are times when the lovers do seem to one another to be disguised, "you as a rumpled elephant—/hide suitcase with white fur,/me as a bramble bush" (*MBH*, 123). At the same time, the poem rejects any representation of aging that is conceived as a simple binary between an outward appearance and an inner self: the inner and outer "aliases" that the aging lovers present to one another work against the notion of the body as distinct from an inner self that is unchanging and essentially youthful (123). Coral Ann Howells has said of this poem that it exposes as illusory any centring of the individual human subject (76), and indeed Atwood's description of the lovers' younger bodies as "all sleight-of-hand and illusion" questions the extent to which identity was ever synonymous with a youthful appearance (*MBH*, 123). Disguise, alias, and illusion are presented as ongoing aspects of identity that are not confined to middle age alone. Comparing herself to a bramble bush, the poet admits, "Well, the hair/was always difficult" (123). Refusing an interpretation of middle age as a catastrophic break with the past and with youth, Atwood instead emphasizes continuities that enable acceptance of the body as it ages as an integral part of the self. Her affirmation, "*Yes./It's still you*," far from being a statement of faith in an inner identity that persists despite bodily changes, is rather an acceptance of change, including the changes of aging, as an essential component of selfhood.

The poet's attitude of acceptance toward the aging body is perhaps most clearly articulated through her emphasis on physical intimacy. Tanis Macdonald has theorized the possibility of a feminist heterosexuality capable of collapsing the distance implicit in the objectifying gaze of much traditional love poetry. Atwood's poem achieves this in a way that voices a specifically middle-aged feminist heterosexuality: by emphasizing touching over seeing, Atwood writes against a cultural tendency to reduce aging to its visible attributes, and directly challenges the view that aging and sexuality are antithetical. The poet fondly remembers youthful sexuality but does not bewail its loss:

> Once we were lithe as pythons, quick
> and silvery as herring, and we still are, momentarily,
> except our knees hurt. (*MBH*, 123)

The middle-aged couple, "content to huddle under the shed feathers of duck and goose," shares an intimacy that is changed but not diminished, as Atwood again represents the life course in a way that stresses continuity over loss.

This emphasis on touch is carried right through to the end of the poem, where the couple is envisioned entering deep old age locked in a kind of Protean embrace:

> But the trick is just to hold on
> through all appearances; and so we do,
> and yes, I know it's you;
> and that is what we will come to, sooner
> or later, when it's even darker
> than it is now, when the snow is colder,
> when it's darkest and coldest
> and candles are no longer any use to us
> and the visibility is zero: *Yes.*
> *It's still you. It's still you.* (125)

While Atwood continues to defy cultural taboo by suggesting the continuance of physical intimacy beyond middle age and into old age, it is at this point that the limits of her use of touch as an affirmation of identity in old age stand revealed. Woodward reminds us that "the loss of the affectionate touch of others" (*Aging* 171) is often a reality of life for the very old, and in view of this, the embrace that in Atwood's poem provides assurance of identity seems especially poignant: "If we are not touched," Woodward observes, "we might begin to suspect that we are not here" (*Aging* 174). Atwood's imagining of an old age when touch is still available might be read as an attempt to expose or even resist this particular form of cultural neglect of the elderly, but it seems equally possible to read it as a kind of evasion: no matter how we may try to anticipate and not fear our own future aging, there are still things that we don't want to imagine.

Indeed, the embrace that concludes the poem is one of several instances in which Atwood's vision of aging is shadowed by residual anxieties. For example, when the poet imagines herself and her partner as "footprints/becoming limestone, or … coal becoming diamond. Less/flexible, but more condensed," notice the way in which that second line break subtly insists on a diminishment that the phrase as a whole works to deny with its consoling images of transformation, permanence, and value (*MBH*, 123). This tension is established with the biological paradox that opens the stanza: "Every cell/in our bodies has renewed itself/so many times …

there's/not much left, my love,/of the originals." Here, aging is figured as a process of renewal that is simultaneously an erosion, one that deprives the lovers of a future (there is not much time left) and also a past (the people that they once were have ceased to exist). While the poet's biological metaphor figures aging in terms of regeneration, it also contains the fear of aging as instead a falling away from an "original," superior self. The reality of cellular deterioration fuels a cultural mythology of identity as formed and fixed in the early stages of the life course, a mythology that implicitly devalues the later ones. The poet's rueful lament for an original self finds a darker counterpart in "Waiting," where middle age is simply a confirmation of childhood fears, an experience that derealises the mature woman and reduces her to a kind of antique child, "a yellowing paper child," crouching on the floor of a house that no longer exists (10).

Likewise in "Shapechangers in Winter," the poet envisions the eventual demise of the domestic space that appears to offer such security:

> The walls of the house fold themselves down,
> and the house turns
> itself inside out, as a tulip does
> in its last full-blown moment, and our candle
> flares up and goes out, and the only common
> sense that remains to us is touch (124)

With this apocalyptic image, the poet attempts to come to terms not only with death but also with other fears associated with growing old, fears of loss, loneliness, neglect. As we have seen, in this middle-aged love poem the poet tries to mitigate this fear of the future by taking comfort in a present moment of physical intimacy. The fact that this intimacy, however, is couched in terms of such a conventional figure for a depleted (female) sexuality—the overblown flower—indicates the difficulty of escaping pervasive cultural stereotypes and finding different ways of imagining age.

Still, with this poem of sympathy and acceptance, we have moved a long way from the uncanny anticipations of "Waiting." The placement of "Shapechangers in Winter" near the end of the collection suggests the evolution of the poet's attitude toward aging, one that is part of what Van Spanckeren has labelled the book's "hard-won trajectory from a self-oriented mode to a more human vision" (106). On their own, Atwood's poems of aging are often haunted by powerful cultural anxieties, but taken together, they do convey some hope that a more habitable attitude might possibly be within our reach.

—University of Alberta

WORKS CITED

Atwood, Margaret. *Morning in the Burned House*. Toronto: McClelland & Stewart, 1995.

———. *Selected Poems II: Poems Selected and New 1976–1986*. Toronto: Oxford University Press.

Chivers, Sally. *From Old Woman to Older Women: Contemporary Culture and Women's Narratives*. Columbus: Ohio State University Press, 2003.

de Beauvoir, Simone. *Old Age*. London: Cox & Wyman, 1972.

Featherstone, Mike, and Mike Hepworth. "The Mask of Ageing and the Postmodern Life Course." In *The Body: Social Process and Cultural Theory*, edited by Mike Featherstone, Mike Hepworth, and B.S. Turner, 371–89. London: Sage, 1991.

Freud, Sigmund. "The Uncanny." [1919]. *The Standard Edition of the Complete Psychological Works of Sigmund Freud*, Vol. 17, translated and edited by James Strachey, 218–56. London: Hogarth Press, 1953–1974.

Gullette, Margaret M. *Declining to Decline: Cultural Combat and the Politics of the Midlife*. Charlottesville: University Press of Virginia, 1997.

Howells, Coral Ann. "*Morning in the Burned House*: At Home in the Wilderness." In *The Contrast and the Culmination: Essays in Honour of Hera Maes-Jelinek*, edited by Marc Delrez and Bénédicte Ledent, 69–78. Liège: University of Liège, 1997.

Lurie, Alison. *The Language of Clothes*. New York: Random, 1981.

MacDonald, Tanis. "Regarding the Male Body: Rhapsodic Contemplation in Lorna Crozier's 'Penis Poems.'" *ESC*, no.28 (2002): 247–67.

Van Spanckeren, Kathryn. "Humanizing the Fox: Atwood's Poetic Tricksters and *Morning in the Burned House*." In *Margaret Atwood's Textual Assassinations: Recent Poetry and Fiction*, edited by Sharon R. Wilson, 102–20. Columbus: Ohio State University Press, 2003.

Woodward, Kathleen. *Aging and Its Discontents: Freud and Other Fictions*. Bloomington: Indiana University Press, 1991.

"Com[ing] Through Darkness": Margaret Atwood's "I"-Opening Lyricism

DAVID R. JARRAWAY

> The writer is thus the original invisible man: not there at all but also very solidly there, at one and the same time ... [since] we can hear a voice. Or so it seems.
> —Margaret Atwood, *Negotiating with the Dead* (148)

...

> the fact that [the place of woman] remains empty does not mean that we cannot find something there. But in it we find only masks, masks of nothingness, which are sufficient to justify the connection between women and semblances.
> —Jacques-Alain Miller, "On Semblances in the Relation between the Sexes" (14)

...

> It's one damn thing after another, and the important word in that sentence is *after*.
> —Margaret Atwood, *Negotiating with the Dead* (158)

With the recent publication of her novel *Oryx and Crake*, Margaret Atwood's extraordinary achievement as a poet may continue to recede for a large number of her readers. This paper aims in the first instance to rekindle interest in that achievement, and will take as its starting point the clear separation Atwood makes between writing poetry and writing fiction in her National Arts Club Medal for Literature acceptance speech from 1997. There, reminiscing about composing comic books on rainy summer days with her brother in their youth, Atwood alludes to the more sunny occasions they also spent "turning over rocks to see what was underneath." She remarks, "People often ask me, 'What's the difference between writing poetry and writing fiction?' And surely it is this: with a lyric poem, you look, and meditate, and put the rock back" rather than (as with fiction) "pok[ing] things with a stick to see what will happen." "But with both," Atwood emphasizes, "there has to be something under the rock first ... and this is where hope and despair ... come into it" ("The Writer" 39).

Let me begin, therefore, with what must appear the despairing side throughout much of Atwood's *Selected Poetry* and the continuous perception that nature (or external reality, or the outside world) is somehow specifically calculated to overwhelm and perhaps even eradicate the lone and hapless self. In poems like "Progressive Insanities of a Pioneer," published in 1968 in *The Animals in That Country* (1968), we first begin reading about an "absence/of order" or the deluge of "unstructured/space" that, like the invasion of some "unnamed whale" (*SP* 48, 49, 50), eventually modulates into the unfamiliar chaos of nature in *The Journals of Susanna Moodie*. Consider "A Bus along St. Clair: December":

> Right now, the snow
> is no more familiar
> to you than it was to me:
> this is my doing.
> The grey air, the roar
> going on behind it
> are no more familiar. (*SP* 91)

Like the menacing outside of snowy space in *Power Politics* and a decade later in *True Stories* poems like "High Summer" continue to render the natural world in purely existential terms as a riddling and baffling Other resisting all manner of appropriation and all method of domestication:

> Wild mustard, hornworms, cutworms
> push at the edge of this space
>
> it's taken eight years to clear.
> ... [Yet,] Nothing
> is owned, not even the graves
> across the road with the names
>
> so squarely marked. (*SP* 275)

Hence, in the opening lines of the very last text from *Interlunar*, the eponymous "Interlunar" opens with a "[d]arkness [that] waits apart from any occasion for it," and, like "[t]he lake, vast and dimensionless" that closes out the poem, "doubles everything" (*SP* 319, 320)—a darkness to which I will return later.

But a larger dimension of despair imparted by the woman writer of these poems arguably arises in the manner in which they inevitably speak to issues of gender and sexuality. Attendees of the 2004 Margaret Atwood Symposium already prepared by the governing thematic of the "Open Eye" may recall that ocular image's more sinister cast within the opening epigraph to Atwood's *Power Politics*: "you fit into me/like a hook into an eye//a fish hook/an open eye." Thus, in keeping with the sinister despair of so many of the poems within that volume, one lyric in particular (from the "Their attitudes differ" sequence) reads:

> Night seeps into us
> through the accidents we have
> inflicted upon each other
>
> Next time we commit,
> love, we ought to
> choose in advance what to kill. (*SP* 127)

The deadly aggression between the sexes, whose primordial blood feud D.H. Lawrence once elegantly attributed to an *egoïsme à deux*, reaches back to poems like those featured in Atwood's *The Animals in That Country* and baldly code the male as lone outlaw and the female as empty space rife for desecration. Sexual aggression also reaches forward in *You Are Happy*, and, in particular, to the excessively morbid "Circe/Mud" sequence so reminiscent of the writing of Ann Sexton and Ted Hughes, in which men bear the heads of eagles or the bodies of pigs, and women are pictured with withered fists chained around their necks.

The continuous thread that runs throughout this poetry—from the early "Speeches for Dr. Frankenstein" through the middling swatch of fragments entitled "Marrying the Hangman" and to the later "Snake Poems" of *Interlunar*—is an inevitable masculine imposition of rational or conscious order upon recalcitrant female matter or substance that psychoanalytic theorists today are prone to descry in the foundationally patriarchal and asymmetrical contours of modern socialized comportment. "[S]uch curtailment," as Elisabeth Bronfman observes, "calls forth a desire to transgress these laws, to enjoy [the power] that belongs to the agent of forbiddance, to the paternal law of authority, so that … What the law prohibits, desire seeks" (177). And because poets, for Atwood, "travel the dark roads" where "[t]he well of inspiration is a hole that leads *downwards*" (*ND* 176, emphasis added), it is tempting to construe a certain part of Atwood's own poetic oeuvre in terms of a psychoanalytic project that would blankly refuse the master/matter conjuncture through the transgression of desire as Bronfman depicts it. "You would hold/the darkness that you fear/turned flesh and embers,/cool power coiling in your wrists," reads a passage from one of the aforementioned "Snake" pieces (*SP* 288). Accordingly, in "A Women's Issue" from the *True Stories* volume, the master discovers that the surge of such power is indeed forbidding since matter is "[e]nemy territory, no man's/land, to be entered furtively,/fenced, owned but never surely" (*SP* 261). Very quickly, then, one learns to go down the (w)hole of Atwood's I-opening lyricism with a considerable degree of circumspection.

My rather weak pun, which takes its cue from Atwood's own poetic linking to some psychic "hole," gains further emphasis when Atwood feels inclined to connect the figure of the poet to Lewis Carroll's "Alice" in her published Empson lectures entitled *Negotiating with the Dead*. But rather than Alice down the rabbit hole, I am considering Atwood's remarks on *Alice Through the Looking Glass*, and the way these help to move the despairing reception of her poetry, now, into a register more decidedly on the side of hope. For as Alice grapples with her mirror, rather than discarding its "'art' side for the hard and bright 'life' side" as the Lady of Shalott does (*ND* 56), "Alice goes the other way." Hence, Atwood observes,

> [Alice] goes *through* the mirror ... Instead of destroying her double, the "real" Alice merges with the other Alice—the imagined Alice, the dream Alice, *the Alice who exists nowhere* ... At this one instant, the glass barrier between the doubles dissolves, and Alice is *neither the one thing nor the other*, though at the same time she is all of these at once. At that moment time itself stops, and also stretches out, and both writer and reader have all the time not in the world. (57–58, emphasis added)

In these cogent remarks, what is fascinating about the poet doubling as Alice who exists "nowhere" and who is "neither one thing nor the other" is the extraordinary coordination that is established with contemporary (i.e., post-Freudian) psychoanalytic theory, and with the notion, as in my second epigraph, of woman as an "empty" construction of what Jacques-Alain Miller refers to as "semblances." Miller explains, "A semblance is something whose function is to mask nothingness ... [and] because we cannot discover Woman, we can only invent her" (14). However, in true Lacanian fashion, rather than "filling the hole in the lack" (as in Freud's analytical investigations), Miller lights upon another solution mirrored by Atwood in the above passage:

> This solution consists not in filling the hole, but rather in metabolizing it, dialectizing it [hence, the two Alices of Atwood's discussion] ... making oneself a being with nothingness. This opens up a whole new clinic of the feminine, a clinic of the lack of identity ... [that is to say,] of being the hole in the Other by giving it a positive form. (16–17)

What is even *more* hopeful in Atwood, it seems, is the rather capacious space she allows in her work by making both woman *and* man a being with nothingness: "The writer as the original invisible man," as stated in the first epigraph, "[is] not there at all but also very solidly there," as Atwood importantly qualifies the case for a more enlarged sense of humanity in general (*ND* 148). And although the lack of identity, as Miller argues, may not be "experienced as intensely in men as in women" (16), is it not the more hopeful case that a whole new clinic of the masculine and feminine opens up in Atwood's poetry when we descend with her into the Underworld—the Other world of metabolized and dialecticized semblances—and negotiate for ourselves an identity not of *one* thing but rather an "I"-opening repertoire, as Atwood herself puts it in the third epigraph, of "one damn thing after another," the important word in that observation, of course, being the word "after" (*ND* 158).

When we turn back to the poetry itself, some of our most immediately despairing responses to Atwood's work become subject to almost instant revision. With a more affirming psychoanalytic epistemology of variorum semblances, for instance, the whole status of determinate self-reflection is not so much a trick, as in "Tricks with Mirrors" from the *You Are Happy* volume, as a self-enclosing trap picked up especially in stanza iii: "You are suspended in me // beautiful and frozen, I/preserve you, in me you are safe. // It is not a trick either, it is a craft:/mirrors are crafty" (*SP* 149). Thus, as Atwood's prickly title implies, and as Alice's infamous and perhaps Lacan's even more infamous mirror stage of misrecognitions corroborates, the looking glass has a rather uncanny ability of returning the self to the Other, and of transforming the Room of One's Own, or even one's very own self, into its abject opposite. Hence, the riposte to *You Are Happy* four years later in *Two-Headed Poems*, in the ironically titled "Marrying the Hangman":

> To live in prison is to live without mirrors. To live without mirrors is to live without the self. She is living selflessly, she finds a hole in the stone wall and on the other side of the wall a voice. The voice comes through darkness and has no face. This voice becomes her mirror. (*SP* 216)

The hole in the wall here aptly functions as a rhetorical displacement for the captive sense of self onto some "other side" and, by implication, onto some other self—the "I" opening onto that unremittingly perpetuated voice "coming through darkness" that I foreground in my paper's title; such a figurative (w)hole thus offers subjectivity up to what the poetic sequence refers to a bit later as "a wid[er] choice" than merely "someone to pull off his shoes, someone to watch him while he talks ... someone in whom to plunge himself for rest and renewal ... someone condemned to death by other men for wishing to be beautiful" (*SP* 217).

Allow me to refer once again to Atwood's observation about writing in general—that "there has to be something under the rock first": if that "something" presents readers with any kind of hope, it's only because the lyric voice "coming through darkness" discloses a wider choice within which to fashion its own unique sense of identity. Indeed, it is a dark hope. But as Atwood herself admits, "writing has to do with darkness, and a desire or perhaps a compulsion to enter it, and with luck, to illuminate it, and to bring something back out to the light" (*ND* xxiv). At that very moment of illumination, it's likely that the despair of the mirror gives place inevitably to the hope of the book: more specifically, in Atwood's poetry, when a text like "Solstice Poem" ("Each has a mirror/which when asked replies not you" [*SP* 234]) gives place to one later like the more aptly named "Orpheus (1)" ("You could not believe I was more than your echo" [*SP* 301]). The point is even more powerfully finessed in an epigraph from Marguerite Duras that opens Atwood's *Negotiating with the Dead*:

> Finding yourself in a hole, at the bottom of the hole, in almost total solitude, and discovering that only writing can save you ... [that is,] to find yourself, once again, before a book. A vast emptiness. A possible book. Before nothing. [And yet,] Before something like living, naked writing, like something terrible, terrible to overcome. (xiii)

"[T]errible, terrible" reminds us, once again, of just how darkly fraught with hope and despair Atwood's "I"-opening lyricism actually is. Along similar lines, Thomas J. Otten observes of Jorie Graham's own American lyricism that "the abyss or gap that is construed both as a field open to new possibilities and as a terrifyingly empty space" is precisely so because the lyricism of the interpersonal "becomes an idiom of the materialized indefinite" (249). Otten bolsters the point by alluding to social theorists like Anthony Giddens whose "I"-opening studies of intimate relations in less "tradition-bound eras" like our own depict subjects as "free-floating, experimental, open, insecure, and risky" (*Modernity and Self Identity* [1991]), and sexuality today as "liberated from its reproductive telos," and therefore as "plastic and malleable" (*The Transformation of Intimacy* [1992] 249). Otten states the case succinctly: "The problem the poem tries to work out is how to give definition to this distance, this gaze—how to imagine it as *something* more than 'dear nothingness,' how to make visible the space across which persons connect emotionally" (245, emphasis added).

As a means of concluding this more hopeful recuperation of the "something" that Atwood herself interlinks with "sacred space" (*ND* 61)—an emotionally charged space of dear nothingness via Duras—that something's further definition as a notional elaboration of rhetorical distance is enormously instructive. When Jacques-Alain Miller ruminates about the "truth" of woman "in Lacan's sense [as that] measured by her subjective distance from the position of motherhood" (17), his formulation is not a brief *against* motherhood, or babies, or more generally the "reproductive telos" of human sexuality. Miller's point is, rather, that no one generic or essential or universal truth can (or ought) to be ascribed to woman since from the agential perspective of Atwood's wider choice, "[t]he true woman can only be invoked case by case" (17). Trying to say something universally definitive about woman is like trying to say something universally definitive about existential reality. According to Atwood, it seems to be a fairly hopeless project, as in "Backdrop Addresses Cowboy":

> I am the horizon
> you ride towards, the thing you can never lasso ...
> scattered with your
> tincans, bones, empty shells, the litter of your invasions
>
> I am the space you desecrate
> as you pass through. (*SP* 57)

Hence, in "Newsreel: Man and Firing Squad" we read, "No more of these closeups, this agony/taken just for the record" since to "interpret/the semaphore of our bending bodies, from a distance we could be dancing" (*SP* 145).

For Elisabeth Bronfman, therefore, only a rhetorical "distanciation" allows for the kind of contingency that "undercuts" the narratives of realism—"Things could have happened differently"—and thus marks "the voice of alterity," and with it "the gesture of accepting our fate of radical alienation within the symbolic and the gesture of living in ironic distanciation from any one law of fate" (211, 212). Put another way, a rhetorical distance opens up at the very point at which we lose the ability "to distinguish between the real and the imagined," or, better yet, when we assume "the attitude that what we consider real is also imagined" (*ND* 7). In psychoanalytic terms, such a distance is further marked, as I observe elsewhere, by a traumatic point or Lacanian "Real" that imaginarily *resists* the kind of lawful symbolization just noted by Bronfman (Jarraway 110). And it is precisely this kind of distanciated presentation of identity that Atwood aims for in the concluding stanzas of a poem like "The Landlady" from as far back as 1968 (in *The Animals in That Country*), and framed significantly by the line "Nothing is mine":

> and when I dream images
> of daring escapes through the snow
> I find myself walking
> always over a vast face
> which is the land-
> lady's, and wake up shouting.
>
> She is a bulk, a knot
> swollen in space. Though I have tried
> to find some way around
> her, my senses
> are cluttered by perception
> and can't see through her.
>
> She stands there, a raucous fact
> blocking my way:
> immutable, a slab
> of what is real,
> solid as bacon. (*SP* 41–42)

If the I-opening subject for Atwood is ideally an invisible one—"not there at all but also very solidly there"—then the very dark rendering of identity here as a Lacanian "slab/of what is real" that is both resistant to sight and at the same time "solid as bacon" comes fairly close indeed. As for her "bulk, a knot/swollen in space," Mieke Bal (2001) descries "two key metaphors" superimposed in such "knotted subjects" that she extrapolates from Bronfman's most recent work—the navel and the fold. But whereas "[t]he navel is inscribed in the body, the fold, hover[s] between touch and vision, necessitates some *distance* from it," and in that sense, concludes Bal, "the navel describes, [but] the fold promises" (348, emphasis added). Reminded of a similar kind of unspoken promise, we might recall that the ancient female sage in Toni Morrison's Nobel Prize address is, like Atwood's landlady (despite her "raw voice/loose in the rooms beneath" the poem's narrator [*SP* 41]) cryptically wordless: "she does not [answer, says Morrison]; she keeps her secret; her good opinion of herself; her gnomic pronouncements ... She *keeps her distance*, enforces it and retreats into the singularity of isolation, in sophisticated, privileged space" (qtd. in Jarraway 4).

As a final comparison to this somewhat more hopeful treatment of the I-opening subject in Atwood's lyricism, we might look to the figure of Eurydice in the eponymously titled text in *Interlunar*. According to Slavoj Zizek, the figure of the *femme à postiche* that he extracts from the work of Miller is precisely the opposite of the void of subjectivity keeping her distance in Morrison's sophisticated, privileged space. Instead, we find the figure of a woman "who takes refuge from the void in the very heart of her subjectivity," and thereby "gives the impression (and has the false satisfaction) of a firmly anchored being, of a self-enclosed life ... and thus serves as the safe protective rock or safe haven to which her man can always return" ("Thing" 232). Hence, in Atwood's "Eurydice": "He wants you to be what he calls real./He wants you to stop light./He wants to feel himself thickening/like a treetrunk or a haunch/and see blood on his eyelids/when he closes them, and the sun beating" (*SP* 303).

To the degree that the female "I" matches up precisely with the male "eye" in this passage, exactly to that extent does the *femme à postiche* as "a firm, self-enclosed substance ... support ... the male identity[?]" (Zizek "Thing" 232). But as Zizek goes on further to remark, such "phantasmatic harmonious coordinations in which one element finally fully fits the other based on the model of the successful sexual relationship ... [is] 'like a key [fitting] into the opening of a lock'" and, hence, is simply that—phantasmatic (236). The rhetorical distance that Atwood's own lyricism will repeatedly put between itself and such eye-catching coordination is, of course, given by the egregious lack of fit between the fish-hook counterpoised to the open eye that we noticed earlier. And this is so in "Eurydice": despite the fact that "[h]e cannot believe without seeing," the lyric voice nonetheless insists, "it's dark in here," and therefore "it's not through him/you will get your freedom" (*SP* 303). The American poet Mark Doty shrewdly observes that "the eye suffuses what it sees with I. Not 'I' in the sense of my story, the particulars of my life ... But 'I' as the quickest, subtlest thing we are: a moment of attention" merely (50). Open in that quite momentary sense, the "I" in Atwood's moving lyricism finds that a certain measure of freedom is perhaps to be gained "through" the self after all—the prospect of the open "I" as a series of "'dividuals,' constantly reinventing themselves, adopting different roles" (Zizek "Ongoing" 303) that Eurydice in her own descent into darkness cannot be "through" anytime soon. It's a history with "no outcome," as Atwood herself makes plain in her indelible "Is/Not" (from *You Are Happy*)—a history in the broader contours of her ongoing poetic project (one hopes) "where we must walk slowly, /where we may not get anywhere/or anything [but] where we keep going/fighting our ways, our way/not out but *through*" (*SP* 187, emphasis added).

—University of Ottawa

WORKS CITED

Atwood, Margaret. *Negotiating with the Dead: A Writer on Writing*. New York: Cambridge University Press, 2002.

———. *Selected Poems: 1966–1984*. Toronto: Oxford University Press, 1990.

———. "'The Writer: A New Canadian Life-Form.'" *The New York Times Book Review*, May 18, 1997. 39.

Bal, Mieke. "Enfolding Feminism." *Feminist Consequences: Theory for the New Century*, edited by Elisabeth Bronfman and Misha Kavka, 321–52. New York: Columbia University Press, 2001.

Bronfman, Elisabeth. "Noir Wagner." In *SIC 3: Sexuation*, edited by Renata Salecl, 170–215. Durham and London: Duke University Press, 2000.

Doty, Mark. *Still Life with Oysters and Lemon*. Boston: Beacon, 2001.

Jarraway, David R. *"Going the Distance": Dissident Subjectivity in Modernist American Literature*. Baton Rouge: Louisiana State University Press, 2003.

Miller, Jacques-Alain. "On Semblances in the Relation between the Sexes." In *SIC 3: Sexuation*, edited by Renata Salecl, 13–27. Durham and London: Duke University Press, 2000.

Morrison, Toni. *Nobel Lecture: 1993*. Ottawa, Canada: The Nobel Foundation, Courtesy of the Swedish Embassy, 1993.

Otten, Thomas J. "Jorrie Graham's _____s." [sic] *PMLA* 118, no.2 (2003): 239–53.

Zizek, Slavoj. "'The Ongoing 'Soft Revolution.'" *Critical Inquiry* 30, no.2 (2004): 292–323.

———. "The Thing from Inner Space." In *SIC 3: Sexuation*, edited by Renata Salecl, 216–59. Durham and London: Duke University Press, 2000.

Power Politics/
Power Politics:
Atwood and Foucault

PILAR SOMACARRERA

POWER HAS TRADITIONALLY been defined as a social relation between two agents who may usefully be called the "principal" and the "subaltern" (Lukes 2), or as the capacity of powerful agents to realize their will over the will of powerless people. However, Michel Foucault's theories have radically replaced unitary and compact conceptions of power with a dynamic model in which power is seen as a net of relations only existing in action: "Power in the substantive sense, '*le*' *pouvoir*, doesn't exist. The idea that there is either located at—or emanating from—a given point something which is a 'power' seems to me based on a misguided analysis" (*Power* 198). He also indicates, "I hardly ever use the word power and if I do sometimes, it is always a short cut to the expression I always use: the relationships of power" ("The Ethic" 11). The philosopher sees several main "hypotheses" in his new definition, of which I would like to highlight three:

(i) That power is co-extensive with the social body. ...

(ii) That relations of power are interwoven with other kinds of relations (production, kinship, family, sexuality) for which they play at once a conditioning and a conditioned role. ...

(vi) That there are no relations of power without resistances (*Power* 142)

For Foucault, power must be analyzed as "something which circulates" (*Power* 98). This notion of power as an energy that permeates everything also appears in Margaret Atwood's definition of the concept: "Power is our environment. We live surrounded by it: it pervades everything we are and do, invisible and soundless, like air" ("Notes" 7). Although Atwood has confessed that her ideas about power do not come from literary theory,[1] the characteristics of invisibility and pervasiveness implied in her definition are also part of Michel Foucault's model of power. Like him, she does not believe that it emanates from a single point. Referring to the nature of dictatorial power during the Second World War, the narrator of her novel *Surfacing* explains, "For us when we were small the origin was Hitler, he was the great evil ... But Hitler was gone and the thing remained ... It was like cutting up a tapeworm, the pieces grew" (*Surfacing*, 123). The writer and the philosopher choose a bottom-up model of power in which it is diffused throughout all social relations rather than being imposed from above. Atwood goes as far as questioning the reality of power: "power after all is not real, not really there: people give it to each other" ("Notes" 16). She has recently expanded this idea by saying that "'give it to each other' is somewhat limited"—they take it from one another as well. "Political leaders," she adds, "can't be so without followers, or enough followers."[2]

This last idea—that politicians need supporters—is also contained in Atwood's definition of politics as she spelled it out in an interview with Jo Brans: "A lot of power is ascription. People have power because we think they have power, and that's all politics is" (149). Likewise, according to Foucault, political power consists in the partial or total cession of the concrete power that every individual holds (*Power* 88). The other aspect included in Atwood's notion of politics is related to questions of passivity and agency: "By politics I do not mean who you voted for in the last election, although that is included. I mean who is entitled to do what to whom; who profits by it; and who therefore eats what" (*SW* 394). This definition presupposes two features of power: the first is that one of its implications is the infliction of violence, and the second, that, again following Foucault's views, power is directly related to economics. Another characteristic of Atwood's approach to power is that she always stresses the connections between the political and the personal: "So many of the things we do in what we sadly think of as our personal lives are simply duplications of the external world of power games, power struggles" ("Notes" 7).

Margaret Atwood has also emphasized the permanent presence of power in literature: "The novel tends to deal with interactions among the levels of power, whether it's political power or social power. It's always there, again because it's there in human life and it's one of the things that humans do."[3] Her own works demonstrate her preoccupation with the issue of sexual and national power, witnessed for the first time, as Shannon Hengen notes, in the subject of Atwood's unfinished Harvard PhD thesis, "Nature and Power in the English Metaphysical Romance of the Nineteenth and Twentieth Centuries" (127). In the early 1970s, this concern is followed up in the poems of *Power Politics*, expanded to include the discourse of national and international politics in her novel *Surfacing*, and continued in the 1980s in her most politically engaged fictions, *Bodily Harm* and *The Handmaid's Tale*. Her most recent novels, *The Blind Assassin*, which includes a history of capitalism in twentieth-century Canada, and *Oryx and Crake*, a dystopia about the effects of economic globalization, follow up the same concerns. In this essay I will use Michel Foucault's model to explore Atwood's fictions about power in an intergeneric itinerary through her works, and will also draw on her essay "Amnesty International: an Address," published in *Second Words*, and her poem "Notes Towards a Poem That Can Never Be Written."

In her politically committed novel *Bodily Harm*, Atwood puts into practice her theory that "art [should be] a mirror held up to life" rather than "a Disneyland of the soul, containing ... all the Escapelands which are much more agreeable than the complex truth" (*SW* 393). Its plot concerns a lifestyles journalist, Rennie, who involuntarily becomes involved in the political uprising taking place on the Caribbean island she visits while writing a tourist piece for a Toronto magazine. As Brooks Bouson observes, the text acts out an important political agenda in its insistent focus on the potential horrors of power and gender politics (133). Sexual politics are patent as early as the opening episode when Rennie comes home to discover that a stranger has left a coiled rope on her bed. At the crossroads between the political and the personal is the novel's discussion of pornography,[4] which Foucault glosses as "an economic and perhaps also ideological exploitation of eroticisation" (*Power* 57). As Jennifer Strauss argues, the protagonist finally learns that sexual politics is different only in kind from other politics when she sees the prisoners tormented by the guards (118):

> She's afraid of men and it's simple, it's rational, she's afraid of men because men are frightening. She's seen the man with the rope, now she knows what he looks like ... Rennie understands for the first time that this is not necessarily a place she will get out of, ever. She is not exempt. Nobody is exempt from anything. (*BH* 290)

Rennie's last thought, which echoes Atwood's own words ("Nobody is immune" [Brans 149]), appears as a paradoxical conclusion for someone who had been promised that the article she had to write about the Caribbean island would be "Nothing political" (*BH* 16). In the Caribbean country, the journalist is bombarded with contradictory views. Paul, the American drug and gun dealer with whom she becomes sentimentally involved, tells her that what happens on the island is "local politics" and "has nothing to do with her" (*BH* 150-51). Dr. Minnow, a Canadian-educated citizen of the fictional island of St. Antoine warns her of the way everyone in his world is involved: "'Everyone is in politics here, my friend,'" says Dr. Minnow. "'All the time. Not like the sweet Canadians'" (*BH* 124). As Helen Tiffin notes, Dr. Minnow's is the one voice in the narrative that could be considered disruptive, with his perspicacious comments on British colonialism in the Caribbean and on the neo-colonialisms of the United States and Canada in the area (123). Diana Brydon has also read the text through a post-colonial lens, an approach that highlights Atwood's idea that all notions of the personal are constructed through the political (93).

Bodily Harm also illustrates Atwood's scepticism about politicians. In her conversation with Jo Brans, she states, "I don't endorse political candidates" (149), and in a more recent interview, she reiterates this view when asked her if she mistrusts politics:

> Everybody mistrusts politics, of course politicians can lie ... they've been known to lie, they always have. However, there are rules about lying, everybody knows that you can lie to the electorate. If you lie to reporters, that's expected, but you are not supposed to lie to Parliament.[5]

In *Bodily Harm* several characters articulate Atwood's lack of faith in politicians. Paul, one of the most cynical characters in the novel, has the following opinion about Dr. Minnow: "'He's a politician so he's a user, they have to be, but he's less of a user than most'" (*BH* 247). Lora, the character who suffers on her own body the crudity of political violence, also disapproves of politicians: "'As far as I am concerned the world would be a lot better if you took the politicians, any kind at all, and put them in the loony bin where they belong'" (265–66). This critical approach contrasts with the quasi-theocratic view the population has of politicians, in a society, like that of the Caribbean, that is immersed in religion. Religious discourse is adopted in the slogans of the candidates: Ellis uses the motto "Ellis is King"; the candidate known as Prince responds to the slogan "Prince of Peace" (37–76, 191), a phrase used by the prophet Isaiah to refer to the Messiah; and Dr. Minnow's is "The Fish lives" (78), which relies on the traditional Christian symbolism of the fish.

In a novel that does not offer a very positive view of politicians, Dr. Minnow is the only character who believes in democracy and shares Atwood's utopian view that it is necessary to "change things" (133) in a country where "nothing is inconceivable" (133). In fact, as Paul points out, on an island like St. Antoine, concepts like democracy, and even human rights, are permanently at stake (240). The fictional portrait of this former British colony allows Atwood to lay bare the crudest dimensions of power: first, that power is ascription, as political leaders are given power at elections, but the elections can be manipulated. Second, that, following Foucault, the historical *raison d'etre* of political power is to be found in the economy (*Power* 89). This is evinced by the fact that Ellis, who controls the economy of the island, is repeatedly elected. Third, that power is subject to inversions, or, to use Steven Lukes's terminology, "a principal in one relation may be a subaltern in other" (2). This idea can also be found in Foucault's model:

> Relations constituted through the exercise of power define innumerable points of confrontation, forces of instability, each of which has its own risks of conflict, of struggles, and of at least one temporary inversion of the power relations. (*Discipline* 27)

To put it in the words of Paul, with his cynical wisdom about political theory: "'There's only people with power and people without power. Sometimes they change places, that's all'" (*BH* 240). Finally, as Atwood herself has remarked, the aim of absolute power is to silence *the voice*, to abolish the words, so that the only voices and words left are those of the ones in power ("An End" 247). According to Foucault, relations of power prevail over language and meaning (*Power* 114), a view that is formulated poetically by Atwood in *Power Politics*: "Language, the fist/proclaims by squeezing/is for the weak only" (*PP* 31). In *Bodily Harm*, when Ellis sees his re-election threatened by the other candidates, he silences the opposition and the potentially subversive voices by killing Minnow and presumably Prince, and having Rennie and Lora imprisoned.

Political repression is also the subject of "Notes Towards a Poem That Can Never Be Written," a poem from the volume *True Stories* which is in many ways a companion piece to *Bodily Harm*. In her previous collection *Two-Headed Poems*, Atwood had already anticipated her concern about the contrast between the various "Escapelands" of our contemporary world and the reality of torture in a poem titled "Footnote to the Amnesty Report on Torture":

> The torture chamber is not like anything
> you would have expected.
> No opera set or sexy chains and
> leather goods from the glossy magazines,
> porno magazines, no thirties horror (46)

As Foucault notes, nothing is more material, physical, and corporal than the exercise of power (*Power* 57–58), and nowhere is power more material than in torture, which is the title of a whole section of "Notes Towards a Poem" about a woman on whom political violence is inflicted. Atwood, once again, strives to find a definition of power: "power/ like this is not abstract, it's not concerned/with politics and free will, it's beyond slogans" ("NTP" 259). In his analysis of the poem, Frank Davey claims that writers of the First World democracies cannot speak "on behalf of" political prisoners when their own "safe" position in culture and politics is so different from the position of that victim (52–53). However, I believe that Atwood's message is that we are all urged to speak up for these victims: "Elsewhere you must write this poem/because there is nothing more to do" ("NTP" 259).

Atwood's next novel, *The Handmaid's Tale*, analyzes the dangers of ignoring acts of political repression. As Silvia Caporale Bizzini argues, it was written as an answer to the spreading of religious and political fundamentalism at the beginning of the 1980s in the United States (28). In its fundamentalist dictatorship, known as the Republic of Gilead, women, forced into servitude as handmaids, are forced to bear babies for the governing elite. The changes that lead to the establishment of the Republic of Gilead are subtle but progressive, and thus ignored by most people, as Offred, the protagonist, explains:

> We lived, as usual, by ignoring … Nothing changes instantaneously … There were stories in the newspapers, of course, corpses in ditches of the woods … but they were about other women, and the men who did such things were other men. (*HT* 66)

The other reason why the population did not perceive the Gileadean system as something strange was that it was a compendium of elements from previous regimes: "there was little that was truly original with or indigenous to Gilead: its genius was synthesis" (289). In addition, it produces its own truth, a fact that has also been contemplated by Foucault: "each society has its regime of truth" (*Power* 131). Since political regimes produce the truth of power that society demands, the Gileadean regime also manipulates the media, "show[ing] only victories, never defeats" (*HT* 78) and telling the population only "what [they] long to believe" (79). Other than by enforcing its truth, the Republic of Gilead imposes its power through brainwashing and strict surveillance undertaken by security forces: the Angels (army), the Eyes ("invisible" police), and the Guardians. The role of an invisible police in the creation of the panoptic state is also discussed by the French critic: "a centralized police, exerci[se]s a permanent, exhaustive surveillance which makes all things visible by becoming itself invisible" (*Discipline* 40).

The control of reproduction, an aspect that Foucault has identified as one of the objectives of power, is crucial for the Gileadean regime and it is supervised by the doctors. According to the philosopher, medicine is concerned with the conservation of the "labour force" (*Power* 171), or, in this case, "the reproduction force":

> "Population," with its numerical variables of space and chronology, longevity and health, emerges not only as a problem but as a source of

> surveillance, analysis, intervention, modification etc. ... The biological traits of a population become relevant factors for economic management, and it becomes necessary to organize around them an apparatus which will ensure not only their subjection but the constant increase of their utility. (*Power* 171–72)

The other pillar underpinning the system is public torture, which Foucault has also dealt with extensively in *Discipline and Punish*, concluding that all public executions are political operations (53). Accordingly, the Gileadean regime makes ample use of repressive devices like the Particicution and the Salvagings, public executions that serve to eliminate "political enemies" (*HT* 319). Especially horrifying is the hanging from a wall of the dead bodies of men who were executed at the Salvagings. This public display of power had already been portrayed in some lines from "Notes Towards a Poem Which Can Never Be Written":

> a flayed body untangled
> string by string and hung
> to the wall, an agonized banner
> displayed for the same reasons
> flags are. (259)

If *The Handmaid's Tale* is a dystopia that takes place in the United States, *The Blind Assassin* is a fictional memoir, "an unofficial history" of Canada in the twentieth century (Howells, "Sites" 31), told from the point of view of an eighty-year-old woman, Iris Chase. Like the previous novels I have examined, it is a story about the struggle for power with the permanent background of war. The powerful are incarnated in Richard Griffen, Iris's husband, the tycoon whose textile empire takes over the factory owned by the narrator's family. Richard represents a narcissistic and dominating figure that has many predecessors in Atwood's writing, with his "wherewithal for grand gestures ... He has become like a statue of himself: huge, public, imposing, hollow" (*BA* 480). Through this character, Atwood makes a critique of the Canadian businessmen who sympathized with the Nazi regime in the 1930s because it kept Communism under control. However, following a shifting of alliances characteristic of power, the situation changed when the Second World War started:

> He [Richard] had been too cozy with the Germans in his business dealings, too admiring of them in his speeches. Like many of his peers, he'd turn too blind an eye to their brutal violations of democracy; a democracy that many of our leaders had been decrying as unworkable, but that they were now keen to defend. (480)

After the war, Richard set out to start his political career, "readying himself for the mantle of command" (507). In a skillful Foucaldian inversion of power forces, the formerly powerless Iris manages to abort her husband's political expectations and even leads him to suicide. As Dorothy Jones has it, speaking out through "The Blind Assassin,"[6] the novel attributed to Iris's sister, Laura, proves more powerful than she could have imagined (60).

The authority of the conservative manufacturing bourgeoisie in provincial Ontario is challenged by the rise of the workers' rights and the spread of Communism in Europe during the years of the Depression. These events introduce political resistance in the novel, which, following Foucault, "is all the more real and effective because it is formed right at the point where relations of power are exercised, it is multiple and can be integrated in global strategies" (*Power* 142). It is through her love story with Alex Thomas, the Communist activist who also personifies resistance to capitalism, that Iris learns about the Red Scare and the Spanish Civil War. As Coral Ann Howells argues, from Iris's point of view, the working class is frequently equated with "foreign" and "immigrant," an earlier version of othering in Canada before the multiracial immigration of the 1960s (*Contemporary* 48). However, during her girlhood, Iris's view is always influenced by voices from the establishment:

> All through October—the October of 1934—there had been talk of what was going on at the button factory. Outside agitators were hanging around, it was said. ...
>
> Not only were they outside agitators, they were foreign outside agitators, which was somehow more frightening ... These were their methods, these ruthless Bolsheviks and union organizers, who were all the same at heart (according to Elwood Murray). They wanted free love, and the destruction of the family, and the deaths by firing

> squad of anyone who had money ... This was what had been done in Russia. So it was said. (*BA* 203)

As Howells ("Sites" 39) and Jones (51–52) have pointed out, the story in the science fiction fable contained in "The Blind Assassin" resembles real events of the twentieth century. The descriptions of the fictional planet of Zyrcon evoke the landscape of the First World War. As in many other Atwood texts, war is an important presence in *The Blind Assassin*, and a whole section titled "House fires" is dedicated to the topic, stressing the sameness of these conflicts throughout history, as well as its devastating effects in the population: "They have a generic look to them, these wars ... Overnight, whole portions of what had been acknowledged as reality simply vanished. This is what happens when there is a war" (*BA* 477–78). For Atwood war is the most obvious and visible form of the exercise of power, of men attempting to dominate each other ("Notes" 13). Foucault also sees power and war as concomitant terms: "power is a war, a war continued by other means" (*Power* 90). In *The Blind Assassin* war is compared to a newsreel, in an image traceable in a poem from *Power Politics* in which Atwood explores the history of the world through the succession of wars, from the Crusades until the two world wars of the first half of the twentieth century.

In Atwood's latest novel, *Oryx and Crake*, the scientist-protagonist Crake concerns himself with the elimination of wars, which he attributes to "misplaced sexual energy ... a larger factor than the economic, racial and religious causes often cited" (*OC* 293). In the society depicted in this fiction, power no longer centres in the state—there is no mention of government at all in the novel—but is spread through the social system via the corporate power of global capitalism. The globalization of power was already foreseen by Foucault in his writings and interviews of the 1970s: "mechanisms of power have been—and continue to be—invested, colonized, utilized ... by ever more general mechanisms and by forms of global domination" (*Power* 99). Atwood also anticipated the effects of globalization in the early 1980s, when in *Bodily Harm* she had Dr. Minnow say, "'There is no place that is not of general interest'" (*BH* 135). More than twenty years later in *Oryx and Crake*, the aim of the Corporations is "to be global" (*OC* 294), launching their product not just "on society as a whole ... but on the planet" (294). The disciplinary control is perpetuated by the private security forces, the "CorpSeCorps," which represent one step further in the

Foucaldian state of police. Power is invisible but more tangible than ever, as, again following Foucault, it is multiple and comes from many locations: "it wasn't just one side you had to watch out for. Other companies, other countries, various factions and plotters" (27).

The novel also corroborates Foucault's view that it is not possible for power to be exercised without knowledge, and that it is impossible for knowledge not to engender power (*Power* 52), as the Corporations' power is based on their scientific discoveries. As in all the authoritarian regimes depicted in Atwood's novels, in the society of *Oryx and Crake* there is also resistance and shifting of alignments: the narrator's mother, a microbiologist at one of the Corporations, eventually suffers a nervous breakdown and joins the resistance. However, Crake's aim is the elimination of all resistance, first by assimilating the scientists who were against the compound system (*OC* 299), and second by creating the Crakers, one of whose main characteristics is total docility: "Whole populations could be created that would have pre-selected characteristics. Beauty, of course; that would be in high demand. And docility: several world leaders had expressed interest in that" (304). Atwood is warning that if resistance and difference disappear, humankind is doomed to fall in the hands of absolute power without even noticing it.

Although critics have usually ignored the democratic-socialist content of Atwood's writing (Hengen 13), politics appears as an essential issue to understanding her works. *Oryx and Crake* summarizes Atwood's nightmares about the abuses of power in the globalized world, in a dystopian vision that is dangerously close to our reality. Foucault's bottom-up model of power and his focus on the way power permeates all relations within a society provide an appropriate theoretical background to analyze Atwood's works from the beginning of her literary career until her latest publications. Power is often conceptualized as the capacity of powerful agents to realize their will over the will of powerless people, and the ability to force them to do things they do not wish to do. However, both Atwood and Foucault criticize this view, arguing that everybody, even the most powerless, holds some kind of power, and that power is something that is performed, something more like a strategy than a possession, a strategy that implies multiple inversions and resistances.[7]

—Universidad Autónoma de Madrid

NOTES

1. Private email correspondence with the author of this essay, in which Atwood also explained that her ideas about power came from reading Shakespeare and books about history and politics, as well as observing historical changes.
2. Private email correspondence with the author of this essay.
3. Unpublished interview with the author of this essay.
4. For a discussion of pornography and feminism in the 1970s in *Bodily Harm*, see Coral Ann Howells, *Margaret Atwood* (105–25).
5. Unpublished interview with the author of this essay.
6. I refer to the fiction embedded in the text as "The Blind Assassin" to distinguish it from the complete novel, which I have italicized as *The Blind Assassin*.
7. This essay was written with the assistance of the financial aid from the Spanish Ministry of Education, Project HUM 2004-00515/FILO.

WORKS CITED

Atwood, Margaret. *The Blind Assassin*. London: Bloomsbury, 2000.
———. *Bodily Harm*. [1981]. Toronto: McClelland-Bantam Inc., 1982.
———. "An End to an Audience." *Dalhousie Review* 60, no.3 (1980): 420–42.
———. *The Handmaid's Tale*. Toronto: McClelland & Stewart, 1985.
———. "Notes on *Power Politics*." *Acta Victoriana* 97, no.2 (1972): 7–19.
———. *Oryx and Crake*. London: Bloomsbury, 2003.
———. *Power Politics*. [1971]. Toronto: House of Anansi Press, 1996.
———. *Second Words: Selected Critical Prose*. Toronto: Anansi, 1982.
———. *Surfacing*. [1972]. London: Virago, 1996.
———. *Two-Headed Poems*. Toronto: Oxford University Press, 1978.
———. *True Stories*. New York: Simon & Schuster, 1978.
Bouson, Brooks. *Brutal Choreographies: Oppositional Strategies and Narrative Design in the Novels of Margaret Atwood*. Amherst: University of Massachusetts, 1993.
Brans, Jo. "Using What You're Given." In *Margaret Atwood: Conversations*, edited by Earl G. Ingersoll, 140–51. Princeton, NJ: Ontario Review Press, 1990.
Brydon, Diana. "Atwood's Postcolonial Imagination: Rereading *Bodily Harm*." In *Various Atwoods: Essays on the Later Poems, Short Fiction, and Novels*, edited by Lorraine York, 89–116. Toronto: House of Anansi, 1995.
Caporale Bizzini, Silvia. "Power Politics: Literature and Foucaldian Analysis." *In-Between: Essays and Studies in Literary Criticism* 5, no.1 (1995): 23–39.
Davey, Frank. "What is a Genre: Atwood's 'Notes Towards a Poem Which Can Never Be Written.'" In *Inside the Poem: Essays and Poems in Honour of Donald Stephens*, edited by W.H. New, 48–54. Toronto: Oxford University Press, 1992.
Foucault, Michel. *Discipline and Punish: The Birth of the Prison*. New York: Pantheon, 1977.

---. "The Ethic of Care for the Self and a Practice of Freedom." In *The Final Foucault*, edited by James Bernauer and David Ramussen, 10–21. Cambridge, MA: MIT Press, 1988.

---. *Power/Knowledge: Selected Interviews and Other Writings 1972–1977.* Edited by Colin Gordon. New York: Pantheon Books, 1980.

Hengen, Shannon. *Margaret Atwood's Power: Mirrors, Reflections and Images in Select Fiction and Poetry.* Toronto: Second Story Press, 1993.

Howells, Coral A. *Margaret Atwood.* London: Macmillan, 1996.

---. *Refiguring Identities: Contemporary Canadian Women's Fiction.* Basingstoke, UK: Palgrave, 2003.

---. "Sites of Desolation." In *Entering the Labyrinth: "The Blind Assassin,"* edited by Gerry Turcotte, 31–46. Wollongong, New South Wales: University of Wollongong Press, 2003.

Jones, Dorothy. "Narrative Enclosures." In *Entering the Labyrinth: "The Blind Assassin,"* edited by Gerry Turcotte, 47–67. Wollongong, New South Wales: University of Wollongong Press, 2003.

Lukes, Steven. *Power and Structure: Essays in Social Theory.* London: Macmillan, 1977.

Strauss, Jennifer. "'Everyone is in Politics': Margaret Atwood's *Bodily Harm* and Blanche d'Alpuget's *Turtle Beach*." In *Australian/Canadian Literatures in English. Comparative Perspectives*, edited by Russell McDougall and Gillian Whitlock, 111–32. Melbourne: Methuen, 1987.

Tiffin, Helen. "Voice and Form." In *Australian/Canadian Literatures in English: Comparative Perspectives*, edited by Russell McDougall and Gillian Whitlock, 119–32. Melbourne: Methuen, 1987.

The Two-Headed Opus

CHRISTINE EVAIN

THE METAPHOR CONTAINED in the title of Atwood's volume of poetry *Two-Headed Poems* not only is central to the eponymous poem and to the volume of poetry itself, but it also resurfaces in all of Atwood's work from her very first book of poetry to the later novels. It is my intention to demonstrate that the two-headed epithet may be used to describe Atwood's work not only because each book of fiction or poetry is based on a principle of duality but also because the two modes of writing themselves are like the two heads of one body. A parallel reading of the prose and poetry suggests that connections between the two are of a different nature in the beginning of her career and in her later work. My study will therefore focus on three periods (1967–1972; 1973–1995; and 1996–2003) when Atwood's poetic output gradually decreases while her production of fiction continues to grow. It has often been commented that themes and aesthetic characteristics filter through from Atwood's poetry into her novels and vice versa, but these capillary links remain a somewhat vague notion. When Atwood herself was asked to comment on the relationships between these two modes of writing in her work, she said, "Each volume of poetry is a seed planted for the next novel" (Evain and Khandpur 107). So I decided to follow the author's advice and examine the work chronologically, endeavouring to link each volume of poetry to the novels that succeeds it. When one given novel and the volume of poetry that precedes it are brought together, the result is a "twoheaded prodigy" (*CG* 48) present throughout the corpus. As I contemplate this unusual creature, the following questions spring to mind: Does "the poetry head" always lead? Does it truly break new grounds for the "fiction head" to discover?

This metaphor of Atwood's work as a "twoheaded prodigy" can also be considered in its plural form: it is possible to juxtapose a series of separate "twoheaded prodigies," each composed of a volume of poetry and a book of fiction, which may vary according to thematic perspectives, but which, if examined as part of a chronological sequence, are still an indicator of the progress of Atwood's work. For example, I can create a link between *Procedures for Underground* and *Lady Oracle*, as the poem "Procedures for Underground" is an invitation to discover an underground world into which Joan descends in *Lady Oracle* when she experiments with automatic writing. However, *Lady Oracle* may also be connected to the prose poems in *Murder in Dark* as their metafictional content is a condensed version of the teachings of *Lady Oracle*. In this exposé, I seek to demonstrate that the poetry is an extremely dynamic head in the Atwood corpus, but that the experience of the fictional head does feed back into the later poetry mainly by stimulating its metafictional dimension.

In the first period under consideration (from 1967 to 1972), it is possible to determine what Atwood's first novels, *The Edible Woman* and *Surfacing*, owe to the first volumes of poetry. Frank Davey's work on Atwood's vocabulary provides an ideal starting point as Davey shows that the typical Atwood vocabulary includes the following expressions: "technological skins" (93), "mirrors" (94), "the gothic" (98), "refugees and tourists" (104), "underground, underwater" (109), "the maze" (114), "metamorphosis" (120), "signposts/totems" (121). All of these images are present in *The Circle Game* and then resurface in the fiction. Atwood's two first novels explicitly stage female acts of liberation that demonstrate the capacity to resist a male-dominated culture. The characters of *Surfacing* and *The Edible Woman* translate into narrative form the experience of *The Circle Game* personae. The general pattern of both novels mimics the movement of many of *The Circle Game* poems as the protagonists descend into the underworld to avoid being dominated or absorbed and then transcend their alienation.

Atwood's personae and protagonists gain greater power when they begin to integrate the ancestral element that reaches as far back as the formation of the world (*The Circle Game* is saturated with cosmological imagery that resurfaces in the novels). As the personae and protagonists learn to decipher the imprints of the earth, they are overwhelmed by a feeling of continuity: each creature is part of a biological chain that becomes tangible through all of our senses. It is through bodily perceptions that the personae and protagonists recognize their multiple heritage, and they deliberately set out to become members of the human race through symbolic actions that are performed by *the body* itself (in *Surfacing* for example, the narrator decides to bear fruit and to become pregnant). Both in the poetry and the novels, the individual melts into the landscape in order to gain tangible proof of his or her identity. The subject is thus mapped out as a biological entity signified by the recurring metaphors of the "body as landscape." The metaphors imply both that the body is a result of biological evolution and that the sensorial body gains a sense of identity by connecting to the past, by sucking in the "salt" of "living" ancestors and by performing sensorial actions through which the individual willingly becomes part of the biological chain.

While this body-centred imagery resonates from the poetry to the novels, further parallels can be drawn between the two forms of writing, since a direct link can be established between scenes from the novels and the poems from *The Circle Game*. The poetry nourishes the fiction, as demonstrated by the following examples: The symbolic value of running away from the camera is at the heart of the poem "Camera" and mirrors Marian's flight in *The Edible Woman* as well as the unnamed character's resistance to David's filming of Anna in *Surfacing*. The poem "A Meal" (*CG* 28–29) precedes the restaurant scene in *The Edible Woman*. Like the persona in the poem, Marian resents the cutting of the food, this cool butchering act, reduced to its purely biological significance, transforming it into a "diagram" or "a china bowl" (28–29). The conversation between the two fiancés in the novel echoes the one in the poem that equally revolves around the subject of safety and control. Furthermore, Marian's resistance to the patriarchal values that Peter stands for resembles the one of the "furtive insect" that "is hiding/… sly and primitive/the necessary cockroach/in the flesh/that nests in dust" (28–29). This insect has the capacity to resist the temptation of love. Like the persona in *Power Politics*, "[t]heir attitudes differ," or like the sibyl in *The Circle Game*, the insect feeds "on other peoples' leavings" (28) and "gorges on a few/unintentional/spilled crumbs of love" (29). The function of that insect is to rescue "the thing that calls itself/I" (50) from the inevitable loss of identity resulting from a lover's submission, and to bring out the subject's prophetic voice.

In *Surfacing*, empowering the sibylline voice implies a descent into Atwood's underground world. When the female subject descends into the underground world, she becomes one with nature and fully integrates the heritage of "the drowned mothers" or "the forest" and the city, "wide and silent ... lying lost, undersea" (*CG* 4). This heritage is an indispensable part of the regeneration process. In "After the Flood, We," the mineral and biological heritage allows for new faces to emerge (*CG* 5). Stone becomes bone in the poem "The Explorers" (*CG* 78–79) as two skeletons wait to be discovered, while in "The Settlers," they become the nourishing substance for future generations (*CG* 81). In *Surfacing* a similar metamorphosis is observed by the narrator (167) who also seeks to participate in the regeneration process in order to become whole.

Atwood's first five volumes of poetry place special emphasis on the symbolic of metamorphosis. The symbols are drawn mainly from images of quasi-Darwinian regressions and mythical figures like Proteus. At the end of Atwood's first period, in her sixth volume of poetry, *You Are Happy*, the personae's search for identity and experience of wholeness is expressed in terms that are related to ordinary daily situations that take on a symbolic value. In the last sequence of the volume, the lovers are one another's equals and relish the present moment as they realize that "There is Only One of Everything"(*YAH* 92). The female subject then experiences a new form of love that no longer cripples her but, on the contrary, allows her to discover her own potential and materialize an expanded identity in which the two components (the sibyl and "the thing that calls itself/I") cohabit harmoniously.

Lady Oracle offers an ironic twist to the perfect balance found in the third sequence of *You Are Happy*. Joan longs for both an intense and ordinary life. When she mocks other women's expectations, she realizes that their fantasy lives are not much different from her own. Nevertheless, she finds her "own arrangement ... more satisfactory" (*LO* 216) because she knows better than to "demand all things of just one man" (216). The irony of Joan's discourse becomes increasingly apparent as her growing dissatisfaction is revealed: "It was true I had two lives, but on off days I felt that neither of them was completely real" (216). Because of Joan's many mistakes (which account for the mess in her life—encapsulated in the last sentence of the novel) the reader is sceptical about her capacity for harmony. The novel thus offers a comic treatment of the themes of the last sequence of the *You Are Happy* volume. Although Atwood's heroine can only make a mess of things, the personae in poems such as "Is/Not," "There is Only One of Everything," and "Book of Ancestors" express the belief that wholeness occurs when the humble and ordinary fellow travelling of lovers is transcended in love. However, Atwood's seventh volume of poetry once again emphasizes the conflict of the two heads, giving each head new symbolic meanings as the poems move from the personal level to the social and political levels. The superimposition of themes in *Two-Headed Poems* can be observed in *Life Before Man*, the novel that succeeds it. According to McCombs, *Two-Headed Poems* marks the transition from Atwood's "Stage I Closed, Divided, Mirroring World" to Atwood's "Stage II realistic, Open World" (69).

Indeed, in the second period, the "Stage I" patterns shift focus and are extended. In the novels following *Lady Oracle*, the voice of the "paralyzed artist" (to use Atwood's expression in the ninth chapter of *Survival*) grows older and more present, as if Atwood's heroines were moving on to a different stage of life and as if they were discovering a more ordinary and yet more complicated and demanding world around them. This complexity not only is the result of greater importance given to political and social issues but it is also linked to a more realistic type of novel writing. Depression is one of the leitmotivs of both *Two-Headed Poems* and *Life Before Man*, where it is linked to imagery in which biological decay dominates: the heart is caught up in its contradiction and stops beating (*THP* 15), flowers that are emblematic of the domestic sphere simply fade away (55), contamination spreads (*THP* 74; *LBM* 238), and biological deterioration foreshadows the end of an era (*THP* 89, 175; *LBM* 238). Language itself fails, as words become biological material subjected to violence.

I would now like to move on to my next "twoheaded prodigy" composed of *True Stories* and *Bodily Harm*, both published in 1981. The dominant themes are those related to the obsession with the true story, political oppression, artificiality of both landscape and feelings, and, finally, loss of love.

The heroine of *Bodily Harm*, Rennie, oscillates between anger and feelings of helplessness and depression like those expressed by the personae in "Late Night," "Hotel," "Earth," "Last Poem," or "Variation on the Word Love." Although Rennie dwells on her past and on her own pain, feeling her wounds as she feels her scar after her mastectomy, she resists the temptation to "regurgitate" (Barthes 191), defined by Barthes as "loquèle"; that is "le flux de paroles à travers lequel le sujet argumente inlassablement dans sa tête les effets d'une blessure" (191). Rennie's remembrance does not lead to repetition. It is not an endless replaying of the past. In the same way the persona of the poem "Rain" moves beyond pain, Rennie discovers a breathing space that helps her overcome her past traumas and experience sexual pleasure: "she enters her body again and there's a moment of pain, incarnation, ... she's grateful, he's touching her, she can still be touched" (*BH* 204).

In both the novel and the poem, this "breathing space" is a state of grace: "This much will have to do, this much is enough" (*BH* 204), "a pause ... a day after a day ... a breathing space" (*TS* 89). The subject's gratitude is expressed in a cry of joy: "the rain/ throwing itself down out of the/bluegrey sky, clear joy" (*TS* 89) and "he's touching her, she can still be touched" (*BH* 204).

The echoes between *Two-Headed Poems*, *Life Before Man*, *Bodily Harm*, and *True Stories* deserve further study (special attention could be paid to symbols such as the hand in *Bodily Harm* and *True Stories*, or the heart in *Two-Headed Poems* and *Life Before Man*, etc.), but space is limited and we must now consider the third period of Atwood's work. From 1983 onward, the corpus enters a new phase: the principles of alternation, of the predominance of poetic output and the thematic unity that characterized the first two periods give way to a gathering together of themes and previously explored forms, a combination that opens the door on a new creative process. I wish to focus on the metafictional aspects of the third period (mainly in *Murder in Dark* and *Good Bones*) before moving on to Atwood's last volume of poetry, *Morning in the Burned House*, in relation to the fiction of that period.

Murder in the Dark marks a turning point in the corpus as Atwood embarks on a new genre of writing. The ambiguity of the new form is underlined by the subtitle of *Murder in the Dark*: "Short Fictions and Prose Poems." Each piece in the volume seems to be both a piece of short fiction and a prose poem.

The filtering through of Atwood's previous work into *Murder in the Dark* is multi-faceted, but I will focus on a couple of elements only, starting with the example of "Women's Novel." The poem "Women's Novel" and *Lady Oracle* both parody and pastiche lowbrow literature.[1] In *Lady Oracle* the element of pastiche stems from the imitation of the "historical romances" genre (*LO* 156), as Joan, the narrator, is a writer of such novels, while the parodic note is derived from a process of exaggeration. In much the same way, "Women's Novel" also uses parody and pastiche and intertwines metafictional commentaries alongside these techniques. The other common factor between *Lady Oracle* and "Women's Novel" is that both the novel and the prose poem work on the principle of an internal mirror in which the persona or the heroine contemplates her multi-faceted image. Like Joan (who is the narrator of *Lady Oracle* and the writer of costume gothics, as well as a consumer of the genre because she is hooked on the very plots she creates), the persona of "Women's Novel" takes on the three distinct roles of writer, consumer of the genre, and protagonist. The reader is also included in this multi-faceted mirror game, as he or she recognizes his or her own image in Joan's triple role. It is as if "Women's Novel" were a miniature construction of the mechanics of *Lady Oracle*, highlighting a set of techniques as well as an underlying ideological discourse.

Unlike "Women's Novel," "Happy Endings" does not refer to any particular genre, but it points to the components of the story and sends back to the reader a reflected image of his or her own credulity as well as an addiction to both plots and romance. This mirror game then leads to the rejection of stories constructed according to such recipes:

> That's about all that can be said for plots, which anyway are just one thing after an other, a what and a what and a what.
> Now try How and Why. (*MD* 70)

Combinatory dexterity is not enough. What the persona finds of greater interest revolves around the questions of "How and Why." Readers qualified as the "true connoisseur" (*MD* 70) will equally appreciate the effort put into working with these two questions.

Many of the prose poems in *Good Bones* also deal with metafictional issues. "Gertrude Talks Back," "Unpopular Gals," "The Little Red Hen Tells All," "There Was Once," "Bad News," and "Let Us Now Praise Stupid

Women" are all poems that participate in the deconstruction of clichés. In order to underline cultural stereotypes, they subvert the ingredients and techniques of literary genres such as the fairy tale and popular novels. Atwood draws on her experience of novel writing to create prose poems that encapsulate the tensions between genres of writing. She also weaves in ironical comments on readers' expectations and habits. Such irony is also present in *Alias Grace*, in which the reader's voyeurism is mirrored in the following comment:

> Confess, confess. Let me forgive and pity. Let me get up a Petition
> for you. Tell me all.
> And then what did he do? Oh shocking. And then what?
> The left hand or the right?
> How far up exactly?
> Show me where. (*AG* 39)

In *The Robber Bride* the three protagonists' eagerness to be chosen by Zenia as her confidante is equally emblematic of the reader's own desire to be the narrator's bosom friend.

In *The Handmaid's Tale* the narrator's power as a storyteller stems from this same narrative strategy of bringing the reader into her confidence. The mechanics and the power of confessional discourses are exposed in the poem "Siren Song," which stages such a voice echoed by its own ironical discourse.

Atwood's novels published after "Siren Song" are clearly constructed on the self-reflective and ironical dynamics of a confession addressed to the reader, which is in keeping not only with the teachings of the poem but also with its double-voiced discourse. One also notices that the prose poems in *Murder in the Dark* and *Good Bones* parody the functioning of such a dynamic, thereby reformulating the main teaching of "Siren Song" and further emphasizing the reader's cheap infatuation with any discourse that speaks of his uniqueness: "you are unique/at last" (*YAH* 39).

To complete our overview of Atwood's third period of poetic work, one needs to consider *Morning in the Burned House*, which is the author's last published volume. *Morning in the Burned House* is divided into five parts. The two last parts are composed of two unique sets of poems on mourning (this theme feeds back into *Labrador Fiasco*, published one year later) and the three first parts allow typical Atwoodian themes to resurface (depression in the first and third part of the volume and female identity mainly in the second part). In the poems touching on female-empowerment, *The Circle Game* themes are revisited and further developed with a supplementary ironical twist. The use of irony in these poems leads to the assertion of an expanded identity made up of two distinct components. The poems thus stage the reconciliation between the two heads of the persona, all the while mocking traditional views that claim that this reconciliation is either impossible or undesirable. The voices such as those of "Miss July Grows Older" (21–23), "Manet's Olympia" (24–25), "Daphne and Laura and So Forth" (26–27), "Ava Gardner Reincarnated as a Magnolia" (30–32), "Helen of Troy Does Counter Dancing" (33–36), or "Sekhmet, The Lion-Headed Goddess of War, Violent Storms, Pestilence, and Recovery From Illness, Contemplates the Desert in The Metropolitan Museum of Art" (39–41) denounce the female icon as a male construct. They refuse to conform; they reject the domination of their lover and thus move beyond the Atwoodian victim position.[2] Each persona integrates the two components of her extended identity and denounces the passivity of her lover(s). The symbolic representations of the personae in *Morning in the Burned House* draw on a store of typically Atwoodian imagery: mythical, biological, technological, gothic, and literary, all of which assert the plural identity of the personae. The vitality and confidence that some of the personae display stem from the successful reconciliation of the different components of an expanded identity, and this reconciliation is expressed through bodily metaphors and through the personae's capacity to mock the voyeur, the lover, or the potential manipulator.

Finally, the experience of being double takes on a new meaning in the two poems "Burned House" (*I* 93–94) and "Morning in the Burned House" (*MBH* 126–27). It then becomes an experience of temporal ubiquity in which the personae inhabit two moments simultaneously: past and present are superimposed. The body itself becomes double: "including the body I had then,/including the body I have now" (*MBH* 127). This amounts to a form of resistance to time, which speaks both of permanence and change. The personae spell out the inevitable movement from life to death ("this house has long been over" (*MBH* 127), which is further underlined by the titles of the two poems. However, at the same time, the personae underline their ability to endure and survive. The experience of ubiquity becomes a moment of sheer joy: the subject experiences life as a gift for which no justification is needed. It is no longer a matter of saying: I exist because…, but, simply: I exist.

In Atwood's first two periods of creative activity, the influence of the author's poetry on her novels is made apparent when the following two-headed prodigies are considered: *The Circle Game/The Edible Woman*, *The Circle Game/Surfacing*. The early work (from *The Circle Game* to *Power Politics*) actually filters through all of the novels, and Atwoodian themes and ideologies become clearly recognizable when the author's body of work is considered as a whole.

The systematic alternation between poetry and novel writing, observed in Atwood's first period, is even more visible in the second period (three volumes of poetry in 1974, 1978, and 1981 and three novels in 1976, 1979, and 1981), as if the author had drawn on the poetic activity in order to renew her artistic potential. *Lady Oracle* offers an ironical treatment of the achievement of harmony between the sexes suggested in the last poems of *You Are Happy*. *Life Before Man* echoes themes and images from *Two-Headed Poems*, mainly siamese duality, spatialization of depression, and suicidal impulses, while the themes of political oppression and loss of love are explored in *True Stories* and then in *Bodily Harm*.

The first two periods of Atwood's work thus illustrate her own comment about the importance of poetry: "If you think of language as a series of concentric circles, poetry is right at the centre. It's where precision takes place. It's where that use of language takes place that can extend a word yet have it be precise" (qtd. in Ingersoll 169).

This chronological approach to Atwood's work clearly reveals that the dynamics of writing start with the poetry. The poetry not only leads to the creation of a body of work (a dozen books of poetry and three volumes of prose poems) with distinctive qualities in itself, but the poetic linguistic work is also later transformed into organic material from which the novels are shaped.

A close examination of the corpus of the third period suggests a different process of creation.[2] The principles of alternation, predominance of poetic output, and thematic unity that characterized the first two periods give way to a mixing of themes and forms that allows for the metafictional games of the prose poems. Finally, in Atwood's last volume of poetry, the two-headed characteristic of the female-empowered poems becomes a cry of victory over cultural and social entrapments.

It is clear that in the two first periods of Atwood's work, much of the innovation in the author's artistic creation finds its origin in the poetry. However, it is important here to point out that the fecundity of poetry is obviously not an exclusively Atwoodian characteristic, but, rather, is inherent to the very nature of poetry itself.

Poetry stretches language into realms of great complexity by exploiting the tension between form and content. Yet, as a result of this tension, poetry cannot settle anything. The fragmented nature of the verse, its deliberate opposition to the continuity of prose writing, is a sign of an impossible reconciliation amply illustrated by Atwood's double-headed image. The reader is forced to play a more active role because of the difficulty involved in coming to terms with the tension between what one sees and what one hears when reading poetry.[3] The play on both language and visual form stimulates the reader to reflect on possible polyphonies and contradictions in the poem and thus use this extremely tight form of writing to explore the paradoxes of our human condition. Poems are not dreams offering a romantic or idealistic vision of life, and since their scope is limited by being addressed to an individual reader, they cannot reform society. But they *do* have something to offer in that they can help us explore restrictions, contradictions, hopes, and desires. Poetry will lead the way to the understanding of the human stuff we are made of, as well as the inevitable paradoxes and new forms of resistance to the social, cultural, and political. Poems do not produce a voice that functions merely as an echo chamber of existing discourses; they work within tensions we eventually learn to see as "permanently unresolved" (to use Munro's expression).[4] This teaching of a better understanding and acceptance of something "permanently unresolved" mirrors the very nature of poetry. It is then hardly surprising that such teachings (which are offered both to the poet and the reader) should result in the production of potential material for novels. Atwood's signature is characterized by two-headedness staged in a multi-faceted manner throughout the corpus. Through working on Atwood's poetry, the reader learns to grow attentive to a polyphony of voices. We learn to listen and to integrate the different components of our extended identity. Like the two-headed beings of "A Sybil," "Shadow Voice," "Miss July Grows Older" or

"Manet's Olympia," and many other poems, we learn to resist the unsatisfactory bargains offered by society, and to cultivate the willpower to remain in this fragile state of equilibrium that allows us to explore both light and darkness. Thus, we follow the voice of the persona of "Interlunar," that says:

> I wish to show you the darkness
> you are so afraid of
>
> Trust me. This darkness is
> a place you can enter and be
> as safe in as you are anywhere;
> you can put one foot in front of the other
> and believe the sides of your eyes.
> Memorize. You will know it
> again in your own time...
> We have come to the edge:...
> The lake, vast and dimensionless,
> doubles everything, the stars,
> the boulders, itself, even the darkness
> that you can walk so long in
> it becomes light. (*I* 102–03)

— École Centrale de Nantes

NOTES

1. Genette's definitions are the following: "[La parodie—ou travestissement, transposition—est] tout texte dérivé d'un texte antérieur par... transformation ou par... imitation"; le pastiche (ou charge, forge): "Le pasticheur se saisit d'un style... et ce style lui dicte son texte" (40). The difference between a parody and a pastiche is that the parody is based on a text (which is transformed and potentially transposed into a different style), whereas the pastiche is based on a specific style.
2. Even in the third period, Atwood's novels owe a great deal to her poetry. Let us mention a couple of images or themes that can be directly traced back to the early volumes of poetry. In *Alias Grace* the opening of the novel (5) is reminiscent of the poem "Visit to Toronto, with Companions" in *The Journals of Susanna Moodie*. In *The Blind Assassin*, the Sybil figure (42) much resem-

bles the one in *The Circle Game*. And *Oryx and Crake* offers an ironic reversal of the Frankenstein theme, such as the one presented in "Speeches for Dr Frankenstein" in *The Animals in That Country*.
3. According to Donoghue, "[Epireaders] read or interpret—the same act—in the hope of going through the words to something that the words both reveal and hide ... [they] say to poems: I want to hear you. Graphireaders say: I want to see what I can do, stimulated by your insignia" (151– 52). Bradford, using Donoghue's terminology, explains that "[the lines] work as a kind of 'score' for vocal performance, observing that when 'read aloud,' the change of [line and rhythm] ... signals a change of emphasis" (33).
4. Alice Munro, *The Moons of Jupiter* (New York: Vintage, 1991), 197.

WORKS CITED

Atwood, Margaret. *Alias Grace*. [1996]. London: Virago Press, 1997.
———. *The Animals in That Country*. Toronto: Oxford University Press, 1968.
———. *The Blind Assassin*. London: Bloomsbury, 2000.
———. *Bodily Harm*. [1981]. London: Vintage, 1996.
———. *Cat's Eye*. [1988]. London: Virago Press, 1990.
———. *The Circle Game*. [1966]. Toronto: Anansi, 1967.
———. *Eating Fire, Selected Poetry 1965–1995*. London: Virago Press, 1998.
———. *The Edible Woman*. [1969]. London: Virago Press, 1980.
———. *Good Bones*. [1992]. London: Virago Press, 1993.
———. *The Handmaid's Tale*. [1985]. London: Vintage, 1996.
———. *Interlunar*. Toronto: Oxford University Press, 1984.
———. *The Journals of Susanna Moodie*. [1970]. London: Bloomsbury, 1997.
———. *Lady Oracle*. [1976]. London: Virago Press, 1982.
———. *Life Before Man*. [1979]. London: Vintage, 1996.
———. *Morning in the Burned House*. Toronto: McClelland & Stewart, 1995.
———. *Murder in the Dark*. [1983]. London: Virago Press, 1994.
———. *Oryx and Crake*. London: Bloomsbury, 2003.
———. *Power Politics*. [1971]. Toronto: Anansi, 1996.
———. *Procedures for Underground*. Toronto: Oxford University Press, 1970.
———. *The Robber Bride*. [1993]. London: Virago Press, 1994.
———. *Surfacing*. [1972]. London: Virago Press, 1979.
———. *True Stories*. Toronto: Oxford University Press, 1981.
———. *Two-Headed Poems*. Toronto: Oxford University Press, 1978.
———. *You Are Happy*. Toronto: Oxford University Press, 1974.
———. *The Journals of Susanna Moodie*. 1970. London: Bloomsbury, 1997.
Barthes, Roland. *Fragments d'un discours amoureux*. Paris: Seuil, 1977.

Bradford, Richard. *The Look of It: A Theory of Visual Form in English Poetry*. Cork: Cork University Press, 1993.
Davey, Frank. *Margaret Atwood: A Feminist Poetics*. Vancouver: Talonbooks, 1984.
Donoghue, Denis. *Ferocious Alphabets*. London: Faber & Faber, 1981.
Evain, Christine, and Khandpur Reena, eds. *Atwood On Her Work: "Poems Open the Doors. Novels Are the Corridors."* Nantes: Éditions du CRINI, *Canadensis* series, 2006.
Genette, Gérard. *Palimpsestes*. Paris: Seuil, 1982.
Ingersoll, Earl G. *Margaret Atwood: Conversations*. Princeton, NJ: Ontario Review Press, 1990.
McCombs, Judith. "Atwood's Fictive Portraits of the Artist: From Victim to Surfacer, From Oracle to Birth." *Women's Studies*, 1986, no. 12: 69–88.
Munro, Alice. *The Moons of Jupiter*. [1982]. New York: Vintage, 1991.

Incandescence: "the power of what is not there" in Margaret Atwood's *Morning in the Burned House*

ROSE LUCAS

these slurred ghosts, never entirely welcome,
even those we have loved the most,
especially those we have loved the most
returning from where we shoved them
away too quickly:
from under the ground, from under the water,
they clutch at us, they clutch at us,
we won't let go. ("Two Dreams, 2"[1] 351)

WE CARRY OUR dead with us. Bent double, we bind them to our backs. Desperate, ravenous, they cling to our shoulders, nails in our hair, hooked in our scalps, wailing endearments into the whorls of our ears. We are their creatures, our blood and bones are theirs, their only frame; their names are inked into our skin, and they whisper on our breath.

We are haunted, and more than half in love; we are their familiars. Not just the ones we've known and lost but every stratum of the past, its myriad faces, its minutiae and its larger patterns, its here and there, its crevices and heights; it is multidirectional, never static. We are drenched in the past, its huge breakers washing over us, cleansing, drowning.

And in the face of it all: the small "I," the candle's flicker on the endless beaches of the past, in the wildness of the storm's gust. A tenuous criss-crossing of currents, a momentary congruence and seeming cohesion of parts from which to speak, to caress another.

Atwood's 1995 collection of poetry, *Morning in the Burned House* is, like much of her oeuvre, both poetic and fictional, concerned with the broad experiences of loss and memory, of the cascade of consequences the past has upon the experience of the present moment. In this discussion, I am particularly concerned with tracing the ways in which poetry, as a specific mode of articulation, can be seen to be analogous to the operations of dream in its evocation of the complex relation between past and present. Both dream and poetry can be understood as acts of mourning where mourning is defined as the endless process of focus and negotiation between the overlapped categories of what is lost, and must be grieved for, and what is continuing and redolent with the possibilities of the future. The present moment, often literally and figuratively enacted in the seemingly continuous presentness of dream and the intensity of the poetic image, is thus brought to a point of radiance and comprehension which, ideally, can operate as a productive point of bidirectionality between the past and the future. The poem blends and interprets, reveals and disguises the past with its fissures and aporia, representing and reordering a trauma that is always too soon, too much to be comprehended as it occurs. In this way, poetry can be understood as a ritualized act of remembering—a remembering redolent with its inevitable shadows of forgetting. Like the dreamwork that produces and interprets the complex web of latent and manifest impulses, the poem gives shape, articulation, image, and sensation to the weave of known and unknown, seen and unseen, what is repressed and what crests the surface of conscious possibility. Its strategies of lyricism, associative language, the suppression of obvious, rational links correspond to those of condensation, displacement, and the surreal to create a textual fabric suggestive of the inevitably endless and repetitive acts of recollection and the acknowledgement of loss.

As a number of critics have noted,[2] the central focus for Atwood's examination of poetry as mourning and facilitation is in Section IV of *Morning in the Burned House*, in the sequence of poems that form a specific elegy for Atwood's father, charting his final illness and death and the range of the speaker's feelings and memories. Like the image of the ancient yet preserved "Man in a Glacier" (340), the figure of the lost father who is "freeze-framed" in memory operates as the emotional pivot of the collection, connecting its various threads of loss, grief, and reconciliation. These poems of very specific, personalized loss, encapsulate the examination of the paradox of loss and the elegiac or recuperative impulses of mourning and retrieval, posing Atwood's central questions: *Is* something of the past "[t]here still," the speaker asks, peering at the newly-discovered image of her youthful father; *is* there a persistent element that continues and defies the deluge of loss, some kind of essence perhaps, or just the inscriptions of memory and desire? Indeed, what is it that is faintly etched on the photographic plate of memory the speaker/poet interprets? A teasing shadow of denial, a fantasy projection of what is irretrievably lost? A trace of continuity? A simulacrum, or imitation of a lost presence that only intensifies the inevitability of extinction, of nothingness?

As a ritualized and articulated act of mourning, always in elegiac relationship to the past, poetry enacts the endless and inevitable returns of that past. Its repetitions or textual ghostings may be read as complexly symptomatic of a desire to regain what is lost, thus potentially remaining fixed in a denial of that loss; to seek cathartic release through a recollection born out of acknowledgement of loss; and/or to offer a kind of consolation for losses through the keening of the text, the ambiguous and visceral poetic wail. As poet, Atwood is intimately concerned with the ambivalent relation between the past and the present—not just to mourn what is done with but also to read its continuing inscriptions in the text of the moment in which "everything recurs/and nothing is elsewhere" (338). And although these traces may be all we have left—talismans like the faded photographic plate or the preserved corpse, excavated from the ice—they move us to remember, to engage with our ghosts and to see the present, with all its imagined futures, as constituted and enriched by the inscriptions of the past.

Even before the specific loss of her father, the collection is haunted by a sense of foreboding and dislocation: the disjunctions of "You come back" (294)—"You know it was you/who slept, who ate here, though you don't/believe it"; the chronic sadness or narcissistic wounding that comes from everyone's eventual sense that "*I am not the favourite child*" (295); and the existential emptiness evoked by the realization that "[t]he sensed absence/of God and the sensed presence/amount to much the same thing" (296) can never satisfy our cravings for comfort and knowledge. In the poem

"Waiting," the "dark thing" that has been feared for so long is also seen to be something that is anticipated, even longed for. And when it comes, suddenly emptied of its imagined and melodramatic manifestations, it is not foreign and invasive but, rather, "strangely like home./Like your own home, fifty years ago" (297). In the "clouded thick yellow light" of childhood memories, in the comfort of domestic detail and the shielding presence of the mother, the "dark thing" is shown to be a long-denied recognition of limitation, of the ephemeral nature of youth and, indeed, of life:

>...you realized for the first time
>in your life that you would be old
>. . . . .
>and the home you were reading the funnies in
>by the thick yellow light, would be gone
>with all the people in it, even you (298)

Like Freud's notion of the uncanny,[3] this dark thing that has flapped like a sinister bat at the edge of consciousness is shown to be "nothing new" but, rather, something old, something once known and repressed yet that continues to exert uncomfortable pressure upon the fragility of the ego, the self constructed in defiance of loss and imminent erasure. Although we can have no mnemonic trace of death, an awareness of limitation and of the possibility of cessation dawns upon us out of the endless present, the *ennui* of childhood, a recognition to be resounded and also resisted until it is finally—and always violently—confronted: "the shocked mouths grief has made/and keeps on making:/round silent Ohs" ("Oh" 352). Significantly, however, the dark thing the speaker of "Waiting" recalls is, of course, not the thing itself, the *petit objet a* that is always deferred, but rather a screen, "a yellowing paper child's fear" (298) of what cannot yet be grasped, a diverting mask for the always traumatic finality of change and death.

As Freud formalized in *The Interpretation of Dreams*, and in the subsequent praxis of psychoanalysis, dreams can offer pictographic and visceral clues to the workings of the unconscious; they are a key mechanism by which we gain a measure of insight into the profundities, subterfuges, and sedimentations of the psyche. By the sometimes oblique methods of displacement and condensation, dreams, just as the associative, imagistic poem, can offer a tantalizing hieroglyph of desire and counter-desire. They also provide a theatre and an internal logic that allows the interpreter to recognize the operations of memory, such that memory functions both as the foundational material out of which any notion of the "self" is fabricated and as the active psychic function that seeks to cohere the fault lines between past and present, between what is available to conscious knowledge and what is not. Thus memory acts not only as a kind of gap filler for the details of the past but also as a dynamic agent of conciliation between the desire to retrieve the past (thus potentially and fundamentally denying its lostness), and the acceptance of that loss, an acceptance that initiates the cascades of grief but that in turn makes possible an engagement with the present moment and its imagined futures.

Thus, when Atwood catapults us into a poetic of dreams, with their logic of extra-rationality and seamless, imagistic movements between past and present tenses, the poetic exposes this paradox of longing implicit in an ethics of mourning. What appears to us through the logic of dreams—"these slurred ghosts, never entirely welcome"—reinforces a sense of process, of endless irresolvability between consciousness and its constitutive repressions:

> In the daylight we know
> what's gone is gone,
> but at night it's different.
> Nothing gets finished,
> not dying, not mourning;
> the dead repeat themselves, like clumsy drunks
> lurching sideways through the doors
> we open to them in sleep; ("Two Dreams, 2" 351)

Ironically, the seeming absolute finality of death is seen to trigger endless repetitions in which a past that cannot be done with and finished will inevitably recur and haunt the present moment's attempts at freshness, at the blank page of the new. According to Freud, when a past is somehow denied, unable to be assimilated into a sustainable present, we are condemned to repeat it, helpless before the increasingly insistent and fractured returns of the (always inadequately) repressed,[4] be they in dreams or other instances of parapraxis. By contradistinction, to use his specific terminology, it may ideally be possible to "remember"—that is, to actively draw together the components of the past into an ordering that is consistent with and sustainable by the present, rather than merely "repeat"[5] the past in unconscious actions. Such an idealized process, originally imagined in the therapeutic context, might also be enacted through the processes of poetry—as a signifying system which, like dreaming, facilitates the images and insights of the unconscious as a repository of memory, through stylized articulations of an alteric perception radically disconnected from the grids of rationality and consciousness. The present moment that might result from such an intervention or process would be one that allowed for the possibility of a "hot" or enriched text, a page made luminous and incandescent by the "power of what is not there."

In the collection's title poem "Morning in the Burned House" (367), Atwood makes explicit the paradoxes of memory and desire by using the language and scenarios of dream. As she comments in "Two Dreams, 2," our dead return to us in the interstices of dream, a momentarily open door that offers a glimpse of the endless process of mourning. The freshness and promise of "morning" is also coupled with the ambiguity of *mourning*, of lamentation for one's own childhood and loved ones, which the poem enacts through the apparent miracle, or surreal logic—is it "trap or blessing"?—of "finding myself back here, where everything/in this house has been long over." Past is miraculously sutured to present, explicable to inexplicable, the impossible hunger of a night of loss is simply satisfied:

> In the burned house I am eating breakfast.
> You understand there is no house, there is no breakfast,
> yet here I am. (368)

The brightness of the morning, "the lake is blue, the forest watchful," is also juxtaposed with the complex and violent imagery of what is "burned." As the poem "A Fire Place" suggests (361), the effects of fire, even one out of control—the destruction of property, bushland, the risk to human life—is not necessarily negative, but might be seen as part of a wider natural scheme of things: "only we can regret/the perishing of the burned place./Only we could call it a wound." The house is "burned," but it is almost impossible to sit in judgment of this as an act of wounding. However, the passage of time may be experienced as a wound, especially to the narcissistic child who has not imagined its transitory nature or the inability of human desire to in any way influence or hold on to what has been most dear. To be burned may be imagined to have been destroyed utterly, changed beyond any recognition; as in "The Pink Hotel," it may also carry the resonances of a trauma that won't be forgotten, a Holocaust-like horror that can't be assimilated despite the passage of time: "it's because of the war/ which won't stay under the waves and leaves./The carpet smells of ashes" (338). Fire also has connotations of an act that metamorphoses—from the spoon and bowl "which [were] melted" and are able, at least in dream, to operate again to a transformation that purifies, an alchemical rendering that removes the dross of distraction to reveal something more fundamental, something that is perhaps beyond the decays of time. "Morning in the Burned House" offers an enactment of the paradox of the simultaneity of past and present, and the complexity of the shifting "I," the voice who speaks and enjoins across the rifts and fiery catharses of the past to at once build and dissolve a self.

The uncertain, often unpredictable movement between surfaces of perception—what operates at conscious/unconscious levels, when the past deluges the present, or where projected personae collide with some secret or private self—is also evoked in the poem "Down" (334). Here, the ordinary world of domestic routine suddenly slips, capsizes: "Plate, cup, knife./ All at once there's no blue, no green,/no warning." The "underworld" is not elsewhere but emerges as simultaneous, coterminous with the world of "ordinary" perceptions. This slide, which might, in other contexts, indicate a moment of mystical revelation, an epiphany of alterity, can equally be figured as a depressive, even a psychotic, break, as the "ordinary mirage" collapses, the "albino voices" flutter at your ears, and the enormity of pain and injustice—your own and the worlds'—floods any "mild routines." In a strategy reminiscent of Plath's "Cut," the speaker's sadomasochistic impulses seek a further conflation of the tenuous boundaries between inside and outside, passivity and activity:

> You make a cut in yourself,
> A little opening
> For the pain to get in.
> You set loose three drops of your blood. (335)

It's risky business. As the pain enters the sealed "subterfuge" of the body's fantasies of wholeness and impermeability, there is the possibility for a seeing that exceeds such limitation, that goes beyond the parochial borders of the self and the comfortable. As a poet, perhaps as an individual of emotional and ethical courage, it is a step that has to be taken in order to unpick the seams of the ordinary, of the surface world, and to expose the layers upon layers of complexity, of sedimentation, of fossilization and its consequences. It's a risk specific to the imaginative journeying of poetry. The "marsh languages" (323) of poetry, as Atwood describes them—with their evocations of plurality, alterity, the deep past, and an infantile, semiotic unconscious—prise open the doors of the ordinary, of rationality and temporality, leading out of and away from the known into the chthonic reaches of the past, off the page of the recognizable and safe:

> Old thread, old line
> of ink twisting out into the clearness
> we call space
> where are you leading me this time?
>
> Past the stove, past the table,
> past the daily horizontal
> of the floor, past the cellar,
> past the believable,
> down into the darkness
> where you reverse and shine. (335)

Poetic language is here the tool of discovery, the cord to allow the speaker to follow back, down, out, and into darkness and possibility. Implicit in such an activity is the danger of loss of any kind of cohering self, of being unable to return, to communicate the experienced alterity. What is unleashed or retrieved in such a movement "down" can be experienced as almost unbearable "pressure," as in the weight of snow and detail in "Shapechangers in Winter" (364), or a pressure that is potentially paralyzing in "Up" (357), in which the speaker can't even get out of bed: "The past, its density/and drowned events [press] you down,/like sea water, like gelatin/filling your lungs instead of air."

Atwood offers a number of potential life lines out of such mortal risk while always emphasizing their uncertainty, their ambiguity. What can the poet offer as strategy and compensation for that weight of the past, as rich as an archaeological dig and as dense, massive, cumulative as an avalanche? In part it is the poetic voice itself that, recognizing loss, still continues to sing, to mark the path, to hold that loss at bay because, as humans, it is the most we can do. In the poem "The Ottawa River by Night" (353) Atwood describes an event in which "two long canoes full/of children tipped" into the icy river:

> …they all held hands
> and sang until the chill reached their hearts.
> I suppose in our waking lives that's the best
> we can hope for, if you think of that moment
> stretched out for years.

If one knows and accepts that drowning in the flood of life's experience is the endpoint of our journey, then perhaps this connection with others is an act which both comforts the self and reaches beyond the self in a compassionate and ethical way. It's an image that reframes rather than denies the tragedy of loss—even though they are children, even though death has come "too soon"—and highlights the wisdom of acceptance rather than struggle. The importance of connection with an other is also emphasized in "Shapechangers in Winter," in which even though age and time renders the lovers different, almost unrecognizable to each other, and even though the security of their domestic lives and love is shown to be only a precarious part of a vast network of multidirectional difference and alterity, the ability to reach out to an other is a lodestone for survival:

> But the trick is just to hold on
> through all appearances; and so we do,
> and yes, I know it's you;
> and that is what we will come to, sooner
> or later, when it's even darker
> than it is now, when the snow is colder,
> when it's darkest and coldest
> and candles are no longer any use to us
> and the visibility is zero: *yes.*
> *It's still you.* ("Shapechangers in Winter" 366)

While the tangible pleasures and possibilities of the self as physical body offer an anchor, a dam wall against the pressure of "the past, its density/and drowned events," the poet also takes us in the opposite direction; she suggests that perhaps the very loss of that cohering self is actually not so terrible, only different. The "obliteration," "erasure," and "nothingness" produced by the whiteout effect of the pressure of the past in "Shapechangers" may be read as part of a more vast natural cycle of "forgiveness" rather than "indifference," a reabsorption into a tabula rasa that doesn't deny the past but is built out of it. In "Statuary" (362) we see the very human resistance to this process of absorption, the pressure of "earthbound" and "nothingness" that chisels away our specificities, drawing us into the swirl of "rubble," "liquid," "the shape of a galaxy," the force of "the power of what is not there" that finally "lets us fly/and embody" (362–63). The risk of the "old line/of ink," the poetic exploration of memory and loss, takes us to a place of hiatus, of heightened possibility and heightened risk of negation. Despite such risks, it's a place to which Atwood's poetry impels us to travel:

> This is the solstice, the still point
> of the sun, its cusp and midnight,
> the year's threshold
> and unlocking, where the past
> lets go of and becomes the future;
> the place of caught breath, the door
> of a vanished house left ajar.
>
> Taking hands like children
> lost in a six-dimensional
> forest, we step across. (366)

The point at which the "past/lets go of and becomes the future" is a point of transition, a vacuum to consume and/or enable passage into another dimension, another possible way of imagining a productive liaison between past and present, a resolution of the backward arc of mourning that keeps us pinned to grief and denial. Through that narrow space of change, "the place of caught breath, the door/of a vanished house left ajar," memory continues to glimmer and the past will press and haunt. However, here, in this burned, vanished house that is and is not present, the ghosts are not dark things of fear but are, rather, the potentially healing insights of the poetic imagination:

> as I sit at this morning table, alone and happy,
>
> bare child's feet on the scorched floorboards
> (I can almost see)
> in my burning clothes, the thin green shorts
>
> and grubby yellow T-shirt
> holding my cindery, non-existent,
> radiant flesh. Incandescent. (368)

Howells describes this moment as one of "transcendence ... where loss is transformed through the construction of an imaginative space of memory in which the narrating subject can find shelter" (78). The impregnated images of radiance and incandescence certainly suggest the possibilities of a triumphant or transcendent escape from those aspects of the flames of loss that destroy, reduce to ashes and nothingness. However, they also embody the notion of a productive and bidirectional haunting, a script of transparency that offers a more sustaining, if ambiguous, model of the relationship between the present and the past and the ephemeral speaking/dreaming "I" that threads them together. The dream-poem offers the reader a visceral synchronicity of past and present in which the self is experienced as well as observed, and where the past and its minutiae both crumble into ashes of loss, and are reformed, remembered, through the almost radioactive agency of the poetic imagination.

—Monash University

NOTES

This paper is dedicated to my father, Ken Lucas, who died April 7, 2004: "Nothing gets finished,/not dying, not mourning."

1. In Margaret Atwood, *Eating Fire: Selected Poetry 1965–1995* (London: Virago, 1998), 294–368. All page numbers cited are to this edition.
2. For example, see Janice Fiamengo, "'A Last Time for this Also': Margaret Atwood's Texts of Mourning," *Canadian Literature*, no. 166 (2000): 145–64; Coral Ann Howells, "*Morning in the Burned House*: At Home in the Wilderness," in *The Contact and the Culmination*, edited by Marc Deirez and Benedicte Ledent, 69–78 (Liege, Belgium: Liege Language and Literature, University of Liege, 1997); Sara Jamieson, "Mourning in the Burned House: Margaret Atwood and the Modern Elegy," *Canadian Poetry*, no. 48 (2000/2001): 38–68.
3. Sigmund Freud, "Recollection, Repetition and Working Through" [1914], in *Freud: Therapy and Technique*, edited by Philip Rieff, 157–66 (New York: Macmillan, 1963).
4. The concept of the return of the repressed is discussed at length in Freud, "Beyond the Pleasure Principle" (1920), in *On Metapsychology: The Theory of Psychoanalysis, Pelican Freud Library,* translated by James Strachey (Harmondsworth: Penguin, 1984), 11:269–338.
5. This distinction is made in the essay "Recollection, Repetition and Working Through."

WORKS CITED

Atwood, Margaret. *Morning in the Burned House.* [1995]. *Eating Fire: Selected Poetry 1965–1995.* London: Virago, 1998. 294–368.

Fiamengo, Janice. "'A Last Time for this Also': Margaret Atwood's Texts of Mourning." *Canadian Literature*, no. 166 (2000): 145–64.

Freud, Sigmund. "Beyond the Pleasure Principle." [1920]. In *On Metapsychology: The Theory of Psychoanalysis*. Vol. 11, *The Pelican Freud Library*, translated by James Strachey, 269–338. Harmondsworth: Penguin, 1984.

———. *The Interpretation of Dreams.* [1901]. Vol. 4, *The Pelican Freud Library.* Translated by James Strachey. Harmondsworth: Penguin, 1975.

———. "Recollection, Repetition and Working Through." [1914]. In *Freud: Therapy and Technique*, edited by Philip Rieff, 157–66. New York: Macmillan, 1963.

Howells, Coral A. "*Morning in the Burned House*: At Home in the Wilderness." In *The Contact and the Culmination*, edited by Marc Deirez and Benedicte Ledent, 69–78. Liege, Belgium: Liege Language and Literature, University of Liege, 1997.

Jamieson, Sara. "Mourning in the Burned House: Margaret Atwood and the Modern Elegy." *Canadian Poetry*, no. 48 (2000/2001): 38–68.

Plath, Sylvia "Cut." *The Collected Poems.* Edited by Ted Hughes. New York: Harper & Row, 1981. 235.

Eye-Openers: Photography in Margaret Atwood's Poetry

REINGARD M. NISCHIK AND
JULIA BREITBACH

> The ultimate wisdom of the photographic image is to say: "There is the surface. Now think—or rather feel, intuit—what is beyond it, what the reality must be like if it looks this way."[1]

WHEN IN 1973 Susan Sontag delved into the discursive depths of photography despite, or rather because of, its deceptively "shallow" appearance, Margaret Atwood had long come up with an answer from her own quest for the medium's ontological secrets. In one of her earliest poems, "This Is a Photograph of Me" (*The Circle Game*), the lyrical "I" instructs the reader: "I am in the lake, in the center/of the picture, just under the surface./[...] if you look long enough,/eventually/you will be able to see me" (ll.17–26).[2] As Sontag would a couple of years later, Atwood here and elsewhere debunks the widely-held idea about photography's "transparency" (Sontag 6) to any given "obvious" subject, revealing instead the potentially "distort[ing]" (l.23) impact of photographic representation. Unlike Sontag, Atwood's critique of the naive belief in superficial verisimilitude transcends the discursive for the performative level: Atwood's case for relative "interpretation" over absolute "transparency" (Sontag 6)—that is the inevitability of accessing even the most "objective" photo by means of language, narration, and (con-)text—gains its force not least by being embedded in a poem.

The following thoughts on those six poems in which Atwood engages with photographic issues (from her first, *The Circle Game*, through her most recent poetry collection, *Morning in the Burned House*) thus aim to deal with this highly versatile writer as an astute appropriator of yet another cultural discourse: the art and theory of photography become the subject of poetry, and are thereby shrewdly subjected to the latter's own means of expression through language. Apart from "This Is a Photograph of Me," the poems to be discussed are: "At the Tourist Centre in Boston" (*The Animals in That Country*), "Daguerreotype Taken in Old Age" (*The Journals of Susanna Moodie*), "Girl and Horse, 1928," "Projected Slide of an Unknown Soldier" (*Procedures for Underground*), and "Man in a Glacier" (*Morning in the Burned House*). All of these texts testify to Atwood's sustained interest in working out, and working with, the ontological qualities of photography. All of them hold at their core—"in the center" indeed ("Photograph," l.17)—some visual epiphany to open the eyes of the lyrical "I" and the reader alike, some pivotal moment to literally change the picture for good. Finally, against the background of contemporary critical debate on photography, all the poems show Atwood at the height of her time, if not preceding pre-eminent "professionals" of photographic criticism of the last decades; though clearly inviting the panopsis with the likes of Sontag and Roland Barthes in particular, Atwood does not adopt but anticipates certain ideas that would later be extensively and influentially articulated in Sontag's *On Photography* and Barthes' *Camera Lucida*. Adding Atwood's aforementioned intertwining of photographic and poetic discourses, the originality of her work stands out even more. Consequently, occasional references to the writings of Sontag and Barthes (or others) in this article by no means intend to reduce these poems to the state of mere illustrations of photo theory. Rather, they provide a helpful analytical vocabulary for coming to terms with the poems' distinctly Atwoodian voice, which typically oscillates between the kind of adamant intellectual alertness that marks Sontag's stance toward photography in the 1970s and the somewhat elegiac lucidity of Barthes' very last book published in the year of his death.

Any study of Atwood's engagement with photography has to start with "This Is a Photograph of Me": not only because it is her first but arguably because it is her most resonant and moreover highly programmatic statement on the topic, stripped down to almost abstract dimensions through the diminishment of all specificities such as plot, time, or place, and rich in interpretative implications for the poems to follow. The reliance on bare essentials on the content level is matched by the unemotional, descriptive tone of the lyrical "I," which nevertheless manages to slowly but surely draw an apostrophized "you" into the abstract maze of poor photographic resolution ("a smeared/print: blurred lines and grey flecks/blended with the paper" ll.3–5). Temporal indicators ("At first" l.2 "then" l.6) further underscore the spatial perspective of successively "scan[ning]" (l.6) the scenery, an apparently "gentle" (l.11) landscape. Just as in the darkroom, where contours and colours gradually emerge from the developing bath, the eerie sight of a human body suddenly materializes in the second part of the poem, "right in the center/of the picture, just under the surface" (ll.17–18). The metaphor of seeing something *in* a photo translates into an in-depth investigation of the picture's third dimension, of what may be the true subject beyond the superficial landscape idyll. Inverting the parenthetical effect of common usage, the conspicuous bracketing of the entire second part marks the poem's centre of attention and meaning. In fact, it is only within these confines that a subject in the narrow sense of the word (i.e., referring to a human being) actually first "comes up"—both to the water's surface and to the onlooker's/reader's awareness. Adding the Atwoodian leitmotiv of a subject's death by drowning (ll.15–16), we have all the thematic constituents to make up the poem's discursive core: engaging with recurring themes of photo theory, "This Is a Photograph of Me" reformulates such time-honoured photographic issues as mortality and revelation within the medium of language and the genre of poetry.

What makes this poem particularly fascinating in this context is its endeavour to expose the means by which photography traditionally gains the aura of unquestionable truth—even in the writings of a Walter Benjamin who, after all, argued for a fundamental distinction between "technically reproducible" (photography, film) and "auratic" arts (painting, sculpture, etc.) in his seminal treatise *Das Kunstwerk im Zeitalter seiner technischen Reproduzierbarkeit* (1936/1955; *The Work of Art in the Age of Technological Reproduction*). Benjamin's "Short History of Photography" ("Kleine Geschichte der Photographie" 1931), in contrast, still aligns him with the common(-sense) reverence of photography for its indexical relation to the allegedly non-discursive external reality. Joining technological means and "magical" effect in his pursuit of the "optical unconscious" (das "Optisch-Unbewusste," Benjamin 50) beyond human sensory perception, Benjamin substitutes the "aura of objective truth"—however miraculous and unfathomable he admits it to be—for that of subjective originality.[3] His thinking may thus serve to sum up an ambivalent discussion at least as old as the phenomenon of Veronica's veil and never more virulent than during the revolution of the photographic age in the nineteenth century. It is the idea of a medium that on one hand is totally neutral and proves without a doubt the historical existence of a certain subject/object by preserving the traces it once physically imprinted itself, and that on the other hand still remains "natively surreal": "What could be more surreal than an object which virtually produces itself?" (Sontag 51f). At first glance—given the shocking manifestation of Benjamin's "optical unconscious" in the form of a drowned body—Atwood appears to merely clad this genuinely photographic discourse in words, with the flatness of the photo (both materially and content-wise) opening up under scrutiny to the sinister truth it held all along. But on second thought, the poem tells a different story, in fact the only story there is: being embedded in the poetic utterance of a lyrical "I," it is through words, not visual data, that the "optical unconscious" in the photo can suddenly be "seen;" it is interpretation, not eyesight, that brings up the subject in the first place. Atwood obviously undermines photography's apotheosis of indexicality by subversively mimicking its own reasoning. Within the bracketed space, she takes up photography's promise of revelation ("if [only] you look long enough" l.24), but then forever defers it to an undefined future ("eventually/you will be able to see me" ll.25–26). Similarly, she alludes to the basic process of picture-taking through the exposure of photosensitive material to light, but simultaneously sabotages the associated poetic "picture" of light being refracted on the water's prismatic surface when she simply turns the metaphoric constituents around—to a "distort[ing]" effect indeed: "the effect of water/on light is a distortion" (ll.22–23). In this way, the poem subtly yet decisively dismisses the idea of a photo being transparent (like water) to some objective truth, and instead argues for the verbal exploration of the only truth there is in any picture: that of the individual interpreter. Barthes' rather elusive concept of the "punctum" may come to mind here, which describes the completely subjective and therefore incommunicable experience of being existentially overwhelmed—"sting[ed]" and "bruise[d]" (27)—by a single detail in an ordinary photo. Correspondingly, the lyrical

"I" in "This Is a Photograph of Me" does not, in fact cannot, give its private "punctum" away, but instead invites the reader to come closer and "see" (l.26), or, better, "say" (ll.19–20) for herself. On looking at a picture of his late mother as a small child, Barthes likewise refuses to grant the reader so much as a reproduction of the photo.[5] However, he takes it as his point of departure for an ontological investigation into photography: "Something like an essence of the Photograph floated in this particular picture. I therefore decided to 'derive' all Photography (its 'nature') from [it]" (73). Apart from the clever vocabulary—"to float" suggesting both a drifting movement on water or air and the photo's suggestiveness itself—Barthes' design is also conspicuously reminiscent of Atwood's poem insofar as they share the theme of mortality and death, and, more interestingly, link it to the photographic discourse via the means of parenthesis. Barthes calls the experience of being photographed "a micro-version of death (of parenthesis)" (14); Atwood puts her (drowned) subject into brackets.

If we have similarly proposed to read "This Is a Photograph of Me" as a programmatic text and predominantly for its discursive "essence," it was not least to steer away from the kind of empathetic (auto-)biographical reading the purposefully misleading title seems to imply. Considering photography's promise of objective referentiality on one hand and the confessional air of poetry on the other hand, one may be tempted to forget about what Sherrill Grace in this volume aptly quotes as the "autobiographical pact" (Philippe Lejeune) between author and reader (Coleridge's "suspension of disbelief" taken to the extreme, if you will). Her convincing case against any "absolute distinctions [...] between testimony at one end of the truth and reality scale and first-person novels at the other (123, this vol.)" is equally applicable to our context as well—with Atwood's negotiation of poetry and photography arguably further challenging the reader's capacity to "tell the difference between types of fictionality and degrees of referentiality."[6] The autobiographical intimation evoked by the title and its frustration, particularly in the second half of the poem, clearly presents us with a young writer who is as much aware of the power and possibilities of photography as of those of her own medium, language, in "reassessing the picture."

Turning from the rather abstract *how* to the concrete *what* of photographic representation, the following poem is a case in point for the theoretical issues dealt with above, as it reflects the latter against a very palpable content: "Unsuspecting/window lady, [...]/Do you see nothing/

watching you from under the water?" (ll.38–41) the lyrical "I" inquires "At the Tourist Centre in Boston," thus transferring the uncanny scenario of the preceding poem onto the contested terrain of intercultural politics. Looking at a map of Canada, the lyrical "I," who strongly identifies with "[her] country" (ll.1–6), finds its representation strikingly out of proportion: the giant land is (necessarily) "reduced to the size of a wall" and wilfully annotated with "10 blownup snapshots/one for each province." First, her reaction seems to be ambivalent, oscillating between the insider's amusement of knowing better and the severe irritation if not downright anger about the arrogant cultural ignorance conveyed by the visual stereotypes, simplifications, and misrepresentations of Canadian cities and provinces through the American tourist industry. Not only do the photos label the product to sell with geographical clichés of "Mountains and lakes and more lakes" (ll.11) in ecologically approved colouring ("blues […]/of an assertive purity" ll.9–10), but they also replace any portrayal of Canadians with staged photos of All-American, that is, US-American, "grinning tourists" (l.16). Cultural imperialism and the cosmetics of marketing work hand in hand here, fabricating a picture of attractive people in "convenient" (l.18) surroundings with too much makeup to be true: "in immaculate slacks by a smokeless fire,/her teeth white as detergent" (ll.21–22). Still somewhat undecided about the (mean) intentions of this representation—is it "a dream"/"manufactured hallucination," "a cynical fiction," or rather "a lure for export" (ll.23–26)?—the lyrical "I" calls up diverging memories of "people, […] also slush, machines, and assorted garbage," only to immediately dismiss them as her "private mirage" (ll.27–30), that is, yet another selective and reductive picture of reality, and, besides, too weak to confront the above master myth. Instead of giving up, however, the lyrical "I" boldly leaves its "victim position" (Atwood) behind and opts to battle on native ground in more than one sense: the "citizens" (l.32) lying in wait in the wilderness to butcher "platoons of tourists" (l.36) come to stand for Canada's "cultural expertise" in the deceitfulness of nature's beauty and magnificence in general and for Atwood's subversive techniques in challenging photography's supreme claim to objective representation in particular. Rather than launching a counter-image/"mirage," Atwood sabotages the opponent's version of reality by taking over its argumentation and suggesting to an "[u]nsuspecting" onlooker, accustomed to trusting the credibility of a picture, that she or he may simply fall short of seeing right this time. This is not a self-righteous judgment either. After all, the question "Who really lives here?" (l.43) goes even deeper—all the way to the Native defence of life and land against the European conquerors ("odd red massacres" l.37). Far from downplaying the incomparably graver dimension of this physical and material assault, the implied analogy between military conquest then and cultural invasion now still manages to blur the categories of victim and aggressor to the extent that at the end of the poem no clear answer, no unequivocal positioning in a long history of imperialist takeovers is available anymore to either the lyrical "I" or the reader.

"Projected Slide of an Unknown Soldier" not only makes war its central theme but is also much more confrontational than the previous poem when it comes to the negotiation of visual data and interpretative words. Published in Atwood's fourth poetry collection, in 1970, the poem is most likely to refer to the Vietnam War as *the* defining fix point in the collective memory of the Western world at that time. In contrast to the other poems to be discussed, Atwood chooses the third-person perspective and, presumably, a press photograph here, thus keeping the reader at a certain critical distance from the start. These markers of detachment further add to the poem's composition according to those stark contrasts that photography is especially apt to convey: collisions of near and far, light and dark, black and white dominate the overall picture, both pertaining to the photo itself and to its "speaking" through language. As the title states, the poem describes the larger-than-life projection of some anonymous soldier's face entangled in dark "leaves, glossy,/perhaps tropical" (l.5). With "clothes [...] invisible,/ the eyes/hidden; the nose/foreshortened" (ll.13–16), the "open mouth" (l.20) becomes the picture's sole means of expression, thrusting forward an unfathomable abyss of darkness against the glaring whiteness of "absolute" (l.21) light on skin and teeth. It does not become entirely clear whether the man is dead or alive, but the reference to a "slippery halo" (l.12) and his "ultimate demand" (l.25) give a tentative preference to the former possibility. The sheer size, the dramatic chiaroscuro effect, and the black hole of a mouth (appearing to swallow ever more light) add up to quite a visual shock on the part of the onlooker as he or she finds zones of brilliant light and pitch-black "pushing" (ll.3, 31) against each other in what seems to be an elemental fight over visual hegemony; common distinctions between figure and ground, foreground and background have already been eliminated in the process ("not making/explicit whether the face was/breaking through [the leaves], wore them/as disguise, was crowned/with them or sent them/forth as rays,/a slippery halo" (ll.6–12). Most strikingly in this context, light and dark become articulate, in the true sense of the word, for they are said to "utter" (ll.2, 31) themselves. Compensating for the mute and likewise incomprehensible "call or howl [...] of agony, ultimate demand or simple famine" (ll.23–25), this visual utterance obviously refers to the way photography typically communicates—that is, through images, not words—and to the specific shortcomings of language. Barthes states, "It is the misfortune (but also perhaps the voluptuous pleasure) of language not to be able to authenticate itself. The *noeme* of language is perhaps this impotence, or, to put it positively: language is, by nature, fictional" (86–87). In contrast to photography's indexical status, language is a symbolic system, of course, and as such always further removed from its real-life referents. Photography therefore seems to be the superior medium: not only does it bridge the temporal and spatial chasm between subject and spectator (cf. Sontag's "pseudo-presence" to be discussed below in more detail) but also its ability to blow up any small detail can even create the illusion of a hyper-real intimacy with the subject.

Still, Atwood would not be Atwood—or a poet for that matter—if she did not insist on the power of words to endow pictures with a meaning they cannot produce on their own. She starts with photography's deficiency of not being able to grant the soldier an audible voice; as in "This Is a Photograph of Me," the crucial point appears in brackets: "(there was no tongue)" (l.24). This muteness is of course diametrically opposed to the poem on the page. In fact, one might even read the black lettering on the white page as transforming the shapeless dark of the open mouth against the white face into communicable signs (given Atwood's awareness of and interest in the materiality of writing—see, for example, her prose poem "The Page" from *Murder in the Dark*). The poem would claim nothing less than giving the soldier a voice. One should, however, not neglect the more refined subtlety of the poem. Considering the implied "canine" imagery ("howl," "canine teeth" l.27), what emerges from the bottomless darkness of the distorted mouth is less a human sound, let alone word, than an untranslatable animal cry. But despite, or rather because of, this denial of language, the poem manages to render the soldier's agony as authentically as possible. Facing the impossible task of objectively describing the horror and suffering of another person through explicit words, Atwood opens up the poem's constituents, that is, its words, to a dimension beyond communication as we know it. Embodied by the "open mouth" (l.30), the poem closes on a mute outcry that transcends the idea of verbalizing the unspeakable for the depiction of the unspeakable itself. Edvard Munch's famous painting "The Scream" may come to mind here, and it may in fact help our understanding of the poem. When Munch extends the depiction of the individual's crying out in utter despair to the lines and colours of the figure's surroundings, he infects the medium itself with the horror of the subject, thereby acknowledging and at the same time overcoming (like Atwood) the inherent inability of traditional media—be they iconic (painting) or symbolic (language)—to be truly "realistic." In the face of incommunicable experiences on one hand and the rivalry of a medium that is particularly effective in producing shock images on the other hand, Atwood (like Munch) lets *her* medium be the (subject's) message.[7]

We have so far analyzed Atwood's poems in relation to each other and, more importantly, to the theoretic framework distilled from "This Is a Photograph of Me." The three poems to follow can also be said to form a subgroup of their own, with the exceptionally resonant "Girl and Horse, 1928" taking the programmatic lead in this case. Theirs is a concern for the particular impact of photographic representation on conceptions and perceptions of time, that is, pertaining to such topics as temporal transience, relativity, linearity, or circularity, and so on. Both "Daguerreotype Taken in Old Age" and "Man in a Glacier" display the most fascinating facets of this discussion. However, for our declared purpose of examining Atwood's negotiation of poetic and photographic means and effects, rather than those of photography as such, we have opted to mainly concentrate on "Girl and Horse, 1928," since the other two poems offer less potential in this particular regard.

Published in the same poetry collection as "Projected Slide," "Girl and Horse, 1928," at first glance, could not be more different in theme and tone. Instead of the detached perspective on the distorted, overexposed face of an anonymous soldier, we get a young girl gently shaded by apple trees in full bloom and intimately addressed by a lyrical "I." Instead of a sensational shot selected for public display, this is most likely an everyday *mise-en-scène* from some family archive. And yet both poems deal with the intricacies of communicating issues of death and mortality through photographic material, be it a soldier's utmost horror in the face of death or a young girl's apparent oblivion of her subjection to transience: "[F]orty/years ago [she was] caught by light" (ll.12–13)—the contingent moment now being read by the lyrical "I" as a Barthesian "prophesy in reverse: like Cassandra, but eyes fixed on the past," telling of certain "death in the future" (Barthes 87, 96). The insignia of spring significantly falling like snowflakes ("Can't you/see the apple blossoms falling around/you, snow, sun, snow" ll.5–7) is indeed the most overt exponent in this poem of the *memento mori* that is forever inscribed into human existence and that has arguably never shown more "vividly" than in photographic representation. As Sontag states, "All photographs are *memento mori*. To take a photograph is to participate in another person's (or thing's) mortality, vulnerability, mutability. Precisely by slicing out this moment and freezing it, all photographs testify to time's relentless melt" (15). From the privileged perspective in the here and now, the lyrical "I" therefore confronts the girl's manner of carefree innocence: "Why do you smile?" She does not get an answer, of course, for she does not get heard in the first place ("you can't hear me" l.12). A seemingly unbridgeable chasm that temporally and spatially divides two historical subjects from each other frustrates any attempt to establish a reciprocal connection.

Atwood's "Daguerreotype Taken in Old Age" is yet another intriguing elaboration of the human subjection to constant "change" (l.1) in time. The technical necessity of a rather prolonged exposure to light—which Benjamin describes as the process of slowly growing into one's image[8]—makes this antiquated forerunner of photography an especially apt medium to record the tormenting experience of continually losing each moment to an irretrievable past (note the passive progressive tense): "I am being/eaten away by light" (ll.23–24). "Daguerreotype" locates the aforementioned temporal chasm between two distinct existences within one and the same person, for example, the Susanna Moodie of Atwood's imagination, unsettled by the documentation of her aged face. It thereby introduces the experience of self-alienation that photography may induce ("I know I change/have changed/but whose is this vapid face" ll.1–3): the portrait on the iodized silver plate appears as remote to the lyrical "I"'s sense of self as the pale moon is to her grounded position on earth. Moreover, it is the moon seen "in a telescope" (l.6), that is, through an optical lens, that shrinks the actual distance in space and isolates the object of observation from its context. Correspondingly, the face appears "suspended in empty paper" (l.5), a contingent flat detail (cf. Barthes' "absolute Particular" or "sovereign Contingency" [4]) subtracted from the woman's body as from her ongoing existence through time. Overcoming this image of utter stasis and immobility, the lyrical "I" unexpectedly starts to enact the lunar analogy. Launched by Atwood's shrewd use of equivocal vocabulary, which may refer to facial and planetary features alike ("vapid," "pitted and vast, rotund," "granular" ll.3–7), she starts "pulling against gravity" (l.9) and enters the moon's orbit. But just as the moon may "revolve" (l.12) on fixed "paths" (l.18) only, the lyrical "I" cannot transgress her predetermined voyage toward eventual death, her moribund existence literally highlighted as the sun leaves her "eye-sockets 2 craters" (ll.16–17). The analogy between the sun casting its brilliant light on the dependent moon and the process of photographic recording through the exposure of photosensitive material to (sun-)light makes for a rather gloomy ending: the poem closes on an elegiac coming to awareness of one's continual fading into nothingness—"I am being/eaten away by light"—that we did not encounter to this (cosmic) extent in "Girl and Horse, 1928," in which the "apple blossoms" are falling, too, but do not yet transcend their earthly origins to turn into "white white spinning/stars" as in "Daguerreotype" (ll.21–22).

Correspondingly, in "Girl and Horse, 1928," it is not the surrender of both the girl's life and all communicative efforts to "time's relentless melt" that constitutes the gist of the poem. Neither its inherent prophecy of eventual death, nor its linkage to a bygone time and distant space makes photography a dead end here. Instead, the medium displays its unrivalled capacity to deconstruct the commonsensical concept of temporal linearity as such, providing an alternative, relative dimension of time and space where contact *is* possible after all. The liberating challenge to supposedly stable temporal categories is already introduced in the first two lines: "You are younger than I am, you are/someone I never knew" (ll.1–2). The reader may wonder, first, whether the girl on the photo was actually born after the lyrical "I" or, more likely in this context, whether she is younger only in this particular picture and from the reference point of the lyrical "I"'s present age, and, second, whether the two historical subjects may know each other at all, and, if yes, in what sense. "You are/someone I never knew" may either simply mean that their ways never crossed or, again more likely under the circumstances, that the lyrical "I" did not know the girl in/of 1928 and thus *never* knew the person in the photo (regardless of a conceivable acquaintance later in life). Still, the lyrical "I" *does* feel she can get to know the girl *now*, or why else would she try to communicate with her? This thorough confusion of temporal categories has been a major issue in photographic discourse. Sontag's statement that any photograph "is both a pseudo-presence and a token of absence" (16) and Barthes' making "every photograph [...] a certificate of presence" (87) are as representative of this debate as the latter is characteristically, and in fact inevitably, resistant to logical argument. In our own, albeit hardly less paradoxical, wording: photography's indexical relation to its subject has the power to (momentarily) save this subject from its passage through time and toward death, endowing it with an air of ontological integrity and independence that substitutes a temporal concept of absolute simultaneity for that of successive linearity. Back to Atwood's poem, this means that to the lyrical "I", the girl in the orchard is as authentically present in the moment the photo is being looked at as is the lyrical "I" itself. Photography freezes the fleeting moment, precisely putting it side by side with any present moment later on. Like no other medium it conveys the image—in the truest sense of the word—of securing the evanescence of all existence against its irrevocable decline into the past, and, for that matter, potentially into oblivion. Thus, carrying the past as "absence" and at the same time denying the linear concept of time that this mediation actually presupposes, photography indeed recreates the past as "pseudo-presence" (16), as Sontag would have it. It is upon this almost tangible "pseudo-presence" produced by the photographic image (cf. Barthes' radical assertion that "what we see on paper is as certain as what we touch" [88]) that Atwood builds her reconstruction of the "whole picture" in the last two stanzas—*pars pro toto* for the integrity of the girl's life as opposed to her moribund existence in the photo. Within the parenthesized space of "poetic freedom" (Barthes' "voluptuous pleasure" of language, 85), Atwood reimagines the temporal continuum from which the photo had once been extracted. She has the girl on horseback literally riding out of the picture, now that "the instant/ is over" (ll.18–19), her undirected "wav[ing]" (l.20) and "smiling"—"as though [she] do[es] not notice" (l.24)—tentatively signifying the girl's awareness of an indefinite beholder (the photographer? the lyrical "I"? the reader?). This minimal communication is said to occur "on the other side/ of the picture" (ll.17–18), a turn in direction we might again interpret as the typically Atwoodian turn from deceitful surfaces to their multi-dimensional context, here coupled with a graphical spatialization of time. In fact, the image of the photo's "other side" aptly describes the aforementioned idea of photography's offering an alternative side/site indeed: a liminal space unfettered by temporal boundaries, a threshold zone to constantly mediate past and present (and future, for that matter) and to allow for the establishing of imaginative relations across generational divides.

Some twenty-five years later, it is the same urge to "connect" that presumably motivates Atwood's writing of "Man in a Glacier" on the experience of her father's slow decline into death. Like "Projected Slide of an Unknown Soldier," the poem starts with a sensational sight for the public eye: an ancient male corpse of "two thousand years [...], or three," "with everything intact," and "still fresh as a mastodon," is found in a glacier—the diagnosis is "death by snow" (ll.2–7). "Then" (l.7) tone and perspective abruptly change from a slightly mocking report of scientific sensation to the very private domestic scene of two siblings projecting a portrait of their father as a young man ("younger than all/of us now" ll.15–16) on the cellar wall. As in "Daguerreotype Taken in Old Age," Atwood works by means of analogy: the "flowers of crystallizing earth" (l.13) on the slides evoke the glacial ice covering the dead man; the "wand of light" (l.14) casting the projection of an old photograph on the wall recalls a glaring searchlight cutting through the ice to expose a well-preserved body.[9] Moreover, as in "Girl and Horse, 1928," it is the confrontation with the past not merely *in* but actually *as* the (pseudo-)present that triggers the realization of photography's startling powers. However, contrary to all previous examples of Atwood's poetic engagement with photography—particularly the programmatic and mockingly autobiographical "This Is a Photograph of Me,"—"Man in a Glacier" introduces with its frankly personal dimension a notion of what we might best describe as a form of self-critical lenience, as Atwood's mournful affection toward her father infiltrates her intellectual dissection of photographic representation in this very particular case. "This was all we got,/this echo, this freeze-framed/simulacrum or slight imprint,/ in answer to our prayers for everlastingness" (ll.25–28): voicing this most explicit statement on photography throughout her poetry, Atwood hits a note of humble honesty here, which resonates with the kind of compassionate tenor we know from Barthes' elegy for the (soon-to-be-) dead *in* and *through* photography in his *Camera Lucida*. Knowing perfectly well that even the indexical quality of photography, that is, its status as "echo" or "imprint" of "real life," produces a mere "simulacrum" of authenticity, the lyrical "I" still wants to believe in, in fact "pray[s]" for, photography's capacity to transcend time and space and overcome death for "everlastingness" (l.28) ; the incompatible registers of religious plea on one hand and "professional" photographic discourse on the other make this inherent contradiction only more apparent. Her uncharacteristically lenient stance toward photography's "spiritual powers" notwithstanding, Atwood loses nothing of her intellectual, (self-)critical fervour. Her invocation of higher powers turns out to appeal not to some benign divinity but to the "bad godmothers": "Chemistry and Physics," who "were present at our birth, who laid/the curse on us: *You will not sleep forever*" (ll.34–37). Photography obviously answers to a "curse" rather than a blessing here, and Atwood knows she is as much an accomplice as anyone who accepts this denial of rest for the comfort of having a beloved person "fixed in that secret/place where we live, where we believe/nothing can change, grow older" ("Girl and Horse, 1928" ll.14–16). From the perspective of a loving daughter, Atwood still puts her finger on the self-serving, appropriative preservation of bygone times and existences through photographic recording. It is this synthesis between intellectual and emotional perspective that distinguishes "Man in a Glacier" as the most overt example of Atwood's idiosyncratic incorporation of both Sontag's analytical acumen and Barthes' elegiac lucidity, thereby creatively joining two rather diverging positions within the wide field of photographic discourse. And it is the "failure" of this synthesis, that is, the poem's irresolvable ambiguity as laid out above, that makes the latter a poetic success. If, at the end of the day, a photograph cannot be truly cherished for its (in-)famous function of preserving the past—because photographic representation smacks of selfish appropriation on one hand, and poor authenticity on the other—it might be a poem (on a photo) instead, which by virtue of its imaginative freedom may transcend both the advantages and drawbacks of photography by creating a symbolic realm of "everlastingness" to better save the past *for* and at the same time *from* posterity.

Looking back on Atwood's critical stance toward and poetic engagement with photography throughout her long career,[10] we see that she obviously finds the medium as resonant with her writing as she continually comes to terms with its paramount issues only, that is to say, *precisely*, through (her own) words, each time hitting photography's weak spot of needing (con-)text and "interpretation" to evolve the "transparency" it promises all along, in the most artistically accomplished of manners.

—University of Constance

NOTES

1. Susan Sontag, "In Plato's Cave," in *On Photography* (New York: Picador 1990), 23; originally published in *The New York Times Review of Books* 20, no. 16 (October 18, 1973).
2. All references to Atwood's poems are based on her *Eating Fire: Selected Poetry 1965–1995* (London: Virago, 1999).
3. "Photography, however, with its time lapses, enlargements, etc. makes such knowledge possible. Through these methods one first learns of this optical unconscious, just as one learns of the drives of the unconscious through psychoanalysis . [...] [P]hotography opens up in this material the physiognomic aspects of the world of images [...]. Now, however, large and formulatable as they have grown, they are able to establish the difference between technology and magic as a thoroughly historical variable." Walter Benjamin in *Classic Essays on Photography*, ed. Alan Trachtenberg (Stony Creek, CT: Leete's Island, 1980), 203.
4. Compare also: "As if only by looking at reality in the form of an object—through the fix of the photograph—is it really real, that is surreal." Ibid.: 80.
5. "(I cannot reproduce the Winter Garden Photograph. It exists only for me. For you, it would be nothing but an indifferent picture, one of the thousand manifestations of the 'ordinary'; it cannot in any way constitute the visible object of a science; it cannot establish an objectivity, in the positive sense of the term; at most it would interest your studium: period, clothes, photogeny; but in it, for you, no wound.)" (Barthes 73).
6. Sherrill Grace, "Atwood and the 'Autobiographical Pact,'" *Margaret Atwood: The Open Eye*, edited by John Moss and Tobi Kozakewich.(Ottawa: University of Ottawa Press, 2006). 121-34.
7. Cf. Marshall McLuhan and Quentin Fiore, *The Medium Is the Message: An Inventory of Effects* (New York: Bantam, 1967).
8. "The procedure itself caused the models to live, not out of the instant, but into it; during the long exposure they grew, as it were, into the image" (Benjamin 204).
9. Cf. Atwood's short story "The Age of Lead" from *Wilderness Tips* for a thematically similar, yet more explicit, analogy between the protagonist's untimely

death and the discovery of the body of a young explorer from the nineteenth century in the arctic permafrost.
10. Cf. Atwood's treatment of photography in other genres, i.e. its prominent role in the novels *The Edible Woman* and *The Blind Assassin*.

WORKS CITED

Atwood, Margaret. "The Age of Lead." *Wilderness Tips*. Toronto: McClelland & Stewart, 1991. 159–78.

———. *The Blind Assassin*. Toronto: McClelland & Stewart, 2000.

———. *Eating Fire: Selected Poetry, 1965–1995*. London: Virago, 1999.

———. *The Edible Woman*. [1969]. Toronto: McClelland & Stewart, 1973.

Barthes, Roland. *Camera Lucida: Reflections on Photography*. New York: Hill and Wang, 1981.

Benjamin, Walter. "A Short History on Photography." *Classic Essays on Photography*. Edited by Alan Trachtenberg. Stony Creek: Leete's Island, 1980.

Grace, Sherrill. "Atwood and the 'Autobiographical Pact'." *Margaret Atwood: The Open Eye*, edited by John Moss and Tobi Kozakewich. Ottawa: University of Ottawa Press, 2006. 121–34.

McLuhan, Marshall, and Quentin Fiore. *The Medium is the Message: An Inventory of Effects*. New York: Bantam, 1967.

Sontag, Susan. "In Plato's Cave." *On Photography*. New York: Picador, 1990.

———. "Melancholy Objects." *On Photography*. New York: Picador, 1990. 51–82.

THE BLIND ASSASSIN AND *ORYX AND CRAKE*

Negotiating with the Looking Glass: Atwood, Her Protagonists, and the Journey to the Dead

PHYLLIS STERNBERG PERRAKIS

WHILE MARGARET ATWOOD has always questioned what Carolyn Heilbrun calls "the once traditional female existence"(124), since her late forties Atwood's writing has increasingly investigated the process by which older women acquire "new attitudes and new courage."[1] Protagonists like Elaine Risley in *Cat's Eye*, Roz, Charis, and Tony in *The Robber Bride*, and Iris Chase in *The Blind Assassin*, in their middle years or older, have begun to experience what Atwood calls "an intimation of transience, of evanescence, and thus of mortality," which drives them to begin a journey into the past and into the confrontation with the dead (*ND* 158).[2] In her book of essays, Atwood explicitly links this process of accommodating growth into older age with the drive or force necessary to write: "*all* writing of the narrative kind, and perhaps all writing, is motivated deep down, by a fear of and a fascination with mortality—by a desire to make the risky trip to the Underworld, and to bring something or someone back from the dead" (156).

In *Negotiating with the Dead: A Writer on Writing*, Atwood makes clear the dangers involved in taking this trip: "Calling up the dead and dealing with them across the threshold" is one thing, but it is a lot riskier to cross over from this world into theirs (*ND* 166, 167). Each of Atwood's recent middle-aged or older women protagonists has taken that dangerous journey, crossing over into the other realm in which the dead reside, and in doing so each of them has come back to tell a story, either to herself or to others. The process of telling this story allows each protagonist to accommodate herself to a new stage in life: middle age for Elaine, Roz, Charis, and Tony, and older age for Iris. In the spiral-like journey back, each protagonist revisits earlier experiences from a new vantage point and acquires new understandings and capacities. But the price for this self-evolution, this movement along the spiral, is what Atwood calls "blood" (*ND* 178). It flows from the protagonist's suffering because, as Iris acknowledges at the end of *The Blind Assassin*, "It's loss and regret and misery and yearning that drive the story forward, along its twisted road" (*BA* 650), and, I might add, also backward. The blood flows from the destruction of the delusions and false understandings that mark the interrelationship with a loved/hated/feared other, and, especially in *The Blind Assassin*, from the acknowledgement of the role that the protagonist plays in the murder, symbolic or literal, of important others. All these forms of loss, destruction, and murder, interpsychic and intersubjective, must be encountered and acknowledged by the protagonist, and accommodated to her present sense of self and stage of life in order to acquire the riches of greater wholeness of being.[3]

Often the experience of peering into a looking glass, both literally and metaphorically, initiates the movement backward for the various protagonists. At the beginning of *Cat's Eye*, back in the city of her childhood for a retrospective of her art, Elaine Risley begins to experience difficulties finding the right distance when looking into a mirror: "too close ... I'm a blur, too far back and I can't see the details" (*CE* 5). Finding the right distance is also necessary for viewing the past. Elaine approaches this task from a "transitional vantage point"(5), not quite old but no longer very young. It is this liminal position that frees her to explore new emotional territory.

For Elaine, the springboard for the trip back is her access to the memories of her girlhood friend Cordelia. Gazing into the mirror of her emotionally abusive relationship with her nine-year-old girlfriend, in which Elaine's behaviour is constantly watched and negatively reflected back, Elaine retrieves the memories that lead up to her near-death experience in the ravine under the bridge where the dead reside, a dangerous place she dares enter only because Cordelia ordered her to, to fetch her hat. Saved by a visitation from the realm of the dead, an archetypal spiritual mother clothed in the guise of Elaine's girlhood spiritual beliefs, Elaine later identifies this symbolic figure with the Virgin of Lost Things and paints her as holding a cat's eye marble in front of her heart, the talismanic expression of Elaine's tenuous hold on her identity during the time of her emotional torture. At that time, to defend against psychic invasion by Cordelia, Elaine had regressed to what psychoanalyst Daniel Stern calls the core sense of self. Seeing the world through the symbolic eye of the cat's eye marble, Elaine had viewed it as a very young infant does, full of shapes and colours one can escape from by turning one's head away, by not looking.[4]

In the narrative present, having remembered and re-experienced her past traumatic experiences and reinterpreted their expression in her art, Elaine is ready to release herself from their lingering power. She has a final crossover experience also involving looking and not looking, not as a regressive defence but, rather, as a moment of holistic integration. Again standing on the bridge over the ravine, Elaine sees that the "sky moves sideways"(442) and there, just to the side of her vision, is nine-year-old Cordelia, awkward, lonely, and afraid. For a moment Elaine feels the old "shame, the sick feeling in my body, the same knowledge of my own wrongness, awkwardness, weakness" (*CE* 443). Then new understanding floods in: "But these are not my own emotions anymore. They are Cordelia's; as they always were" (443). Understanding now that Cordelia's cruelty had been an acting out and projection onto Elaine of Cordelia's own disturbed family relationships and tormented inner world, Elaine can finally let go of the fear and pain connected to her childhood memories. Integrating a powerful, nurturing, and spiritual potential into her sense of self, Elaine can become the Virgin of Lost Things for the lost Cordelia imprisoned in her psyche, offering her acceptance and forgiveness: "*It's all right*, I say to her. *You can go home now*" (443). Elaine's ability to accommodate a new sense of self emanating from a new centre of her being is the gift from the dead she has brought back from her painful journey into the past.

If the way back in *Cat's Eye* starts out by seeing through the mirror of another self, a dark twin, whose relationship to the self has not been fully acknowledged or accepted, it begins to grow more complex in Atwood's next novel of spiral adventuring by middle-aged women. In *The Robber Bride*, the way back seems once again to be the gaze into the mirror of another crossover figure, but this time the dark twin is explicitly connected to the power of storytelling. Gazing into Zenia's blue-black eyes, Tony, whose narration begins and ends the novel, listens to Zenia's story of her horrific past, and "sees her [Tony's] own reflection: herself as she would like to be. … Herself turned inside out" (*RB* 193). As if to force us to focus on Zenia's role as the embodiment of storytelling power, Atwood triples Zenia's manipulative game so that we see her use her mesmerizing stories to insinuate herself in the lives of not one but all three protagonists. Elsewhere I argue that "[d]espite its apparent insidiousness, Zenia's function is ultimately transformative, forcing the three protagonists out of submissive relationships and making possible new modes of self-other interaction" ("Atwood's *The Robber Bride*" 152). Here I want to focus on how the line begins to blur between Zenia's role as a threatening Other whose interaction with the three women triggers their retrospective journeys, the role Cordelia plays for Elaine, and Zenia's symbolic function as the storyteller whose tales hold up a mirror to each of the protagonists' inner worlds, enabling them to access the dark underside of the self for the first time. When at the end of the novel Tony concludes that Zenia is "insubstantial," a kind of magician who "did it with mirrors," and "[t]he mirror was whoever was watching" (*RB* 535), she emphasizes not the storyteller but the role of story itself as the vehicle through which the three protagonists journey into the past in order to consolidate new senses of self in the present. In each case the transformative power of narrative for the three protagonists is directly related to their ability first to listen to Zenia's story and then to dare to articulate their own. It is Zenia's intersubjective attunement to each of the protagonists' troubled inner worlds through her stories that subsequently frees them to dare for the first time to shape their own difficult past experiences into a story, either to be told to another or to themselves.[5]

Sharing for the first time her inner world with another, Tony "begins to fit together the 'shiny fragments' of her memory of her mother and to create for the first time a self-narrative of her painful childhood" (Perrakis, "Atwood's *The Robber Bride*" 158). Charis, more deeply traumatized than the other two protagonists, does not share her past with Zenia, but she dares to allow back into her consciousness and to shape as narrative the previously repressed memories of when she was Karen, physically abused by her mentally ill mother and sexually abused by her uncle.[6] If being able to remember and formulate previously unavailable narratives of their early relations with the (m)other are freeing for the other two protagonists, in Roz's case she must reformulate her self-narrative to include her relationships with both her parents, but particularly those of her mysterious father whose return fills her girlhood with both wonder and doubt. In choosing to trust Zenia's story of her father as a hero, Roz is initially free to rewrite the story of the father she resembles but distrusts. Eventually, however, she must learn to tell stories about herself that do justice to the strengths and weaknesses of both her parents and both sides of her personality.[7] In each case, Zenia, by telling her own stories, which are neatly tailored to mirror the pain and confusion experienced by each of the protagonists in the past, serves as the vehicle that encourages and enables each of the protagonists to formulate (or reformulate) her own self-narrative. She thus enables the three protagonists to overcome the obstacles that hold them in stasis, tied to a past they have not fully acknowledged and therefore cannot escape, and to finally move forward to a present they can fully inhabit.

With *The Blind Assassin* Atwood foregrounds the act of writing itself as the mirror through which Iris not only connects with her past and the murderous role she has played but also through which she accommodates herself to her own approaching death.[8] Here Atwood confronts more directly the "fear of and fascination with mortality": the impetus to write (*ND* 156). While Iris's immediate motivation for writing her story comes from the emotions stirred in her from handing out the award in Laura's name at the high school ceremony, an act that opens the "old wound" connected to Laura's death, allowing "the invisible blood [to] pour forth," the urgency of her response comes from her realization that time is running out, that "soon I'll be emptied" (*BA* 52). In *The Blind Assassin* Atwood also develops more fully Roz's insight in *The Robber Bride* that women play all the roles—the parts of the aggressors as well as the victims. Iris is a different kind of protagonist than the previous ones. Ostensibly an insider rather than an outsider, trained at least partially to be obedient to the social rules governing women's behaviour, which the earlier protagonists trespass through their inability to conform, or through their ignorance or clumsiness, Iris in some ways embodies the murderous forces that lie beneath the surface of women's blindness to their own needs and their desire to recognize and please the other. Sold off to a business magnate to pay her father's business debts, and taught to play the role of a society wife to further her husband's career, Iris finally rebels against the scripts offered her after understanding the roles that she and her husband have played in her sister's death. In reaction, more consciously although indirectly, Iris contributes to her husband's suicide.

Only in older age, however, as death approaches, does Iris have the psychic strength and motivation to begin the spiral back and to write down what she discovers, which is both her story and that of her sister, Laura. It is her decision to write down what she finds that distinguishes Iris from the earlier protagonists and connects her most intimately with her creator. Furthermore, it is Iris's earlier book, "The Blind Assassin," the book she writes to memorialize her affair with her left-wing lover, Alex Thomas, that becomes the mirror through which Iris and the reader see Iris's story. The final *Blind Assassin* is structured so that after the crucial first chapter, in which Iris describes how she learns of Laura's death, we are introduced to the prologue and to the first four chapters of the inner "Blind Assassin" before we get to the chapters in the final novel's narrative present, in which Iris describes sitting down to write her story. Furthermore, we slowly realize that the metaphors from the inner "Blind Assassin" comment on and finally come to shape the final book that Iris writes. The mute sacrificial maiden of Sakiel-Norn becomes Laura as a six-year-old pushed off the ledge by Iris for believing literally that her mother is with God; later she is Iris herself as she is married off to Richard to save her father's business. Still later she will be Laura again, pushed over the edge into suicide by the blind assassin Iris, whose jealous, unguarded words inform Laura that Alex is dead and that he was her, Iris's, lover. Finally, it is the left hand of her dead sister Laura, the disconnected hand at the edge of the picture in the photo of Iris and Alex at the picnic, the description of which begins and ends the inner "Blind Assassin," that provides the metaphor for the older Iris's ability to finally acknowledge and embrace Laura's part in her story.

Gazing into the mirror of the inner "Blind Assassin" is the first step in Iris's gradual understanding of Laura's role in her story. Writing the inner "Blind Assassin" had been Iris's first attempt to negotiate with the dead. She admits having written it originally to keep alive her memories of her lover, Alex. Then she published it under Laura's name to both punish her ex-husband Richard and keep Laura's name alive. Furthermore, as she meditates on the metaphors in her first book, she comes to understand that Laura had been her "collaborator" in the "spiritual sense" (*BA* 644) when Iris wrote "The Blind Assassin." Without consciously understanding it, Iris now realizes she was already subliminally influenced by Laura's ability to see the implications of the sterile world surrounding Iris. In writing the second, larger *Blind Assassin*, Iris consciously comes to terms with Laura's role in awakening her [Iris] from her lifelong sleep and in guiding Iris's hand, her denied left hand, "the hand that will set things down" (650) (her characterization of it at the end of the inner "Blind Assassin"), the hand of the writer. But Laura is not another Cordelia or Zenia. She is not the disturbed child who projects her shame and insecurities onto a girlhood friend, or the adult femme fatale who enjoys playing with the weaknesses of other women. Laura's power is more ordinary and more potentially accessible. Trying to account for Laura's difference, Iris concludes that "perhaps Laura wasn't very different from other people after all. Perhaps she was the same—the same as some odd, skewed element in them that most people keep hidden but that Laura did not and this was why she frightened them" (112). What Iris does not realize until very late in her story is that Laura's openness to that odd potential in herself, what Iris elsewhere calls her "tranquil single-mindedness"(122), and Laura's search for ways to actualize that potential in the world around her, also protects Laura from the social lies and compromises that Iris so willingly accepts. Laura's fidelity to her inner spiritual vision allows her to accurately assess other people's inner natures, and to intuit the self beneath their polite social veneers. She tries to share this insight with Iris when she leaves her the message of the tinted wedding photos, revealing the red flames emanating from Richard's head and hands, the self-sacrificing radiant yellow enveloping Laura's figure, and the bleached-out eyes, nose, and mouth of Iris's fog-covered face (566). But Iris is only prepared to take Laura's messages seriously after the blood has flowed. Following Laura's suicide, Iris looks into the schoolgirl notebooks left in her drawer and finds the record of the times that Richard has sexually exploited Laura.

If Iris is the blind assassin whose jealous words drive Laura to her death, she is also implicated in the death of Aimee, Iris's daughter, as well. It is not impatience and jealousy but fear, guilt, and undeveloped intersubjective capacities that cause Iris's complicity in her daughter's death. From the beginning, Iris had doubted her "capacity to love" her newborn daughter, or "to love her as much as she'd need" (*BA* 541). Struggling to meet the demands of her role as Richard's wife, desperately missing Alex who was away fighting in the Spanish Civil War (we learn this later), and worried about Laura, who had been institutionalized by Richard supposedly for a mental breakdown, Iris feels, "I was spread too thin as it was. I did not think there would be enough of me left over" (541).

Iris is spread too thin in another way as well. Trained from childhood to deny her own needs and feelings and to give primacy to those of the powerful other, Iris seems unable to nurture either herself or her daughters, real and surrogate. She feels blind and helpless to assess the truth or find out what has really happened when Laura is committed to the institution, and she portrays the same helplessness when she loses Aimee to Winifred. Iris's intersubjective difficulties are most visible when she visits the grown Aimee, now with a daughter of her own, relying on drugs and alcohol to soothe her pain. Iris cannot find the words to allay Aimee's suspicion that Laura, not Iris, is her real mother, nor can she provide Aimee with the love and acceptance she so desperately cries out for. Iris fails on all three levels of intersubjective communication discussed by Daniel Stern. She fails on the level of core relatedness, the domain in which the young infant becomes aware of "itself as a coherent willful, physical entity" separate from the mother (Stern 26). Iris is not able to communicate with her daughter in this domain; she cannot hold out her arms and physically respond to the sobbing, hysterical Aimee. She also fails in the domain of intersubjective sharing, the next mode of communicating developed, in which the infant realizes that he or she possesses inner subjective states that can be shared with another (140–42). Iris is not able to imagine what her daughter feels and to empathize with her. Finally, Iris fails in the domain of verbal communication, the domain that allows a child "to objectify the self, to be self-reflexive, to comprehend and produce language" (28). She cannot find the words to bridge the space between them, as she could not in her earlier dealings with Laura. Aimee's desperate need for an intersubjective bridge between her tormented world and a caring other becomes only too apparent when three weeks later she dies from a fall down the stairs. She had already been starting to fall when Iris saw her.

Only near the end of her life, as Iris spirals back to these earlier painful times and interactions, does she have the strength to imagine different outcomes. Commenting on how Winifred took Aimee away from her, Iris notes that "Winifred wouldn't have won that battle now, but she did then" (*BA* 544). Already stronger by the time Winifred gains custody of Sabrina, Aimee's daughter, after Aimee's death, Iris thinks that had she taken Sabrina she would have loved her, unlike Winifred (545). Indeed, it is Iris's ability in the narrative present to imagine loving Sabrina that provides the most powerful gauge as to what Iris has gained from her written record of her spiral journey back. When Iris began her story she did not know for whom she was writing. At one point early on she thinks she simply needs to leave her mark, a record of her voice. It is only near the end of her story that Iris can acknowledge that the purpose of her writing is to communicate with her granddaughter, to find the words that will heal and make possible a relationship that was not available in her actual experience. To do this Iris has had to consciously cross over to the realm of the dead, invoking the Furies, welcoming the wolves that Alex has told her are a part of every story, and finally accepting the "[d]ead women with azure hair and eyes like snake-filled pits" (623), the symbols of all that Iris had repressed in her life.

Iris's newfound strength is seen in her ability at the end of her story to imagine another kind of crossover—not to the dead but to her living but unknown granddaughter. Her daydream meeting with the grown-up Sabrina occurs in what Iris had earlier called another dimension, this time involving the future and not the past, created not out of memory but out of empathetic imagination, intuition, and love. Iris can now conjure up a meeting with the granddaughter to whom she had not dared reveal herself earlier when she used to secretly watch the teenaged Sabrina sitting with friends in the local hangout. Iris can find now the words and gestures she would use with Sabrina because she is strong enough not only to acknowledge her guilt in the deaths of the three people closest to her but also to acknowledge the penetrating vision and strange power of her artistic muse, her left hand, Laura.

In *Negotiating With the Dead* Atwood describes how the writer, in reaching back into the realm of the dead, where the stories are, is also changed; she "gets clairvoyance, and the completion of her identity as a poet" (*ND* 178). In *The Blind Assassin* Atwood reveals more clearly than ever before the secrets of her encounter with the dead and the nature of what she discovers. Perhaps because Atwood herself is approaching a time when the fear and fascination with mortality become more pressing, she raises the veil a little and allows us to see her left hand pulling the strings behind the curtain. When Alex comes back from the dead to revisit Iris near the end of the inner "Blind Assassin," he shows her the city going up in flames, the city that she recognizes as Sakiel-Norn, their joint fantasy creation. But, perhaps as a warning to Iris, Alex also connects that fantasy city to some city in Europe that is fire bombed during the Second World War (588–89). Perhaps Atwood is also trying to warn us. What Iris now knows, and what Atwood has brought back from the dead to tell us, is that the only way to avoid being destroyed by the burning city whose coercive institutions have blinded some of us and rendered others mute is to accept our left hand, to open ourselves to the skewed, potent, clear-sighted power of the self beneath our conditioning. Questioning the meaning of the words that those around us accept as clichés, responding to peoples' true colours and not to their tinted costumes, daring to search for the presence of spirit in our daily lives, and connecting these skewed insights to a level-headed understanding of the workings of everyday life, perhaps we may find ourselves empowered with enough new vision and new speech to save the city from burning—or perhaps not.

—University of Ottawa

NOTES

1. Carolyn Heilbrun has commented that "[f]or women who have awakened to new possibilities in middle age or who were born into the current women's movement and have escaped the usual rhythm of the once traditional female existence, the last third of life is likely to require new attitudes and new courage" (124).
2. Although I am concentrating on female protagonists in this paper, the male protagonist of *Oryx and Crake* also fits this retrospective pattern. Grace Marks of *Alias Grace* is younger than the other protagonists and her motivations for her journey back are less clear and more complex.
3. In discussing the spiral-like development of Atwood's protagonists, I draw upon, among others, the model of human development called "Spiral Dynamics" pioneered by Clare Graves, who describes it as follows: "The psychology of the mature human being is an unfolding, emergent, oscillating spiraling process marked by progressive subordination of older, lower-order behavior systems to newer, higher-order systems as an individual's existential problems change" (qtd. in Wilber 5– 6).
4. I develop these insights more fully in my article "The Female Gothic and the (M)other in Atwood and Lessing."
5. Suzette A. Henke, writing about the therapeutic value of women's self-narrative, notes that "[a] great deal of evidence now suggests that the formulation of narrative cohesion can reconfigure the individual's obsessive mental processing

of embedded traumatic scripts" (xviii). She also quotes Judith Herman, who explains that the primary goal of therapy for post-traumatic stress victims is "to put the story, including its imagery, into words" (Henke xviii).
6. Zenia's role with the three protagonists enables them to pass through stages of recovery somewhat analogous to those of the post-traumatic stress victim discussed by Judith Herman. Suzette A. Henke, paraphrasing Herman, explains the stages of recovery as "establishing safety, reconstructing the trauma story, and regaining a sense of community" (xvii). Through sharing her stories with the protagonists, Zenia creates a safe space where the three women can dare to create or repair their self-narratives and feel a bond of shared understanding with Zenia. After she deserts them, the three protagonists are able to share their self-narratives with each other.
7. For a fuller discussion of Roz's recreation of her story, see my article, "Atwood's *The Robber Bride*" 163–66).
8. Iris's motives for writing her story seem to have much in common with those of the women writers discussed by Suzette A. Henke. She theorizes that "a major impetus behind autobiographical literature in general, and women's life-writing in particular, may be the articulation of a haunting and debilitating emotional crisis, that, for the author, borders on the unspeakable" (xviii–xix).

WORKS CITED

Atwood, Margaret. *Alias Grace*. Toronto: McClelland & Stewart, 1996.

———. *The Blind Assassin*. Toronto: Seal Books, 2001.

———. *Cat's Eye*. Toronto: McClelland & Stewart, 1988.

———. *Negotiating with the Dead*. Cambridge: Cambridge University Press, 2002.

———. *Oryx and Crake*. Toronto: McClelland & Stewart, 2003.

———. *The Robber Bride*. Toronto: McClelland & Stewart, 1993.

Heilbrun, Carolyn. *Writing a Woman's Life*. New York: Ballantine, 1988.

Henke, Suzette A. *Shattered Subjects: Trauma and Testimony in Women's Life-Writing*. New York: St. Martin's Press, 1998.

Perrakis, Phyllis Sternberg. "Atwood's *The Robber Bride*: The Vampire as Intersubjective Catalyst." *Mosaic* 30, no. 3 (1997): 151–68.

———. "The Female Gothic and the (M)other in Atwood and Lessing." *Doris Lessing Newsletter* 17, no. 1 (1995): 1, 11–15.

Stern, Daniel. *The Interpersonal World of the Infant: A View from Psychoanalysis and Developmental Psychology*. New York: Basic, 1985.

Wilber, Ken. *A Theory of Everything: An Integral Vision for Business, Politics, Science, and Spirituality*. Boston: Shambhala, 2001.

The Body of/as Evidence: Margaret Atwood, *The Blind Assassin*, and the Feminist Literary Mystery

WENDY ROY

IN HIS REVIEW of Margaret Atwood's *The Blind Assassin*, Thomas Mallon of *The New York Times* complains that

> [t]he answer to the book's chief matter of suspense—the source of the Zycron stories—answers itself so obviously and early that Iris [the framing narrator], while disclosing the truth in the book's last pages, feels obliged to concede to the reader, "you must have known that for some time" (*BA* 643). (7)

Mallon's criticism misinterprets Atwood's book in several significant ways. The first is that while *The Blind Assassin* repeatedly evokes conventions of the mystery novel, it is not a conventional mystery, and thus its author is under no obligation—and indeed in all likelihood has not intended—to keep the reader guessing until the final pages. Secondly, contrary to Mallon's assertion, the question of which character tells the story of the blind assassin in the short modernist text embedded within Atwood's novel is just one of its many mysteries, and not even its most compelling. Intentionally more compelling, I would argue, are the related mysteries focused on women's bodies.

What is the significance of the severed female hand in the photographs, to which the multiple narrators repeatedly refer? Who is the model for the sexualized protagonist of the short novel-within-the-novel? What is the metaphorical connection between the mutilated women of Sakiel-Norn (a fictional place described in that embedded novel) and the mid-twentieth-century women of the other parallel narratives? Who is the father of narrator Iris Chase Griffen's child? What is her sister Laura's embodied experience of coercion and abuse, and why and how does she die? Atwood repeatedly poses questions about women's bodily experiences in the various levels of narrative of *The Blind Assassin* in order to interrogate gendered and sexual relationships in mid-twentieth-century North America. The book appropriates and revises the mystery novel's conventional violation of order and eventual return to order through the assemblage of a body of evidence, in part by highlighting the hidden violation of women's physical bodies that is inherent to that order. What Mallon identifies as the "truth" disclosed at the end of the mystery plot is revealed as a subjective concept, since the "truth" of the female protagonists' bodily experiences is either unrecognized or actively suppressed by their families and their societies.

A novel's reception is often determined by the conventions of the genre to which it is judged to belong. In criticizing *The Blind Assassin* as though it were a detective story, Mallon is responding to generic principles such as those put forward in S.S. Van Dine's "Twenty Rules for Writing Detective Stories," first published in 1928 to which mystery writers such as Dorothy Sayers subscribed and at the same time revised and undermined. Van Dine's Rule 15 is: "The truth of the problem must at all times be apparent—provided the reader is shrewd enough to see it" (191). But Mallon fails to mention Atwood's concession to Rule 7: "There simply must be a corpse in a detective novel, and the deader the corpse the better" (190). This rule is abundantly obvious in titles of classics of detective fiction such as Sayers's *Whose Body?* (1923) and Agatha Christie's *The Body in the Library* (1942). The body in *The Blind Assassin* is that of Laura Chase, whose death is described in the opening paragraph by Laura's older sister, Iris. As Iris graphically informs readers, after Laura drove her car off the bridge into the ravine, "Nothing much was left of her but charred smithereens" (3). That this is Laura's body is beyond doubt (in contrast to Christie's and Sayers's books, in which the identity of the body is central to the mystery). The original mystery of *The Blind Assassin*, introduced by the first lines of the book, is the cause of Laura's death. What readers hope to discover by reading Iris's narrative is who drove Laura to propel her body over the edge of that ravine.

Throughout the novel, "clues" are presented that might answer this central mystery in four separate levels of narrative. As well as Iris's retrospective narration of her life history and that of her sister, the story progresses and is undermined and challenged through fictional newspaper articles (and an excerpt from one real magazine, 439–40) that put forward alternate versions of the events Iris narrates. Even more clues are presented in the two embedded fictional narratives: a short modernist novel, also called "The Blind Assassin" and purportedly written by Laura Chase and published by her sister after her death, and the fragmented futuristic/historical story of a blind assassin told by one of that novel's two protagonists.[1] The clues strewn throughout these parallel, echoing, contradictory, and intersecting narratives are not just about Laura's fate but also about the other mysteries that gain prominence—including, as Mallon implies, the question of the authorship of the novel-within-the-novel.

Because Iris repeatedly describes herself writing, and because *The Blind Assassin* addresses the question of authorship and puts forward clues through embedded textual artefacts, it falls into the genre of literary mystery. Examples of this genre are A.S. Byatt's *Possession* and Carol Shields's *Swann*. Both novels gesture toward the codes and conventions of mystery novels in their examinations of fundamentally literary mysteries, yet both provide radical revisions to those traditions. Each novel attempts to unravel a woman writer's life through acts of writing and reading. In Byatt's novel two contemporary literary researchers examine the texts left behind by two nineteenth-century poets for clues about their personal relationship and its influences on their poetry. In *Swann* four contemporary people connected in some way to reading and writing—a literary critic, a biographer, a librarian, and a publisher—deconstruct and reconstruct the life and works of "poète naïve" Mary Swann to try to answer the question: How does art come out of "common clay" (96)? Although these novels use literature as their basis, like *The Blind Assassin* they are also very much about bodies, and in particular women's bodies. An especially present ghost throughout *Swann* is the body of Mary Swann, murdered and dismembered by her husband. *Possession*, meanwhile, harks back to the origins of mystery novels in eighteenth- and nineteenth-century Gothic and sensation plots by revolving around the family secret of concealed pregnancy and mistaken parentage. In *The Blind Assassin*, as in these two earlier novels, women's sexuality, physical and sexual abuse, and hidden parentage are among the central concerns and core mysteries.[2] And these concerns are played out in, through, and between the various levels of literary narrative.

The framing narrative with which the book begins and ends is that of Iris, who at the time she begins to write her story is eighty-two years old. As her narrative makes clear, her body is physically deteriorating toward death from heart failure. The words that she sets down during her final year delineate the way in which women like her in twentieth-century North America are determined by their bodies and are at the same time controlled by the bodies of men. Iris reports that, after her mother died, she and Laura were raised by a father who believed, according to Laura, that the two girls were "*left on his hands*, as if we were some kind of a smear" (484). When Iris becomes an adolescent, she discovers that as far as her father is concerned, "[s]exuality … [is] to be nipped in the bud" (198). Yet, at the same time, he hires a male teacher who verbally and physically abuses both girls, and sexually abuses Laura. The teacher's version of Latin is the study of narratives of rapes of "the kinds of girls we were apparently destined to be" (204). As Iris writes in retrospect, "There was nothing he wanted more than to get a foot on each of our necks" (204).

Iris then writes of herself as an object of exchange, as she is married off to a business acquaintance of her father in an attempt to save her family's failing factory. The language of exchange is explicit in the words Iris's father uses to describe the transaction: "'You'd be in good hands,'" he tells her. "'And Laura too'" (285). Iris soon discovers that, like their former teacher, her new husband, Richard Griffen, planned to keep "a hand always on me, lightly, somewhere" (305) and that he also "wanted to get Laura under his thumb, he wanted her neck under his foot, however lightly placed" (481).

The photo of Laura during this time, from the dustjacket of the novel she is supposed to have written, shows her as "A tabula rasa, not waiting to write, but to be written on" (58). (And this comment about Laura as blank page rather than as writer is a clue to the authorship of the novel-within-the-novel.) Yet Iris also writes of her own body as sand, snow, "written on, rewritten, smoothed over" (469). Her sister-in-law, Winifred, sees her as "a lump of unmoulded clay" (293), to be shaped, dressed up, and coifed. Iris learns that her body must be "[a] topography like wet clay, a surface the hands would glide over" (382). Those hands are her husband's: she writes that she is "taking shape—the shape intended for me, by him" (382).

Another image that Iris has of herself is as an artist's drawing or a figure in a colouring book: "[e]ach time I looked in the mirror a little more of me had been coloured in" (382). Some of those colours are bruises in places that will not show, "purple, then blue, then yellow": "I sometimes felt as if these marks on my body were a kind of code, which blossomed, then faded, like invisible ink held to a candle" (469).

Although Iris's body has been and is being written on, that writing is often invisible to others. Her beautiful new clothes both cover up the bruises and are seen by her twentieth-century North American society as adequate compensation for the sexual violence she endures. Iris's description of the societal order as she experiences it is chilling: "[p]lacidity and order and everything in its place, with a decorous and sanctioned violence going on underneath everything, like a heavy, brutal shoe tapping out the rhythm on a carpeted floor" (468). Indeed, that "carpeted floor" muffles brutality through complicity and silence, which is one reason Iris cannot perceive or believe the sexual abuse that her sister endures, first at the hands of their teacher (206, 496), then at the hands of Iris's husband.[3]

This sexual victimization, as Brooks Bouson notes, places Laura by the end of the novel in the position of a Gothic heroine: she is "the sexual victim of a socially powerful man who has her declared mad and confined to an institution" (265). Mystery's roots in the Gothic are also evident in *The Blind Assassin*'s emphasis on family secrets, in particular as they relate to women's child-bearing bodies. Iris writes that her grandmother died of a cancer that must have been gynecological because it was never named; her mother died after a miscarriage that was unsuccessfully concealed from her children; the girls' former caregiver gives birth to a daughter whom Iris speculates may be her own half-sister (490); Laura is forcibly aborted of the child that is a product of the sexual coercion of her brother-in-law; and Iris bears a child whose paternity is kept secret. An unspoken and, until the end of the book, unreported part of Iris's life story is her sexual relationship with the probable father of her child, union activist Alex Thomas.

While clues in Iris's narrative link her and Alex to the protagonists of the embedded modernist novel, the two narratives are just as firmly connected by their parallel emphasis on societal sanctioning of the sexualizing and silencing of women. In its sexual power and rawness, the short fragmented novel of love and desire is reminiscent of Elizabeth Smart's 1945 Canadian modernist classic *By Grand Central Station I Sat Down and Wept* (to which the fictional critics in *The Blind Assassin* also compare it, 358). Unlike Smart's first-person narrative, though, this novel is told in the third person through the consciousness of both its unnamed female and male protagonists. When the narrative is focalized through the male character, he speaks and thinks of women as all body: "tits and ass" (134), a "*Cunt on stilts*" (348), "Bird Brain, or Big Boobs, ... Or Beautiful Blonde" (350). He notices a bruise on the woman character's thigh, but instead of reading it for what it is, sexual and physical abuse, he wishes he had made it himself (348).[4] In the search for clues that might identify the writer and the female protagonist, the reader can retrospectively connect this bruise to the bruises that Iris develops as a result of her husband's violence but that seem to her to be like "invisible ink" because they are ignored by the people around her (469). Meanwhile, the unnamed female protagonist looks for the published version of one of the stories her lover has told her, because it is "a clue that proved his existence, a piece of evidence, however absurd" (576).

The stories that he tells—primarily about a blind assassin but also about two male interplanetary adventurers who encounter women who turn to peach-flavoured mush when they are struck—are further linked to the retrospective narrative Iris is writing through their emphasis on women's bodies.[5] In the other "dimension of space" of the blind assassin, which is at once futuristic and harks back to bleak historic examples, society is exaggeratedly oppressive in terms of class and gender, yet clearly parallels Iris's own cultural milieu. Like the wives in Sakiel-Norn sold into slavery to redeem their husbands' debts, Iris is sold into marital slavery to redeem her father's debts. The girls' caregiver, Reenie, has warned them about white slavers, but it is Iris's husband who will enslave them, as Laura understands more consciously than Iris when she calls him "a lying, treacherous slave-trader" (539). The silenced, sexually coerced, and sacrificed virgins of the twentieth-century North American narrative are thus just a few steps removed from the tongueless, raped, and sacrificed virgins of Sakiel-Norn. Laura even identifies her coerced sexual consent as a "sacrifice" (611).[6]

Issues of the gendered body, literariness, and mysteries intersect in Atwood's *The Blind Assassin* through an emphasis on one specific part of the body: the hand that oppresses but that also resists oppression by writing. Iris as narrator is aware of the power of hands: as a child she used her own to pull Laura from a river, and also to push her off a ledge. Much later, words stand in for hands as Iris reveals her affair with Alex and thus metaphorically pushes Laura off the bridge, at the same time as she remembers pushing her off the ledge. "My fingers itched with spite," she tells her reader. "I knew what had happened next. I'd pushed her off" (612).

At the end of the novel, Iris leaves her narrative in her granddaughter's hands, identifying that granddaughter as her desired reader. The text Iris has left behind and the modernist novel that she eventually reveals she also wrote are connected even more firmly by photos containing an extra hand. Both the prologue and epilogue of Iris's novel describe, in almost identical words, a photograph of a man and a woman that is striking because over to one side is "a hand, cut by the margin, scissored off at the wrist, resting on the grass as if discarded" (8; see also 650). As the epilogue notes, the hand is that of "the other one, the one who is always in the picture whether seen or not. The hand that will set things down" (650). Iris's framing narrative, meanwhile, describes different versions of a tinted photo of Laura, Alex, and Iris that Laura has produced: one for each young woman, with the other excised except for her hand (277–78). Like the photos of Iris's wedding, which Laura also shapes and colours in (565–66), these pictures make visually concrete her own unspoken interpretation of her and her sister's violated bodily experience.[7]

When Iris refers to the process of writing—and she does so repeatedly—she often implies that it is only her hand that is doing that writing: "my hand has taken on a life of its own," she writes, "and will keep on going even if severed from the rest of me" (471). When she confesses to her reader that she is the author of Laura's book, she again characterizes herself as "a bodiless hand" (643). She notes that while critics of Laura's supposed novel have interpreted Iris as "an appendage: Laura's odd extra hand, attached to no body" (363), Iris believes that their metaphorical and physical relationship gives the two women power through bodily collaboration: "Laura was my left hand, and I was hers. We wrote the book together" (644). The image of the severed hand, an image of disability, is thus reversed as each woman appropriates that third hand to allow her to convert herself from a body that is written on to one that records her version of her bodily experience.

Writing and various hidden aspects of women's bodies are thus at the core of the mystery in *The Blind Assassin*, as they are in Atwood's earlier experiments with the genre: *Lady Oracle* from 1976 and *Alias Grace* from 1996. In *Lady Oracle*, a writer of costume gothics scripts fakes her own death, while in *Alias Grace* a woman convicted of a historical Canadian murder becomes both character in and narrator of a subsequent investigation into her ostensible guilt. These earlier books also centre their mysteries on women's bodies. Joan Foster's youthful obesity is one of the secrets of *Lady Oracle* and, after her "death," Joan unsuccessfully tries to alter her appearance so that she will not be recognized. In *Alias Grace* the spiritual possession of Grace Marks's body by another woman—a woman whose death from an abortion is the result of seduction at the hands of an employer—is the possible "solution" to the mystery of Grace's guilt. In these books, as in *The Blind Assassin*, women's bodies become the site of evidence not only for literary suspense but also for societal crimes.

It is no accident that elements of Gothic narratives feature in all three books. As Maggie Kilgour notes, "The gothic … offers to its readers a momentary subversion of order that is followed by the restoration of a norm, which, after the experience of terror, now seems immensely desirable" (8). In her investigation of feminist revisions to the mystery genre, Maureen T. Reddy argues that, as with its forbear, "The classic crime novel begins in disorder or in violation of order and proceeds more or less linearly to order." Reddy suggests that such a progression proclaims "that it is not only desirable, but actually possible, to banish or to destroy disruptive social elements, and that the greatly to be desired continuation of bourgeois, patriarchal society depends upon general acceptance of the control of a masculine authority figure." That authority, Reddy argues, establishes "a single version of reality, which he calls 'truth,' that we are required to accept if we are to move with the text toward closure" (5–6). By leaving the fate of Iris's manuscript unresolved—Iris speculates that it may either be burned by her purported half-sister or read by her estranged granddaughter—Atwood's novel refuses the closure that Reddy points to as a requirement of conventional mysteries. In such mysteries, the return to order is achieved through examination of the body of the murdered person and the assemblage of a body of evidence that reveals the "truth" that will solve the mystery. Mallon suggests in his review of *The Blind Assassin* that Iris reveals the "truth" of her own and her sister's story at the end of her narrative. But while Iris suggests several times that she will attempt to write the truth, first by assuming that what she writes will never be read (357) and then by writing what she imagines as well as what she remembers (643), she also concedes that a search for "truth" is in fact futile. "You want the truth, of course," she tells her reader. "You want me to put two and two together. But two and two doesn't necessarily get you the truth" (498). The reader of *The Blind Assassin,* instead of feeling relief at a revelation of truth through the establishment of a body of evidence and the resulting resumption of order, is left with the unsettling knowledge that truth is subjective, and that conventional order rests on the unacknowledged violation of women's bodies.

The final clues that Iris as literary detective reveals to the reader about the causes of Laura's death are ones she finds in school notebooks—each with its ironic and only somewhat inaccurate subject title—written in by Laura with the help of her third hand (625–28). *Latin* contains Laura's translation of the concluding lines of Book 4 of the *Aeneid,* in which another Iris aids in the suicide of a troubled woman.[8] *History* contains Laura's coloured and cropped copy of the photo of her and Alex with Iris's hand. *Geography* is Laura's description of the town where she and Iris were raised and where she was first sexually abused by both her teacher and her brother-in-law. And *Math* is simply a list of dates, with Xs indicating when Laura was raped by Richard, and an O indicating the resulting pregnancy. As Iris concludes after reading these notebooks, "Everything was known, but nothing could be proven" (629). Laura has written her narrative of abuse, but the crimes will never be brought home to their perpetrators because only by continuing to turn a "blind" eye to women's bodily experience can Laura's society maintain its conventional order: "everything in its place, with a decorous and sanctioned violence going on underneath."

—University of Saskatchewan

NOTES

1. Other critics have noted the presence of these "clues": Patricia Paillot suggests that Atwood's text "is riddled with often obsessive clues which contribute to creating distance, difference, disguise and pretence" (123); Earl G. Ingersoll calls the book a "whodunit" and argues that the reader is "constructed as a 'detective'," "energized by the desire to pay attention to the clues which will connect Iris to the woman in the novel-within-a-novel" (543–544); Karen F. Stein suggests that readers are invited to participate in the "game" of "[u]ntangling … narrative threads" (135) at the same time as Iris "must unravel clues" in order "to understand her sister's life" (138); and Brooks Bouson writes that Iris must "piece together" the "cryptic written and visual clues" that Laura leaves behind (265).

2. Examples of eighteenth- and nineteenth-century novels that revolve around hidden parentage and other family secrets include Horace Walpole's *The Castle of Otranto* (1764), Sophia Lee's *The Recess* (1785), Charlotte Brönte's *Jane Eyre* (1847), and Wilkie Collins's *The Woman in White* (1860). For brief discussions of family secrets and the Gothic genre as evident in *The Blind Assassin* see Stein (150), Ingersoll (554), and Bouson (265).
3. Bouson suggests that *The Blind Assassin* illustrates "women's cultural blindness to, and thus collusion with, their own victimization as well as the victimization of other women" (252). Because of her blindness to her sister's plight, Iris has been interpreted by some readers as her sister's metaphoric, if not physical, killer. However, as Ingersoll argues, "if Iris functions as her sister's 'assassin' it is vital to stress the modifier 'blind,' especially in the context of the novel-within-the-novel in which the blind assassins have themselves been the victims of cruel horrors" (550).
4. Many literary researchers identify this man with Alex. He is, however, only a character constructed by the fictional author (eventually revealed to be Iris), who through this medium presents her perspective on her lover and her imagined reproduction of his thoughts.
5. Marta Dvorak points out that he gives the other character a choice of genres, including romance, science fiction, or mystery (65).
6. As Brooks Bouson suggests, through "repetitive retelling of the story of women's sexual victimization," including the "traumatic sexual sacrifice of the two sisters" and the planned sacrifice of the tongueless virgin, Atwood "probes the cultural—and historical—repetition of sexual violence against women" and reveals "the link between institutionalized misogyny and the sexual traumatization of women" (251).
7. The severed hand, at least initially, points to the young women's powerlessness. In the wedding photos, which Iris finds impossible to interpret, Richard's green colour in one (similar to that of the Lizard-men villains from the embedded novel) and red hands and flames shooting up around him in the other hint at the evil that he perpetrates with his hands. Iris's blue or bleached tinting points to her passivity and ignorance, while Laura's radiant yellow indicates her separation of spirit from body since, as Iris tells her reader, Laura long ago "developed the ability to subtract herself" (205).
8. Iris was a messenger of the gods who was sent by Juno to cut Queen Dido's golden hair, which had kept her soul attached to her body after she tried to kill herself over her love for the departing Aeneas.

WORKS CITED

Atwood, Margaret. *Alias Grace*. Toronto: McClelland & Stewart, 1996.
———. *The Blind Assassin*. Toronto: Random House, 2000.
———. *Lady Oracle*. Toronto: McClelland & Stewart, 1976.
Bouson, J. Brooks. "'A Commemoration of Wounds Endured and Resented': Margaret Atwood's *The Blind Assassin* as Feminist Memoir." *Critique* 44, no. 3 (2003): 251–70.
Byatt, A.S. *Possession*. London: Vintage, 1990.
Dvorak, Marta. "The Right Hand Writing and the Left Hand Erasing in Margaret Atwood's *The Blind Assassin*." *Commonwealth Essays and Studies* 25, no. 1 (2003): 59–68.
Ingersoll, Earl G. "Waiting for the End: Closure in Margaret Atwood's *The Blind Assassin*." *Studies in the Novel* 35, no. 4 (2003): 543–59.
Kilgour, Maggie. *The Rise of the Gothic Novel*. London: Routledge, 1995.
Mallon, Thomas. "Wheels within Wheels." Review of *The Blind Assassin*, by Margaret Atwood. *The New York Times Book Review*, September 4, 2000. 7.
Paillot, Patricia. "To Bind or not to Bind: Irony in *The Blind Assassin* by Margaret Atwood." *Études canadiennes/Canadian Studies*, no. 53 (2002): 117–25.
Reddy, Maureen T. *Sisters in Crime: Feminism and the Crime Novel*. New York: Continuum, 1988.
Shields, Carol. *Swann*. Toronto: Stoddart, 1987.
Stein, Karen F. "A Left-handed Story: *The Blind Assassin*." In *Margaret Atwood's Textual Assassinations: Recent Poetry and Fiction*, edited by Sharon R. Wilson, 135–53. Columbus: Ohio State University Press, 2003.
Van Dine, S.S. (Willard Huntington Wright). "Twenty Rules for Writing Detective Stories." [1928]. In *The Art of the Mystery Story*, edited by Howard Haycraft, 189–93. New York: Grosset, 1974.

The Dead Are in the Hands of the Living: Memory Haunting Storytelling in Margaret Atwood's *The Blind Assassin*

HELENA HYTTINEN

MARGARET ATWOOD'S NOVEL *The Blind Assassin* encompasses a diversity of literary genres that are reworked in order to bring about alternative effects as they transcend their traditional forms, functions, and gender codes. Atwood is hence highly involved in scrutinizing not only social and political structures but also the structures prevailing within the realm of literature, from a perspective that highlights power structures and gender discourse. In this essay, the focus will be on one of the genres encompassed in her novel: the gothic romance. The genre will be elucidated and discussed in relation to gender and Susanna Becker's theory of the "feminine gothic."

In her work *Gothic Forms of Feminine Fictions*, Susanne Becker discusses and then rejects the term "female gothic" in favour of her more encompassing and fruitful term "feminine gothic." The distinctions she makes between these two terms elucidate her awareness of a problematic subdivision of the gothic. Becker sees the earlier classification of works into the realm of "female gothic" as unproductive since it focuses on the sex of the author rather than the qualities of the work itself. Becker's term, on the other hand, puts *the text* in focus as she formulates her definition of feminine gothic as a work encompassing gothic characteristics as well as a "necessarily gendered subjectivity" that makes the gothic feminine in its very form in the following three ways:

> [A]s a split subject it feminises the romance into an "interrogative text"; as a subject-in-process it turns the gothic into the story of gender construction; and as subject-in-relation with a gothic figure like the "monstrous-feminine" it posits a radical attack on the constraints of "Woman": the female ideal in a specific cultural historical context. (41)

What follows is that female subjectivity not only provides a formal challenge to "textual and ideological orders" but also challenges these orders from a thematic and theoretical perspective. These challenges are clearly displayed in self-reflexive neo-gothic texts such as Atwood's novels, in which she skilfully masters a multitude of narrative strategies through which she, as Becker points out, "turns the subject-in-process into a 'subject in excess'" (41). One of these strategies is her reworking and transcending of genres.

Among the many genres Atwood intricately uses and transcends in her novel *The Blind Assassin* we find the gothic romance with its key characteristics of mystery and betrayal, of lies and the unspoken, of the unspeakable, and of buried life (Stein 136–38; Bouson, "Commemoration" 264–65).[1] The gothic and its characteristics will be the focus of this essay in order to explore the impact of haunting on storytelling and memory. In *The Blind Assassin* the narrator-protagonist Iris—who has survived her sister—narrates her and her sister Laura's story because she wants to, needs to, and is forced to do so by her guilty conscience and by her dead sister who haunts her into remembering:

> Officially, Laura had been papered over. A few years more and it would be almost as if she'd never existed. I shouldn't have taken a vow of silence, I told myself. What did I want? Nothing much. Just a memorial of some kind. But what is a memorial, when you come right down to it, but a commemoration of wounds endured? Endured, and resented. Without memory, there can be no revenge.
>
> *Lest we forget. Remember me. To you from failing hands we throw.* Cries of the thirsty ghosts.
>
> Nothing is more difficult than to understand the dead, I've found; but nothing is more dangerous than to ignore them. (*BA* 508, original italics)

After her sister's death in 1945, the protagonist is haunted into writing her sister into history/*her*story to prevent her from being "papered over" and to create a memorial for her, a memorial in which she tries to set things right through the unconventional but—for her—*only* possible way: through distortion. The haunting hence represents a central motive for why the protagonist writes her novella and, later, her autobiography. Other motives are that of revenge and justice. In 1947 Iris's novella "The Blind Assassin" is published—but the authorship is attributed to her deceased sister. And as "Laura's" novella it has the effect desired: it destroys the reputation of Iris's oppressive and abusive husband Richard and—as an extension—destroys Richard himself, who is found dead on their boat, a copy of the novella beside him. The novella thus works as a powerful tool of revenge for Iris who, for a long time, does not take any responsibility for what she has set down.

Although the novella serves as a memorial in helping to preserve Laura's name, it simultaneously obscures who Laura was, since readers interpret it as an autobiographical account of *Laura's* secret life of romance. As a consequence the novella distorts the story of both sisters' lives and it unintentionally comes to serve as a tool that also blindly hurts and destroys the innocent: the children. As the years go by, Iris painfully becomes aware of the danger in meddling with words as the danger implicit in rewriting and obscuring history is manifested in the tragic loss of her daughter. Iris thus acknowledges her own culpability in losing her daughter not once but twice through her distortion of history. By hiding the truth about the father of her daughter—the disguised parental heritage that is a common gothic trait—Iris not only loses custody of her and, later, of her granddaughter to her witch-like sister-in-law Winifred but also loses them both as the lies alienate them from her and literally destroy her daughter, who takes her refuge in drugs and dies young.

For more than fifty years, Iris's distortion comes to serve as the public version of Laura's life. Then an urge to set things straight, confess, and write her own and her sister's story erupts in the late 1990s and so, at the age of eighty-three, the protagonist embarks on her laborious and painful journey into her memory and buried emotions. She feels she owes this to the dead: to her daughter, lover, and sister. She knows that the living are in the hands of the dead, because of "ancestral voices that never shut up" (334) and therefore are hard to ignore. The living are in the hands of the dead, but the dead are simultaneously in the hands of the living, who decide if they are to be "papered over" or not. The protagonist also knows that she has blood on her hands and, since she cannot wash it off, she needs to dig up history, to dig up the buried bones and secrets that still haunt her. She needs to acknowledge the blood that also tints her hands red. And, finally, she owes it to her sole surviving relative, her granddaughter, to set *her* story straight despite the distortions caused by time, memory, and guilt. Atwood's novel hence illustrates the gothic excess through the use of its multiple female stories written through multiple agendas across time. The doubleness and double perspective that characterize Atwood's novels here transcend into the spectral realm, particularly when it comes to writing Laura and her life through multiple voices. Here, the distinction between Iris and Laura becomes blurred—as are most of the overt or implied references as to whose hand is writing and/or arranging the novel's multiple texts and discourses. And as this distinction becomes blurred, the boundaries between victim and victimizer, haunter and haunted perpetually shift—as does the power.

This double perspective that characterizes Atwood's novels can be further illustrated by turning to Zenia in Atwood's 1993 novel *The Robber Bride*. The writing of Zenia into history is at least double—or should I say triple—since there are three narrators who record her stories into theirs. Hence Zenia becomes history, or, rather, "She will only be history if Tony chooses to shape her into history ... because she is dead, and all of the dead are in the hands of the living" (*RB* 461). This remark by Atwood's female military historian refers both to turning someone into history in the sense that the person is acknowledged to belong to the past as a closed chapter—that is, to stop someone from the past from interfering and haunting the present—but the phrase is simultaneously a recognition of how history is produced and made up by multiple, subjective stories. Howells illustrates this through Tony, who

> has a postmodern attitude to her discipline (more like Offred's than Professor Pieixoto's), recognizing the subjective element in any narrative construction of the past. History is a discontinuous text with many gaps, so that different interpretations of the facts are always possible. ... [T]he narratives of history always reconstruct the available facts of the past for readers in the present according to ideologically congenial perspectives ... ("*The Robber Bride*" 149)

The power inherent in the process of writing someone into history is thus manifold: the power of the writer to shape—or refuse to shape—someone into history and the empowerment that, at the same time, is bestowed onto the shaper of history and the one(s) being shaped into it. This Iris knows.

In *The Blind Assassin* Iris is haunted into *re*-membering and *re*-assembling the bones and voices of the buried and recording them into herstory. The remaining part of my essay will therefore investigate how, from a gender perspective, Atwood's use of the gothic romance genre relates to the intertwined relationship between history, memory, haunting, and storytelling in *The Blind Assassin*.

Although Atwood has used the themes and narrative strategies employed in *The Blind Assassin* in her earlier novels, my argument is that she now takes storytelling farthest, and here the haunting becomes spectral as the self is created out of conflicting discourses (including gaps and silences) and through a network of narratives across time, place, and space. Iris is haunted by Laura for at least two reasons: her guilty conscience and the evasiveness of Laura. This evasiveness is manifested in that although Laura inscribed herself through her actions, she simultaneously did not, since Iris never heard *her* story. The last message Iris receives from Laura before she dies is *"Tell Iris I'll talk to her later"* (491) and only after her death does Iris finally hear her sister's story again, and again, and again, because "she tends to repeat herself, as the dead have a habit of doing. They say all the things they say to you in life; but they rarely say anything new" (491).

Atwood's use of the gothic romance genre in her novels is an effective narrative strategy to metafictively discuss the relationship between story and history, facts and fiction, memory and storytelling. David Punter characterizes the gothic as

> a way of imagining the unimaginable, whether it be the distant depths of history or the even more distant soundings of the unconscious. The gothic is a distorting lens, a magnifying lens; but the shapes which we see through it have nonetheless a reality which cannot be apprehended in any other way. (97–98)

Punter's definition illustrates what the genre does for Atwood's novel, since the protagonist has to (re)gain her vision to be able to see beyond the lies, gaps, and distortions to understand what happened to her sister. As is characteristic of the gothic genre, the protagonist needs to find the hidden coded message to gain knowledge of the unspeakable: here represented by the tragic and gothic story of her sister's life and *her* sacrifice. When Iris does find, and manages to interpret, the messages—hidden in old notebooks and hand-tinted in her wedding photos—she is faced with a horrific story: a story that "had been there all along, right before my very eyes. How could I have been so blind?" (500). The gothic elements thus progressively multiply, as do the stories, and the genre overtly inscribes itself when the first two *public stories* of the deceased sister crumble and a third version—Iris's interpretation of Laura's coded version—surfaces.

William Patrick Day echoes Punter's notion of the gothic as a distorting lens through which "the whole world" can be seen, and goes on to describe the relationship between the gothic and "the conventional world" as "parodic," and the gothic parody thus "creates a state of metaphysical uncertainty and anxiety" (59–60). Even if the distorting lens metaphor of these two critics is somewhat uncomfortable indicating as it does that there is *One* Reality (whose?) hidden behind it, Day's emphasis on parody is useful to my argument as it strengthens and elucidates the "doubleness" or "multiplicity" and ambiguity inherent in Atwood's writing—not least concerning gender and genre in relation to the poetics of excess.

The narrative strategy of excess—or the poetics of excess—is another characteristic of Atwood's novels, and is manifested in her use of, for example, parody, irony, allusion and multiple female stories. And, as her novels inhabit the feminine gothic realm, her narrative strategy of excess thus enters into the realm of gothic excess where it becomes a powerful device that helps break down secure and comfortable reading positions and, through provocation, creates an uncomfortable feminist position from which the reader cannot shun away.[2]

The Blind Assassin, with its narrative and gothic excess, thus provides the reader with (at least) three accounts of Laura's life. The first is carefully orchestrated by Richard and Winifred *prior* to the publication of the novella, by alleged author Laura Chase, in 1947. Their public version is, significantly, represented by newspaper clippings throughout the novel as well as accounted for in the novel's framing narrative narrated by eighty-three-year-old Iris Chase Griffen. And it is in *their* version we find the gothic story of the madwoman. Richard and Winifred have Laura incarcerated at a mental institution under the pretext that she has had a mental breakdown. Here, the gothic theme about the madwoman is turned even more gothic as the reader learns that the clinic is an abortion clinic to which sixteen-year-old Laura has been sent away in order to cover up Richard's sexual assault. Hence, Richard represents the formulaic gothic villain stereotype of an older, powerful, rich, and threatening man. Consequently, Atwood's novel also includes the "marital gothic," since Richard sexually abuses both his young wife and even younger sister-in-law.[3] The marital gothic is further emphasized in the novella's science fiction story in which the veiled virgin about to be sacrificed to the goddess is compared to a "pampered society bride" (29) who, on the night before her throat is cut, is to be raped by the Lord of The Underworld—a lucrative new tradition that can be seen as a grotesque inversion of the wedding night.

In Becker's discussion of marital gothic and gothic excess (31–40), adultery is justified for the heroine in a loveless, brutal marriage, and the treatment of the sexual woman as monstrous or mad is thus redefined. In *The Blind Assassin*, adultery for a woman is accepted by Toronto's High Society in the 1930s and "[a]s long as she does it on the Q.T., nobody will say boo" (423). Instead, it is the women—and teenage girls like Laura—who are not concerned with sex who are looked upon as being "more than a little odd" (422). As long as Iris keeps her love affair a secret it is accepted by her community, as well as "justified," according to Becker, since the affair provides an escape from a brutal husband and a loveless marriage. However, Becker also stresses that for the heroine to run from the villain to the hero is no solution since the hero only provides *temporal* escape. If Iris is to break free from her abusive husband and the lies, she has to come up with her own solution rather than rely on someone to provide it for her. Her lover can only provide temporal relief and help her see—just as Laura tries to make Iris wake up and open her eyes. But, as is characteristic of the gothic genre, Laura has a hard time getting her message across to her sister due to messages that disappear.

Laura's letters, telegrams, and phone calls never reach Iris because of Richard and Winifred. Disappearing letters and messages is a gothic trait present throughout the novel and illustrates how Iris is kept in the dark about her father's death, her husband's abuse, and her sister's situation when incarcerated at the clinic. However, these missing messages are gothic for yet another reason: they contain the real horrors of Laura's life, which would have been revealed—although perhaps not believed—had they reached their addressee. Gothic excess thus marks the *form* of the novel with its mixture of genres, multiple female stories (both the heard and the silenced ones), and adds to the gothic emotions of horror and fear—most clearly displayed in Laura who has got her eyes open and *can* spot a gothic villain when she sees one.

After the publication of the novella and the renewed public interest in the circumstances of Laura's death ("someone made an anonymous phone call—now who could that have been?" [509]), which led to the digging up of Richard's revealing correspondence with the manager of the suspect clinic, and also to the digging up of its backyard (where the fetuses supposedly had been disposed of), Richard's distorted story of Laura is hereby replaced by Iris's distortion. Furthermore, it takes more than fifty years for Iris to acknowledge her own involvement in the first two public distortions and, finally, revise them into a third version. However, the degree to which the third version is a public or a private story is problematized as Atwood leaves this question, as well as the interlinking question about the identity of the novel's arranging narrator(s), unresolved in a gothic manner.

The three versions of Laura's life are, as has been illustrated, dictated as well as narrated by others, and only in the third one is *her* hidden and coded version inserted and decoded. At least, this is what the narrator-protagonist tells the reader, but, since she is the one who finds, decodes, and inserts this version after having helped distort the previous ones, the element of unreliability shakes and shifts her narrative, as does the distortion of memory across time. These gothic characteristics thus problematize storytelling and—through its anti-realism—the concepts of reality and truth. Throughout the novel, Atwood illustrates the difficulty in telling one's story by having the narrator acknowledge that what she has set down is not the truth, "not because of what I've set down but because of what I've omitted. What isn't there has a presence, like the absence of light" (395). Hence, the crucial pieces of information are found not in what is said and written down but among the many gaps and silences that represent the unspeakable.

Furthermore, gothic narrative is, Sedgwick writes, characterized by "incorporating tales within tales, changes of narrators, and such ... devices as found manuscripts or interpolated stories" (9). This is true also of *The Blind Assassin*. Although Iris is the main narrator-protagonist, Atwood's novel incorporates a multitude of voices across temporal and spatial boundaries, which means that the role, function, and identity of the narrator *and* the arranging narrator(s) remain a haunting mystery to the readers. At the open-ended end of the novel the readers are consequently left with the question of who the arranging narrator(s) is (are). The readers conclude that it is not the narrator-protagonist Iris who has arranged all the texts, but how many, if any, remains unknown.

Also, the incorporation of tales within tales is skilfully carried out in order to have the multiple tales enter into dialogic discourse since they not only intersect but also interact with each other as well as with other texts, thus inviting an intertextual reading of the novel. The novel holds a novella entitled "The Blind Assassin," and the novella in turn incorporates a pulp science fiction story about a blind assassin. Karen F. Stein, however, argues that "although it is set on the planet Zycron it is really a Gothic adventure romance of conspiracy and intrigue" (139). In my view, the story of the blind assassin is both. As a science fiction story it is removed from reality and earth, which allows the male Bolshevik storyteller to pugnaciously inveigh against the 1930s Canadian capitalist and class-bound society. The predominantly male pulp science fiction genre is thus presented as a (male) forum for publishing controversial political ideas in 1930s Canada without running the risk of being censored. The story about the assassin that he tells his lover during their secret rendezvous is, however, never completed but left open-ended. Or, rather, it has three endings. His lover comes up with a suggestion for the gothic romance's happy ending (including sweet revenge) in which the assassin and the young, tongue-less girl he rescues and falls in love with not only escape their persecutors but also actively aid in their destruction, and then live happily ever after. Her suggested ending is, however, immediately discarded by her lover, who counters by retelling her version but substituting her happy ending with an ending that is "true to life" (344), in which he kills off everyone including the lovers. When *his* story is published in a pulp science fiction magazine, his lover is dismayed to discover that he left out the love plot altogether and instead had the people of Zycron join together across class boundaries to fight off the alien attack launched against them. When—and this is my concluding point of this essay—the male narrator tells his lover the story in private he transgresses into the gothic romance, although he refuses to include its formulaic happy ending. But *his* published written story strictly follows the formula of the male pulp science fiction genre, including the formal demands on closure. The relationship between gender and genre and *their* relation to public and private stories are evident here.

The formal demands of closure are met in the science fiction story that the male protagonist publishes in a pulp magazine, but in the novella the *orally* narrated version resists closure—as does Atwood's novel. And by having the fictive novella incorporate orally narrated science fiction/gothic romance stories, and having a female narrator actively participating in telling them *and* commenting on the published version, as well as recording the secret meetings of the two unnamed lovers/storytellers in a novella, Atwood not only mixes and transcends the traditional genre boundaries—she also exposes their gendered nature.

—Karlstad University

NOTES

1. This postmodern transgressing of literary genres in general and of the gothic and gothic romance in particular is not a new strategy in Atwood's writing. The gothic romance is present also in *Surfacing* with its gothic wilderness combined with a ghost story; in *Lady Oracle*, in which the genre is parodied; and in *The Robber Bride*, which is a postmodern gothic romance partly set in Toronto in the 1990s (Howells, "Transgressing" 139–56)—as is part of *The Blind Assassin*.
2. For a more detailed discussion of feminist reading positions, see Bouson, *Brutal Choreographies*.
3. "Marital gothic" is a term coined by Michelle Massé (20), and it is of central importance to Becker's discussions of gothic excess and its perception of marriage and adultery (Becker, 31–40).

WORKS CITED

Atwood, Margaret. *The Blind Assassin*. New York: Doubleday, 2000.

———. *The Robber Bride*. London: Bloomsbury, 1993.

Becker, Susanne. *Gothic Forms of Feminine Fictions*. Manchester: Manchester University Press, 1999.

Bouson, Brooks. *Brutal Choreographies*. Amherst: University of Massachusetts Press, 1993.

———. "'A Commemoration of Wounds Endured and Resented': Margaret Atwood's *The Blind Assassin* as Feminist Memoir." *Critique: Studies in Contemporary Fiction* 44, no. 3 (2003): 251–69.

Day, William. *In the Circles of Fear and Desire: A Study of Gothic Fantasy.* Chicago: University of Chicago Press, 1985.

Howells, Carol. "*The Robber Bride*; or, Who Is a True Canadian?" In *Atwood's Textual Assassinations*, edited by Sharon R. Wilson, 88–101. Columbus: Ohio State University Press, 2003.

———. "Transgressing Genre: A Generic Approach to Margaret Atwood's Novels." In *Margaret Atwood: Works & Impact*, edited by Reingaard M. Nischik, 139–56. Rochester: Camden House, 2000.

Massé, Michelle. *In the Name of Love: Women, Masochism, and the Gothic.* Ithaca, NY: Cornell University Press, 1992.

Punter, David. *The Literature of Terror: A History of Gothic Fictions from 1765 to the Present Day.* Vol. 1. Burned Mill, NY: Longman, 1996.

Sedgwick, Eve Kosofsky. *The Coherence of Gothic Conventions.* New York: Methuen, 1986.

Stein, Karen F. "A Left-Handed Story: *The Blind Assassin.*" In *Atwood's Textual Assassinations*, edited by Sharon R. Wilson, 135–53. Columbus: Ohio State University Press, 2003.

Margaret Atwood and the Critical Limits of Embodiment

SALLY CHIVERS

> Why should any child get stuck with cerebral palsy, or autism, or schizophrenia, or Huntington's chorea, or the many other maladies that genes are heir to? They shouldn't if there's a remedy, and there is. (Atwood, "Arguing Against Ice Cream" 344)

IN A GROUNDBREAKING special issue of *Public Culture*, Carol A. Breckenridge and Candace Vogler reinsert embodiment into the emerging contested terrain of the *New Disability Studies*. The disabled body is a "problem" for disability scholars not because its aberrance must be contained or fixed by the helping professions but because it signifies difference from other forms of difference studies based on gender, race, or class.[1] Social construction, an appealing escape from the objectifying gaze of medical and psychiatric models, threatens to elide yet again the already ignored disabled body. However, insistence on the physicality of disability threatens to reify the assumed limits of bodily difference. Breckenridge and Vogler explain:

> New work in disability studies ... challenges established habits of thought about "having" a body. Disability studies dissolves deeply entrenched mind-and-body distinctions and further destabilizes the concept of the normal, whose charted internal ambiguities have themselves become too familiar. An ethics and a politics of disability

are crucial to the work of the university—pedagogically, theoretically, and institutionally. But reconfiguring knowledge in light of disability criticism is a project that is likely to take longer than making public space accessible. (348–49)

Disability Studies scholars reconsider what Rosemarie Garland Thomson terms "extraordinary" embodiment as a multiplication of lived circumstances constructed both physically and socially. Most of them would not choose the remedy suggested in my epigraph but rather would insist that society fix itself.

Disability Studies scholars working in the humanities turn to the cultural record for signs and significations of bodily difference. While it is difficult to find a literary work that does *not* represent disability (at least as a background concern), it is more difficult to find literary works that represent disability well enough to incite new thinking about its social, cultural, historical, and physical circumstances. Further, while disability is everywhere within the Western cultural record, it is rarely examined. Margaret Atwood's prevalence not only as a Canadian literary giant but also as a global icon,[2] along with her abundant publishing record, make her work a suitable locus for the scrutiny of contemporary disability representation. Further, her unique approach to embodiment stimulates critical questions about the role literary production might play in well-known questions of accessible public space and little-known disability perspectives on human rights and inclusion.

Margaret Atwood's oeuvre illuminates Disability Studies discourse at the same time that patterns of disability representation provide a crucial context for the scrutiny of her writing. While disability scholars become frustrated that the Western literary record for the most part presents disabled figures merely as metaphoric symbols of social failing, Atwood to some degree contests the institutional frameworks that typically attempt to contain the cancerous body ("Hairball" and *Bodily Harm*), the mentally ill body (*Alias Grace*), the tortured body (*True Stories*), blind, mobility-impaired and elderly bodies in *The Blind Assassin*, and genetically modified bodies in *Oryx and Crake*. Her investment in the body as integrated into politically defined social and built environments recurs in writings from *The Edible Woman* to *Oryx and Crake*. While she often sidesteps the disabled body in frustrating ways (as I discuss below), Atwood's depictions of physical difference insist on an engagement with the physically "anomalous" body that refuses simple categorization and, as such, her works provide a crucible for narrating the phenomenology of the disabled body as well as the disabled body as a mere symbol that reinforces normative physicality.

I. "HAIRBALL": CUTTING EMBODIMENT

At the conclusion of Margaret Atwood's frequently anthologized short story, "Hairball," the central character Kat takes her well-preserved dermoid cyst, packages it with truffles, and sends it to her lover and his wife with the note: "Gerald, Sorry I couldn't be with you. This is all the rage. Love, K" (62). Throughout the story, the cyst challenges institutional attempts to contain it—Kat revels that it is labelled "benign" in hopes that the "thing had a soul and wished her well" (44). More than anything, she wants her "hairball" to be deviant, a sign of her unique embodiment. Her doctor disappoints her when he claims that the cyst's hair, bones, nails, and teeth are *not* abnormal:

> Some people thought this kind of tumour was present in seedling form at birth, or before it. It might be the woman's undeveloped twin. What they really were was unknown. They had many kinds of tissue, though. Even brain tissue. Though of course all these tissues lack structure. (60)

Kat, however, rejects the sibling hypothesis and interprets the rejected tumour as "her child with Gerald, her thwarted child, not allowed to grow normally. Her warped child, taking its revenge. 'Hairball,' she says, 'You're so ugly. Only a mother could love you." (60). While not a representation of disability, this rival interpretation of bodily difference signals the complex array of contextual markers that create disability and marginalize people with disabilities.

It is tempting to read "Hairball" in terms of psychiatric disability: that is, as a manifestation of a feverish fantasy wherein a woman wreaks revenge on her feckless lover by imposing (or even just imagining imposing) herself (through a body part) into his own living room, a domestic symbol of the marriage she interrupted. Kat's pun on "rage" invites a figurative reading of the tumour. But I think the very concreteness of the cyst in the story invites another reading that competes with the delusional narrator's interpretation. As the story explains:

> Hairball speaks to her, without words. It is irreducible, it has the texture of reality, it is not an image. What it tells her is everything she's never wanted to hear about herself. This is new knowledge, dark and precious and necessary. It cuts. (60)

Kat's "hairball" is not merely a metonym for the diseased (and hence immoral) other woman; it does not simply stand in for her rejection. It also encapsulates the mutability of bodily form and the fraught attempts of a fashion editor to come to terms with her new embodiment. Beyond that it is a concrete signification of not just lived physical difference but also a *desire* for lived physical difference.

II. *ORYX AND CRAKE*: CUTTING DIFFERENCE

In this paper, I hold up "Hairball" as a constructive backdrop for Atwood's most recent foray into speculative fiction, *Oryx and Crake*. While the ever-potent normalcy yields its sceptre in both works, the elimination of physical difference from *Oryx and Crake* frighteningly illuminates the necessity for Kat's reverence for her own pathology. Physical conformity as a common human (and inhuman) goal blatantly dominates *Oryx and Crake*. The work is unique in its complete elision of disability. The demise of humankind proposed in the novel depends entirely on widespread investment in a normative bodily frame, so much so that the description of ideal human qualities does not even mention disability (as desired or reviled). There is no Tiny Tim to make readers (and other characters) feel powerful and charitable; there is no Ahab seeking treacherous revenge. Physical disability has already been eliminated from even the earliest historical moment of this novel, and its silent demise could well predict the devastation of a wider swath of human existence.

While there *may* be support for Atwood's postulation, cited in my epigraph, that physically disabling "maladies," especially those that involve great physical pain, ought to be remedied (or rather prevented as she suggests), there is no way to argue that individuals or the world would be better off without blindness, deafness, or ambulatory variation without revealing terrifying assumptions about power and normalcy. In this way, Atwood's novel—in having already eliminated disability—makes an argument, albeit subtle, that the eugenic logic that motivates the pursuit of the new physical normalcy begins with the extermination of disability.

Also, because of the novel's restricted bodily compass, physical signs not currently considered disability are read as such. The very markers of Jimmy/Snowman's humanity, for example, signify his status as a "cripple" slouching toward the Crakers for sustenance.

Although the corporate competition that dominates *Oryx and Crake*'s pre-apocalyptic world depends upon and encourages the pursuit of a physical ideal that is all too familiar to twenty-first-century readers, cognitive normalcy is not desirable; rather, it is derided. Crake, the ultimate mastermind of this new world, takes pride in his near-autistic qualities (this is the novel's categorization, not mine). In the only embrace of disability (and only one of three overt mentions of disability) in the novel, the students of Watson Crick rename their school Asperger's U "because of the high percentage of brilliant weirdos that strolled and hopped and lurched through its corridors. Demi-autistic, genetically speaking; single-track tunnel-vision minds, a marked degree of social ineptitude" (193–94). Those not fortunate enough to attend Watson Crick earn the moniker Neuro-typical and find themselves, like Jimmy, in the corporate departments that most resemble what we currently call advertising because these "NTs" lack the "genius gene" (194). The study of genetics is left to those selected for their chromosomal uniqueness; the selling of products designed to make up for flawed genetics is ironically left to those who lack aberrant DNA.

In *Oryx and Crake*, which divides "numbers people" (like Crake) from "word people" (like Jimmy), the apparently deregulated corporations frighteningly understand that they need the former to create products and the latter to sell them. In addition to the profit motive, the two perspectives conjoin through a fundamental commitment to the idea of human perfectibility through permanent changes to human physical form. The corporations that dominate a central narrative of *Oryx and Crake* all take genetic experiments to their seemingly inevitable apocalyptic conclusion. The novel depicts these "advancements" in a progression, from the hybridization of pigs with humans, through the development of "vitamins" that promise to improve human embodiment, and finally to genetically spliced human-like creatures. This progression proposes, perhaps satirically, that no amount of technology or biomedical understanding can eliminate the centrality of the human body to social and individual welfare. Attempts to make the body redundant in this novel prove more than fatal.

The eerily familiar products featured throughout *Oryx and Crake* each appeal to consumers through the promotion of a belief that though the wallet has limits, the body does not. As Jimmy's father asks him rhetorically:

> What well-to-do and once-young, once-beautiful woman or man, cranked up on hormonal supplements and shot full of vitamins but hampered by the unforgiving mirror, wouldn't sell their house, their gated retirement villa, their kids, and their soul to get a second kick at the sexual can? (55)

Accordingly, Jimmy annotates the subtext to his own uninspired slogan, *"Live in the moment"*: "Why chain your body to a clock, you can break the shackles of time, and so on and so forth. The picture was of a woman with wings, taking flight from a pile of dirty old wrinkled cloth, or possibly skin" (265–66). Jimmy's cynicism about his role does not prevent him from investing in the process that allows the destruction of humankind in the novel. Designated a "words person," Jimmy's job has been to convince a variety of minds that their bodies require these products:

> Cosmetic creams, workout equipment, Joltbars to build your musclescape into a breathtaking marvel of sculpted granite. Pills to make you fatter, thinner, hairier, balder, whiter, browner, blacker, yellower, sexier, and happier. It was his task to describe and extol, to present the vision of what—oh, so easily!—could come to be. Hope and fear, desire and revulsion, these were his stocks-in-trade, on these he rang his changes. Once in a while he'd make up a word—*tensicity, fibracionous, pheromonimal*—but he never once got caught out. His proprietors liked those kinds of words in the small print on packages because they sounded scientific and had a convincing effect. (248)

Jimmy's arts-based education at the Martha Graham institute prepares him only to convince potential customers of the endless possibilities of physical and self-change, and the process relies on as much deceit as does Crake's science. Jimmy's senior thesis on "self-help books of the twentieth century" ironically prepares him to fulfill the same purpose as those books, but more overtly as the agent of industry.

With the polar terms—mind and body—as his past professional guideposts, the post-apocalypse manifestation of Jimmy, a character now named Snowman, has philosophical moments about the physicality of the present world and reifies the Cartesian mind-body split that drives the novel:

> When did the body first set out on its own adventures? Snowman thinks; after having ditched its old traveling companions, the mind and the soul, … It must have got tired of the soul's constant nagging and whining and the anxiety-driven intellectual web-spinning of the mind … It had dumped the other two back there somewhere, leaving them stranded in some damp sanctuary or stuffy lecture hall while it made a beeline for the topless bars, and it had dumped culture along with them: music and painting and poetry and plays. Sublimation, all of it; nothing but sublimation, according to the body. Why not cut to the chase? But the body had its own cultural forms. It had its own art. Executions were its tragedies, pornography was its romance. (85)

The enforced division does not really succeed because Jimmy/Snowman can only interpret the body through art and language. In *Surfacing*, Atwood's central character explains, "The trouble is all in the knob at the top of our bodies. I'm not against the body or the head either: only the neck, which creates the illusion that they are separate" (76). Just as Kat cannot bear to dispose of Hairball because it is fundamentally a part of her social existence and self-understanding, Snowman tries to separate the body from art, but ultimately can only conceive of physicality as culturally embedded.

Though his unknowingly injected immunity to Jetspeed Ultra Virus Extraordinary (JUVE) leaves Jimmy the almost sole survivor of the human-destroying plague, the new planetary conditions reduce him, as Snowman, to the limits of his body. The entire book revolves around his attempts to survive and to understand how his body has come to encounter a hostile environment so poorly. Rather than presenting a transcendent robotic future existence, Atwood restricts readers to the quotidian bodily functions of a minor player in the genetic revolution. To some extent, Snowman buys into the arguments presented by the companies who employed him. For example, he ties his emotions entirely to his physicality and thinks of the products that could cure them: "These things sneak up on him for no reason, these flashes of irrational happiness. It's probably a vitamin deficiency" (41). Although he lives within the devastating effects of the destruction such thinking achieves, he cannot prevent himself from buying into the project and desiring self-change in the terms of a genetically modifiable world:

> "Who gives a rat's ass?" says Snowman. "He doesn't care about the iron in his blood or the calcium in his skeletal frame; he's tired of being himself, he wants to be someone else. Turn over all his cells, get a chromosome transplant, trade in his head for some other head, one with better things in it." (109)

He is left without an imagination to rethink his situation, so his only framework to think about change is biological and, specifically, genetic.

Although there is no blindness, deafness, mobility impairment, or even prosthetic limbs in the near-future world of *Oryx and Crake*, the absence of what a twenty-first-century reader thinks of as physical disability speaks volumes. As Tom Shakespeare points out in an article about the new eugenics, disability is the "missing term in the debate around the popular and scientific discourse of genetics" (669). Cognitive disability holds power (if stereotypically destructive) in Atwood's novel, and, in concert, the fear of physical inferiority and the lust for a physical ideal create the conditions for human destruction. The entire notion of the ideal rests upon the absented disabled bodies. Because the cause of extinction comes hidden in a pill that promises immunity to sexually transmitted diseases, creates sexual prowess, and prolongs youth, the promised and actual results of the pill, supposedly drastically different, in fact share a eugenic logic. The democratizing bliss promised by BlyssPluss and the democratizing disintegration caused by it equally eliminate human differentiation and, therefore, most humans.

David T. Mitchell and Sharon L. Snyder explain the process by which Disability Studies has shifted the terms of debate around physical difference:

> By moving disabled bodies into a social and political context and away from their historical mooring as medical and supernatural oddities, disability studies transformed the understanding of

physical and cognitive difference from that of malfunction within particular bodies to the scenario of a cultural production, writ large. Historical representations do not disappear with the passing of an era or cultural formation; they continue to manifest traces in our own, contemporary moment. (381)

In *Oryx and Crake*, Jimmy/Snowman becomes the trace of the disability that is otherwise absent. Next to the Crakers, who "look like retouched fashion photos, or ads for a high-priced workout program," the limited omniscient narrator describes Snowman in terms often reserved for people with disabilities (100). Jimmy's human traits, such as a hairy chest, brown eyes, and a tendency to wear clothes, mark him as different from the Crakers, and different in a way that signifies disability: "Compared to them he is just too weird; they make him feel deformed" (42). Crake's notion of the physically ideal has always relied upon that difference. Though Atwood moves her post- (and even pre-) apocalyptic vision away from an imagination of disability, its lexicon remains. When Snowman encounters the Crakers, "[h]is whistle is like a leper's bell: all those bothered by cripples can get out of his way" (153). He feels the need to warn them so that those uncomfortable with his monstrous (i.e., human) physicality will not be subjected to it.

The children, especially, take interest in this aberrant creature, and he gradually transforms from deviant to mythological. This is what he seeks in choosing his own nickname: "The Abominable Snowman—existing and not existing, flickering at the edges of blizzards, apelike man or manlike ape, stealthy, elusive, known only through rumours and through its backward-pointing footprints" (7–8). At first, his sensitivity to sunlight makes him mysterious: "For the children who are thick-skinned and resistant to ultraviolet, he's a creature of dimness, of the dusk" (6). The children play with him as though he is a monstrous bogeyman: "Every so often they ask him to take off his sunglasses and put them on again: they want to see whether he has two eyes really, or three" (7). But he fears that he will never actually become more than a game because this world is without story, past readers, and beyond art: "He's humanoid, he's hominid, he's an aberration, he's abominable; he'd be legendary, if there were anyone left to relate legends" (307). His occupation as a words person has left the world without words to tell his story.

III. THE CRITICAL LIMITS OF THE SCIENTIFIC IMAGINATION

In his *Canadian Literature* "Opinions & Notes" contribution on *Oryx and Crake*, geneticist Anthony Griffiths insists that "If *Oryx and Crake* is to be taken as serious commentary, then it should stand up to some reality checks about its science" (192). Griffiths claims that because the technologies in the novel seem possible in the current moment, the book cannot be read as merely speculative and therefore should not deviate as far as it does from the realistic bounds of scientific inquiry. Speaking of the hybrid forms of animals throughout the novel, he asks, "Where did Atwood get the idea that such forms are a realistic possibility?" (193) The answer to this needling question is quite straightforward: the imagination. Griffiths's investment in the very division that the book critiques is chilling. For Mitchell and Snyder, the reinsertion of the body into Disability Studies depends precisely on novels like *Oryx and Crake*. They explain that "to narrate a phenomenology of the body requires an approach that can capture its defining elasticity—not as an established fact, but rather as a mutable, temporal, 'first-person' organism. Such is the domain of literature and art" (381). In *Oryx and Crake* Atwood manipulates this creative domain to argue that science is not equipped to handle the elasticity of human physicality where literature and art demand and promote it: "*Watch out for art,* Crake used to say. *As soon as they start doing art, we're in trouble.* Symbolic thinking of any kind would signal downfall, in Crake's view" (361). Scientist Crake can reduce bodily functions to their biological effect, whereas wordsmith Jimmy cannot escape the body's integration into a cultural and social web. Their argument over caecotrophs shows the integral role of the body in this cross-disciplinary debate. While Jimmy argues that the ingestion of "semi-digested herbage, discharged through the anus," boils down to "eating your own shit," Crake tries to reduce the process merely to nutrition:

> Caecotrophs were simply part of alimentation and digestion, a way of making maximum use of the nutrients at hand. Any objections to the process were purely aesthetic.
>
> That was the point, Jimmy had said.
>
> Crake had said that if so it was a bad one. (158–59)

The catch is that the biologically based ideal that Crake masterminds is premised on a socially prescribed aesthetic, that of magazine image-imposed beauty, which goes unquestioned.

Kat's desire in "Hairball" for physical anomaly might have functioned as the unsightly antidote for *Oryx and Crake*'s JUVE virus. In that short story Atwood pinpoints the irreducibility of the always-deviant lived body, and that crucial understanding of physicality persists throughout her writing. Disability scholar Michelle Jarman explains the constitutive function of normativity by saying,:

> [The] fantasy of the "norm" or the "pure" has no tangible core; their meanings are derived from a careful delineation of their opposites—such as "abnormal" or "deviant." These imposed socio-political designations position a contingent group of people in material contrast to the social fantasies of an *ableist* majority. (566)

Whereas Jimmy/Snowman regrets his bodily "deformities" and can only interact with "normal" characters through a parody of his "abnormalities," Kat embraces the physical evidence that her body is *not* a carbon copy of "other" women's, and that her connection with the medical world has re-established a differentiation that she began to lose in her lover relationship. Kat's "fantasy" of the *im*pure drives her character to rebel against the norm, against her own containment within constricting narratives available to women. Jimmy, who can only embrace extremes of his bodily presentation, is doomed to live out the physical disintegration his own participation in this world has brought about.

Margaret Atwood's bodies work together to argue for a conceptual model that holds the social mediation of lived physical difference in tension with the irreducibility of embodiment. As examples of the broader contribution to rethinking embodiment throughout Atwood's writing, these two narratives work in contrast to support the fundamental proposition that desire for physical difference is necessary not only to art but also to human functioning. As W.J.T. Mitchell puts it:

> We will all ultimately become disabled in one way or another, and we all began life that way. To recognize this is not to deny the very real difference that actual physical disabilities make in the lives of

individuals, nor to question the urgency of concrete political and ethical action on behalf of the disabled. It is rather to question the whole model of the self-sufficiency, mastery, and perfect ability (not to mention perfectibility) that governs our picture of the human individual. (397)

—Trent University

NOTES

1. For an explanation of the concept of the "problem body," see Nicole Markotic's introduction to a special issue of *Tessera*, "Coincidence of the Page," Vol. 27 (1999): 6–15.
2. With thanks to Laura Moss for exploring Atwood as icon at the Ottawa conference (April 23, 2004).

WORKS CITED

Atwood, Margaret. "Arguing Against Ice Cream: *Enough: Staying Human in an Engineered Age* by Bill McKibben." *Moving Targets: Writing with Intent, 1982–2004*. Toronto: Anansi, 2004. 339–50.

———. "Hairball." *Wilderness Tips*. New York: Bantam Books, 1991. 41–62.

———. *Oryx and Crake*. Toronto: McClelland & Stewart, 2003.

———. *Surfacing*. Toronto: McClelland & Stewart, 1972.

Breckenridge, Carol A., and Candace Vogler. "The Critical Limits of Embodiment: Disability's Criticism." *Public Culture* 13, no. 3 (2001): 439–57.

Griffiths, Anthony. "Genetics According to Margaret Atwood." *Canadian Literature*, no. 181 (2004): 192–95.

Jarman, Michelle. "Producing 'Normalcy': Absence at the Core of Aberrancy." In "Theorising Disability as Public Subjectivity: work by the UIC Disability Collective on political subjectivities." Michelle Jarman et al. *Disability and Society* 17, no. 5 (2002): 555–69.

Mitchell, David T., and Sharon L. Snyder. "Re-engaging the Body: Disability Studies and the Resistance to Embodiment." *Public Culture* 13, no. 3 (2001): 367–89.

Mitchell, W.J.T. "Seeing Disability." *Public Culture* 13, no. 3 (2001): 391–97.

Shakespeare, Tom. "'Losing the Plot': Medical and Activist Discourses of Contemporary Genetics and Disability." *Sociology of Health and Illness* 21, no. 5 (1999): 669–88.

Thomson, Rosemarie G. *Extraordinary Bodies: Figuring Physical Difference in American Culture and Literature*. New York: Columbia University Press, 1997.

Frankenstein's Gaze and Atwood's Sexual Politics in *Oryx and Crake*

SHARON R. WILSON

FROM AS EARLY AS the poem first published in a rare book as *Speeches for Doctor Frankenstein* (1966), Margaret Atwood has been concerned with creation parables like Mary Shelley's *Frankenstein*. The theme and several images in this poem recur in Atwood's recent and alarming novel, *Oryx and Crake*. Also published in *The Animals in That Country* (1968), "Speeches for Dr. Frankenstein" is about an artist who "dared/to attempt impious wonders" but is unable to foresee the results. He loses control over the creation, which is aborted, deformed, monstrous. "Insane with skill" but wincing "before this plateful of results," by the end of the poem, the doctor, not the monster, is the shadow:

> You sliced me loose
>
> And said it was
> Creation. I could feel the knife.
> Now you would like to heal
> That chasm in your side,
> But I recede, I prowl.
>
> I will not come when you call. (42–47)

In *Oryx and Crake* most readers overlook the extent to which this Frankenstein's unethical vision contributes to the sexual politics and human folly. While Atwood's early texts often focus on protagonists' distortions of vision, especially through mirrors and cameras (see Wilson, "Atwood's Eyes" 226–27; "Camera Images" 29–32), this image has received little comment in recent texts. Most noticeably in *Life Before Man*, *The Handmaid's Tale*, *The Robber Bride*, and *The Blind Assassin*, blindness and distorted vision put male as well as female bodies, and even the newly gendered bodies of this Frankenstein's created species, in jeopardy.

Atwood's little-known visual art makes this sexual politics tangible. Although the rare book, *Speeches for Doctor Frankenstein*, was illustrated with her friend Charles Pachter's visual art, Atwood created two untitled watercolors, later published as "Frankenstein I and II" (Wilson, *Margaret* 48, Plates 6 and 7) for this poem. Suggesting the same kind of dynamics and visual contrast as in Mary Queen of Scots I and II, in which the female figures have a cut off hand or head, Frankenstein I features a robotic male figure (the "monster") without face, arms, or hands, "holding" a fluid, passive female (Elizabeth). In "Frankenstein II," showing the dead Elizabeth and mourners watched by the doctor or possibly his "monster," the male and female are separated by different frames and apparently occupy different realities.

In their childhood and adolescence, Jimmy and Crake, monstrous in their own ways, spend much of their time on pornographic websites, including Hot Totts, Tart of the Day, Superswallowers, and Noodie News, that commodify women's and sometimes men's bodies. Significantly, we first see Oryx, the beautiful woman who captures Jimmy's heart, in the same voyeuristic way that Jimmy and Crake do, as the object of a scopophiliac gaze (Mulvey 440) on a kiddie porn show, and she continues to function as an object in this book filled with images of walled, one-eyed, fish-eyed, ruptured, blind, and ultimately empty-socket vision. Jimmy watches Oryx through the peepholes into the Crakers' secret space and the hallway outside Crake's private quarters. After her death, she is reduced to a voice in Jimmy/Snowman's head. Always part of a Sedgwick triangle in which the central erotic figures are the two men vying for power (524), it is her voice that reminds Snowman to watch over the Crakers, that gives him a reason for being, and, muse-like, inspires his tale. But it is also she who, possibly unknowingly, spreads the virus that may make the human species extinct, with her body at the centre of the novel's sexual politics.

In *Oryx and Crake* even war and other violence are recognized as "misplaced sexual energy." Thus, the new humanoid species created by Crake, this novel's principle Dr. Frankenstein, no longer feels either lust or jealousy, no longer rapes or wages war, mates cyclically every three years when the females go into heat, and neatly drops dead at thirty. Nevertheless, both Crake and the Abominable Snowman/Jimmy are caught in the sexual politics that drives the novel's plot. Although *Oryx and Crake* is unresolved, unlike Atwood's other fiction, this novel seems to offer no rebirth for either male or female bodies, which are literally dismembered and eaten. One of the profoundly ironic possible endings we are offered is a wild-West shoot-out in which the created beings are unlikely to survive precisely *because* they are innocent of violence. As in *Bodily Harm*, *The Handmaid's Tale*, and *The Robber Bride*, sexual politics is not only a metaphor of global disaster but also one of its major causes. Still, this novel that awakens us from our blindness and warns us about our Dr. Frankensteins leaves us in a double bind: continuing on our current blind path ensures extinction, but attempting to eradicate aggression could ensure the same thing.

Atwood writes in a speculative fiction and dystopian tradition that not only includes Orwells's *1984* and *Animal Farm*, Huxley's *Brave New World*, and H. G. Welles's *The Time Machine* and *The Island of Dr. Moreau* but also so many canonical and popular cultural texts that *Oryx and Crake* constitutes an overview of literature and culture as well as a critique of ancient and modern values and modes of being. As narrator, Snowman is one of the long stream of narrators, from Job (the Bible) to Melville's Ishmael (*Moby Dick*) to Shelley's Walton (*Frankenstein*) to Vonnegut's John (*Cat's Cradle*), to bear witness to the folly and grief that constitute human experience. Paradoxically, however, these stories of destruction inevitably shape new creations. Melville chooses Job's story, which he associates with Jonah's, for Ishmael's epilogue to his narrative of disaster: "And I only am escaped alone to tell thee" (432). Job, Ishmael, Walton, and John are not only forced to see the wreck of all conceivable projects of vanity but they are also self-conscious narrators who must tell their stories, creating art from destruction sometimes paradoxically caused by monstrous creation. Ironically, only Job can transcend human apocalypse and the boundaries of fiction to regain and even double what was taken from him.

Shelley's *Frankenstein* uses alchemy, the golem, and the Faust legend, as well as myths of pride, disaster, and fall, in its story of destructive creation. In *Frankenstein* it is appropriate that we first encounter all three self-conscious narrators in this tale-within-a-tale-within-a-tale when they are shut in by ice. From his colonial perspective, Walton sees the created being as "savage" rather than nobly European, as he thinks Dr. Frankenstein is (20–21). Thus, he identifies with the monstrous creator whose quest for the Absolute culminates in a shadow self, a "child" he cannot accept and for whom he feels no pity. Not surprisingly, having never experienced Lacanian parental mirroring (*Écrits*), education, or any kind of "warmth," the being ironically wants to die on a funeral pyre: the symbol of lost love. Shelley's Dr. Frankenstein is not only Prometheus, Faust, and Satan, in his cold and prideful striving to create life out of death, but also the archetypal bad father who steals the female ability to create life and who takes no responsibility for his "child" or his actions. As narrators, Walton and Frankenstein are at least as unreliable as the murderous "monster" who admits his flaws and wants to be punished for his crimes. In their abilities to wall themselves in ice, both Walton and Dr. Frankenstein prefigure the creator of ice-nine as well as Atwood's central creator-monster, Crake, who not only remotely designs apocalypse, watches and then abandons the species he creates, but even gets someone else to distribute the pills that increase sexual pleasure *while* they kill humanity. As in *Frankenstein* and Atwood's poem, Crake's supposedly perfect species develops in directions he does not foresee. When the Crakers make an image of Snowman to call him back, Jimmy recognizes that

> [s]ymbolic thinking of any kind would signal downfall, in Crake's view. Next they'd be inventing idols, and funerals, and grave goods, and the afterlife, and sin, and Linear B, and kings, and then slavery and war. (361)

John of *Cat's Cradle*, who says he should have been Jonah because he was compelled to be at certain places at certain times, ends up telling a different story than the one he had intended, "The Day the World Ended," about the atomic bomb. *Cat's Cradle* is a useful introduction to the absurd universe *Oryx and Crake* penetrates. In *Cat's Cradle* it is still possible to laugh at science and technology so irresponsible and chaotic that a childish scientist deprived of tinker toys could create both the atomic bomb and ice-nine. Supposed to freeze mud for the convenience of the military, ice-nine gets out of hand and freezes the earth. Defoe's *Robinson Crusoe* (McCombs), Shelley's *The Last Man*, Dodgson's *Alice in Wonderland and Through the Looking Glass* (Gussow 2), Swift's *Gulliver's Travels* (epigraph), Woolf's *To the Lighthouse* (epigraph), Piercy's feminist dystopia/utopia *Woman on the Edge of Time* (1976), and "mad scientist" films depicting irresponsible experiments in creating or prolonging life also inform *Oryx and Crake*. For example, Marge Piercy's feminist dystopia/utopia anticipates both Atwood's use of multicoloured beings as a proposed tool for the eradication of racism, and social manipulation of language to condition values. Unlike Crake's scheme to create what he advertises as Paradice (as in "pair of dice") by ending war, aggression, sexual violence and angst, overpopulation, environmental pollution, fear of aging and death, and racism, Piercy's utopia also tackles sexism by using *per* as a gender-neutral substitute for *his* and *her* and making all births by test tube.

Crake resembles the many mad scientists of film, such as the numerous *Frankensteins* frequently featuring Boris Karloff (Whale 1931) and their parodies,[1] *The Invisible Man* (1933), *Island of Lost Souls* (1933) and two remakes, *The Island of Dr. Moreau* (1966, 1977), *Forbidden Planet* (1956), and *The Fly* (1958, 1986), whose Faustian efforts to rival God inevitably spell disaster. Like Professor Morbius of *Forbidden Planet*, Crake transcends normal humanity but creates "a Monster from the ID ... when ... machineries for good bec[o]me engines of ill will" (Chapman). While overtly doing the establishment will, his buried resentment over his father's murder helps precipitate the disgust that culminates in species murder. Crake is even a kind of Dr. Jekyll whose Hyde personality, his dark double, remains hidden behind computer screens and technological experiments (see Stevenson's *The Strange Case of Dr. Jekyll and Mr. Hyde* [1886] and the many films based on it). He is also a Dr. Strangelove (*Dr. Strangelove: Or How I Learned to Stop Worrying and Love the Bomb* [1963]), whose "strange love" is his attraction to extinction. It is Jimmy who, seeming to be *The Invisible Man*, is left alone with the world Crake creates.

Crake, like his model resembling Prometheus, Faust, God, and Satan, most closely resembles Shelley's Dr. Frankenstein. His complex dome, "like a bubble of ice" (228), with watch towers resembling those of the 1932 film, even recalls the frozen island that mirrors the doctor's inner as well as outer landscape at *Frankenstein's* end. Actually named Glenn and modelled on the Canadian pianist Glenn Gould, whom Atwood believes suffered from Asperger's disease (qtd. in Bethune 46), Glenn adopts the name Crake, after the nearly extinct red Australian bird, as his username on the secret terrorist site of the video game show Extinctathon. As his gateway and to irritate Jimmy, Crake uses the picture of Oryx, or someone who looks like her, that he has secretly saved since he and Jimmy were voyeurs of Hot Totts, a child pornography site. Like Victor Frankenstein, however, Crake is physically remote and repressed. Although Crake later frequently touches Oryx, an employee acquired through Student (sexual) Services, his touch says, "Mine, mine" (313), and is ultimately as deadly as Victor's. In both novels, women are passive objects of exchange. Long before his creature kills Elizabeth to punish Victor, Shelley's Victor dreams of holding her dead body, which he associates with his mother's (49). Crake provides Oryx's body to get Jimmy's cooperation. Jimmy thinks that if Crake dies, he expects Oryx to sacrifice herself on a funeral pyre, but as soon as she has spread the virus, Crake slits her throat in front of Jimmy.

Ironically, just as Dr. Frankenstein's attempt to create life is doomed by his selection of dead body parts, the species that Crake creates to replace human beings is implicitly marked for extinction by being called *Crakers*. Like Dr. Frankenstein, who defies God by egotistically creating life and working to eliminate the distinction between natural and man-made, Crake and his fellow scientists eradicate the distinction between real and fake, parodying religion by offering the new species as "floor models" to be adjusted to consumer preferences, and by selling the Moses Model rock, which gives water when struck (302, 200). Despite his distrust of religion and efforts to "edit out" religious impulses—including questions about origins and the desire to know the creator—*Crake* is the name by which he is later "worshipped."

Just as Dr. Frankenstein locks up his creature, Crake locks up not only his new species but also the entire group of anti-social scientists in the RejoovenEssense compound. As extensions of today's exclusive gated communities, compounds can be one of the secret, forbidden spaces, including also the grandmasters' section of the Extinctathon website (216), resembling the forbidden doors in the Grimm fairy tale to which Atwood frequently refers. Such forbidden doors[2] hide the dismemberment and sometimes cannibalism that function symbolically in "Speeches for Dr. Frankenstein" as well as in *Oryx and Crake*. As head of an outlaw group called MaddAddam, Crake also resembles the robbers of life in the Grimm tale, representing not just one mad scientist but an entire mad segment of society (Wilson, *Margaret* 198–228).

Both Crake and Jimmy are monsters in their contrasting ways of seeing without seeing. It is no accident that Crake's dome complex is described as a "blind eyeball" and that it has only slits for windows. Although Crake's pseudolove intensifies his blindness, Oryx admires Crake's "vision" (313, 322). Like other scientific geniuses rewarded by society, Crake is a demi-autistic "brainiac" who ironically functions as a mutant on another planet as he proceeds toward exterminating humanity on this one (174, 193). He reduces art to a desire to have sex and dismisses female artists as misguided; however, except for competition with Jimmy to possess Oryx and the single-minded effort to eradicate a society obsessed with sex and war games, he seems to feel little human emotion himself.

In addition to sometimes doubling as both the doctor and the monster creation, desiring Oryx as his bride (169), Jimmy is the deformed Igor figure, usually played by Bela Lugosi in Frankenstein films. Jimmy's deformity is feeling unloved and not good enough. We first see him as Snowman, another image of coldness despite his tendency to sunburn and of the monstrous as in "abominable." He is wearing one-eyed sunglasses after a life of "structured" ignorance and blindness that contributes to the apocalypse: "He'd grown up in walled spaces, and then he had become one. He had shut things out," turned a "blind eye" (184, 260). As a child, he cultivates a fish-eye stare (277). After he sees his mother's filmed execution following a riot scene from a *Frankenstein* remake and other interjections, even the sunrise is "blinding":

> Everything in his life was temporary, ungrounded. Language itself had lost its solidity; it had become thin, contingent, slippery, a viscid film on which he was sliding around like an eyeball on a plate. An eyeball that could still see, however. That was the trouble. (260)

After he has allowed Crake to destroy everything he values, Jimmy opens and closes his eyes, realizing that he can't regain the past and will be destroyed by the present if he looks at it too closely (147). Because the

Crakers see him as a prophet, in a sense he is a blind Tireseus. He is a time traveler without a time-machine and thus unable to return to his time (106). As the self-conscious narrator of the book we read and the creator of myths for the Crakers, he, too, is a creator. His head always filled with words and voices, he hopes to prevent words from becoming extinct but allows his gift with language to be commodified in Crake's service.

If Crake and Jimmy are blind Frankensteins and Oryx is the object of exchange that fuels the book's sexual politics, their society is the epitome of a world out of control created by and creating Frankensteins. According to Amanda's pleebland roommates, their current society, only slightly more vicious than ours, is monstrous:

> its main products being corpses and rubble. It never learned, it made the same cretinous mistakes over and over, trading short-term gain for long-term pain. It was like a giant slug eating its way relentlessly through all the other bioforms on the planet, grinding up life on earth and shitting it out the backside in the form of pieces of manufactured and soon-to-be-obsolete plastic junk. (243)

This is a society in which the body, "having ditched its old traveling companions, the mind and the soul, … has set out on its own adventures" (85). While the species Crake creates cannot read and does not even understand the concepts of war and rape, it is superior to Crake's fellow human beings in many respects, including its reverence for the environment and living beings, as well as its comic communal healing through purring. But these advantages exist because of genetic pre-programming and thus make the Crakers seem less free than the human beings that precede them. Crake does his best to prevent Crakers from being able to develop civilization, including art, technology, or the kind of human achievements pitted against human atrocities on the game show Blood and Roses (78–79), but there are already signs that they are beginning to develop in directions Crake thinks he has edited out. Thus, even if their innocence does not mark them for extinction, there is no assurance that they will not eventually develop the self-destructive characteristics that lead human culture to death. True, the current world seems hopelessly messed up and Crake's motives might be good. On the other hand, he always enjoys playing intellectual games to see whether he can do what he conceives. The novel poses a number of ethical issues: Is it really impossible for human beings to change? Is it really necessary to program sex and death and adapt humans to eat what they defecate? At the end of the novel, Snowman, at least three other human beings, and the Crakers are still alive. The choice seems to be theirs—and ours.

—University of Northern Colorado

NOTES

1. Crake might appreciate current self-parodying websites such as MadSciNet, "a collective cranium of scientists providing answers to your questions."
2. The Grimms' "Fitcher's Bird" features a door to a forbidden room of Fitcher's previous, dismembered brides. He gives the third sister keys to every room but forbids her to enter this one. Jimmy is dimly aware of the dangers of doors being unlocked: his mother's job is to make "locks" for cell "doors" (29); he worries about the forbidden door swinging open both when his mother leaves home and when he discovers "a stream of secret lives" on the Extinctathon site (216), and, long after it is too late, he dreams of being locked into a vault with Oryx (43).

WORKS CITED

Atwood, Margaret. *The Animals in That Country.* Toronto: Oxford University Press, 1968.

———. *Oryx and Crake.* New York: Doubleday, 2003.

———. *Speeches for Doctor Frankenstein.* Illustrated and printed by Charles Pachter. Bloomfield Hill, MI: Cranbrook Academy of Art, 1965.

Bethune, Brian. "Atwood Apocalyptic." *Maclean's* 116, no. 17: 44–49.

Chapman, Douglas. "To a New World of Gods and Monsters: Mad Scientists and the Movies." [online]: <http://www.strangemag.com/madscientists/madscientists.html> (accessed February 12, 2004).

Dr. Jekyll and Mr. Hyde. Dir. Victor Fleming. Metro-Goldwyn-Mayer, 1941.

Dr. Strangelove: Or How I Learned to Stop Worrying and Love the Bomb. Dir. Stanley Kubrick. GB, 1963.

Forbidden Planet. Dir. Fred M. Wilcox. Warner Studios, 1956.

Frankenstein. Dir. James Whale. Universal, 1931.

Gussow, Mel. "Handwringer's Tale of Tomorrow." *New York Times,* June 24, 2003. [online]: <http://NYTimes.com> (accessed June 24, 2003).

Lacan, Jacques. *Écrits: A Selection.* Translated by Alan Sheridan. New York: Norton, 1977.

MadSciNet [online]: <http://www.madsci.org> (accessed February 12, 2004).
McCombs, Judith. "Rewriting *Crusoe:* Atwood's Cautionary: Future-Shock *Oryx and Crake.*" Paper presented at ACSUS. Portland, OR, 2003.
Melville, Herman. *Moby-Dick or The Whale.* Edited by Alfred Kazin. Boston: Houghton Mifflin, 1956.
Mulvey, Laura. "Visual Pleasure and Narrative Cinema." In *Feminisms: An Anthology of Literary Theory and Criticism,* edited by Robyn R. Warhol and Diane Price Herndl, 438–48. New Brunswick, NJ: Rutgers University Press, 1997.
Piercy, Marge. *Woman on the Edge of Time.* New York: Knopf, 1976.
Sedgwick, Eve K. "Gender Asymmetry and Erotic Triangles." In *Feminisms: An Anthology of Literary Theory and Criticism,* edited by Robyn R. Warhol and Diane Price Herndl, 524–31. New Brunswick, NJ: Rutgers University Press, 1997.
Shelley, Mary W. *Frankenstein, or The Modern Prometheus.* New York: Macmillan, 1973.
Stevenson, Robert Louis. *The Strange Case of Dr. Jekyll and Mr. Hyde.* [1886]. New York: Norton, 2003.
Swift, Jonathan. *Gulliver's Travels: An Annotated Text with Critical Essays.* Edited by Robert A. Greenberg. New York: Norton, 1961.
Vonnegut, Kurt Jr. *Cat's Cradle.* New York: Dell, 1963.
Dir Fred M. Wilcox. *Forbidden Planet.* Warner Studios, 1956.
Wilson, Sharon R. "Atwood's Eyes and I's." In *International Literature in English: Essays on the Major Writers,* edited by Robert L. Ross. Garland Reference Library of the Humanities, Vol. 1159. 225–39. New York and London: Garland, 1991.
———. "Camera Images in Margaret Atwood's Novels." In *Margaret Atwood: Reflection and Reality.* Living Authors Series, edited by Beatrice Mendez-Egle, 6. 29–57. Edinburg, TX: Pan American University, 1987.
———. *Margaret Atwood's Fairy-Tale Sexual Politics.* Jackson: University Press of Mississippi, 1993.

The Representation of the Absent Mother in Margaret Atwood's *Oryx and Crake*

NATHALIE FOY

THERE IS A burgeoning genre of writing about the meaning of motherhood in twenty-first-century industrialized society, with books that range from humorous works of fiction (Allison Pearson's *I Don't Know How She Does It* and Helen Simpson's *Hey Yeah Right Get a Life*) to sardonic life writing (Marni Jackson's *The Mother Zone* and Andrea Buchanan's *Mother Shock: Loving Every (Other) Minute of It*), and from sociological inquiry (Diane Eyer's *Motherguilt: How Our Culture Blames Mothers for What's Wrong with Society* and Sharon Hays's *The Cultural Contradictions of Motherhood*) to a topic closer to home: academic employment (*The Family Track: Keeping Your Faculties While You Mentor, Nurture, Teach, and Serve*). Each of these works engages with the impossible ideal of the perfect mother and with mothers' attempts to balance the competing claims of their maternal and non-maternal roles. In *The Mommy Myth: The Idealization of Motherhood and How It Has Undermined Women*, Susan Douglas and Meredith Michaels examine how this romanticized vision of perfectible motherhood has become a normative aspect of mainstream North American values. Under the rubric of "new momism"—"the insistence that no woman is truly complete or fulfilled unless she has kids, that women remain the best primary caretakers of children, and that to be a remotely decent mother, a woman has to devote her entire physical, psychological, emotional, and intellectual being, 24/7, to her children"—Douglas and Michaels examine trends in print and televised media that promote a definition of motherhood in which the standards of perfection are impossible to meet (4). Mothers, they contend, are either beatified or demonized by the media, and this polarization serves to police women's maternal activity by forcing women to sublimate all of their negative emotions as they strive to meet the omnicompetent ideal. They claim "new momism" as the direct descendant of Betty Friedan's feminine mystique, and they chart a backlash against women that operates under the guise of discussions that posit motherhood as an unequivocally positive role. They offer this droll account of how the spurious concept of post-feminism has worked to redomesticate women:

> Feminism won; you can have it all; of course you want children; mothers are better at raising children than fathers; of course your children come first; of course you come last; today's children need constant attention, cultivation, adoration, or they'll become failures and hate you forever; you don't want to fail at that; it's easier for mothers to abandon their work and their dreams than for fathers; you don't want it all anymore (which is good because you can't have it all); who cares about equality, you're too tired; and whoops—here we are in 1954. (25)

Consistent with Douglas and Michaels's sense of déjà vu, Margaret Atwood's characterization of Sharon in her futuristic *Oryx and Crake* appears less post-feminist than pre-feminist. At some stage, Sharon had balanced work outside of the home and motherhood, but the details of that period are not provided. The reason for Sharon's leaving her job as a microbiologist at OrganInc Farms is skirted, but after leaving work to stay at home with her son, she sinks into a deep depression. She seems a caricature of the woman who suffers from Betty Friedan's "problem that has no name," the deep dissatisfaction that many women in 1950s North America felt with their immersion in their roles as wives and mothers, a dissatifaction that they felt unentitled to articulate because domestic feminity was so universally lauded as a woman's calling. The representation of her move out of depression and into activism recalls a 1970s style of consciousness-raising, as she is seen at rallies and becomes part of an increasingly militant margin that challenges the status quo. The narrator of the novel describes a very bleak future, and the novel is unrelenting in its assault on the reader with instance after instance of environmental, corporate, social, and moral calamity. The story is clearly a warning about the dangers of unchecked corporate control of human societies and unchecked genetic experimentation. One of the interesting challenges the novel poses, however, is for the reader to find an iteration of that warning that is not compromised by its complicity with the very system it denounces. Jimmy/Snowman, through whom the novel is focalized, was never much of a critic of the abuses he describes. Sharon, however, emerges as a positive figure of hope and agency in an apparently hopeless future. She represents a positive alternative to her son Jimmy's apathy, to Crake's pathological solution to the imperfections of human societies, and to the Crakers' repugnantly engineered perfection. When we juxtapose these negative alternatives with the trajectory of Sharon's move from depression to activism and with her actions as a critic of genetic engineering, the novel seems to endorse her choices. The fact that the novel is focalized through her son, however, poses a major threat to this endorsement. The reader is initially overwhelmed by the pathos of the representation of Jimmy as an abandoned child, and the positive aspect of Sharon's escape is obscured by his recalled sense of loss and anger.

With her representation of the absent mother in this novel, Atwood negotiates the tenets of "new momism" with her signature resistance to absolutes. She demonstrates the absurdity of a woman's immersing herself in motherhood to the exclusion of all other goals, while simultaneously offering a sensitive depiction of a child's sense of loss when his mother does not fulfil the maternal ideal. Of course, from Jimmy's point of view, the devotion of his mother's entire physical, psychological, emotional, and intellectual being to his welfare would have been all to the good. His mother is negatively compared to his nanny Dolores, who "had smiled and laughed and cooked his egg just the way he liked it, and had sung songs and indulged him," and who had been made redundant by Sharon's decision to stay home with Jimmy (30). Atwood handles the sense of anxiety and loss occasioned by his mother's depression and absence with a certain compassion. She acknowledges a child's need to be at the centre of his mother's universe, and she empathetically depicts Jimmy's reaction to his mother's failure to fulfil that need. At the same time, however, Sharon's actions are endorsed by the ironic gap created between Atwood and her self-absorbed narrator. Jimmy's sense of loss is satirized, for example, by his yearning for a well-cooked egg. Sharon's depression obviates any of the supposed benefits of a woman's immersing herself in her maternal role, no matter how much her son may have desired or benefited from that immersion. Motherhood cannot compensate for her despair at the escalation of the abuses of genetic engineering, and she has to abandon the maternal role in order to combat those abuses. That Jimmy cannot credit her leaving with any positive motive is especially ironic given his senior thesis on twentieth-century self-help literature. Sharon's absence, therefore, takes on two mutually exclusive meanings: her own sense of self-actualization and Jimmy's sense of abandonment.

The novel begins with Snowman's waking, his coming into consciousness, and it is that consciousness that determines the narrative structure of the novel. The third-person narration is focalized through Snowman as he negotiates life in the post-apocalyptic world and remembers his pre-apocalyptic life as Jimmy. Shifts in narrative time correspond to shifts in the identity of the focalizer, and a gap emerges between the pre-apocalyptic Jimmy and his post-apocalyptic incarnation as Snowman. Interesting slippages occur because of the multiplicity of focalizing identities: third-person narrator, Snowman, and Jimmy. What this choice of narrative voice allows Atwood to accomplish is her astonishingly deft (and rather dizzying) way of advancing and withdrawing Snowman as a credible voice of dissent both to Crake's atrocity and to his mother's activism.

The obvious irony that undermines Snowman's credibility is that it was his very complicity with Crake's plan that resulted in his being apparently the only remaining human left on earth. As Crake's "wordman," Jimmy wrote the advertising copy for the commercially successful BlyssPluss pills, which delivered the hemorrhagic disease that has obliterated human life. As Crake's second in command, he was left with a means to survive the disease and tend to the Crakers. Alone, he is now the unwilling shepherd to Crake's flock, and there is a degree of poetic justice to his plight. Though Snowman may have unknowingly participated in bringing about the apocalyptic plague, he had never been very critical of the abuses of scientific knowledge that led to it, and he must now live with the horror of the final outcome of Crake's plan.

On the other hand, one means by which Atwood accentuates the credibility of the narrative voice is to establish a separation between the post-apocalyptic Snowman, who has seen Crake's capacity for evil taken to its fullest extent, and Jimmy, who benefited from Crake's friendship and patronage. In a moment of retrospection, Snowman recalls his teenaged self: "Jimmy had been full of himself back then, thinks Snowman with indulgence and a little envy. He'd been unhappy too, of course. It went without saying, his unhappiness. He'd put a lot of energy into it" (71–72). Snowman's tone is wry, and his perspective is frankly critical. Though we know that a major source of his unhappiness is his absent mother, Snowman undercuts the pathos of that yearning by recalling how Jimmy had nurtured his sense of loss rather than try to overcome it. At the same time that Atwood underscores Snowman's capacity to judge himself harshly, however, she undermines Snowman's credibility. Snowman thinks of his former self "with indulgence and a little envy" (71). Indeed, during his worst moments of despair, Snowman reverts to a childish self:

> "I didn't do it on purpose," he says, in the snivelling child's voice he reverts to in this mood. "Things happened, I had no idea, it was out of my control! What could I have done? Just someone, anyone, listen to me please!" What a bad performance. Even he isn't convinced by it. (45)

The pathos—in this instance, of Snowman's profound loneliness and despair—is undercut by the narrator's admitting to its performative aspect. Furthermore, Snowman's *mea culpa* is not really a confession but, rather, a denial, and he still rejects his share of the responsibility for the outcome of the BlyssPluss plague. To the extent that there is any criticism of Jimmy, then, it is focalized through a self who is still limited in his ability to accept his share of responsibility for precipitating the end of humanity. While this limitation is offset by Snowman's keen sense of the fraud of pathos, the result is an unstable narrative voice.

The consequence of the instability of the narrative voice is that it is difficult to find purchase on a site within the novel from which to contest Snowman's limited sense of the power of the individual and his portrayal of events that make Crake's ascendancy and success appear inevitable. Snowman is capable of shrewd appraisals of Jimmy's behaviour, decrying Jimmy's blindness and apathetic indifference to the implications of Crake's power, yet there is still a sense of his apathy and disbelief in his own power to have effected positive change. The reader is on constantly unstable epistemological ground with Snowman/Jimmy as narrative focalizer, and by choosing this narrative voice, Atwood activates a suspicious reading of the novel, a reading necessarily suspicious of absolutes since no absolute readings are possible (Snowman is understandably anguished and deserves our pity, *and* Snowman is hamming it up and deserves our scorn). Furthermore, the kind of suspicion Atwood activates is in direct contrast to Jimmy's tendency to either read his world in absolute terms of good and evil or retreat into a state of apathy or drunken oblivion in which the difference between good and evil ceases to matter. From Jimmy's point of view, the world is far too big for his actions to make any difference, and he mocks his mother's activism for its naivety. However, by separating the discussion of the mother from the son who is responsible for narrating her into existence, it becomes possible to find a place from which to contest the limits of the narrative voice and of the narrative focalizer's ethics.

Jimmy's descriptions of his mother before her disappearance are poignant in their evocation of the confusion of a child who is indifferently or improperly mothered. In Jimmy's recollections, his mother is often characterized as monstrous in her mood swings:

> Snowman has a clear image of his mother—of Jimmy's mother—sitting at the kitchen table, still in her bathrobe when he came home from school for his lunch. She would have a cup of coffee in front of her, untouched; she would be looking out the window and smoking. The bathrobe was magenta, a colour that still makes him anxious whenever he sees it. As a rule there would be no lunch ready for him and he would have to make it himself, his mother's only participation being to issue directions in a flat voice. ... Once in a while there would be a real lunch waiting for him, a lunch that was so arranged and extravagant it frightened him, for what was the occasion? ... His mother would be carefully dressed, her lipstick smile an echo of the jelly smile on the sandwich, and she would be all sparkling attention, for him and his silly stories, looking at him directly, her eyes bluer than blue. (31–32)

This passage not only highlights the profound and lingering impact of witnessing his mother's depression (magenta still makes him anxious) but it also illustrates the intractability of Jimmy's anxiety. His mother's resolve to put on a brave face is no solution at all; that face exacerbates rather than calms Jimmy's uneasiness.

Because of his mother's erratic moods, Jimmy experiences a frightening ambivalence as a child. As Rozsika Parker notes, ambivalence is not mixed feelings; it is a "concept developed by psychoanalysis according to which quite contradictory impulses and emotions towards the same person co-exist. The positive and negative components sit side by side and remain in opposition" (*Torn in Two* 5–6). In children the coexistence of love and hate for the mother facilitates a positive stage of individuation. Parker notes the contradiction that

> [a]lthough most psychoanalytic writers view the capacity to experience love and hate towards the mother as a positive achievement for the developing infant, ambivalent feelings towards her baby are more often than not considered to be a problem for a mother. ("Production and Purposes" 17)

They are a problem because they interfere with the mother's ability to feel that she has given her child the hate-free and constant love required of the ideal mother. Parker argues that ambivalence itself is not problematic for either mother or child; rather, it is the feelings of shame about ambivalence that are problematic, and Jimmy and his mother both struggle with that shame (37). In addition to wrestling with her mixed feelings about living off of the avails of genetic engineering, it is clear that Sharon also experiences shame and despondency about her capacity to mother effectively. As Sharon's depression deepens, the extremes of Jimmy's ambivalence also escalate. As a young child, and immediately following his mother's decision to stay at home, he develops a behavioural pattern of attraction and repulsion in reaction to her mood swings:

> She often tried to explain things to him; then she got discouraged. These were the worst moments, for both of them. He resisted her, he pretended he didn't understand even when he did, he acted stupid, but he didn't want her to give up on him. He wanted her to be brave, to try her best with him, to hammer away at the wall he'd put up against her, to keep on going. (21)

As he gets older and as his mother's depression deepens, Jimmy experiences correspondingly heightened feelings of love and hate:

> More than anything, Jimmy had wanted to make her laugh—to make her happy, as he seemed to remember her being once. ... As he grew older and more devious, he found that on the days when he couldn't grab some approval, he could at least get a reaction. Anything was better than the flat voice, the blank eyes, the tired staring out of the window. ... She would shake all over, gasp for breath, choking and sobbing. He wouldn't know what to do then. He loved her so much when he made her unhappy, or else when she made him unhappy: at these moments he scarcely knew which was which. He would pat her, standing well back as with strange dogs, stretching out his hand, saying, "I'm sorry, I'm sorry." And he was sorry, but there was more to it: he was also gloating, congratulating himself, because he'd managed to create such an effect. (31–33)

His ambivalence is even more exacerbated by her departure and extends into his adolescence. The potential positive outcomes of Jimmy's ambivalence, separation, and individuation are short-circuited by his mother preempting the gesture of separation. She, not he, has initiated an abrupt and painful separation that seems to leave him stranded in emotional childhood. When he sees his vanished mother in news footage of a demonstration, the ambivalence is described in stark terms: "Love jolted through him, abrupt and painful, followed by anger" (181).

Whereas Jimmy's ambivalence as a child was with reference to a mother whose (albeit oppressive) presence was a given, in this last instance, his feelings of love and hate are overlaid by his anger that she took decisive action and left him. It is the pathos of the descriptions of Jimmy as the abandoned child that most overwhelms the possibility of a positive characterization of the absent mother. Of course, in effect, Sharon's absence began before her disappearance, with her depression, and Jimmy had to learn to fend for himself from an early age. Because of his dysfunctional family, and in the absence of genuine friendships at school, Jimmy identifies Killer, his pet rakunk, as his "secret best friend" (59). When Sharon absconds with Killer, then, she commits two grave wrongs, robbing her son of his beloved pet as well as of his mother. That Killer is only a postscript to her farewell note adds insult to injury:

> *P.S., she'd said. I have taken Killer with me to liberate her, as I know she will be happier living a wild, free life in the forest.* Jimmy hadn't believed that either. He was enraged by it. How dare she? Killer was his! And Killer was a tame animal, she'd be helpless on her own, she wouldn't know how to fend for herself, everything hungry would tear her into furry black and white pieces. (61)

Sharon's releasing Killer to a certain death is a gesture that thoroughly demonizes her and cements Jimmy's status as wronged victim: "In secret, in the night, he yearned for Killer. Also—in some corner of himself he could not quite acknowledge—for his real, strange, insufficient, miserable mother" (61–67).

Sharon's releasing Killer also, however, verges on comedy rather than tragedy: even as it makes Jimmy's abandonment more emotionally wrenching, it pushes the element of pathos into hyperbole. Sharon's execution at the hands of the CorpSeCorps agents, and the sign that she holds up that reads "Remember Killer," are also hyperbolic in their pathos. Jimmy had never endorsed Sharon's reasons for leaving, as is apparent from his paraphrase of her parting note: "*Dear Jimmy*, it said. *Blah blah blah, suffered with conscience long enough, blah blah, no longer participate in a lifestyle that is not only meaningless in itself but blah blah blah*" (61). From Jimmy's point of view, her motives remain misguided to the end: her injunction to remember Killer reinforces the pain she inflicted with her naïve idea of a free life in the forest rather than serving as a rallying cry to her cause. Jimmy, therefore, is not alone in being the object of Atwood's satire.

The pathos of Killer's being sent to a certain death and his mother's desertion are also undercut by Jimmy's use of the story to his own ends. He had used his mother's depression and his parents' disintegrating marriage at school with the "major piece of treachery" of his Evil Dad and Righteous Mom hand puppet act: "This lunchroom show of his was a hit; a crowd would collect, with requests. *Jimmy, Jimmy—do Evil Dad!* ... Jimmy felt guilty sometimes, afterwards, when he'd gone too far. ... But the other kids egged him on, and he couldn't resist the applause" (60). Similarly, he later uses the fact of his mother's absence to attract women:

> Snowman is ashamed to remember how he'd used that story—a hint here, a hesitation there. Soon the women would be consoling him, and he'd roll around in their sympathy, soak it in, massage himself

with it. ... When he got to the part where she'd stolen Killer the rakunk away from him he could usually wring out a tear or two, not from himself but from his auditors. (191)

Significantly, the only woman who does not empathize with Jimmy's story of abandonment is Oryx: "*So Jimmy, your mother went somewhere else? Too bad. Maybe she had some good reasons. You thought of that?* Oryx had neither pity for him nor self-pity" (191). Oryx, Jimmy thinks, has a larger claim in the wounded psyche department, and he pesters her with questions about what he sees as her years of victimization at the hands of her mother and the string of perverted men who exploited her. His outrage is ironic given that he first sees her as he is consuming child pornography:

> Then she looked over her shoulder and right into the eyes of the viewer—right into Jimmy's eyes, into the secret person inside him. *I see you*, that look said. *I see you watching. I know you. I know what you want.* ... [For] the first time he'd felt that what they'd been doing was wrong. Before, it had always been entertainment, or else far beyond his control, but now he felt culpable. (91)

Formerly unable to appreciate the wrong in his behaviour or to appreciate his agency in perpetuating a global demand for child pornography, he responds by understanding the morality of the sex trade in absolute terms of good and evil, but also in the limited terms of Oryx as an individual victim. He wants to include her in his sense of righteous indignation, but Oryx remains a cypher in his play of outrage. She refuses to provide him with the details that would bolster his view of the world in which she is exclusively a victim:

> ... she might say, "I don't know. I've forgotten." Or, "I don't want to tell you that." Or, "Jimmy, you are so bad, it's not your business." Once she'd said, "You have a lot of pictures in your head, Jimmy. Where did you get them? Why do you think they are pictures of me?"
>
> He thought he understood her vagueness, her evasiveness. "It's all right," he'd told her, stroking her hair. "None of it was your fault."
>
> "None of what, Jimmy?" (114)

Whereas Jimmy's resentment of his mother persists, Oryx is able to forgive her mother for selling her into prostitution. She has a pragmatic sense of the social and economic context that drove her mother to do what she did and a reasoned approach to making the best of her value:

> She herself would rather have had her mother's love ... but love was undependable, it came and then it went, so it was good to have a money value, because then at least those who wanted to make a profit from you would make sure you were fed enough and not damaged too much. (126)

Oryx understands her mother's behaviour in a wider socio-economic context than Jimmy's individual familial perspective on his mother's absence. Similarly, although Sharon's decision to leave is an individual choice, it is not self-serving. She leaves to fight for causes that represent a wider interest than her son's happiness. Ironically, it is on the very site of absence (Jimmy's yearning for the impossibly perfectible mother and for his real, flawed, and absent mother) that Atwood constructs hope—through Sharon's activism. Notwithstanding the heightened emotion of Sharon's execution, the novel's bleakness is redeemed by Sharon's exercising of choice and of individual conscience. Oryx's perspective on her mother's actions, and Sharon's decision to leave her family in order to contribute to a greater good both operate as alternatives to Jimmy's understanding of the world through individual victimization and to his limited sense of an individual's ability to effect change.

Parker argues that the value of maternal ambivalence is that it can be a source of creative insight (*Torn in Two* 120). When a mother has to negotiate her ambivalence, she is forced into thinking about rather than simply responding to her emotions and her relationship with her child. Similarly, the value of the unstable narrative voice in this novel is that it constantly prompts the reader's suspicion and leads the reader past the limitation of Jimmy's/Snowman's perspective. The instability of the narrative voice makes it possible to question Jimmy's perspective of his absent mother and find a redemptive side to her desertion.

The novel ends with Snowman suffering from a badly, and possibly lethally, infected foot and with him on the verge of encountering other surviving humans. We do not know if Snowman survives the infection or the encounter, but we do know that a narrator survives to tell the tale. We also know that the narrator has a sense of humour, unlike the Crakers. When Snowman first sees them, he asks Crake if they can make jokes. "'Not as such,' said Crake. 'For jokes you need a certain edge, a little malice. It took a lot of trial and error and we're still testing, but I think we've managed to do away with jokes'" (306). The joke, it appears, is on Crake: he has not managed to do away with all human life after all.

Given his yearning for a perfectible mother and his attraction to the purity of absolute outrage in response to Oryx's history of exploitation, it is curious that one of the characteristics of the Crakers that make them repugnant to Jimmy is their perfection:

> They look like retouched fashion photos, or ads for a high-priced workout program. Maybe this is the reason that these women arouse in Snowman not even the faintest stirrings of lust. It was the thumbprints of human imperfection that used to move him, the flaws in the design. (100)

His preference for a flawed woman is a preference we are meant to sanction, and we are encouraged to take the step that Jimmy cannot take and celebrate his mother's imperfections as well. As the novel illustrates, Crake's pursuit of the alternative, a perfect species, is pathological. Through the figure of Snowman's absent mother, the novel charges its readers to hope, not in the tabula rasa of new beginnings—the Crakers disprove any such hope of new beginnings—or in the perfectibility of mothers, but rather in our ability to reconcile ourselves to our flaws, using that recognition as a spur to improvement, not perfection. It is at the site of the absent mother that the reader can locate resistance to the hopelessness of the future Atwood describes. Snowman's mother is the antidote to the passive surrender to corporate culture and to the abuses of scientific knowledge. She escapes to fight those abuses, but, significantly, she is not flawless. She is by no means beatified. The injunction to seek out the absent mother as a source of hope is not an injunction to deify her. The novel, rather, calls for a reading that will serve as a corrective to the polarized view of beatified and demonized mothers.

—University of Toronto

WORKS CITED

Atwood, Margaret. *Oryx and Crake*. Toronto: McClelland & Stewart, 2003.
Buchanan, Andrea. *Mother Shock: Loving Every (Other) Minute of It*. New York: Seal Press, 2003.
Coiner, Constance, and Diana H. George. *The Family Track: Keeping Your Faculties While You Mentor, Nurture, Teach, and Serve*. Chicago: University of Illinois Press, 1998.
Douglas, Susan, and Meredith Michaels. *The Mommy Myth: The Idealization of Motherhood and How It Has Undermined Women*. Toronto: Free Press, 2004.
Eyer, Diane. *Motherguilt: How Our Culture Blames Women for What's Wrong with Society*. Toronto: Random House, 1996.
Hays, Sharon. *The Cultural Contradictions of Motherhood*. New Haven: Yale University Press, 1996.
Jackson, Marni. *The Mother Zone*. Toronto: Vintage, 2002.
Parker, Rozsika. *Torn in Two: The Experience of Maternal Ambivalence*. London: Virago, 1995.
———. "The Production and Purposes of Maternal Ambivalence." In *Mothering and Ambivalence*, edited by Wendy Holloway and Brid Featherstone, 17–36. London: Routledge, 1997.
Pearson, Allison. *I Don't Know How She Does It*. New York: Alfred K. Knopf, 2003.
Simpson, Helen. *Hey Yeah Right Get a Life*. London: Vintage, 2000.

Resistance in Futility: The Cyborg Identities of Oryx and Crake

MICHÈLE LACOMBE

I. OPEN SESAME

Crake moved to the girl's left eye, clicked on the iris. It was a gateway: the playroom opened up.
Hello, Grandmaster Crake. Enter passnumber now.
Crake did so. (Atwood, *OC* 215–16)

OPEN SESAME: "ADAM *named the animals. MaddAddam customizes them*" (*OC* 216). Open sesame: "It was the picture of Oryx, seven or eight years old, naked except for her ribbons, her flowers" (215). When Jimmy first encounters the image of the prepubescent Oryx on Crake's computer when they are both teenagers, he starts feeling guilty about surfing the net, but also that he feels "hooked through the gills" (91). Years later, he still seems more concerned about Crake's use of the image—"his own private thing" (215)—than he is about the site's more sinister implications or Crake's manipulation of him. The voyeur's clouded vision subsequently gives way to the scavenger's partial insight, sunglasses with one missing lens complicating the picture.

In *Oryx and Crake*'s manichean world of triangles, trinities, and triumverates gone wild, it is not clear who is Adam, Eve, or Lucifer, who is prostitute or madam, who is john or pimp. The image of MaddAddam, for all its post-cyberpunk indebtedness to William Gibson, is nothing if not redolent of Sylvia Plath's Nobodaddy. As for the nuclear family unit, there too we might well ask, as does Crake, "what is real?" For those not sold into prostitution as children, the most serious concern is how to deal with a parent or a spouse who might betray the culture of the Compound. When Jimmy, peering through the one-way mirror into Paradise (*pace* Coleridge), finally zeroes in on his vision of the naked, adult Oryx, he initially confuses her with one of the Crakers whom she is disguised to resemble. The look is unmistakeable, even as the eyes are a luminescent green. The pet rakunk in her arms, a fixture from his own childhood, is a dead giveaway and should have been his first clue, but by now Jimmy is fully conditioned to fall for Crake's plan—hook, line, and sinker. Re-baptized as Snowman, Jimmy ponders his prior ignorance, comparing it to an "unformed, inchoate" state—"not willed, exactly." Bearing the usual scars, "he'd grown up in walled spaces, and then he had become one" (184). At what point does Jimmy/Snowman begin to see the "top of Crake's charmed dome" (228), beyond the physical and cultural ruins of the Paradise compound—that "blind eyeball," rising above the vegetation (296)? As much as on Crake's Faustian ambition, the cautionary tale's narrative hinges on, among other things, Jimmy's all-too-human failure to see and to act in a timely fashion. Atwood revisits C.P. Snow's two cultures, seeing them together as an asymmetrical, co-dependent odd couple unaware of the serious difficulty in which they are mired—the mad scientist and lofty poet as mirror image of one another. In this reading, the mask of Oryx is not Jimmy's and Crake's juvenile muse so much as a veiled commentary, in my opinion, on Gayatri Spivak's sense of the subaltern, Judith Butler's understanding of gender, and Baudrillard's image of the simulacrum.

Some years ago, in my article "The Writing on the Wall: Amputated Speech in Margaret Atwood's *The Handmaid's Tale*," I attempted a feminist Lacanian deconstructive reading of that novel. No longer cocooned in her safe marriage and easy job converting books to electronic media, and unable to conceive, the heroine of that novel must reconsider her previous life as well as her present dilemma. I argued, among other things, for the saving grace of laughter in the face of despair, if indeed the forgotten, forbidden "noise coming up, coming out, of the broken place, in my face" can simply be called laughter. Her sexuality and identity repressed, Offred gives way to hidden hysteria, hands crammed in her mouth in the cupboard of her room in the Commander's house. In *Oryx and Crake* it is with head down on two fists and "weeping with laughter"(259) that Jimmy explains to Crake the story of his mother abandoning him together with his beloved pet rakunk Killer—having just seen on the Internet what appears to be her execution for crimes against the state. If Crake is the obvious psychopath in this novel, Jimmy's cynical sense of detachment and tendency to hide all emotion are also symptomatic: "Oh how to lament? He's a failure even at that" (335). Yet his sardonic sense of humour remains his saving grace, as the reader is led to mourn as well as to celebrate the passing on of Jimmy's funnybone, especially in his all-too-brief reincarnation as the Abominable Snowman.

II. THE BORG

In my piece on *The Handmaid's Tale*, the amputated speech and writing on the wall referred to one of the nameless hanged men encountered on a shopping trip: the white hood covering his cut-out tongue is perceived by Offred as a red zero, the faceless men as "snowmen with the eyes and the carrot noses fallen out," their faces melting, although the blood reminds her that they are "not snowmen after all." This reading of *Oryx and Crake* takes its cue from Donna Haraway's feminist essay "A Manifesto for Cyborgs" from her 1991 book *Simians, Cyborgs, and Women: The Reinvention of Nature*. Briefly, Haraway defines cyborgs as "creatures simultaneously animal and machine, who populate worlds ambiguously natural and crafted" (149). In a world in which "modern production seems like a dream of cyborg colonization work, a dream that makes the nightmare of Taylorism seem idyllic" (150), the myth of the cyborg represents not a dream "of a common language, but of a powerful infidel heteroglossia" (181). The cyborg is blasphemous, "resolutely committed to partiality, irony, intimacy, and perversity" (192). Haraway argues for the cyborg as a fiction that maps our bodily and social reality: in the "border war between organism and machine," she argues for "pleasure in the confusion of boundaries and for responsibility in their construction" (150). Conceiving of "nature" as, in her words, coyote or trickster, for her the key question is the challenge of

> historically specific human relations with "nature" [that] must somehow ... be imagined as genuinely social and actively relational; and yet the partners remain utterly inhomogeneous. "Our" relations with "nature" might be imagined as a social engagement with a being who is neither "it", "you", "thou", "he", "she", nor "they" in relation to

> "us". The pronouns embedded in sentences about contestations for what may count as nature are themselves political tools, expressing hopes, fears and contradictory histories. Grammar is politics by other means... (3)

In short, "some differences are playful; some are poles of world historical systems of domination. Epistemology is about knowing the difference" (202–03).

Populated by cyborgs of several kinds, it could be argued that *Oryx and Crake* is at least in some ways consistent with Haraway's vision. From cameos to protagonists, some of whom are emerging from different states and stages of abjection, Atwood's characters all operate, at different moments of their being, on a shifting scale of cyborg identities and cyborg politics ranging from dominant to subaltern spaces in the machine. Haraway could easily be speaking of Atwood's vision when she claims that in cyborg writing's

> fraying of identities and in the reflexive strategies for constructing them, the possibility opens up for weaving something other than a shroud for the day after the apocalypse that so prophetically ends salvation history. (199)

However, Atwood's poetic vision seems considerably more sanguine about the worrisome implications of cybernetics and genetic splicing than is Haraway's theoretical piece, although she would likely agree with her that "we can learn from our fusions with animals and machines how not to be Man, the embodiment of Western logos" (215). To the extent that it is a stand-in for unfettered capitalism, irresponsible applications of science and technology, and misguided human ambition, the metaphor of Borg functions in ways similar to that of the Plague in writers such as Mary Shelley, Albert Camus, and Garcia Marquez. And within the world of the Borg, of course, we are all cyborgs, as we are all infected by the plague and subject to the flood. In short, like women and children, cyborgs are boundary creatures, and as such are "literally *monsters*, a word that shares more than its root with the word, to *demonstrate*. Monsters signify" (2).

III. THE ABOMINABLE SNO/WOMAN

If monsters signify, then let us consider the following of Jimmy's several morphings as Snowman, this time in the eye of the storm, in the chapter entitled "Twister. " If his muddied toga and wounded foot are reminiscent of Philoctetes and Achilles, not to mention Tiresius, and if his broken sunglasses remind us of Oedipus and the Cyclops, in my opinion Atwood's indebtedness to Mary Shelley and Jonathan Swift (not to mention twentieth-century popular culture) revisits feminist theory's understanding of de Beauvoir's woman-as-monster by transforming the aging Jimmy into a parody of a woman. Specifically, when "some previously fried solar circuit must have been refried" (236), he is reborn as a performance of a woman—the transvestite as drag queen, sweaty and grumpy, with Oryx's internalized voice from long ago as the ghost driving his machine. Huddling at the receptionist's desk beneath the former watchtower command post in the RejoovenEssence compound, all bundled up in a fresh bedsheet (now no longer white but floral and scrolled), his legs dangling over the arms of the former receptionist's ergonomic chair in order to protect his tender tootsies from the snats, the Abominable Snowman—who once whimpered, Job-like, to the ghost of Crake, "'Why am I on this earth? How come I'm alone? Where's my Bride of Frankenstein?'" (167)—now is Frankenstein's bride, not to mention Lewis Carroll's Alice and Corporal Klinger from M.A.S.H, all rolled into one. In her flowered sarong, sun-proof khaki shirt, two-eyed sunglasses (finally!), and "authentic replica Boston Red Sox baseball cap" (4)—her atavistic command of enough obscure words to win the mother of obsolete spelling bees still intact—the new Abominable S/no/woman bursts upon the scene and heads for the smoke signals.

Yet when he finally sneaks up on three of his fellow survivors, presumably the Paradice staff previously known as Rhine, Beluga, and White Sedge—two male and one female—who have just finished roasting a rakunk (so much for dreams of "a precious can of imitation Spam, if serendipity strikes" [152]), Jimmy is—except for his baseball cap and his stungun—almost as naked as the day he was born. No longer merging monster and mad scientist, he is not to be confused with Mary Shelley's last man, nor even with that blithely troublesome, postmodern everyman figure, reality TV's would-be survivor. In the end, Snowman's Zero Hour—aside from the blooming condition of his Achilles' heel (whether due more to an excess of bourbon or pigoons is not clear)—is born from the as-yet undetermined possibility of community in the midst of isolation, of talk as two-way communication rather than as issuing from the mouths of stunguns, despite the ongoing contingencies, limitations, and dangers of such talk. For a fleeting moment the reader may be allowed to believe that Jimmy the Snowman is no longer merely a "white illusion of a man" (224), no longer "some caged, wired-up lab animal, trapped into performing futile and perverse experiments on his own brain" (45), no longer merely that familiar, endearing but self-deluded suburban figure, the wordsmith as hired hand, the guy upstairs in the striped pyjamas (233). A newly endangered species once again, Atwood's abominable s/no/w/"man" (only the "o" is missing) reconsiders "his" condition and identity as a wielder of language and maker of symbols.

IV. POLLY WANTS A CRAKER

Questions of gender aside (assuming one can ever set these aside entirely), if human nature is a contagious malady, can it be passed on to the Crakers? Not robots so much as floor models, we are told, they are hardwired for dreaming, singing, and the "capital G" spot, if only because Crake was unable to eliminate those features from the prototype. While Crake petulantly insists that the capacity to ask questions about origins has been edited out, Oryx quietly replies that Crakers do in fact ask those kinds of questions. Fast emerging from abjection, as subaltern creatures, to give voice to a new life of their own, the Children of Crake put the lie to Snowman's remembered or imaginary anthropology handbook, even as they do indeed suggest "a whole new take on *indigenous*" (97). In this sense the cyborg is

> a creature in a postgender world; it has no truck with bisexuality, pre-Oedipal symbiosis, unalienated labor, or other seductions to organic wholeness ... the cyborg has no origin story in the Western sense; a "final" irony since the cyborg is also the awful apocalyptic telos of the West's escalating dominations of abstract individuation, an ultimate self untied at last from all dependency. (Harraway 192)

Snowman tends to think of the Crakers as vulnerable mental midgets and of himself as their reluctant caregiver, partly out of promises made in the memory of Oryx, partly out of a misguided sense of superiority, and partly out of a submerged lust for power. Yet when his variable and paltry weekly fish ration—he wishes he had asked for more—materializes on the Snowman Fish Path, he feels suspiciously like an animal in a zoo.

Atwood's take on Craker sex is playful. At times their hauntingly beautiful chants, a cross between crystals singing and ferns unscrolling—"something old, carboniferous, but at the same time newborn, fragrant, verdant" (104)—seems to echo Haraway's comment that "cyborg 'sex' restores some of the lovely replicative baroque of ferns and invertebrates." At other moments, this romantic vision is undercut by the no-less endearing comic image "of a circle of naked car mechanics, each holding a wrench" like "some campy chorus line from one of the seedier nightclubs" (155). Hinting at the complex, contradictory origins of Craker social structures, such parody points to their indebtedness to their maker. Whether or to what extent the short-lived, childlike Crakers are, like the narrator, able to enjoy irony is an open question: it is hard to tell given their innately polite manners with their betters and their apparent lack of experience in the ways of the world. Abraham Lincoln seems "dubious" but remains dutiful, for instance, when Snowman insists that Crake watches over him in the daytime and Oryx at night. Simone de Beauvoir (who reminds Snowman of Dolores, Jimmy's "long-lost Philippina nanny"), serenely intones that "Crake always watches over us," while Marie Curie repeats that, indeed, "he takes good care of us ... You must tell him that we are grateful" (161).

I would argue that the greatest difference between the Crakers and Snowman, at this early stage of the game, is that he has almost given up on mirrors, whereas they have not quite discovered them yet. According to Atwood in a *Globe and Mail* excerpt from the 2004 Kesterton lecture, "A society without the arts would have broken its mirror and cut out its heart. It would no longer be what we recognize as human" (A19). If Jimmy's mother paid the price, and assuming the jury is still out on the Crakers, it may not be too late for Snowman.

V. ENTER ORYX

However she is perceived, or for that matter invented, by Jimmy, Crake, and the Children of Crake (and in direct contrast to Jimmy's mother), it is Oryx who, in my opinion, most clearly illustrates the mixed inheritance and qualified potential of cyborg identities suggested by Donna Haraway. Snowman reflects upon the instance when he glimpsed Oryx in Paradice as the fatal moment in his life:

> But which fatal moment? *Enter Oryx as a young girl on a kiddie porn site, flowers in her hair, whipped cream on her chin;* or, *Enter Oryx as*

> *a teenage news item, sprung from a pervert's garage;* or *Enter Oryx, stark naked and pedagogical in the Crakers' inner sanctum;* or, *Enter Oryx, towel around her hair, emerging from the shower;* or, *Enter Oryx, in a pewter-grey silk pantsuit and demure half-high heels, carrying a suitcase, the image of a professional Compound globewise saleswoman?* Which of these will it be, and how can he ever be sure there's a line connecting the first to the last? Was there only one Oryx, or was she legion? (307–08).

Let me suggest several other versions of Oryx besides Jimmy's. To begin with, at the receiving end of the male gaze, she reminds me of the headless, corpse-like nude lying in a field in the famous peephole painting "Étant Donné" by Marcel Duchamp. While this does not render her voiceless, within this masculine libidinal economy, the voice, like "the look" that seems forever to "blend innocence and contempt and understanding" (255), is seriously misread by both Jimmy and Crake. They want a talking version of the Duchamp woman as cyborg, a vision not far removed from that which hovers on the edge of Snowman's peripheral field of vision, when he briefly stops to "take stock of himself in the oval mirror," of the post-apocalyptic suburban house that resembles his childhood home: "Behind him in the glass the husk of the woman in the bed seems almost like a real woman; as if at any moment she might turn towards him, open her arms, whisper to him to come and get her" (231).

A related image resurfaces in the airlock corridor, just before Crake slits Oryx's throat: "he had his other arm around Oryx, who seemed asleep; her face was against Crake's chest, her long pink-ribboned braid hung down her back" (328–29). In this version, the slaughter of the sacred cow in the film *Apocalpse Now* is displaced by the ritual sacrifice of the antelope-like Oryx, and it is in this pose that her faceless body, and in particular her antlered/beribonned head, freeze-frames into position as a death mask. (Crake, for his part, seems to parody Peter O'Toole in his crazed, blood lust rampages in *Laurence of Arabia*, complete with homoerotic undertones). In yet another version, when Oryx subsequently resurfaces in Snowman's drug- or drink-induced dreams, he especially welcomes her incarnation as a winged angel or mermaid, typically "floating on her back in a swimming pool, wearing an outfit that appears to be made of delicate white tissue-paper petals. They spread out around her, expanding and contracting like the valves of a jellyfish" (43).

The swimming pool as pastoral setting is telling. A cyborg body, according to Haraway, "is not innocent; it was not born in a garden; it does not seek unitary identity and so generate antagonistic dualisms without end (or until the world ends); it takes irony for granted" (180). And so, even as she plays the game, Oryx will not let Jimmy off the hook, which from his standpoint of course merely makes her that much more intriguing than his previous girlfriends. Unlike them, and unlike him, for instance, she is not taken in by his self-dramatization of the monstrous martyred mother:

> Only Oryx had not been impressed by this dire, feathered mother of his. *So Jimmy, your mother went somewhere else? Too bad. Maybe she had some good reasons. You thought of that?* Oryx had neither pity for him nor self-pity. She was not unfeeling: on the contrary. But she refused to feel what he wanted her to feel. (191)

Neither deity nor demon, in keeping with Haraway's reading of the indigenous woman Malinche, "mother of the mestizo 'bastard' race of the new world, master of languages, and mistress of Cortes" (175), Oryx appears as the doomed harbinger of an outcast race. Like the Craker woman Sacajawea, and like Jimmy's mother, Oryx speaks for and from the margins of power, of the Malinche figure as "transformed from the evil mother of masculinist fear into the originally literate mother who teaches survival" (177). In this sense Oryx is not a victim, nor she who refuses to be a victim, so much as she who deconstructs the early (and no less tongue-in-cheek) binary logic of *Survival*. When Jimmy, contrasting himself to the men who abused her in the past, claims not to do things to her against her will, especially now that she is grown up, she merely laughs, and asks, "What is my will?" (141). And when he refuses to "buy" her apparent lack of buried rage, she asks him, tenderly, "What it is that you would like to buy instead?" (142). Oryx provocatively illustrates Haraway's observation that with

> no available dream of a common language or original symbiosis promising protection from hostile "masculine" separation, but written into the play of a text that has no finally privileged reading or salvation history, to recognize "oneself" as fully implicated in the world frees us of the need to root politics in identification, vanguard parties, purity, and mothering. (176)

In this sense, her fondness for eating Chickienobs, pizza, and soy chips, and for eating them with her fingers, might raise a few eyebrows, but it effectively distinguishes her from the more consistent and single-minded Gardeners for God who set free the hapless Chickienob creature. Their open activism and her surface passivity each in its own way possesses its merits as well as its pitfalls.

The book of Oryx is, for all that, a cautionary tale. For me, it is more reminiscent of the poems in *True Stories* than of those in *Morning in the Burned House*. If Oryx serves to remind the reader that women, like cyborgs, are not born but made, the quintessential cyborgs in Haraway's model are the Third World female factory workers—and who knows what really goes on in the pleeblands? Certainly not Jimmy and Crake. The pleebland women have even less control than Jimmy's mother over either the system or the conditions and perceived worth of their labour, although one assumes that, like Oryx, they have mastered the skills for surviving, if not for subversion. According to Haraway, "Contrary to orientalist stereotypes of the 'oral primitive,' literacy is a special mark of women of colour" as cyborg (174). Given a chance, Oryx presumably bears at least the potential to lead the Children of Crake out of the compound—but, like Jimmy's mother, she dies before we can find out if this would have come about. Even at that, Atwood's dark vision is as ambiguously open-ended as ever. Haraway reminds us that

> the home, work place, market, public arena, the body itself—all can be dispersed and interfaced in nearly infinite, polymorphous ways [that have] large consequences for women and others—consequences that themselves are very different for different people and which make potent oppositional international movements both difficult to imagine and essential for survival. (163)

Jimmy, who helped invent Oryx, must now, like the Crakers, make do without her. In his voyeuristic gaze she is displaced, in Atwood's closing scene, by the scarecrow effigy of a woman roasting a rakunk: "thin, battered, ... tea-coloured ... in the remains of a uniform of some kind—nurse, guard? Must have been pretty once, before she lost all that weight; now she's stringy, her hair parched, broomstraw" (373). In relation to her and her companions, Jimmy notes that "he has nothing to trade with them, nor they with him. Nothing except themselves" (373).

VI. CYBORG ART

A consideration of the question of Craker art lies beyond the scope of this brief paper. But if irony is one kind of mirror on the path to the social and other arts, I would hold out qualified hope for the Crakers no less than for Jimmy/Snowman. In Haraway's reading, cyborg identities are "not about the Fall, the imagination of a once-upon-a-time wholeness before language"; rather, cyborg writing is "about the power to survive not on the basis of original innocence, but on the basis of seizing the tools to mark the world that marked them as other" (217). If the jury is still out about Craker art (except for their beautiful singing, which is also healing), there are several clear instances of cyborg art (including examples of art for art's sake) in the novel.

Jimmy's relationship to words would be worth an essay in itself; here, I restrict myself to a few comments on the uses that the novel makes of visual rather than verbal language as encoding cyborg art, which is most prominent (outside the compounds) in educational institutional contexts. The ways in which this art is gendered should come as no surprise, starting with the contrast between Martha Graham and Watson Crick universities and the sculptures that adorn their gates. It should be noted that in a world in which there is little room for art beyond disguises for air purification systems, cyborg art, necessarily marginal and oppositional, is both part of the Borg and about it. The cyborg artist and her art also can not escape commodification.

Briefly, the novel offers two cameo portraits of cyborg art, both taking the form of performance art. One is the website "At Home with Anna K" (84), where the performance artist reads all the parts from *Macbeth* out loud while sitting on the toilet of her completely and permanently wired living quarters. (One assumes that Anna got good grades in "Advanced Mischaracterization" at Martha Graham U; the appeal of her work is its post-punk espousal of art-for-art's sake, all irony and all citation). The other is the mixed media, multi-dimensional, randomly interactive, dead/live animal installation art of Amanda, one of Jimmy's old girl-friends, a "Pictorial and Plastic Arts" product of the pleeblands and fellow Problematics major. Her "Vulture Sculptures" (244) organize truckloads of dead animals into the shape of four-letter words, with the ensuing turkey vulture feeding frenzy photographed by helicopter. You will recall that when she briefly and very tentatively breaks out of her writer's block to attempt the word "love," Jimmy decides that it is time for a new girlfriend. Like Anna K, Amanda is not very far removed from contemporary definitions of life, art, and politics in the world outside Atwood's novel.

Embedded in Jimmy's memory banks and—one would like to think—in some of his future storytelling, these artist figures are playful stand-ins for and commentaries on Atwood's own art. Unlike *The Handmaid's Tale*, however, which offers in lieu of a conclusion a future conference recontextualizing and reappropriating the handmaid's fragmentary voice, *Oryx and Crake* does not give us a postscript and framing device that would allow for Oryx's voice to emerge, however partially, in a future proto-feminist commentary on Jimmy's fragmentary text. The signature ambiguity of Atwood's open ending in *The Handmaid's Tale* is compounded in the multi-layered text that is *Oryx and Crake*. As in all her work, Atwood's metafictional commentary on and example of cyborg writing offers the reader—within carefully crafted limits—the freedom and pleasure of reaching her own partial conclusions.

—Trent University

WORKS CITED

Atwood, Margaret. "The Art of the Matter." *Globe and Mail* (Toronto), January 24, 2004. A19.

———. *Oryx and Crake*. Toronto: McClelland & Stewart, 2003.

Haraway, Donna J. *Simians, Cyborgs, and Women: The Reinvention of Nature*. New York: Routledge, 1991.

Lacombe, Michèle. "The Writing on the Wall: Amputated Speech in Margaret Atwood's *The Handmaid's Tale*." *Wascana Review* 21, no. 12 (1986): 3–23.

Oryx and Crake: Atwood's Ironic Inversion of *Frankenstein*

HILDE STAELS

SINCE THE 1970s, we have lived in a world in which biotechnology is in the service of corporate profit. In the United States, western Europe, and Japan, techniques of genetic engineering have been developed that cross the line between nature and artifice. In her widely acclaimed novel *Oryx and Crake*, Margaret Atwood depicts a futuristic world in which the total rule of technoscience involves the radical exclusion of Nature—capitalized in the novel because Mother Earth's creative, organic processes are distinguished from manufactured nature. In this world, creations like Frankenstein's monster, a manufactured (human) nature, become the norm rather than the exception.

When commenting on the genre to which *Oryx and Crake* belongs, Atwood does not wish to categorize her novel as science fiction but, rather, as speculative fiction. Though she agrees that the novel contains dystopian elements, she would not define it as a classic dystopia like *The Handmaid's Tale*. In her view it is rather "an adventure romance—that is, the hero goes on a quest—coupled with a Menippean satire, the literary form that deals in intellectual obsession" ("*The Handmaid's Tale*" 517).

Atwood's satire warns against the techno-scientific preoccupation with the abolition of all human imperfection. She explores what it means to be human in a highly technocratic society that tries to exclude what it perceives as chaos in favour of total order and control. For a description of this society's politics of radical expulsion and its effects on the protagonist, I rely on Julia Kristeva's influential study *Pouvoirs de l'horreur: Essai sur l'abjection*. Subsequently, I shall try to demonstrate that *Oryx and Crake* not only alludes to Mary Shelley's *The Last Man* but also mainly parodies or ironically inverts her gothic novel *Frankenstein*. I rely on Linda Hutcheon's definition of parody as imitation characterized by ironic inversion or repetition with critical difference (*A Theory of Parody* 6). Atwood's parodic technique and her treatment of "monstrousness" requires a close investigation of her method of characterization, that is, the main character's discourse, world view, and behaviour, and especially his repetitive, symptomatic behaviour and language. Specific attention will be given to the textual foregrounding of unconscious processes, such as the untameable and non-rational human desires and anxieties in the relationship of the protagonist toward his natural mother, his repressed Other, and Nature.

I. THE RADICAL EXCLUSION OF "CHAOS"

Atwood presents two futuristic worlds of the twenty-first century: the novel is set in an apocalyptic world during the second decade of the twenty-first century and provides flashbacks of a past technological wasteland. The protagonist Jimmy, alias Snowman, lives in this present apocalyptic world as one of the last men who survived a worldwide plague caused by a viral-biological attack. Mary Shelley's *The Last Man* (1826), the first futurist catastrophe novel that tried to forecast what the end of the twenty-first century might be, may very well be another intertext, for Shelley's novel is in Rosemary Jackson's terms

> a remarkable fantasy of cultural annihilation ... it tells of a global plague which spreads gradually across the world. Its panorama of decay presents a complete erasure of the human species. Only Verney, the last man ... remains to tell the tale of order lapsing into undifferentiation and decay. (103)

The text is a third-person, anonymous omniscient narrative. Jimmy is the central focalizer reflecting on the present, yet mainly journeying through the past. Particularly useful for a proper understanding of Jimmy's conscious and unconscious mental processes is Julia Kristeva's notion of abjection. In *Pouvoirs de l'horreur* she defines the abject as that which evokes horror, disgust, or revulsion, such as excrement, decay, infection, disease, corpses—everything that reminds us of our mortality, animality, and corporeality. Kristeva places the abject on the side of the maternal body or in the space of the pre-Oedipal mother. The latter becomes abject when the child enters into "the symbolic order" and starts obeying the law of the father. The abject is the radically excluded object, because it threatens the social system, the existing order, and one's identity. It is the place where "I" am not, or the space of the non-ego and of drive energy. While the abject evokes fear, we also identify with it because, according to Kristeva, it forms a repressed part of the self. However much we try to expel the abject, it defies boundaries and resists the unitary subject: it is the in-between, the ambiguous, the composite. Maud Ellman explains the term as follows:

> The word abject literally means cast out, though commonly it means downcast in spirits: but abjection may refer to waste itself as well as to the act of throwing it away. It is the ambiguity of the abject that distinguishes it from the object, which the subject rigorously jettisons (ob-jects). The abject emerges when exclusions fail, in the sickening collapse of limits. (181)

The protagonist of *Oryx and Crake* is the product of a past technological society that expels "chaos," associated with organic natural processes, to "the other side" (27). This past society is characterized by a topographical dichotomy between the "civilized" compounds of genetic engineers and the "savage," contaminating pleeblands (plebeian lands). The rational, Apollonian world of the engineers creates a border, which deposits the abject on the other side, to separate the self from that which threatens the self. The dualistic geographical space coincides with the division between social purity and social hybridization as well as with the polarity between thoughts, intellect versus emotions, and drives. To the scientific rationalists living in the compounds, the pleeblands represent the lower class of the Freudian id—the part of the personality that contains our primitive appetites and impulses, the plebs of the psyche, as opposed to the ego, that is, intelligence and reason. The scientists demonize the unknown pleeblands on the other side of the dividing line as a dangerous space of chaos, violence, disruption, and uncertainty. Within this dualistic logic, the other side is an object of disgust, perceived as a threat to social order and a stable identity, as evil, barbaric, and vulgar; yet, it is at the same time a source of attraction and furtive desire.

To Jimmy, who remembers himself as an ordinary boy with average intellectual capacities, the pleeblands were a source of longing and fascination:

> There, it was rumoured, the kids ran in packs, in hordes. They'd wait until some parent was away, then get right down to business—they'd swarm the place, waste themselves with loud music and toking and boozing, fuck everything, including the family cat, trash the furniture, shoot up, overdose. Glamorous, thought Jimmy. But in the Compounds the lid was screwed down tight. (73)

As a child, Jimmy longed for visiting the pleeblands as much as for going to the sea, yet the latter is also abject, because "boundless" chaotic Nature (196) is associated with the primal mother.

Crake used to be Glenn, one of Jimmy's friends at a private high school for future scientific geniuses. Crake is Glenn's computer code name, after the Australian Red-necked Crake, an almost extinct Australian bird. Jimmy adopted the code name Snowman, after the legendary Himalayan apeman also called the Yeti. Jimmy now lives in a nightmarish space caused by Crake's plague, where Nature is almost extinct, replaced by instrumentalized nature, by transgenic animals such as wolvogs (wolf dogs) and snats (snake rats) that are a threat to what may be the last man on earth. He keeps company with the innocent Children of Crake, who incarnate Crake's ideal:

> [T]here's no more unrequited love these days, no more thwarted lust; no more shadow between the desire and the act. ... No more prostitution, no sexual abuse of children, no haggling over the price, no pimps, no sex slaves. No more rape. (165)

In other words, in his attempt to perfect the world, to "improve" the human condition and to establish an ideal new order, Crake has "cleared away the dirt" (103), thus eliminating abject bodily processes.

II. ATWOOD'S IRONIC INVERSION OF MARY SHELLEY'S *FRANKENSTEIN*

Crake is an operator in genetic experimentation, who uses the abject for his own profit by killing in the name of a new, perfectly controlled life. Whereas the scientists do not allow transgressive energies in "civilized" human beings, transgressive border crossing is the rule in genetic engineering. A Faustian overreacher, Crake creates cloned transgenic human-animal hybrids who emerge from a technological womb and who lack an unpredictable inner life, an unconscious mind, or shadow self. As head of the Paradice compound, a biotechnological genetics laboratory, he displaces God and Nature by creating these artificial children. Thus, he usurps both divine power and female, procreative power. Crake's children are pristine surrogate human beings—humans without subjectivity—who have no mother and cannot therefore experience the (original) loss of the mother. In his children, Crake expels the human feelings, desires, and bodily drives that he wishes to extinguish in himself, and which he sees grotesquely reflected in Jimmy, his repressed dark shadow.

Scientific overreaching and man's alienation from Nature remind us of Mary Shelley's novel *Frankenstein, or the Modern Prometheus*, which is indeed a central intertext in *Oryx and Crake*; especially the desire for the loved, lost mother links both novels. A significant detail supporting this idea is the epigraph to Atwood's novel, which is an extract from Virginia Woolf's *To the Lighthouse:*[1] "Was there no safety? No learning by heart of the ways of the world? No guide, no shelter, but all was miracle and leaping from the pinnacle of a tower into the air?" In this passage, Lilie Briscoe is looking out to sea and grieving the loss of Mrs. Ramsay, the archetypal mother. In Mary Shelley's novel, Victor Frankenstein's mother dies before his departure for the University of Ingolstadt. Victor, who cannot accept his mother's death, wants to bring her body back to life. He also merges with his dead mother by creating a fake nature, thus becoming a mother himself.

Like Victor and his monster, who deplores that "no mother had blessed [him] with smiles and caresses" (117), Crake and Jimmy are solitary individuals who desire happiness, maternal love, and affection. Crake, however, tries to conform to the masculine, technocratic world of the compounds, and completely seals off his inner life. He expels the maternal body, which reminds him of his own mortality and corporeality, to the other side. Thus, he witnesses the horrifying death, the slow decay of his mother's body, yet refuses to be overwhelmed by irrational "unmanly" emotions. Jimmy, by contrast, who functions as his dark double, cannot control his emotions. Throughout the narrative text, his desire for his lost mother is a visible source of obsession and a furtive object of study for Crake, who "jestingly" says to Jimmy: "I like to watch you suffer" (174).

The absence of Jimmy's mother during early childhood caused Jimmy's unspeakable sadness. Depressed, dissatisfied with what she judged to be her husband's unethical bioengineering experiments, and disappointed with her child, Jimmy's mother left the house when he was eight years old, choosing to live in exile on the other side, where she was eventually killed as a subversive by the secret police, the CorpSeCorps. Jimmy cannot overcome the trauma of emotional and physical deprivation. As a result, he struggles with a repetitive sense of failure and guilt, sorrow and pain, and with a sentimental longing for an imaginary happy mother who loves him unconditionally. Jimmy cherishes the word "home," an archaic concept in Crake's apocalyptic world, yet a human being's deepest object of desire. Now, Jimmy's home is a tree near the ocean on the East Coast of the United States. The ocean is the closest he can get to the archaic mother; it fills him with a death wish, a subconscious desire to return to the oceanic primordial state inside the womb, in which the self disintegrates.

Atwood does not simply create a contemporary version of *Frankenstein* but, rather, a parody, an ironic inversion of Mary Shelley's novel. In *Oryx and Crake* the unhappy, alienated monster is the protagonist, rather than Crake's manufactured children. In Atwood's novel, a "monstrous" human being replaces the human monster as a victim of society. The thoughts, feelings, and emotions that give Frankenstein's physically deformed creature an aspect of humanity, become traces of monstrosity in Atwood's protagonist. In both novels, monstrousness or deviance is associated with the idea of betweenness. Like Atwood, Judith Halberstam views the monstrous as the hybrid or the mixed. With regard to Mary Shelley's monstrous creature, Halberstam says:

> But in *Frankenstein* the complexity of the monster—it walks, it talks, it demands, it pursues, it rationalizes and shows emotion—confuses the politics of purity in which every dirty thing is marked and will pollute if not eliminated. The monster mixes humanity with physical deformity, a desire for community with an irreducible foreignness, great physical strength with femininity. (44)

Similarly, Jimmy is monstrous because he belongs simultaneously to, and is torn between, two incompatible realms of experience.

As soon as Jimmy's mother flees to the pleeblands, the other side becomes a source of phobic fascination for the boy; he becomes obsessed with the absent, forbidden (m)Other. His patterns of behaviour and speech are symptomatic of unconscious affects, emerging from what Julia Kristeva calls a "semiotic" space (*From One Identity to An Other* 133). Kristeva associates the semiotic with the maternal body (the *chora* or womb) and the transverbal language of the unconscious mind. The semiotic is abject in a totalitarian technocratic society because it is a site of transgression, containing the potential expression of repressed instinctual drives. Technocratic society perceives the semiotic as a threat to a fixed identity and to the paternal, rule-governed social order, because it is the cause of disruption and renewal. In Atwood's characterization of the protagonist, textual traces of unconscious, transgressive semiotic activity can be found in rhythmic and repetitive symptomatic language and compulsive behaviour, in articulations of Jimmy's instinctual drives and unconscious affects, such as anxiety, pain, sorrow, and rage, as well as pleasure and rapture.

The abject, which hides within Jimmy, does not respect socially imposed limits, and thus engulfs him. From adolescence onward, he turns into a multiple addict: smoking weed and drinking alcohol to dull the emotional pain, satisfying his sexual drives in brief relationships with unhappy girls by whom he is both attracted and repulsed, furtively and compulsively watching "disgusting" porno Internet sites (85). Jimmy's intoxications are symptomatic of his suffering, whereby Dionysian irrationalism—his primitive instincts and drives—overwhelms him. In Crake's apocalyptic world, he is like the monster of Frankenstein, an alien impure creature among "perfect," homogeneous hormone robots who "make him feel deformed" (42), and who have "accepted Snowman's monstrousness" (101). He is the sole remnant of what was once a human being with natural and normal human feelings and desires, yet he is afraid that to the children "[h]e's humanoid, he's hominid, he's an aberration, he's abominable" (307). He feels guilty about the concealed squalor of affect inside his body that uncontrollably erupts and breaks the barrier of repression. He perceives himself as "a creature of dimness" (6), whose primitive instincts and excess of emotions become visible to others.

During adolescence, Jimmy transgresses borders by profaning his parents in a malicious comic play, and is an expert at "fake vomiting and choking to death" (54). By playing with his corporeal limits, he displays his "monstrousness." Like his father, who admits to being "a monster" (20) when making jokes, the protagonist compulsively makes tendentious jokes. Underlying his hostile and obscene jokes, which are meant to produce pleasure in the listener, are repressed aggressive impulses and a sense of (sexual) dissatisfaction. According to Sigmund Freud tendentious jokes circumvent outright aggressiveness (*Jokes and Their Relationship to the Unconscious* 185). Crake does away with jokes in the mind of his children, because as he says: "For jokes you need a certain edge, a little malice" (*OC* 306).

Jimmy's speech teems with curses such as "shit," "fuck," "asshole," and obscene terms such as "*Saggy boobs ... Bunfaced tofubrain ... Bladderheaded jerk*" (249). His abuses, curses, profanities, and improprieties are symptomatic of a destructive force inside him, an archaic rage that results from feelings of unhappiness and isolation.[2] He resembles the monster of Frankenstein, who is only malicious, capable of an uncontrollable "fiendish rage," because he is miserable (141). The fact that Jimmy is Crake's uncanny alter ego is especially visible at the unexpected outbreak of the plague, when Crake loses control, becomes violent, and exposes his knowledge of Jimmy's secret desires: "'Every time you went to the pleebs to wallow in the mud and drown your lovesick sorrows.'" "'How did you know?' said Jimmy. 'How did you know where I, what I wanted?'" (328).

Atwood's method of characterization portrays Jimmy as a tragi-comic, unchanging protagonist. Even though he is in his late twenties at the moment of narration, Jimmy is a perpetual adolescent, trapped in an unresolved love-hate relationship with his mother. This love-hatred is an archaic drive that reminds us of Joan Foster in Atwood's *Lady Oracle* who is similarly haunted by a trauma suffered in the past, and trapped in a circle of accusation against her unhappy and unloving mother. Self-debunking in both characters is symptomatic of their negative self-image. Like Joan Foster, who repetitively judges her actions as "ridiculous," "ludicrous," and "stupid," and who compares her "monstrous" body to that of freaks and figures of fun such as Dumbo, the flying elephant, Jimmy says about himself: "Here's Snowman, thick as a brick, dunderhead, frivol, and dupe ... He's a failure" (335).

Jimmy retrospectively wonders whether his insufficiency as a child was the true cause of his mother's unhappiness and departure. He repetitively perceives himself as a "bad boy" and a failure in his mother's eyes: "He felt he'd disappointed [his mother], he'd failed her in some crucial way" (68). Yet in the fossilized childhood story that entraps him, he also perceives his mother as alienated from Nature, interpreting her unexpected departure as an act unnatural for a true mother. Thus, he wonders, "Wasn't there supposed to be a maternal bond?" (61). Similarly, Victor Frankenstein rejects his creation and flees from the abhorrent monster who feels "spurned" and "abandoned" by his creator (213).

III. JIMMY'S AFFECT-DRIVEN RELATIONSHIP TOWARD HIS MOTHER, HIS REPRESSED OTHER, AND NATURE

As a result of his upbringing in the absolutely safe compounds, which involved a limited exposure to the "chaos" on the other side, the protagonist is trapped in a fantasy, believing that unambiguous feelings such as true love or true happiness can be achieved in real life, and that such feelings can be provided by an ideal mother. Thus, his wounded, sentimental self proves to be in search of pure, uncontaminated feelings and singularity of meaning. In this way, he is also the Doppelgänger of Crake, whose ideal of absolute perfection and stability, which is the opposite of the "monstrous" abject, appears to be achieved in his children.

Jimmy's dreams in the present and the past reveal the conflictual relationship with his mother, and his unfulfilled desires. He repetitively dreams about Alex the parrot, who gets "fed up" and leaves home, saying: "I'm going away now," which displaces the sudden loss of his mother, the traumatic childhood event that underlies his isolation and misery:

> No, he never dreams about his mother, only about her absence. He's in the kitchen. Whuff, goes the wind in his ear, a door closing... How much he'd hated her at that moment. He could hardly breathe, he'd been suffocating with hatred, tears of hatred had been rolling down his cheeks. But he'd hugged his arms around himself all the same. Her arms. (277)

Such wish dreams about the child's desire to be truly loved by its mother are juxtaposed with Jimmy's repetitive anxiety (day)dreams about female demons and mermaids toward whom he has ambiguous feelings of attraction and repulsion: "Creatures with heads and breasts of women and the talons of eagles will swoop down on him, and he'll open his arms to them, and that will be the end. Brainfrizz" (11). In Atwood's novel *Alias Grace*, the psychoanalyst Simon Jordan suffers from similar fantasies. His perversions result from having an overprotective, possessive mother. Underlying both characters' anxiety dreams is an archaic fear and desire of fusion with the primordial mother, the archetypal Great Goddess in the image of the terrible mother who inhibits their independence. In both novels, Atwood inscribes the Great Mother archetype, who splits into two opposing images of the good and the terrible mother. The good mother is the healer and protector, a benevolent and redeeming figure, embodied by the adult Oryx in *Oryx and Crake*.

At age fourteen, Jimmy becomes lovesick for and haunted by Oryx, who lives on the other side, a seven- or eight-year-old cyberspace porno child of Asian origin. The code name refers to the almost-extinct East African herbivore Oryx Beisa. Jimmy narcissistically projects onto Oryx his dark secret feelings and unconscious desires. He imagines they share an inner essence, that of the unhappy child who at age seven or eight was abandoned by its mother, and is therefore homeless and emotionally deprived:

> Any moment now she would open herself up, reveal to him the essential thing, the hidden thing at the core of life, or of her life, or of his life—the thing he was longing for—the thing he was longing to know. The thing he'd always wanted. What would it be? ... she was in him, or part of her was in part of him. (314–315)

When Jimmy finally meets the real adult Oryx, who crossed the border to the Paradice compound, he wants her to share his negative energy, his rage, pain, and grief. He desperately desires to be truly loved and to be made happy by Oryx. Yet she refuses to be fixed in time by Jimmy and to coincide with the fantasy object he has made her into. She repeatedly questions the fantasy story he has created about her by confronting him with multiple, contradictory "truths" about herself and her childhood. Jimmy remembers her unbearable evasiveness and retrospectively wonders whether it was possible to ever know the real Oryx: "But she's always been evasive, you can never pin her down" (110); "There must once have been other versions of her" (114).

In contrast to Jimmy, who has always been artificially separated from life on the other side, Oryx has always lived amidst "chaos" and otherness. Atwood juxtaposes Jimmy with Oryx, whereby the former is associated with darkness, (self-)destruction, ignorance, and mental stasis, while the latter is a protean character, associated with knowledge and wisdom, light and positive energy. Performing the function of Jimmy's repressed Other, Oryx tries to heal his wounded self by appealing to the light side of his soul. She counters his dominant and negative self-image by speaking to him tenderly: "You're doing really well" (238); "Oh Jimmy, this is so positive … You have a Paradice within you, happier far" (308); "You're a good boy" (321), for Jimmy represents the Jungian archetype of the *puer aeternus*, the eternal boy. Yet Jimmy is afraid of a risky, unpredictable regeneration of his inner self. The product of a society that demonizes "chaos," he keeps excluding and fails to explore the unknown part of him hidden inside the unconscious mind, which may be a source of light, wisdom, transformation, or a new start in life. When Crake finally kills his beloved Oryx, Jimmy murders him in a fit of archaic rage, thus acting once more like Frankenstein's monster, who took revenge on his creator after being denied the solace of a female companion.

The almost exact mirroring of the beginning and end of the novel hints at the mythical "hero's" cyclical journey back "home," his tree near the shore, after a spiritual journey into the past:

> Snowman wakes before dawn. He lies unmoving, listening to the tide coming in, wave after wave sloshing over the various barricades, wish-wash, the rhythm of heartbeat. He would so like to believe he is still asleep.
>
> On the eastern horizon there's a greyish haze, lit now with a rozy, deadly glow. Strange how that colour still seems tender. (3)
> …
>
> Snowman wakes before dawn. He lies unmoving, listening to the tide coming in, wish-wash, the rhythm of heartbeat. He would so like to believe he is still asleep.

> On the eastern horizon there's a greyish haze, lit now with a rozy, deadly glow. Strange how that colour still seems tender. He gazes at it with rapture; there's no other word for it. *Rapture.* (371)

In Crake's apocalyptic wasteland, Jimmy is struck by the fact that he is capable of feeling tenderness toward his new home, the remnants of Mother Earth: the rhythm of waves, the sounds of rustling leaves and shrieking birds, the colours of Nature. The few remainders of Nature's beauty appeal to his primitive instincts and make him feel at home in the world. Frankenstein's monster, who feels miserable in the human world, similarly derives consolation from nature, for he says: "My spirits were elevated by the enchanting appearance of nature. ... My senses were gratified and refreshed by a thousand scents of delight and a thousand sights of beauty" (Shelley 112–13). Jimmy's sense of rapture, a supposedly obsolete, ecstatic feeling, temporarily counters his unspeakable suffering. The "inexplicable surge of tenderness and joy" (41) he sometimes feels as a disinterested observer of Nature's beauty resembles his sentimentalizing since adolescence over extinct words. He compares these lost, useless words to abandoned children like himself, aching for love: "*wheelwright, lodestone, saturnine, adamant.* He's developed a strangely tender feeling toward such words, as if they were children abandoned in the woods and it was his duty to rescue them" (195). Savouring the musicality, the pure materiality of these beautiful words similarly causes a release of unconscious affects, for it provides an aesthetic pleasure and a consolation that temporarily fills an emotional void. Beauty is indeed the other world of the depressed, when melancholia resulting from a traumatic experience of loss is temporarily overcome.

At the end of the novel, Jimmy is lethally wounded after having stepped with his bare foot on a piece of broken glass. Like the speaker in T.S. Eliot's poem *The Waste Land* (1922), which appears to be one out of many other intertexts, Jimmy is impotent in the sense of being spiritually and emotionally in need of healing. However, as there is no sign of a spiritual death-rebirth or salvation, the novel ends in darkness and on a note of uncertainty. To Jimmy there are still many questions to which there are no final answers, such as whether his mother really loved him. The novel, after all, closes with his memory of her unbearably ambiguous last words to him: "*I love you. Don't let me down."* This memory triggers off an instinctual death drive, a longing for a desireless stable state, suggested by Jimmy's final words: "Time to go" (374). The womb image in the final chapter shifts from connoting a desire for absolute safety and regression into a pre-Oedipal relationship with the primordial mother to a death wish. His death drive converges with that of Frankenstein's monster who, before being "borne away by the waves" at the end of Mary Shelley's novel, says to Walton, "'I shall die. I shall no longer feel the agonies which now consume me, or be the prey of feelings unsatisfied, yet unquenched'" (214).

CONCLUSION

The analysis leads to the conclusion that Atwood's concern, in the portrayal of her tragi-comic character, is with the human, which becomes "monstrous" when the language of the body and the life of the soul (desires and affects) are relegated to a forbidden, banished realm of chaos. Traces in the text of the central character's "monstrousness"—his vulgar speech, his uncontrollable bodily drives and intoxications—mark his imperfection and therefore, ironically, his humanity. In her parody of Mary Shelley's novel *Frankenstein*, Margaret Atwood seems to side with a human condition that celebrates unfixed identity, and a desiring-becoming subject, because in order to be fully human, a balance between order and chaos, between conscious and unconscious processes, and a mediation between reason and affect, is required.

—University of Leuven

NOTES

1. The other epigraph is an extract from Swift's *Gulliver's Travels*. Concerning this novel, Rosi Braidotti makes a remark that throws an interesting light on Margaret Atwood's menippean satire. According to Braidotti, *Gulliver's Travels* deals with "the horror of the female body" and as a genre "the satirical text is implicitly monstrous, it is a deviant, an aberration in itself" (79–80).
2. To Julia Kristeva in "From One Identity to An Other," obscene words in Louis-Ferdinand Céline's novels have "a *desemanticization* function analogous to the fragmentation of syntax by rhythm. Far from referring, as do all signs, to an object exterior to discourse and identifiable as such by consciousness, the obscene word is the minimal mark of a situation of desire where the identity of

the signifying subject, if not destroyed, is exceeded by a conflict of instinctual drives linking one subject to another" (142).

WORKS CITED

Atwood, Margaret. "*The Handmaid's Tale* and *Oryx and Crake* in Context." *PMLA* 119, no. 3 (2004): 513–17.

———. *Oryx and Crake*. New York: Doubleday, 2003.

Braidotti, Rosi. *Nomadic Subjects: Embodiment and Sexual Difference in Contemporary Feminist Theory*. New York: Columbia University Press, 1994.

Ellman, Maud. "Eliot's Abjection." In *Abjection, Melancholia and Love: The Works of Julia Kristeva*, edited by John Fletcher and Andrew Benjamin. London: Routledge, 1990. 178–200.

Freud, Sigmund. *Jokes and Their Relation to the Unconscious*. Translated by James Strachey. New York: Pelican Books, 1981.

Halberstam, Judith. *Skin Shows: Gothic Horror and the Technology of Monsters*. Durham: Duke University Press, 1995.

Hutcheon, Linda. *A Theory of Parody*. London: Methuen, 1985.

Jackson, Rosemary. *Fantasy: The Literature of Subversion*. London: Methuen, 1981.

Kristeva, Julia. *Pouvoirs de l'horreur: Essai sur l'abjection*. Paris: Seuil, 1980.

———. "From One Identity to An Other." In *Desire in Language: A Semiotic Approach to Literature and Art by Julia Kristeva*, edited by Leon S. Roudiez. New York: Columbia University Press, 1980. 121–47.

Shelley, Mary. *Frankenstein, or the Modern Prometheus*. 1818. Edited by Maurice Hindle. London: Penguin, 1992.

Atwood's Global Ethic: The Open Eye, The Blinded Eye

DIANA BRYDON

TAKING MY LEAD from Atwood's commentary, I have shaped this paper around the themes of "negotiating with the dead" and the dangers of the one-eyed imagination. In what sense is the open eye also the blinded eye and what is the relationship between blindness and vision? Reading *Oryx and Crake*, I kept thinking of that old saying, "In the world of the blind the one-eyed man is king." Both Crake and Jimmy/Snowman are one-eyed men; Crake cedes his empire to Snowman after he has destroyed one world and set another in motion. *Oryx and Crake* attacks the one-eyed imagination to imply that the world is in need of a global ethic, one that can align discourses of human rights with those of responsibilities, and human endeavours in the sciences with those in the arts. There are many ways one might describe the singular perspective that defines the lens through which Crake and Snowman view their world, symbolized by the one missing lens in Snowman's sunglasses (4). At its simplest, each sees through a mindset frozen in adolescence, through the dynamic of his relation to his father. Crake, it seems, is more alert to how power functions in his world, whereas Jimmy, Snowman's first incarnation, chooses to blind himself to this. But Snowman also believes that he can see things Crake could not. These choices reflect a broader reality: the relative value assigned to science and art in their society. Through the story of Crake and Jimmy, this novel deplores the separation of Science and Art that widened during the course of the twentieth century (C.P. Snow's "two cultures"), eventually producing the world of walled enclaves of knowledge that predominates today, and that Atwood extrapolates into an apartheid future, where the separation of art and science, rich and poor is further institutionalized and where science is reduced to technology, art to advertising.

As I worked on this paper, Canada's social science and humanities academic communities debated our research council's proposal to rename our collective work the "human sciences." Just like Jimmy, most of my colleagues deplore the narrowing of the imagination that the word "science" currently implies, yet doubt the capacity of the adjective "human" to broaden its scope (as SSHRC initially proposed through its replacement of the humanities and social sciences by the literal translation of the French term *"les sciences humaines"* into "human sciences"). By mid-2004, this proposal was withdrawn. Yet the *"dysphoria"* of the critique that led to the defeat of this proposal reflects a crisis of imagination that arises as the eighteenth-century notion of the human, which has sustained thinking for the last two centuries, comes under increasing pressure on at least two fronts: advances in genetics and transplant technologies are problematizing the drawing of the line separating human from animal, and advances in technology have blurred the line separating human from machine.

Both render traditional jurisdictions for the arts suspect. Joseph Epstein attacks Alice W. Flaherty's belief that "[s]cience ... is the mouthpiece of determinism, and literature the last holdout of free will" (40). I share this critique, but note the popularity of this view: there is a general sense, in society at large and in *Oryx and Crake* in particular, that this last holdout of free will, literature, and the forms of literacy that it inspires is eroding fast, replaced by forms of television, Internet, and performance programming where there may be little room for free will or anything else that once anchored definitions of the human since the Enlightenment.

In the world that Atwood depicts, what passes for the arts does not humanize, yet the idea of art remains the locus of the text's hope. This is the paradox I see at the heart of the novel. It records the passing of a way of life that took its sustenance and its direction from literature, but the only solace that it can offer is a return to the literary values of the past. In making this case, the novel is very much in tune with the arguments put forward by Helen Vendler in her 2004 National Endowment for the Humanities

Jefferson Lecture, "The Ocean, the Bird, and the Scholar," and with Edward Said's posthumously published Columbia lectures on American culture, *Humanism and Democratic Criticism*. Yet Vendler and Said, in tune perhaps with the genre of the public lecture, are more sanguine about the possibility of restoring literature and humanist study to the breadth of their past values.

In *Oryx and Crake*, dystopia is the genre and *dysphoria* sets the tone. I borrow the term "*dysphoria*" from Hans Ulrich Gumbrecht's use of it to define the current crisis of faith in literary studies, in his article entitled "*Dysphoria*: How (Some) Literary Scholars Feel about Literary Studies." As he describes it, the scholars invited to contribute to a special issue of the *Canadian Review of Comparative Literature* on "The Future of Literary Studies" differ considerably in the substance of their responses yet "uncannily" share a tone that exemplifies "simultaneity between bad humour and a seeming disinterest in constructive alternatives" (14). That is not a bad description of Jimmy/Snowman, who is the reader's guide into the apparently near-future world of *Oryx and Crake*.

The names "Oryx" and "Crake" signal the crisis of disappearing species brought about by humanity's increasing domination of the globe. In taking on the names of birds and animals, Atwood's characters imply their dawning realization that the human also, as the human and as the generator of and audience for the humanities, is bound to the fate of these other creatures and may well also be on the road to extinction. This interpretation shows the connections between what might otherwise seem very disparate links to non-governmental organizations on the official Oryx and Crake website: to People for the Ethical Treatment of Animals and to various human rights organizations, like the Medical Foundation for the Care of Victims of Torture. From the perspective of globalization studies, these constitute an idiosyncratically selective mix. Absent from such links are any of the thousands of NGOs devoted to global governance questions or democratic reform. Such groups are almost entirely excluded from the world of *Oryx and Crake*, in which the only oppositional collective seems to be "God's Gardeners," a group dedicated to protest rather than reform and apparently anarchic in inspiration. Jimmy's mother's opposition remains unspecified, but again mostly linked to street demonstrations. Her motivation and efficacy are left in doubt, and the novel's interest in her activity is confined to its effects on her son, Jimmy/Snowman.

As a representative of the humanities, Jimmy cuts a sorry figure, but because he is granted the role of narrator and survivor, when Oryx and Crake are gone, he commands a degree of readerly sympathy despite his flaws. He rejects the name of an endangered animal species, assigned to him by Crake, choosing instead to rename himself Snowman, after the mythical "Abominable Snowman," the North American monster that survives in the northern wilderness. Snowman seems an appropriate name for the only survivor of the ironically named Paradice, so spelled perhaps in homage to Coleridge's "Kubla Khan," which memorably rhymes paradise with ice. This conflation of two concepts through a deviant spelling links utopian desire to cold (as in Shelley's *Frankenstein*) while also suggesting Jimmy's frigid emotional state and the frozen North (itself a longstanding Atwoodian fascination).

In her article "Orwell and Me," Atwood suggests that

> [t]he [twentieth] century could be seen as a race between two versions of man-made hell—the jackbooted state totalitarianism of Orwell's *Nineteen Eight-Four* [sic], and the hedonistic ersatz paradise of *Brave New World*, where absolutely everything is a consumer good and human beings are engineered to be happy. (4)

She continues, "But with 9/11, all that changed. Now it appears we face the prospect of two contradictory dystopias at once—open markets, closed minds" (4). This is the world that has produced the vulnerable but emotionally immature Jimmy, whose version of events, as always with Atwood's narrators, leaves readers in a state of puzzled uncertainty. Many reviewers have suggested that *Oryx and Crake* asks a fundamental question about the role of science in contemporary life: Where do we draw the line? Such responses imply that the scientific imagination should be restrained for the public good. Although they take their cue from Jimmy's unhappy feeling on seeing the experiments underway at Crake's school, that "some line has been crossed" (206), I am unhappy with such interpretations for two reasons.

The thinking behind the metaphor of "drawing the line," as Atwood knows well, can easily be turned against the writerly imagination. Current attempts to alter Canadian law to remove the defence of artistic merit from writing addressing pedophilia and the sexuality of children could easily be extended to censor the depiction of Oryx in Atwood's novel. Although the novel clearly deplores child prostitution, pornography, and the global trade in slaves, it must describe some dimension of these activities to create opposition to them. This aspect of the novel is just as important as its account of genetic experiments and so-called reality shows; more than that, the book seeks to show that the various ills it depicts are linked through an overall world view that no longer values the sanctity of life or the human as a capacious category. Instead, there are people and there are disposable people, and these categories leak. Thus, I don't see the book as a critique of science going too far but, rather, of humanity losing its defining power as the anchor of either a national or a global ethic.

To me, *Oryx and Crake* is asking not where we draw the line but how we reconnect the dots. Can we reconnect the dots to understand the ways in which open markets and closed minds are linked? Can we reconnect the dots to bring the scientific and the artistic imaginations together in the service of the earth and all its creatures? I think the novel implies, through its citations of literature, that this reconnection can only occur through reviving the literary imagination in all its ambiguities, yet the danger here is that readers trained to personalize the big issues will simply identify a villain in Crake and miss the larger picture.[1] Joan Smith, in her review of the novel in the *Observer*, concludes that "in the end, *Oryx and Crake* is a parable, an imaginative text for the anti-globalization movement that does not quite work as a novel" (2). I am turning this judgment on its head. The book does not work as a critique of globalization precisely because of its devotion to the established protocols of the novel, where an investment in Jimmy's personal story is allowed to drown everything else.

I bring my own preoccupations with globalization research to my reading of Atwood's text and it is a testament to her genius that her work can sustain multiple interpretations of the kinds that proliferate throughout this collection. My delight in the text arises from the complexity of its intertextual resonances with many of the canonical works of the Western tradition and especially from the sly reworkings of these that Atwood proposes. I am interested in the implications of these reworked citations, and the ways that they operate, mostly indirectly at the level of the plot rather than through direct quotation. These intertextualities inevitably complicate our interpretation of the text while also pulling it back into an established web of meaning. For example, the name "Snowman" recalls the affinity of Frankenstein's monster for the frozen wastes of the North, while invoking enduring settler fears of the North American environment, embodied in the figure of the "Abominable Snowman," fears that still fuel an urge to conquer nature while acknowledging its power. Yet in dropping the prefix "Abominable" from his new name, after invoking it as an explicit context, Jimmy also recalls the everyday and mortal figure of the "snowman," usually made by children and always destined to melt as the seasons change. Perhaps there is also a more sinister echo of Orwell's nasty Snowball from *Animal Farm*.

But this paper advances a different train of analysis, to suggest that Atwood's insights into the ideological debates of today may be obscured as much as advanced by her mastery of the genre—the novel—that she knows so well. Simply put, if the novel as a genre arose roughly alongside Enlightenment notions of the human to give it imaginative substance, then the novel lets us down when it attempts to confront post-human times. If we accept Benedict Anderson's notion that the rise of print capitalism and of the novel in particular enabled the rise of nations as imagined communities, then what we see in *Oryx and Crake* is a novel addressing post-national global 'scapes through a medium ill-suited to their depiction.[2] As a result, *Oryx and Crake* seems to fall back on the novel's most intimate staples: the singular figure of Crusoe on his island; the nuclear family reduced to mother, father, and child; the eternal triangle of an idealized woman and the two men who bond through their love for her. These are models for the patterning of human relations that do not sufficiently capture the interwoven relations of global capitalism.

Atwood has identified Orwell as a major influence, but I see Faust, Hamlet, Oedipus, Coleridge's "Rime of the Ancient Mariner," and Robinson Crusoe as equally important intertexts drawing together the visionary capacity and the blindnesses of a novel that is almost claustrophobically local in its setting. *Oryx and Crake* addresses the ethical implications of that complex convergence of the contemporary that we term globalization: the triumph of positivism, neo-liberal economics, and the worship of technology; scientific advances, especially in eugenics, beyond the prohibitions of earlier times; renewed investigation of avenues of research closed since the defeat of the Nazis at the end of the Second World War; the near collapse of the social contract that followed that war, leading to increased polarization between rich and poor, the death of cities, the rise of gated communities, new pandemics, an apparently huge increase in the number of people globally termed "disposable"; increasing anxiety about the so-called decline of the Western, nuclear family. But it develops its global ethic through the filter of Snowman's story of Jimmy. For readers still devoted to the traditional novel, this constitutes its strength, but for those who seek engagement with contemporary complexities, that strength also constitutes its blindness.

As a representative of the humanities, Jimmy can be disappointing. The mythology that he teaches the Children of Crake is an embarrassing New Age concoction. But Crake's own imagination, despite his technical skills in creating new life and finding new ways to destroy it, is equally limited. Indeed, he fears and distrusts the world of art, trying to program his new people without the ability to dream or the urge to sing. He fails in his efforts to expunge these, concluding that people, even newly engineered people, seem to be hard-wired for dream and song, but even so, the "new" people he creates are a joke, a living satire of the errors of the utilitarian imagination, and Atwood has a lot of fun with them. The point seems to be that neither art nor science can exist alone. They are interdependent and require interaction to reach their full potential. Oryx, avatar of Faust's "eternal feminine," completes the triangle linking Crake's talent for science with Jimmy's talent for words, but fails to enable the missing convergence.

Some readers attribute the one-dimensionality of Oryx and Crake as characters to failures of Atwood's imagination. I disagree. They lack substance partly because they are seen through Jimmy/Snowman's deficient vision and partly because all three have entered a post-human mode of being that Atwood finds deficient. Jimmy's is a claustrophic and emptied world full of disconnected images and fakery. Like Naomi Klein in *No Logo*, he focuses on the North American consumer obsession with brands, but the worlds outside the gated compounds of privilege remain beyond his imagination and his interests, except for the immediate escape they seem to offer him from the boredom of his own world. Jimmy has been blinded by the gods of his world, the proliferation of media images, so that he can only see what is nearby. He sees everything in terms of the nuclear family unit—father, mother, child—which then becomes replicated in the homosocial triangle of friend, lover, and self. When an unhappy science fiction reviewer complains that Atwood is "satirizing yesterday in the language of the day before yesterday, 1990 in the language of 1960" (Clute 3), I agree with the analysis but contest the negative judgment. Atwood is not writing about the future; she is writing about the present, in what has been the dominant narrative mode of the last two hundred years. When she describes a 1950s family existing in her supposed near future, she is speculating about where current United States obsessions with "family values" might lead, and disputing our era's dominant faith in the inevitability of progress. As in *The Handmaid's Tale*, she shows that hard-won rights may be quickly reversed and that supposedly secure values may be twisted.

At the novel's beginning, Oryx and Crake, two of the novel's three main protagonists, are already dead. Crake is Jimmy's albatross, whose story he is condemned to retell. This "ancient mariner" laments what neo-liberal globalization has thoughtlessly jettisoned. His only hope lies in history repeating itself. Utopian attempts at creating a brave new world or in evolving humanity beyond itself into Nietszchean categories of ultimate man or superman have gone disastrously wrong.

Although Jimmy sees Crake as a type of Faust, his narrative suggests that, like Hamlet, Crake plots in secret to avenge his father's death, quite possibly murdering first his mother, then his stepfather, and eventually most of the world. In grounding her plot in such classic tales of the Freudian family romance, Atwood implies that human nature is stable. If the motto of the World Social Forum bravely affirms that "another world is possible," then Atwood's novel seems to reply with two possible answers, neither of them encouraging such optimism. On one hand, the dystopian world that Jimmy, Oryx, and Crake inhabit implies that if another world is possible, then it is likely to be even worse than the world we inhabit now. On the other hand, the behaviour of the Children of Crake when they are on their own in the outside world, as when they crave the unnecessary hair that Jimmy calls "feathers" and the flowered sheet worn by Jimmy on his return from his scavenging expedition, suggests that another world will not be possible because even new creatures created by idealistic human beings will be hard-wired for the old human, all-too-human traits of acquisitiveness, frivolity, envy, and competition. Of course, one might interpret the child's desire for the unfamiliar sheet worn by Jimmy as the first stirrings of an artistic need for something beyond the merely utilitarian, but even so, that artistic urge, as Atwood presents it, seems intertwined with those less desirable and more dangerous kinds of urges that Crake had hoped to extinguish. I am arguing, then, that far from endorsing an anti-globalization agenda, Atwood's novel questions that agenda's faith in human agency and the possibility of a better future. What Atwood's novel continues to endorse is not humanity's capacity for collective action toward social change but, rather, its inextinguishable individualism, not its capacity for reason but its susceptibility to emotion. Such an endorsement fits comfortably with the orthodoxies of our time.

Although there are moments of critique that suggest an eco-critical concern, the novel's form works against that concern. If eco-criticism de-privileges the human subject, as some have argued, to foreground instead the ecosystem of which the human is a part, then Atwood's novel is clearly not eco-critical so much as humanist in its orientation. Atwood's commitment to the fetish of the individual writer as privileged seer exists in tension with the power of what she sees when she writes. In "Survival Then and Now" (48), for example, she ignores the nation as site of belonging and agency to celebrate instead her personal citizenship in "the republic of letters, where desire is the key to the gateway, and where all who wish may enter." That republic and the globally open citizenship that it envisions depend on the technologies of writing and reading, and the imaginative sympathies that literacy can open through narrative; however, these skills in turn may also depend on governance structures guaranteeing the democratic educational systems, peace, and order that her credo ignores. These are systems and skills that are becoming obsolete in the world of *Oryx and Crake*. The book is a call to revive them. But Atwood's republic of letters also depends on a broader scientific, political, and "transnational literacy" that encourages readers to see beyond Atwood's individual characters to the world that has made them what they are.[3] In documenting their disappearance from Jimmy's world, Atwood seems to assume that readers today can still bring these perspectives to her work, but I am less sure.

Specific attention to matters of global concern in this novel are muted in favour of attention to what the contemporary media might term Jimmy's "human story." Jimmy is not capable of connecting the dots. Like Crake, he entertains a vague conspiracy theory of global commerce but is incapable of analyzing how this world works and what links the world in which he grows up with that of Oryx's childhood on the other side of the world. What I miss in any elaborated sense in Atwood's novel is an awareness of Alan Bewell's observation, in *Romanticism and Colonial Disease*, that globalization's "new epidemiological reality [described by Le Roy Ladurie as a 'common market of bacilli'] is one of the legacies of colonialism" (4). Instead of connecting the dots linking globalization back to colonialism, Jimmy sees colonialism as another slightly absurd costume drama, laced with hypocrisy: "They would have been told to wear solar topis, dress for dinner, refrain from raping the natives" (*OC* 5), he observes cynically. Near the book's end, colonialism is again recalled as "images from old history flip through his head" (366), this time of the savagery that can accompany cross-cultural encounters throughout a range of colonial experiences. The past has become a series of fashion shoots and action shots, making it impossible to see it as the source of the present.

For Crusoe, finding the human footprint in the sand led to the subjugation of Friday. Where it might lead for Jimmy/Snowman is left open: will these other survivors hear his tale, as we readers just have, or will they kill him? Either way, he will certainly die, but humanity, now dispersed into species as varied as Crakers and pigoons, will survive. Yet will it any longer be human? The novel suggests that when science fails, storytelling will remain, and the human as we have known it will somehow survive. Anyone reading a novel like this is likely to find this conclusion a comforting if self-reinforcing prophecy. I am suggesting that beneath these pieties lies a deeper fear—that such stories no longer help in making sense of ourselves or our world. Atwood has said that "if there's a clock in it, you know it's a novel" (*Search* 9). In *Oryx and Crake* the clocks have stopped.

In this sense, the novel is as richly enigmatic as Jimmy's mother's final words: "remember Killer." There is so much to remember about Killer that we cannot know what she wished to convey. Is she reminding Jimmy of how he came to name his pet in defiance of his father's limited expectations of his imaginative potential (that is, of Jimmy's capacity for rebellion) or is she reminding him that he was once capable of genuine love for another (that is, of his capacity for selfless love)—even if that love was based on profoundly unequal relations? In other words, is she recalling the potential of the animal/human bond for establishing intimate alliances or is she noting the societal restrictions that deny that potential? Is she making an anti-pet statement insisting on the animal's need to be free or reminding him that domesticated animals are unlikely to survive in the wild, and hence urging him to value safety over freedom? Is she reminding him that she took away his beloved pet and therefore cannot be trusted, or implying that the pain he felt when she did this can be his first impetus beyond the sterile passivity of his current life toward meaningful action? Is she reminding him that names are not always reliable indicators of essence, that rakunks are not killers, so that pleasure may be derived from the deceptive play of meaning even within a totalitarian state, or is this disjuncture a warning against Orwellian doublespeak? In "Orwell and Me," Atwood notes that current dogma stating that "[f]or the sake of freedom, freedom must be renounced" is "a concept worthy of doublethink" (3). Although most of the novel obsessively recounts Jimmy's fragmented memories of this world, despite "the blank spaces in his stub of a brain" (4), it begins and ends in a differently conceived space, that of a world defined by the "absence of official time" (1), the demise of the old rules (7), and the absence of mirrors (8). Atwood's novel implies that Jimmy/Snowman's apocalyptic vision of a space cleared where newness may enter may be an illusion. Certainly the Snowman's "backward-pointing footprints" (8) and his retrospective narrative cannot lead readers into the future. But his blindnesses may encourage his readers' vision, contributing to the dialogues upon which a global ethic may be advanced.

—University of Western Ontario

NOTES

1. The review by Kakutani in the *New York Times* is typical of such a reaction, dismissing the didacticism, plotting, and satire as implausible and praising only the character of Jimmy.
2. I take the notion of global 'scapes from Arjun Appadurai's influential analysis in *Modernity at Large: Cultural Dimensions of Globalization* (Minneapolis: University of Minnesota Press, 1996).
3. "Transnational literacy" is Gayatri Spivak's term, elaborated in *A Critique of Postcolonial Reason: Toward a History of the Vanishing Present* (Cambridge, Mass.: Harvard University Press, 1999).

WORKS CITED

Anderson, Benedict. *Imagined Communities: Reflections on the Origin and Spread of Nationalism*. 2nd ed. Lodon: Verso, 1991.

Atwood, Margaret. *In Search of Alias Grace*. Ottawa: University of Ottawa Press, 1997.

———. *Oryx and Crake*. Toronto: McClelland & Stewart, 2003.
———. "Orwell and Me." *Guardian* (Manchester), June 18, 2003. 1–4.
———. "Survival Then and Now." In *The Canadian Distinctiveness into the XXIst Century*, edited by Chad Gaffield and Karen L. Gould, 47–55. Ottawa: University of Ottawa Press, 2003.
Bewell, Alan. *Romanticism and Colonial Disease*. Baltimore: Johns Hopkins University Press, 1999.
Clute, John. "Croaked." Excessive Candour. [online]: <http://www.scifi.com/sfw/issue325/excess.html> (accessed November 17, 2003), 1–4.
Epstein, Joseph. "Writing on the Brain." *Commentary*, April 2004. 37–41.
Gumbrecht, Hans Ulrich. "*Dysphoria*: How (Some) Literary Scholars Feel about Literary Studies." *The Future of Literary Studies/L'avenir des études litteraires*, edited by Hans Ulrich Gumbrecht and Walter Moser. *Canadian Review of Comparative Literature* 26, nos. 3–4 (2001): 12–22.
Kakutani, Michiko. "Books of the Times; Lone Human in a Land Filled with Humanoids." *New York Times*, May 13, 2003. Late Edition—Final, Section E, Column 3, page 9.
"Margaret Atwood: Oryx and Crake." [online]: <http://www.randomhouse.com/features/atwood/orysandcrake/links.html> (accessed July 1, 2004).
Said, Edward W. *Humanism and Democratic Criticism*. New York: Columbia University Press, 2004.
Smith, Joan. "And pigs might fly…" *Observer*, May 11, 2003. 1–2. [online]: <http://www.observer.guardian.co.uk/review/story/0,6903,953240,00.html> (accessed November 17, 2003).
Vendler, Helen. "The Ocean, The Bird, and the Scholar." The 33rd Jefferson Lecture in the Humanities, sponsored by the National Endowment for the Humanities, delivered May 6, 2004, Washington, DC. [online]: <http://www.neh.gov/whoweare/vendler/lecture.html> (accessed June 28, 2004).

POSTSCRIPT

Propositions from a (Reap)praising Margaret Atwood Conference

FRANK DAVEY

1. OPENING CEREMONIES

No one can sound more jaded than Margaret Atwood:
Paul Gessell, *The Ottawa Citizen*.

There are more than 100 registrants from fourteen countries:
organizer, John Moss, addressing communicants.

Hordes of academics from around the world
descending on Ottawa to dissect every line: Paul Gessell.

For publication, papers should be sent to Professor Moss:
Tobi Kozakewich, conference assistant.

You don't read them because it would drive you mad:
Margaret Atwood, responding to Gessell.

North is over there: John Moss.

2. CELEBRITY

Margaret Atwood needs both to affirm and disvalue celebrity:
Lorraine York.

Why do you do this?
Margaret Atwood asking John Moss about scholars at conferences.

Icons begin their lives as iconoclasts: Laura Moss
on transnational imagination.

There are forty-one metres of Atwood papers in the Fisher deposit:
Robert McGill, novelist.

Canadians are balloon puncturers: Margaret Atwood,
prefacing a slide show.

3. ARCHIVE CHATTER

An abandoned draft has been abjected: Robert McGill.

An abjected draft becomes a commodity when archived:
someone's notes.

Abandoning & archiving drafts is a mode of self-fashioning:
someone's notes.

The purpose of an archive is
to lift the veil on a writer's life
to make money
to assist critics
to mislead critics
to control critics: Robert McGill.

4. OVERHEARING

Writers must own their privately produced property in order
to participate in a market economy: Renée Hulan.

What is heard is different from what is said: Barbara Godard.

We know all about her and we do not know her at all: John Moss.

The private is constructed for public suitability: Lorraine York.

It would be your worst nightmare if I had attended your sessions:
Margaret Atwood, still prefacing.

5. NATURE

All the characters in *Oryx and Crake* are cyborgs:
Michèle Lacombe.

If humans are natural, and naturally produce cyborgs,
are cyborgs natural?
Atwood reader.

Margaret Atwood is a cyborg?
Passing student.

Here I am as half a windmill: Margaret Atwood showing a slide
of two four-year-old girls dressed as one windmill.

6. DESTINY

History is written backwards: Coral Howells.

This is me at the Bohemian Embassy, listening
to Sylvia Fricker: Margaret Atwood.

The novel is unsuitable for addressing postnational
posthumanistic culture: Diana Brydon.

You can tell which one's the Queen by the hairdo:
Margaret Atwood.

Love is always inadequate to actual experience:
Tae Yamamoto.

Here I am getting married: Margaret Atwood.

And here I'm reading Tarot cards: Margaret Atwood.

(Reprinted by permission of the author from his chapbook, *Risky Propositions*, from above/ground press, 2005.)

Index

adultery, 185–193, 379, 382 n3
"After the Flood, We" (CG, Atwood), 308
"Age of Lead, The" (WT, Atwood), 108, 259, 260–264, 345 n9
"Aging Female Poet on Laundry Day" (SP II, Atwood), 269
aging self, 267–277, 349–358
Alias Grace (AG, Atwood), 11, 12, 27, 53, 59, 66, 107, 110, 111, 112–116, 121, 211, 312, 316 n2, 367–368, 442; construction of personality in, 159, 160, 217–230; dissident subject, 207–215; social class in, 231, 236–238, 239, 240 n2
"Amnesty International: an Address" (SW, Atwood), 293
animal suffering, 171–184
Animals in That Country, The (ATC, Atwood), 82, 281–282; "Landlady, The," 85–86, 287–288; "Progressive Insanities of a Pioneer," 280; "Speeches for Dr. Frankenstein," 317 n2, 397

archive, living, 93–106
"Arguing Against Ice Cream" (MT, Atwood), 385
As Ten as Twenty (ATT, Page): "Element," 87, 91 n6; "If It Were You," 82; "Landlady, The," 85, 246; "Personal Landscape," 82, 87
"At the Tourist Centre in Boston" (ATC, Atwood), 332, 335–337
autobiographical pact, 121–134, 335
"Ava Gardner Reincarnated as a Magnolia" (MBH, Atwood), 313

"Backdrop Addresses Cowboy" (SP 1966–1984, Atwood), 246–247, 286
"Bad News" (GB, Atwood), 311
Blind Assassin, The (BA, Atwood), 10, 13, 22, 27, 28–29, 35, 129, 131, 192 n1, 213, 231, 232, 238–239, 293, 298–300, 316–317 n2, 346 n10; gothic romance genre, 368, 373–382, 398; history/herstory,

107, 112, 116–119, 375, 377;
  as a literary mystery, 361–370;
  protagonists, 349–350, 353–358
Bodily Harm (BH, Atwood), 67, 108, 129, 240 n3, 293–296, 300, 302 n4, 309–310, 314, 399
body-centred imagery, 307, 361–370
"Bog, Man, The" (WT, Atwood), 259, 260–261, 263–266
"Book of Ancestors" (YAH, Atwood), 309
Breitbach, Julia, 13, 331–346
Bromberg, Pamela S., 13, 257–267
Brydon, Diana, 14, 27, 294, 447–458, 463
"Burned House" (MBH, Atwood), 313–314
"Bus along St. Clair: December, A" (SP 1966–1984, Atwood), 280

"Camera" (CG, Atwood), 85, 307
Campbell, Wanda, 13, 243–255
Caroll, Lewis, 282–285, 401, 425
Cat's Eye (CE, Atwood), 97, 108, 231, 232, 235–236, 239, 258, 260, 349–351
Chivers, Sally, 14, 270, 385–396
"Circe/Mud" (YAH, Atwood), 282
Circle Game, The (CG, Atwood), 65, 66, 306–308, 313, 314, 316–317 n2; "After the Flood, We," 308; "Camera," 85, 307; "Explorers, The," 308; "Man With a Hook," 82; "Meal, A," 307; "Messenger, A," 82; "Settlers, The," 147, 308; "Some Objects of Wood and Stone," 82; "Sybil, A," 82, 315; "This is a Photograph of Me," 86–87, 331, 332–335, 338, 339
"Comic Books vs. History" (SP 1966–1984, Atwood), 248

copyright law, 49–64
cyborg identities, 421–432
"Daguerrotype Taken in Old Age" (JSM, Atwood), 332, 339, 340–341, 343
Dancing Girls and Other Stories (DG, Atwood): "Rape Fantasies," 243, 248–249, 251
"Daphne and Laura and So Forth" (MBH, Atwood), 313
Davey, Frank, 10, 12, 61 n3, 117, 161, 231–240, 296, 306, 461–463
"Death by Landscape" (WT, Atwood), 88–89, 91 n7, 108, 129, 146, 147–148, 149, 258
depression, 309–310, 313, 409–410, 412–414, 438
disability, 385–396
Djwa, Sandra, 11, 91–93, 147, 153 n2, 154 n12, 183 n3, 243–244
"Down" (MBH, Atwood), 325–326
duality, principle of, 305–317
dystopian vision, 197, 293, 298, 399, 433, 449, 450, 544

"Earth" (TS, Atwood), 309–310
Eating Fire: Selected Poetry 1965–1995 (EF, Atwood): "Oh," 322; "Shapechangers in Winter," 326, 327–328; "Statuary," 328–329; "Two Dreams, 2," 319, 323, 324; "Up," 326
Edible Woman, The (EW, Atwood), 85, 89–90, 121, 185, 232, 306, 307, 314, 346 n10, 386
Edmonds, Regina M., 12, 217–230
embodiment, limits of, 385–396
environment, the, 29, 108, 182, 262, 455
"Eurydice" (SP 1966–1984, Atwood), 288–289

Evain, Christine, 13, 305–318
"Explorers, The" (CG, Atwood), 308
feminism, 24, 26, 27, 29, 108, 111, 139, 165, 166, 180, 182, 195–205, 234, 239, 274, 302 n4, 361–371, 378, 401, 407–410, 423, 425
Fiamengo, Janice, 12, 14, 171–184, 330 n2
fiction vs. poetry, 280, 305–317
"Fire Place, A" (MBH, Atwood), 324–325
"Five Poems for Grandmothers" (SP II, Atwood), 272–273
"Footnote to the Amnesty Report on Torture" (THP, Atwood), 296
Foucault, Michel, 13, 52, 96, 102, 161–162, 163, 208, 209, 213, 214 n2, 232–233, 279, 291–303
Foy, Nathalie, 14, 407–419
Frankenstein theme, 397–406, 424–426, 433–446

"Gertrude Talks Back" (GB, Atwood), 311
ghosts, 2, 118, 137–158, 172, 258, 329, 363, 383 n1, 425
"Girl and Horse, 1928" (PU, Atwood), 332, 339–340, 341–343
global ethic, 293, 300, 447–457, 449, 451, 452–456
Godin, Julie, 12, 207–215
Good Bones (GB, Atwood), 66, 243–255, 310; "Bad News," 311; "Gertrude Talks Back," 311; "Let Us Now Praise Stupid Women," 311–312; "Little Red Hen Tells All," 311; "There was Once," 311; "Unpopular Gals," 311
gothic romance, 6, 13, 84, 113–114, 138, 140, 148, 152, 190–191, 234, 272, 368, 373–382

Grace, Sherrill, 9, 10, 30 n1, 121–134, 153 n3, 161, 172, 335, 345 n6

"Hack Wednesday" (WT, Atwood), 257, 266–267
"Hairball" (WT, Atwood), 395
Handmaid's Tale, The (HT, Atwood), 10, 27, 29, 30 n5, 42, 53, 66, 108, 121, 129, 207, 232, 239, 245, 312, 398, 422, 423, 432, 433, 454; power politics, 293, 296–298, 399; role of narrative, 195–205
"Happy Endings" (MD, Atwood), 311
"Helen of Troy Does Counter Dancing" (MBH, Atwood), 248, 313
"High Summer" (TS, Atwood), 280–281
history/herstory, 107–120, 207–215, 375, 377
"Hotel" (TS, Atwood), 309–310
Howells, Coral Ann, 9–10, 11, 107–120, 274, 298, 299–300, 302 n4, 330 n2, 376–377, 382 n1, 463
Hulan, Renée, 11, 49–64, 462
humour, use of, 243–255, 309
hypnosis, 212–214, 223–228
hysteria, 210–214, 218, 223, 423
Hyttinen, Helena, 13, 373–383

"I" lyricism, 82, 259–260, 279–289, 331, 333–337, 339–342. *See also* autobiographical pact
iconicity, Atwood's, 1, 9, 20–33, 35–47, 66, 67–68, 185–193, 269–277, 462
In Search of Alias Grace (Search, Atwood), 110, 113, 114, 116, 456
"Interlunar" (Atwood from I), 281, 316

Interlunar (I, Atwood), 288; "Interlunar" (Atwood from I), 281, 316; "Snake Poems," 282
irony, use of, 111, 164, 165, 168, 185–193, 211, 245, 246, 251, 252, 261, 266, 284, 308, 312, 313, 314, 316–317 n2, 378, 437–441
"Is/Not" (YAH, Atwood), 289, 309
"Isis in Darkness" (WT, Atwood), 259

Jamieson, Sara, 13, 269–277, 330 n2
Jarraway, David R., 13, 91 n3, 279–290
Journals of Susanna Moodie, The (JSM, Atwood), 5, 27, 84, 121, 124, 129, 130, 146, 154 n13, 280; "Daguerrotype Taken in Old Age," 332, 339, 340–341, 343; history/herstory, 107, 110–111, 113–114; "Visit to Toronto, with Companions," 316 n2

Kozakewich, Tobi, 9–15, 185–193, 345 n6, 461
Kristeva, Julia, 99, 434–435, 439
Kröller, Eva-Marie, 11, 65–79
Lacombe, Michèle, 14, 421–432, 463
Lady Oracle (LO, Atwood), 11, 12, 13, 43–44, 76 n6, 103, 108, 129, 147, 249, 267 n1, 306, 308–309, 311, 367–368, 440; adultery as metaphor, 185–193; gothic romance genre, 190–191, 234, 368, 382 n1; irony, use of, 185–193, 191–192, 308, 314; sexual politics, 185–193; social class, 233–235
"Landlady" (ATC, SP 1966–1984, Atwood), 85–86, 246, 287–288
language and the individual, 196, 203, 231–233

"Last Poem" (TS, Atwood), 309–310
"Late Night" (TS, Atwood), 309–310
"Let Us Now Praise Stupid Women" (GB, Atwood), 311–312
Life Before Man (LBM, Atwood), 232, 233, 309, 310, 314, 398
"Little Red Hen Tells All" (GB, Atwood), 311
living archive, 93–106
Lucas, Rose, 13, 319–330

madness, 159–169
"Magnet's Olympia" (MBH, Atwood), 313, 316
male/female relationships, 88–90, 108, 185–193, 195–205, 281–282, 293–294, 306, 397–405
"Man in a Glacier" (MBH, Atwood), 260–261, 320–321, 332, 339, 343–344
"Man With a Hook" (CG, Atwood), 82
"Marrying the Hangman" (SP 1966–1984, Atwood), 282, 284–285
McGill, Robert, 11, 95–106, 462
"Meal, A" (CG, Atwood), 307
memories, 217–230
"Messenger, A" (CG, Atwood), 82
Metal and the Flower, The (MF, Page), 83; "Event, The," 88–90; "Man With One Small Hand," 82; "Permanent Tourists," 82
metamorphosis, 82, 110, 247, 264, 270, 306, 308, 325, 424–426
metaphor, use of, 87–89, 177–182, 306, 307, 362, 399, 450–451
"Miss July Grows Older" (MBH, Atwood), 313, 315
"Morning in the Burned House" (MBH, Atwood), 313–314, 324–325

Morning in the Burned House (MBH, Atwood), 13, 129, 250, 269–277, 310, 312–314, 319–330, 430; "Ava Gardner Reincarnated as a Magnolia," 313; "Burned House," 313–314; "Daphne and Laura and So Forth," 313; "Down," 325–326; "Fire Place, A," 324–325; "Helen of Troy Does Counter Dancing," 248, 313; "Magnet's Olympia," 313, 316; "Man in a Glacier," 260–261, 320–321, 332, 339, 343–344; "Miss July Grows Older," 313, 315; "Morning in the Burned House," 313–314, 324–325; "Ottawa River by Night, The," 327; "Pink Hotel, The," 325; "Sekhmet, The Lion-Headed Goddess of War, Violent Storms, Pestilence, and Recovery From Illness, Contemplates the Desert in the Metropolitan Museum of Art," 313; "Shapechangers in Winter," 273–277; "Waiting," 271–272, 273, 276–277, 322

Moss, John, 1–7, 10, 161, 345 n6, 461, 462

Moss, Laura, 10–11, 19–33, 75 n2, 396 n2, 462

Moving Targets: Writing with Intent, 1982–2004 (MT, Atwood), 53; "Arguing Against Ice Cream," 385

Murder in the Dark (MD, Atwood), 101, 213, 306, 310–311, 312; "Happy Endings," 311; "Page, The," 101, 338; "Woman's Novel," 311

mystery, literary, 361–370

mythology, 12, 24, 73, 82–84, 88, 89, 109, 110–114, 118, 248, 276, 308, 313, 393, 404, 424, 443, 450

narcissism, 270, 298, 321, 324, 442

nationalism, 67, 72, 137–140, 195

Negotiating with the Dead: A Writer on Writing (ND, Atwood), 13, 30 n1, 51, 53, 103, 128, 257–267, 279, 285, 357; autobiographical pact, 126–131, 132 n4; Lewis Carroll's "Alice," 282–283; "Negotiating with the Dead," 152; protagonists, 349–350, 353

"Negotiating with the Dead" (ND, Atwood), 152

"Newsreel: Man and Firing Squad" (SP 1966–1984, Atwood), 286

Nischik, Reingard M., 13, 20, 121, 132 n3, 245, 250, 331–346

"Notes Towards a Poem That Can Never Be Written" (NTP, TS, Atwood), 293, 296, 298

"Oh" (EF, Atwood), 322

Orwell, George, 29, 195, 196–197, 399, 450, 452, 457

Oryx and Crake (OC, Atwood), 2, 10, 14, 27, 28, 29, 66, 130, 185, 239–240 n1, 251–252, 262, 279–280, 316–317 n2, 358 n2, 391, 393, 434, 437–441, 447–457; absent mother, 407–418, 441–445; cyborg identities, 421–432; Frankenstein theme, 397–406, 424–426, 433–446; power politics, 293, 300–301, 397–405

Other, the, 13, 112–113, 161–169, 204 n6, 270, 280–281, 283, 284, 434, 443

"Ottawa River by Night, The" (MBH, Atwood), 327

Page, P.K., 11, 81–93; *Metal and the Flower, The*, 82, 88–90; *As Ten as*

Twenty, 82, 85, 246; *Unit of Five*, 86
"Page, The" (MD, Atwood), 101, 338
paradox, 137–158, 163–164, 173–174, 204 n7, 218–219, 257–267, 275–276, 324, 325, 342
parody, use of, 69, 89, 153 n2, 182 n3, 212, 243–244, 250, 311, 312, 317 n1, 378, 382 n1, 434, 437–441, 445
Perrakis, Phyllis Sternberg, 14, 349–359
photographic representation, 331–346, 361, 367
"Pink Hotel, The" (MBH, Atwood), 325
poetry: vs. dreams, 320–330; vs. fiction, 280, 305–317
pornography, 293, 302 n4, 391, 402, 416, 451
power politics, 291–302, 397–405
Power Politics (PP, Atwood), 13, 66, 280–281, 293, 296, 300, 307, 314; "you fit into me," 3, 87, 281
"Procedures for Underground" (PU, Atwood), 147, 306
Procedures for Underground (PU, Atwood), 306; "Girl and Horse, 1928," 332, 339–340, 341–343; "Procedures for Underground," 147, 306; "Projected Slide of an Unknown Soldier," 332, 337–339, 343
"Progressive Insanities of a Pioneer" (ATC, Atwood), 280
"Projected Slide of an Unknown Soldier" (PU, Atwood), 332, 337–339, 343

Quebec, Atwood in, 65–79
"Rape Fantasies" (DG, Atwood), 243, 248–249, 251

realism, 84, 185–193, 245, 309
Robber Bride, The (RB, Atwood), 66, 129, 192 n1, 239, 267 n1, 312, 376, 382 n1, 398, 399; history/herstory, 107, 111–113, 117; protagonists, 349–350, 351–353
Roy, Wendy, 13, 361–371

Second Words (SW, Atwood), 243, 248, 249, 292; "Amnesty International: an Address," 293; "What's so Funny? Notes on Canadian Humour," 252; "Witches," 124
"Sekhmet, The Lion-Headed Goddess of War, Violent Storms, Pestilence, and Recovery From Illness, Contemplates the Desert in the Metropolitan Museum of Art" (MBH, Atwood), 313
Selected Poems: 1965–1975 (SP, Atwood): "This is a Photograph of Me," 259–260
Selected Poems 1966–1984 (SP 1966–1984, Atwood), 2–3, 243, 244–247, 281, 288–289; "Backdrop Addresses Cowboy," 246–247, 286; "Bus along St. Clair: December, A," 280; "Comic Books vs. History," 248; "Eurydice," 288–289; "Landlady, The," 246, 287–288; "Marrying the Hangman," 282, 284–285; "Newsreel: Man and Firing Squad," 286; "Speeches for Dr. Frankenstein," 282; "The Landlady," 246; "Women's Issue, A," 2–3; "you fit into me," 244
Selected Poems 1975–1986 (SPII, Atwood): "Aging Female Poet on Laundry Day," 269; "Five Poems for Grandmothers," 272–273

"Settlers, The" (CG, Atwood), 147, 308
sexual politics, 185–193, 199–200, 293–294, 397–405
sexuality, 273–277, 281–282, 363–364, 365, 370 n6, 427
"Shadow Voice" (ATC, Atwood), 315
"Shapechangers in Winter" (EF, MBH, Atwood), 273–277, 326, 327–328
"Siren Song" (YAH, Atwood; SP 1966–1984, Atwood), 312, 248
"Snake Poems" (I, Atwood), 282
social class, 231–240
Somacarrera, Pilar, 13, 291–303
"Some Objects of Wood and Stone" (CG, Atwood), 82
"Song of the Worms" (SP 1966–1984, Atwood), 247
"Songs of the Transformed" (SP 1966–1984, Atwood), 247
"Speeches for Dr. Frankenstein" (ATC, SP 1966–1984, Atwood), 282, 317 n2, 397
Staels, Hilde, 14, 203 n5, 214 n2, 214 n6, 433–446
"Statuary" (EF, Atwood), 328–329
Stein, Karen, 10, 197, 244, 245, 369–370 n1-2, 374, 381
suffering, 171–184
Sugars, Cynthia, 12, 14, 137–158
Sullivan, Rosemary, 10, 50, 51, 53, 61 n4, 91 n1, 110, 124, 138–139
Sun and the Moon, The (SM, Page), 84, 88–89
Surfacing (Surfacing, Atwood), 5, 11, 12, 27, 75 n4, 82, 85, 88, 89–90, 108, 128, 129, 192, 196, 203, 232, 292, 293, 306, 307, 308, 314, 391; gothic romance genre, 152, 382 n1; madness in, 159–169; suffering in, 171–184; Tom Thomson, 137–158
Survival (Survival, Atwood), 24, 27, 28, 30 n1, 92 n10, 109, 147, 151, 171, 172, 176, 309, 429
"Sybil, A" (CG, Atwood), 82, 315

"Their Attitudes Differ" (SP, Atwood), 281
"There is Only One of Everything" (YAH, Atwood), 308, 309
"There was Once" (GB, Atwood), 311
"This is a Photograph of Me" (CG, SP, Atwood), 86–87, 259–260, 331, 332–335, 338, 339
"Tricks with Mirrors" (YAH, Atwood), 284
Trigg, Tina, 12, 159–169
"True Stories" (TS, Atwood), 111
True Stories (TS, Atwood), 314, 430; "Earth," 309–310; "High Summer," 280–281; "Hotel," 309–310; "Last Poem," 309–310; "Late Night," 309–310; "Notes Towards a Poem That Can Never Be Written" (NTP), 293, 296, 298; "Variation on the Word Love," 309–310; "Women's Issue, A," 282
"True Trash" (WT, Atwood), 259
"Two Dreams, 2" (EF, Atwood), 319, 323, 324
two-headed epithet, 305–317
Two-Headed Poems (THP, Atwood), 67, 284, 309, 310; "Footnote to the Amnesty Report on Torture," 296
Two Solicitudes (TSS, Atwood), 71, 72–73, 253

"Uncles" (WT, Atwood), 258
Unit of Five (UF, Page), 82; "Photograph" (UF, Page), 86

"Unpopular Gals" (GB, Atwood), 311
"Up" (EF, Atwood), 326

"Variation on the Word Love" (TS, Atwood), 309–310
"Visit to Toronto, with Companions" (JSM, Atwood), 316 n2

"Waiting" (MBH, Atwood), 271–272, 273, 276–277, 322
"Weight" (WT, Atwood), 258
"What's so Funny? Notes on Canadian Humour" (SW, Atwood), 252
"Wilderness Tips" (WT, Atwood), 142
Wilderness Tips (WT, Atwood), 82, 108–109, 257–267; "Age of Lead, The," 108, 259, 260–264, 345 n9; "Bog, Man, The," 259, 260–261, 263–266; "Death by Landscape," 88–89, 91 n7, 108, 129, 146, 147–148, 149, 258; "Hack Wednesday," 257, 266–267; "Hairball," 395; "Isis in Darkness," 259; "True Trash," 259; "Uncles," 258; "Weight," 258; "Wilderness Tips," 142
Wilson, Sharon, R., 14, 250, 397–406
"Witches" (SW, Atwood), 124
"Woman's Novel" (MD, Atwood), 311
women's bodies, 361–370
"Women's Issue, A" (SP 1966–1984, TS, Atwood), 2–3, 282
Woolf, Virginia, 2, 5, 65, 401, 437

Yamamoto, Tae, 12, 195–205, 463
York, Lorraine, 10, 35–47, 461, 462
You Are Happy (YAH, Atwood), 289, 314; "Book of Ancestors," 309; "Circe/Mud," 282; "Is/Not," 289, 309; "There is Only One of Everything," 308, 309; "Tricks with Mirrors," 284
"you fit into me" (PP, SP 1966–1984, Atwood), 3, 87, 244, 281

REAPPRAISALS: CANADIAN WRITERS

Reappraisals: Canadian Writers was begun in 1973 in response to a need for single volumes of essays on Canadian authors who had not received the critical attention they deserved or who warranted extensive and intensive reconsideration. It is the longest running series dedicated to the study of Canadian literary subjects. The annual symposium hosted by the Department of English at the University of Ottawa began in 1972 and the following year University of Ottawa Press published the first title in the series, The Grove Symposium. Since then our editorial policy has remained straightforward: each year to make permanently available in a single volume the best of the criticsim and evaluation presented at our symposia on Canadian literature, thereby creating a body of work on and a critical base for the study of Canadian writers and literary subjects.

Gerald Lynch
General Editor

Titles in the series:

THE GROVE SYMPOSIUM, edited and with an introduction by John Nause

THE A.M. KLEIN SYMPOSIUM, edited and with an introduction by Seymour Mayne

THE LAMPMAN SYMPOSIUM, edited and with an introduction by Lorraine McMullen

THE E.J. PRATT SYMPOSIUM, edited and with an introduction by Glenn Clever

THE ISABELLA VALANCY CRAWFORD SYMPOSIUM, edited and with an introduction by Frank M. Tierney

THE DUNCAN CAMPBELL SCOTT SYMPOSIUM, edited and with an introduction by K.P. Stich

THE CALLAGHAN SYMPOSIUM, edited and with an introduction by David Staines

THE ETHEL WILSON SYMPOSIUM, edited and with an introduction by Lorraine McMullen

TRANSLATION IN CANADIAN LITERATURE, edited and with an introduction by Camille R. La Bossière

THE SIR CHARLES G.D. ROBERTS SYMPOSIUM, edited and with an introduction by Glenn Clever

THE THOMAS CHANDLER HALIBURTON SYMPOSIUM, edited and with an introduction by Frank M. Tierney

STEPHEN LEACOCK: A REAPPRAISAL, edited and with an introduction by David Staines

FUTURE INDICATIVE: LITERARY THEORY AND CANADIAN LITERATURE, edited and with an introduction by John Moss

REFLECTIONS: AUTOBIOGRAPHY AND CANADIAN LITERATURE, edited and with an introduction by K.P. Stich

RE(DIS)COVERING OUR FOREMOTHERS: NINETEENTH-CENTURY CANADIAN WOMEN WRITERS, edited and with an introduction by Lorraine McMullen

BLISS CARMAN: A REAPPRAISAL, edited and with an introduction by Gerald Lynch

FROM THE HEART OF THE HEARTLAND: THE FICTION OF SINCLAIR ROSS, edited by John Moss

CONTEXT NORTH AMERICA: CANADIAN/U.S. LITERARY RELATIONS, edited by Camille R. La Bossière

HUGH MACLENNAN, edited by Frank M. Tierney

ECHOING SILENCE: ESSAYS ON ARCTIC NARRATIVE, edited and with a preface by John Moss

BOLDER FLIGHTS: ESSAYS ON THE CANADIAN LONG POEM, edited and with a preface by Frank M. Tierney and Angela Robbeson

DOMINANT IMPRESSIONS: ESSAYS ON THE CANADIAN SHORT STORY, edited by Gerald Lynch and Angela Robbeson

MARGARET LAURENCE: CRITICAL REFLECTIONS, edited and with an introduction by David Staines

ROBERTSON DAVIES: A MINGLING OF CONTRARIETIES, edited by Camille R. La Bossière and Linda M. Morra

WINDOWS AND WORDS: A LOOK AT CANADIAN CHILDREN'S LITERATURE IN ENGLISH, edited by Aïda Hudson and Susan-Ann Cooper

WORLDS OF WONDER: READINGS IN CANADIAN SCIENCE FICTION AND FANTASY LITERATURE, edited by Jean-François Leroux and Camille R. La Bossière

AT THE SPEED OF LIGHT THERE IS ONLY ILLUMINATION: A REAPPRAISAL OF MARSHALL MCLUHAN, edited by John Moss and Linda M. Morra

HOME-WORK: POSTCOLONIALISM, PEDAGOGY, AND CANADIAN LITERATURE, edited and with an introduction by Cynthia Sugars

THE CANADIAN MODERNISTS MEET, edited and with an introduction by Dean Irvine

www.ingramcontent.com/pod-product-compliance
Lightning Source LLC
Chambersburg PA
CBHW070803300426
44111CB00014B/2411